Peaceful Jihad

Online resources to accompany this book are available at [www.bloomsburyonlineresources.com/peaceful-jihad]. If you experience any problems, please contact Bloomsbury at: onlineresources@bloomsbury.com

Critical Studies on Islamism Series

The series Critical Studies on Islamism examines Islamism as a multifaceted, intricate, and evolving phenomenon. The aim of the series is to provide new and original interpretations of Islamism from a scholarly multidisciplinary, and interdisciplinary perspective. The series covers a wide range of topics that relate to Islamist movements, groups, networks, parties and actors. The scope of the series is global and it covers the nature, dynamics and evolution of Islamism at different contexts and regions from the Middle East and North Africa, South East Asia and Australia, to Europe and North America. To achieve disciplinary diversity, manuscripts from all related disciplines are welcomed including, but not limited to: political science, sociology, religious studies, history, political economy, sociolinguistics, media and cultural studies and international relations. The emphasis is on producing books that provide original approaches theoretically and empirically.

Series Editor:

Dr. Khalil al-Anani
Associate Professor of Political Science, Doha Institute for Graduate Studies, Qatar

Advisory Board:

James Piscatori, Australian National University, Australia

Emad El-Din Shahin, Hamad Bin Khalifa University, Qatar

Nathan Brown, George Washington University, USA

Peter Mandaville, George Mason University, USA

Jillian Schwedler, City University of New York's Hunter College, USA

Heba Raouf Ezzat, Ibn Haldun University-Istanbul, Turkey

Nader Hashemi, University of Denver, USA

Francesco Cavatorta, Laval University, Canada

Omar Ashour, Doha Institute for Graduate Studies, Qatar

Peaceful Jihad

The Islamic Civil Rights Movement in Saudi Arabia

Peter Enz-Harlass

I.B. TAURIS
LONDON • NEW YORK • OXFORD • NEW DELHI • SYDNEY

I.B. TAURIS
Bloomsbury Publishing Plc
50 Bedford Square, London, WC1B 3DP, UK
1385 Broadway, New York, NY 10018, USA
29 Earlsfort Terrace, Dublin 2, Ireland

BLOOMSBURY, I.B. TAURIS and the I.B. Tauris logo are trademarks of Bloomsbury Publishing Plc

First published in Great Britain 2023
This paperback edition published 2024

Series design by Adriana Brioso
Cover image © Ahmed al-Osaimi under CC BY-SA 3.0

A catalogue record for this book is available from the British Library.

A catalog record for this book is available from the Library of Congress.

ISBN: HB: 978-0-7556-4716-3
PB: 978-0-7556-4720-0
ePDF: 978-0-7556-4717-0
eBook: 978-0-7556-4718-7

Typeset by Deanta Global Publishing Services, Chennai, India

Series: Critical Studies on Islamism Series I CSI

Contents

Figures

Acknowledgements

This book is based on my doctoral thesis, which I submitted at the University of Vienna in late 2000 CE, and it was the persistent support of many people that ultimately turned it into this book.

My doctoral supervisor Univ. Prof. Mag. Dr Rüdiger Lohlker from the Department of Near Eastern Studies at the University of Vienna kindly took me on as a doctoral candidate when I knocked at his door in the summer of 2017 CE, a somewhat chaotic first draft of my research proposal under my arm.

Dr Markus Rheindorf from the University of Vienna made me realize that writing in English instead of my native German had the benefit of forcing me to formulate my thoughts more clearly.

Professor Mgr. Pavel Ťupek, PhD from Charles University Prague, showed me the complexity of the phenomenon of Salafism and insisted on precise and well-crafted descriptions of the different Islamic scholars and theories of the history of Islamic thought.

Professor Dr Erdal Toprakyaran, from Eberhard Karls University in Tübingen, reminded me that the great debates of Islamic discourse are still ongoing and that what Muslims say in one era and place can be relevant for Muslims in other eras and places.

The enthusiasm and professionalism of Sophie Rudland and the editorial team of I.B. Tauris as well as the suggestions of the anonymous reviewers showed me how one's passion for a specific subject could be conveyed in the form of a book that people might even enjoy reading.

Above all, I owe a huge debt of gratitude to my family. My wife always knows when I need encouragement and when I need a break without being able to admit it. I am thankful for our many small discussions about Saudi Arabia, which helped me find the right path when I was uncertain about how to proceed. She is and will always be my most important critic. The greatest patience was probably demanded from my two daughters, who often only reluctantly accepted that I had to withdraw into the study once again and who cheerfully pulled me out of out my study chamber when it was necessary.

To all these people, I say: Thank you.

شكرا

Vienna, March 2022

Introduction

So come to the ship of civil jihad
to ferry from rule by oppression to rule by consultation.
For there are no civil rights without political rights
and there are no political rights without jihad against oppression until martyrdom.
Do we not see how, out of their bodies, the ants build a solid bridge?
Is it not after tens of victims that they cross a torrential stream?
Do we not see how the bees put up resistance against a giant hornet?
Is it not after tens of victims that they throw it out of the hive?
Moving from the jurisprudence of the rights of the ruler to the jurisprudence of the rights of man
Is the beginning of going out of the snail shells of supplication to the places of self-sacrifice.[1]

Since the 1990s CE, Islamically inspired political movements in many countries of the Islamic world have been striving to combine Islam with modernity, democracy and human rights. More and more activists and intellectuals have been arguing that Islam calls for political freedom and a democratic form of government and that the protection of the people's God-given rights is a major obligation of Islam. From the political opposition in Iran in the 1990s CE[2] to Islamically inspired intellectuals and political parties in Egypt in the 2010s CE,[3] from political and social movements in Turkey[4] to activists in Pakistan[5] and groups in post-Suharto Indonesia,[6] many have been criticizing the political logic of authoritarianism as well as the doctrines of classical Islamists and have been presenting new ideas about the compatibility of Islam with modern political concepts. Even before the Arab Spring, political opposition movements in countries like Egypt, Iran, Kuwait and Lebanon endorsed nonviolent struggle for rights and reforms.[7] Very often, those who believed that Islam required political freedom and peaceful activism were not religious scholars. They were Islamic intellectuals. They were trained lawyers, teachers and engineers, but also devout Muslims and able to formulate Islamic arguments. It was important for them that what they were doing was legitimate in Islam, and they provided their own Islamic justifications for their ideas and their activities.

Beginning in the 1990s CE, the Kingdom of Saudi Arabia experienced its own wave of Islamically inspired politically oppositional activism, which combined Islamic reasoning with calls for the protection of the citizens' rights and political reforms. It included scholars, intellectuals and activists, who insisted that the protection of citizens' rights was a fundamental Islamic duty. They called for a constitution built on values like freedom and pluralism, which they claimed were Islamic principles, and they argued that a democratic system, not an absolute monarchy, was the form of government most in line with Islamic teachings. Soon, some of them translated their ideas into action and started to call for the protection of civil rights in the context of newly founded civil society networks and associations.

The most prominent of these associations was the Saudi Civil and Political Rights Association, or HASM for short. It was founded in 2009 CE by a group of fourteen Saudi academics and activists and soon became a hub for independent thinking and civil rights activism in the kingdom. Its members pointed out that there were serious human rights abuses in Saudi Arabia. They criticized the Saudi government for claiming that it was implementing the sharia, when in reality its continuing violations of citizens' rights and its oppression of dissent could not be justified by Islam. According to HASM, selfless commitment to the struggle for civil rights was a kind of peaceful, political, civil jihad required by Islam. The founding members also declared that it was the aim of HASM to fight against human rights abuses and to construct an Islamic theory of human rights and a culture of peaceful jihad. Soon, the members of HASM put these ideas into practice. They did not only publish books and hold lectures, in which they explained their Islamic theory of civil society activism, but they also actively supported the victims of rights violations and publicly called on the government to implement reforms.

Thus, in the 2000s CE, Saudi Arabia's Islamic civil rights movement was born. The members of its main organization, HASM, organized civil society activities for basic rights, supporting the victims of rights abuses and calling for political reforms, until HASM was banned and its members arrested in the 2010s CE. In their texts, they presented a complex theory, which framed concepts like civil rights, democracy, constitutional rule and civil society in Islamic language. They were mobilizing Islamic concepts against the political status quo, which they perceived as unjust. Significantly, they did not limit themselves to presenting a new theory. Their ideas were always intended as the theoretical framework of practical activism for civil rights. They argued that peaceful civil jihad against oppression was an Islamic obligation, and they went out and waged peaceful civil jihad themselves. In the end, they did not appear to support all of the rights that are enshrined in international human rights documents.[8] However, their focus on political civil rights and practical activism in an Islamic framework was genuine and definitely new in Saudi Arabia's political opposition. In this book, I prefer to call them an Islamic movement rather than describing them as an 'Islamist' or 'post-Islamist' movement, as others have done,[9] because 'Islamist' is both an ideologically charged term and extremely vague, encompassing different sets of ideas, groups and individuals in different contexts.[10]

The story of the Islamic civil rights movement did not last very long. From the beginning, the official Saudi authorities and the religious establishment were suspicious of the group. Soon, its members faced arrests and court trials, having been accused of crimes like inciting disorder and civil disobedience or insulting the king and senior religious scholars. At times the trials against HASM members seemed like ideological battles over the interpretation of key religious terms rather than actual criminal trials, as the prosecution also tried to delegitimize the ideas behind HASM's activism. By the end of 2013 CE, most prominent members of HASM had been given long prison sentences and HASM had been officially dissolved by the Saudi authorities. In April 2020 CE, Abdallah al-Hamid, founding member of HASM and the main ideologue of the group, died while in Saudi custody. At the time of this writing, the rest of the group's founding members remain in prison. However, the declarations, books and videos that outline the Islamic theory behind the group's activism are still being shared online and have left their mark on the very fluid and multifaceted Islamic discourse in the country and beyond the kingdom's borders.

The ideas and actions of the Islamic civil rights movement have been received very differently by observers inside and outside of Saudi Arabia. On the one hand, some journalists and Islamic scholars from Saudi Arabia who are close to the Saudi government harshly criticized the group and welcomed the Saudi state's repression.[11] On the other hand, international NGOs and journalists who reported on the association's ideas and activities publicly lauded the group's efforts in the field of civil rights and criticized the state's repression against dissent in general. Some of the movement's members received international human rights prizes and awards.[12] Many people from outside Saudi Arabia who are interested in the group seem to agree that it is comparable to human rights organizations all around the world.[13] Thus, the Islamic civil rights movement is seen very differently by various groups and individuals. While some seem to consider it a threat to the stability of Saudi Arabia and the pureness of Islamic thought, others seem to understand them as liberal advocates of universal human rights.

This book attempts to go beyond these simplistic labels by thoroughly analysing the ideas behind the Islamic civil rights movement. It focuses on the theory that drove the activities of the movement and examines it through the lens of discourse analysis. In their writings and lectures from the 1990s until the mid-2010s CE, the protagonists of the Islamic civil rights movement outlined a coherent system of thought, which primarily refers to Islamic sources, uses Islamic language and meaningfully combines classical Islamic concepts like sharia, shura (consultation) and jihad with supposedly 'foreign' ones like democracy, civil rights, constitutional rule and civil society. In doing so, they simultaneously challenged the political status quo and the official religious discourse, which serves as a source of legitimacy for the status quo. Thankfully, Stéphane Lacroix and Madawi al-Rasheed have already produced excellent studies on the history of the movement and the social background of its members.[14] However, they mainly focused on historical and social aspects and did not thoroughly analyse the Islamic theory behind the activism of the movement. A detailed discourse analysis of the movement's ideas, their arguments, their underlying concepts and their place in the contemporary Islamic political debate has not been produced yet.

Such an analysis is the aim of this book, which will examine the ideas behind Saudi Arabia's Islamic civil rights movement and elucidate the workings of its Islamic civil rights discourse. After shortly discussing the historical context of the movement (Chapter 1), the book will briefly analyse the social background of the movement's members and their position as Islamic intellectuals (Chapter 2). Then, it will present the most important ideas of the theory of the movement (Chapter 3). After a discussion of how the movement was received inside and outside of Saudi Arabia (Chapter 4), the book will turn to a close analysis of the ideas of the movement, as they have been presented in the lectures, books and declarations by its members. The analysis will focus on the sources and authors they refer to (Chapter 5), the language they use and the arguments they accept (Chapter 6), and the basic theoretical concepts their theory is based on, like their interpretation of jihad and human rights (Chapter 7). Finally, we will examine how their general understanding of Islam and politics affects the openness and flexibility of their theory (Chapter 8).

Such an analysis contributes to our understanding of Saudi society and politics. Judging by international media reports about the kingdom, Saudi society appears to be in the process of a social transition. In June 2018 CE, the headline of the British weekly magazine *The Economist* read, 'The Saudi revolution begins.' The magazine referred to recent changes under the new, powerful crown prince Muhammad ibn Salman (*Muḥammad ibn Salmān*), including the end of the ban against women driving cars, the opening of cinemas and concert venues, and the official announcement to make it easier for foreigners to travel to the country as tourists. At the same time, *The Economist* remarked that the crackdown on the opposition and everyone who was even remotely suspected of being a dissident was continuing unabatedly.[15] The gruesome reports about the murder of Saudi journalist Jamal Khashoggi in October 2018 CE and the fact that, even after women were formally allowed to drive cars, Saudi women's rights defenders who had been lobbying for that very right were still locked away in Saudi prisons only seemed to confirm the impression that Saudi Arabia was still far away from actual political reform. In the context of these changes and continuities, understanding Saudi Arabia's Islamic civil rights movement and its role inside Saudi society will contribute to a more comprehensive and nuanced understanding of the kingdom. The Islamic civil rights movement is part of the kingdom's complex society and its political debate.

However, Saudi Arabia's Islamic civil rights movement is relevant not only for understanding the debate inside Saudi Arabia. It is part of a diverse trend of Islamic intellectuals in many parts of the world, who have been trying to meaningfully combine Islamic thought with modernity, democracy and human rights. Thus, this book can be read as a case study of a movement that has tried to formulate a coherent Islamic theory that can cope with the challenges faced by contemporary Muslim societies. Through their texts and their actions, the movement's members joined the worldwide discussion among Muslims about what kind of politics is required by Islam and how Muslims should participate in the politics of the states they live in. The debate about the relationship between Islam and politics and the compatibility between Islam on the one hand and democracy, pluralism and human rights on the other hand is both old and heated and has gained new momentum since the Arab Spring. The members of the Islamic civil rights movement were clearly aware of this broader context. In their texts, they used references to contemporary thinkers from all over the Islamic world, and their books and texts continue to be read by activists in exile in Great Britain and Canada. Via social media, they built relationships with Muslims and non-Muslims from the Middle East, Asia, Europe and America. Their theory might be their own creation, but they were influenced by Muslim activists and thinkers in other parts of the world, and in many respects their ideas are similar to those of Islamic scholars and intellectuals elsewhere. Through their writings and their activism, they made a contribution to this wide-ranging, ongoing, pan-Islamic debate. Therefore, an analysis of the ideas of Saudi Arabia's Islamic civil rights movement can only enhance our understanding of this debate.

Finally, a few words concerning transcriptions and translations are necessary. In this book, I am generally using the well-known transcription system of the Deutsche Morgenländische Gesellschaft (DMG). As this system of transcription is relatively widespread in academic literature and quite close to the original Arabic orthography, Arabic speakers should find it easy to identify the original Arabic roots of transliterated words. Words that have acquired a reasonably widespread usage in a simplified transcription – like sharia or jihad – are mostly written in their widespread form, although I have occasionally added the scientific transcription in brackets. The same applies to names of individuals, which, for reasons of readability, will usually be written in a simplified transliteration, but occasionally the reader will find the scientific transcription in brackets. Unless otherwise stated, the translations of Arabic texts quoted here are mine.

1

The history of the Islamic civil rights movement

Saudi Arabia's Islamic civil rights movement developed in the late 2000s CE. From the beginning, it was a distinct civil society movement, which openly criticized the policies of the Saudi government and presented its own, well-defined Islamic theory, which formed the basis for their activism. However, it cannot be understood without looking at the context in which it developed. The Islamic civil rights movement was not the first movement to challenge the ruling political discourse, and it certainly was not the last. Since the founding of the Kingdom of Saudi Arabia, there was always opposition to the Saudi leadership and its political discourse. It came from various groups with different ideological and social backgrounds. The Islamic civil rights movement thus stands in a long line of political dissent and is part of this history of resistance to the ruling political conditions and the discourse that legitimizes them. It belongs to the history of political discourse in Saudi Arabia.

Saudi political discourse: Power and dissent

The history of the Kingdom of Saudi Arabia is closely linked to the so-called Wahhabi form of Islam, and Wahhabi Islam has been shaping political discourse in the kingdom since its earliest days. Virtually all studies on the history of the kingdom agree that it begins with the alliance between the firebrand preacher Muhammad ibn Abd al-Wahhab (*Muḥammad ibn ʿAbd al-Wahhāb*), the eponym of Wahhabism, and Muhammad ibn Saud (*Muḥammad ibn Saʿūd*) of the Al Saud (*Āl Saʿūd*) family, a local central Arabian ruler, in 1744 CE. Muhammad ibn Abd al-Wahhab understood himself as an uncompromising religious reformer and argued that Islam had to be purified from supposedly false traditions, which diverted worship away from God. He endorsed a strict and literal implementation of the rulings of Islam and claimed that anyone who did not implement the rules of Islam in this way was no true Muslim and had to be converted or fought by way of armed jihad.[1]

The alliance between the preacher Muhammad ibn Abd al-Wahhab and the political leader Muhammad ibn Saud created a symbiosis, which turned out to benefit both the message of Wahhabism, as the school of Muhammad ibn Abd al-Wahhab was later called,[2] and the political ambitions of Muhammad ibn Saud and the Al Saud family.

Muhammad ibn Saud promised to accept the religious authority of Muhammad ibn Abd al-Wahhab, adopt his ideas and put his political resources at the disposal of his religious mission. In return, Muhammad ibn Abd al-Wahhab accepted the political authority of Muhammad ibn Saud and granted him religious legitimacy.[3] With the ideological support of Wahhabi scholars, the Al Saud family led several successful military campaigns, which led to the founding of three consecutive states on the Arabian Peninsula ruled by the family: first the Emirate of Diriya (1744–1818 CE), then the Emirate of Najd (1824–91 CE) and finally the Kingdom of Saudi Arabia, which was officially founded in 1932 CE. The conquests of the Al Saud family went hand in hand with the spreading of Wahhabi teachings. Wahhabism became the official form of Islam of these states, and the states ensured that the people living inside its territories adhered to the very strict rules set down by the Wahhabi scholars.[4] Bodies, which had a decidedly Wahhabi character, played an important part in integrating new territories into the Saudi state. Two important examples are the so-called mutawwaun (*muṭawwaʿūn*, literally 'volunteers'), trained ritual specialists who ensured that daily life was in accordance with Wahhabi teachings,[5] and the so-called Ikhwan (*iḫwān*, literally 'brothers'), highly radicalized Bedouin warriors, who led many of the military campaigns that led to the founding of the Kingdom of Saudi Arabia.[6] The ideological hegemony of Wahhabism is further buttressed by the fact that scholars of the Wahhabi tradition have been filling virtually all the important posts in the judiciary and in educational institutions.[7]

Wahhabism has always been an important legitimizing factor in Saudi politics. Political discourse is very much influenced by Wahhabi ideas and language. The Saudi rulers have always insisted that they protect 'pure Islam', and that the Saud state was one where the rules of Islam were properly implemented. In difficult times, the kings of Saudi Arabia have often enlisted the support of the official Wahhabi establishment in legitimizing the political decisions of the Saudi leadership. For example, when Abdulaziz ibn Saud (*ʿAbd al-ʿAzīz ibn Saʿūd*), the founder of the Kingdom of Saudi Arabia, was confronted with a rebellion of his Ikhwan warriors in the late 1920s CE, he sought the formal approval of the Wahhabi scholars for his counter-offensive with the support of the British.[8] When King Fahd called for the support of the United States during the Gulf War of 1990–1 CE, he asked the Wahhabi establishment to endorse this decision.[9] Likewise, when King Abdallah strove to counter the effects of the Arab Spring at home and abroad after 2011 CE, he also counted on the religious support of the Wahhabi scholars.[10] In general, Wahhabi scholars have always insisted that Islam calls on ordinary Muslims to obey their rulers. Of course, Islam never was the only ingredient of official political discourse. For example, since the late 1990s CE, the Saudi leadership has increasingly been using nationalist rhetoric and has been trying to foster a sense of national belonging, for example, by celebrating secular national holidays or organizing cultural festivals.[11] However, due to the kingdom's history and the structure of its state institutions, religious arguments continue to be one of the main influences on political discourse in the kingdom.

Despite the obvious importance of Wahhabism for political discourse in Saudi Arabia, the Saudi leadership also sometimes openly defied the official Islamic establishment and took decisions against their advice, if the leadership saw political value in them. In fact, various Saudi kings have at times made decisions that were deemed sinful by the Wahhabi scholars, like the introduction of laws concerning commerce and banking in the 1960s and 1970s CE, which, according to the scholars of the time, violated the Islamic ban on usury (*ribā*) and the primacy of the Islamic sharia. Another example is the Saudi leadership's enthusiasm for international student exchange programme since the 2000s CE, which was criticized by the Islamic scholars because it supposedly carried the risk of mingling with 'unbelievers' and adopting 'un-Islamic' practices.[12] In 2018 CE, the Saudi government legalized cinemas, even though the grand mufti had warned against it only a year earlier. Thus, Saudi Arabia never was a full-fledged theocracy entirely controlled by Wahhabi scholars. Nevertheless, due to the historical alliance and the importance of Wahhabism for political discourse in Saudi Arabia the Saudi rulers have been trying not to anger the Wahhabi scholars and their followers too much, and they often relied on them for strengthening their political legitimacy.

Since the earliest days of the Kingdom of Saudi Arabia, there has always been political opposition to the Saudi leadership and the ruling political discourse. Sometimes, this opposition was inspired by particular interpretations of Islamic teachings, sometimes it was based on nationalist ideas or local grievances. In the late 1920s CE, even before the Kingdom of Saudi Arabia had been officially founded, Abdulaziz ibn Saud had to quell a revolt of his fanatic Ikhwan warriors, who rejected Abdulaziz's pragmatic alliance with the British and accused him of straying from the true way of Islam.[13] In the Hijaz in the west of the kingdom, the rule of Abdulaziz ibn Saud was challenged by an active regionalist opposition during the 1920s and 1930s CE.[14] In the 1950s and 1960s CE, an opposition movement called the Free Princes (*al-Umarāʾ al-aḥrār*), which called for liberal reforms and a constitutional monarchy, developed inside the royal family itself.[15] From the 1950s until the 1970s CE, there was a wave of socialist and nationalist opposition movements.[16] In the 1960s CE, the Sunni movement of Rejectionism, initially an apolitical, puritanical group, developed into a political opposition movement, accusing the Saudi leadership of not taking the rules of Islam seriously enough. In 1979 CE, a radical splinter group of this movement was responsible for a bloody attack on the Great Mosque in Mecca.[17] In the east of the kingdom, where the Shia minority had long been complaining about systematic discrimination and aggressive anti-Shia rhetoric by many Wahhabi scholars, Shia-led opposition activism increased after the 1970s CE.[18] In the 1980s CE, Saudis thinkers and militants like Osama bin Laden (*Usāma ibn Lādin*) contributed to the emergence of the ideology of Jihadism in Afghanistan. While not originally directed against the policies of the Saudi leadership, the Jihadis later turned against the Saudi government, accusing it of being stooges of a global alliance of 'enemies of Islam'.[19] Thus, by the 1990s CE, the Saudi leadership and its policies had already been challenged by several different opposition movements with various backgrounds.

The Islamo-reformist debate of the 1990s, 2000s and 2010s

In the wake of the Gulf War of 1990–1 CE, Islamically inspired opposition activism in Saudi Arabia received a boost, which would profoundly change Saudi opposition discourse and determine the language and ideas of the opposition for decades to come. In the 1990s, 2000s and 2010s CE, the Saudi leadership was challenged by three waves of Islamically inspired political activism, which all referred to the unprecedented mobilization after the Gulf War. It is in this context that the Islamic civil rights movement and its ideas developed and spread.

The rise of Islamically inspired political activism in this period is closely linked to the so-called Sahwa movement (*aṣ-ṣaḥwa*, literally 'awakening'), a social and political movement that developed in Saudi Arabia after the 1960s CE and fused the strict theology of Wahhabism with the Muslim Brotherhood's spirit of social activism. Young scholars belonging to the Sahwa shared Wahhabism's insistence on the need to purify Islam, but in contrast to the Wahhabi establishment, they did not consider blind obedience to the ruler an obligation of Islam. Instead, they called on their followers to actively change the world around them. The alternative discourse of the Sahwa grew particularly popular among university students and young, educated Sunnis in general, who did not feel represented by the closed, strictly hierarchical Wahhabi establishment.[20] However, until the 1990s CE, supporters of the Sahwa had not openly challenged the Saudi political leadership.

This changed after the Gulf War of 1990–1 CE. The decision of the Saudi leadership to invite American troops into the country was deeply unpopular among large parts of the Saudi population. Many accused the Saudi government of having invited 'infidel' soldiers into Saudi territory and of allying themselves with colonial powers. From the beginning, Sahwa scholars were among the loudest critics of this decision. Soon, the debate intensified and young scholars and ordinary Saudis began to question the political status quo and whether it really was in line with the rules of Islam, like the Wahhabi scholars claimed.[21] In 1991 and 1992 CE, Sunni opposition activists published two petitions addressed to the king: the 'Letter of Demands' (*Ḫiṭāb al-maṭālib*) and the 'Memorandum of Advice' (*Muḏakkirat an-naṣīḥa*). They contained political demands, like the call for the establishment of an elected parliament, the protection of the people's basic rights and an end to alliances with foreign powers, and argued that these demands were backed by Islamic teachings. Both petitions were clearly inspired by the Sahwa, but they were supported by hundreds of Islamically motivated activists with various backgrounds.[22] In 1993 CE, some of the supporters of the petitions founded a short-lived non-governmental organization called Committee for the Defence of Legitimate Rights (abb. CDLR, *Laǧnat ad-difāʿ ʿan al-ḥuqūq aš-šarʿīya*). It called for the protection of the citizen's basic rights and for political reforms but insisted on a strict Islamic framework for both these rights and reforms.[23]

In its response to this wave of dissent, the Saudi government followed a two-sided approach. On the one hand, it implemented a number of largely cosmetic reforms.[24] On the other hand, the Saudi security services began to persecute the supporters of the petitions. Many were arrested for vague offences like 'actions undermining national security' or forced into exile.[25] In the end, the wave of opposition activism collapsed. The intellectuals and activists who had joined forces to call for reforms in Islamic language scattered into different currents. Some cut deals with the Saudi government and promised to abstain from political activism in return for a release from prison and financial support. Others turned towards Jihadism and supported the wave of al-Qaeda attacks in Saudi Arabia in the 2000s CE. Finally, a third group continued to peacefully call for political reforms in Islamic language despite the government persecution.[26] Some European researchers soon began to call it 'Islamo-liberal'.[27] However, it is probably best described by the term 'Islamo-reformist', not least because the term 'liberal' is rather vague and has very different connotations in a European or a Middle Eastern setting and because the members of this group themselves mostly referred to themselves as reformists (*iṣlāḥiyūn*).[28]

In the early 2000s CE, Saudi Arabia experienced a short period of relative political openness called 'Riyadh Spring',[29] and it was in this period that the Islamo-reformists launched a second wave of Islamically inspired opposition activism, which referred to many of the ideas that had been spread in the 1990s CE. Encouraged by signs indicating that the government would allow a more open public debate, some activists began to publish newspaper articles and books that were critical of some of its policies. Others organized regular discussion groups in private homes. In addition, several new petitions calling for political reforms were published by members of the Islamo-reformist current. They included the petitions 'Vision for the Present of the Homeland and Its Future' (*Ru'yat li-ḥāḍir al-waṭan wa-mustaqbalihi*)[30] and 'Calling on Both the Leadership and the People: Constitutional Reform First' (*Nidā'an ilā l-qiyāda wa-š-ša'b ma'an: al-Iṣlāḥ ad-dustūrī awwalan*),[31] which were both published in 2003 CE, as well as the 2007 CE petition 'Milestones on the Way of the Constitutional Monarchy' (*Ma'ālim fī ṭarīq al-malakīya d-dustūrīya*).[32] The authors of the petitions called for constitutional reforms, the creation of an elected legislative council, an independent judiciary and the protection of the basic rights of the citizens, and they used Islamic language and arguments to strengthen their demands.

Initially, Crown Prince Abdallah seemed open to some of the demands, but soon the Saudi leadership decided that it was not in its best interest to encourage this kind of debate. Like it had done before, the Saudi government enacted some minor reforms.[33] At the same time, many of the supporters of the new petitions were arrested and tried for crimes like 'inciting civil disobedience' or 'actions damaging to national security'.[34] By 2008 CE, the second wave of Islamic opposition activism had effectively ended.

Only three years later, in the wake of the Arab Spring in 2011 CE, the opposition received a fresh impetus and the kingdom experienced a third wave of Islamically inspired political activism. From the start, the uprisings in countries like Tunisia and Egypt were immensely popular with young Saudis, while the Saudi government soon began to actively counter them, fearing that the Arabian Peninsula would also be gripped by the same revolutionary fervour.[35] In March 2011 CE, the leadership of the Wahhabi establishment published a fatwa condemning the demonstrations as harmful and 'un-Islamic'.[36] This did not deter Saudi activists from trying to organize protests inside Saudi Arabia. However, through a combination of generous financial handouts and pressure by the security forces the government managed to prevent large-scale demonstrations.[37] Nevertheless, small protests in support of specific issues, like the plight of political prisoners or women's rights, continued well into the mid-2010s CE.[38] In addition to these activities, Sunni opposition activists began a new wave of petitions, which, mostly, contained the same demands that had already been raised in the petitions of the 1990s and 2000s CE, including constitutional reforms, greater accountability of government and the protection of the citizen's basic rights. Two important examples are the petition 'Towards a State of Rights and Institutions' (*Naḥwa daulat al-ḥuqūq wa-l-mu'assasāt*) of February 2011 CE[39] and the 'National Declaration of Reform' (*I'lān waṭanī li-l-iṣlāḥ*) of March 2011 CE.[40]

Inspired by the Arab Spring, several Islamo-reformist authors in Saudi Arabia wrote books that openly challenged the official religious and political discourse. Many were influenced by Kuwaiti Salafist scholar Hakim al-Mutayri (*Ḥākim al-Muṭairī*),[41] who had argued in the late 2000s CE that Islam's original political message, which had been one of liberation and empowerment, had been gradually distorted since the time of the prophet Muhammad, in effect turning Islam into a tool of political oppression. In order to regain their political independence, Muslims had to abandon the predominant Islamic political discourse, which preached obedience, and return to the real Islamic discourse, which was one of liberation.[42] This idea found resonance among Islamic activists and intellectuals in Saudi Arabia. In 2012 CE, Saudi Islamic scholar Salman al-Awda (*Salmān al-'Auda*),[43] an influential Sahwa veteran, published the book *Questions of Revolution* (*As'ilat aṯ-ṯawra*).[44] In it, he argued that revolutions, like the ones that were happening in countries like Tunisia and Egypt, were the logical result of oppression and injustice. Like al-Mutayri, al-Awda accused the mainstream Islamic discourse of having distorted the original political message of Islam. He insisted that Islam called for justice and political participation, and that it was the God-given right of Muslims to revolt against oppression. The writings of Saudi Islamic scholar Muhammad al-Abd al-Karim (*Muḥammad al-'Abd al-Karīm*)[45] brought forward very similar arguments. His 2011 CE book *Civil ihtisab* (*al-Iḥtisāb al-madanī*)[46] aimed at formulating a coherent Islamic theory for civil society activism, and his 2013 CE book *Deconstructing Oppression* (*Tafkīk al-istibdād*)[47] provided an elaborate Islamic legal refutation of Islamic argument that had been used to justify oppressive political systems. Saudi academic Abdallah al-Maliki (*'Abdallāh al-Mālikī*)[48] went even further in his controversial book *The Sovereignty of the Umma before the Implementation of the Sharia* (*Siyādat al-umma qabla taṭbīq aš-šarī'a*),[49] which was published in 2012 CE. He argued that, while the authority of the Islamic sharia was generally uncontested among Muslims, this did not mean that anyone had the right to create an Islamic state without the explicit consent of the people. In Islam, the people were the holders of political power and this even meant that, if they decided not to apply the rules of the sharia, this had to be accepted. Finally, Muhammad al-Ahmari's (*Muḥammad al-Aḥmarī*)[50] 2012 CE book *Democracy. The Roots and the Problems of Implementation* (*ad-Dīmuqrāṭīya. al-Ǧuḏūr wa-iškālīyat at-taṭbīq*)[51] made a strong case for democracy. Its main message was that democracy was not a foreign invention, but rather a universal human practice and that Islam endorsed a democratic system of government.

Like before, the wave of opposition activism of the 2010s CE was soon suppressed by the Saudi government. Beginning in 2011 CE, many Islamo-reformist opposition activists and intellectuals, including authors like Salman al-Awda, were arrested and charged with crimes like 'inciting civil disobedience'. Some were later sentenced to long prison sentences by the Specialised Criminal Court (*al-maḥkama l-ǧazā'īya l-mutaḫaṣṣiṣa*), which had been created in 2007 CE as a counter-terrorism court.

Others went into exile in countries like the UK, where they continued their oppositional activism.

The strategy seems to have worked, at least in the short term. Since the mid-2010s CE, there has not been an opposition movement in Saudi Arabia that could be compared to the three waves of Islamic oppositional activism of the 1990s, 2000s and early 2010s CE. However, Saudi opposition groups, like the London-based NGO ALQST,[52] the opposition platform Diwan London[53] and the National Assembly Party (*Ḥizb at-taǧammuʿ al-waṭanī*),[54] as well as independent activists like Canada-based Omar Abdulaziz az-Zahrani or US-based women's rights activist Hala Aldosari have been continuing to call for political reforms in the country from their exile in Europe or North America.

Rise and fall of the Islamic civil rights movement

The Islamic civil rights movement, and its main organization, the Saudi Civil and Political Rights Association (English abbr. ACPRA, *Ǧamʿīyat al-ḥuqūq al-madanīya wa-s-siyāsīya fī s-Suʿūdīya,* Arabic abbr. HASM), grew out of the Islamo-reformist current and developed in the context of the three waves of Islamically inspired opposition activism of the 1990s, 2000s and 2010s CE. The members of HASM were part of the Islamo-reformist debate at the time and made their own contribution to it. Many of its members had actively participated in the campaigns for the opposition petitions, and some had even been involved in the writing of some of the petitions. In general, many ideas that had circulated in the Islamo-reformist discourse were also present in the texts of HASM's members, and they were clearly influenced by the broader debate that had been going on since the 1990s CE.

However, the Islamic civil rights movement was a new movement inside the Islamo-reformist current. Its members presented a complex and coherent theory, which included new ideas. In contrast to the broader Islamo-reformist current, which was rather an open space for debate and not a homogeneous movement with a well-defined set of beliefs, the members of HASM all seemed to subscribe to the same theory. They all identified with HASM and its ideas and showed a remarkable internal coherence. The texts, declarations and lectures of its members seemed to speak of the same issues and used the same arguments and the same language. Finally, while many members of the broader Islamo-reformist current confined themselves to writing texts, the members of HASM also focused on the practical side of Islamically inspired political discourse, and especially the issues of basic rights, thereby combining theory and practical civil society activism. Thus, while it is certainly true that the Islamic civil rights movement was part of the Islamo-reformist current, which had existed since the 1990s CE, it was also a new movement inside this current and had its own theory.

HASM was founded in October 2009 CE by a group of fourteen Saudi men, most of whom had been initiators and supporters of the reformist petitions of the 2000s CE. The group of its founders was rather diverse. It included veteran opposition activists, like the former university professor of Arabic literature Abdallah al-Hamid, who had

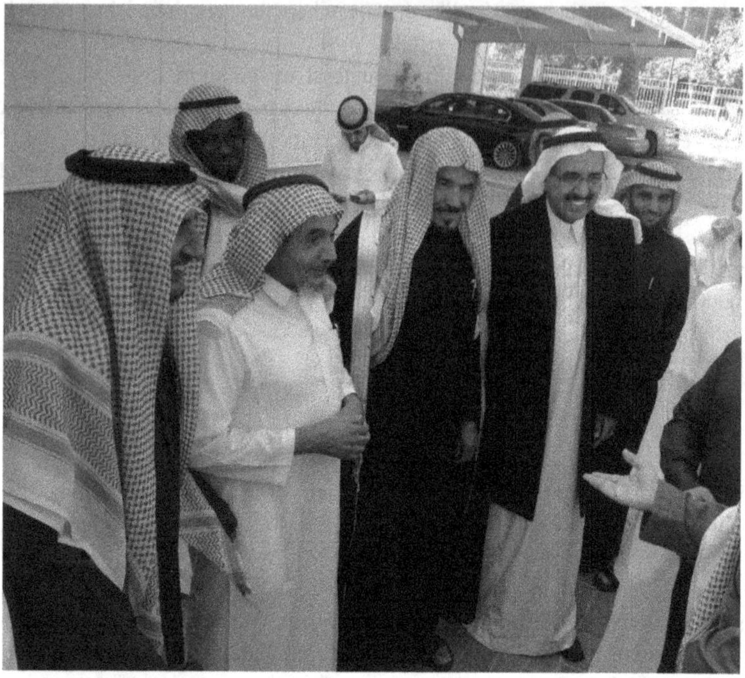

Figure 1 HASM members Abdallah al-Hamid (3rd from right) and Sulayman ar-Rashudi (5th from right) together with other HASM members and supporters, 2012. Wikimedia Commons/Sultan al-Ajmi.

been a part of the opposition since the 1990s CE and had participated in the writing of some of the opposition petitions of the 1990s and 2000s CE, and the former judge Sulayman ar-Rashudi (*Sulaymān ar-Rašūdī*), who had also been a vocal supporter of opposition petitions since the 1990s CE. Both Al-Hamid and ar-Rashudi had been members of the short-lived opposition group Committee for the Defence of Legitimate Rights in the 1990s CE. The group of HASM's founders also included activists who were relatively new to opposition activism, like the economist Muhammad al-Qahtani (*Muḥammad al-Qaḥṭānī*) and the businessman Muhammad al-Bajadi (*Muḥammad al-Bağādī*). Despite their slightly different backgrounds, the founding members of HASM shared the conviction that it was necessary to establish an independent civil rights group.

On 12 October 2009 CE, they published HASM's founding declaration online. It was a comprehensive text abounding with references to Islamic concepts and passages from the Quran. The founding declaration revived many of the demands of the Islamically inspired opposition petitions of the 1990s and 2000s CE, added a strong emphasis on the protection of human rights and basic freedoms, and presented all this in the form of a well-structured, passionate political declaration, which was firmly grounded in Islamic thought. The mood of the declaration was evident from its first words, which stressed the importance of the protection of human rights in Islam:

> Fourteen centuries before the appearance of the international laws which protect human rights and to which governments are committed, the Islamic sharia came to protect human dignity, to safeguard the rights of man and to end injustice. The Almighty God said: 'We have conferred dignity on the children of Adam' [Quran 17:70], and 'Whenever you judge between people, judge with justice' [Quran 4:58].[55]

The authors of the founding declaration argued that the establishment of an independent civil rights organization like HASM was necessary because grave human rights violations were occurring in Saudi Arabia. The situation was exacerbated further by the fact that the Saudi state wrongly claimed to be applying the Islamic sharia when oppressing dissidents. These violations and their religious justification had to stop, according to the founders of HASM. Only collective activism for the protection of basic rights and for political reform would lead to a better life for all the citizens of the state. In fact, the cooperation of individuals for a good cause like this was a form of the Islamic obligation of enjoining virtue and forbidding vice (*al-amr bi-l-maʿrūf wa-n-nahy ʿan al-munkar*), and under the right circumstances could be considered peaceful, political, civil jihad.[56] Therefore, they declared that HASM's aim was to peacefully combat rights abuses in the kingdom and to work towards a fundamental political reform that would eliminate the structural causes of these abuses.

Their aim was a more inclusive and just political system, which would embody basic Islamic principles and ensure that the Islamic sharia was properly implemented. The Saudi state had to be moved in the direction of a constitutional monarchy, with

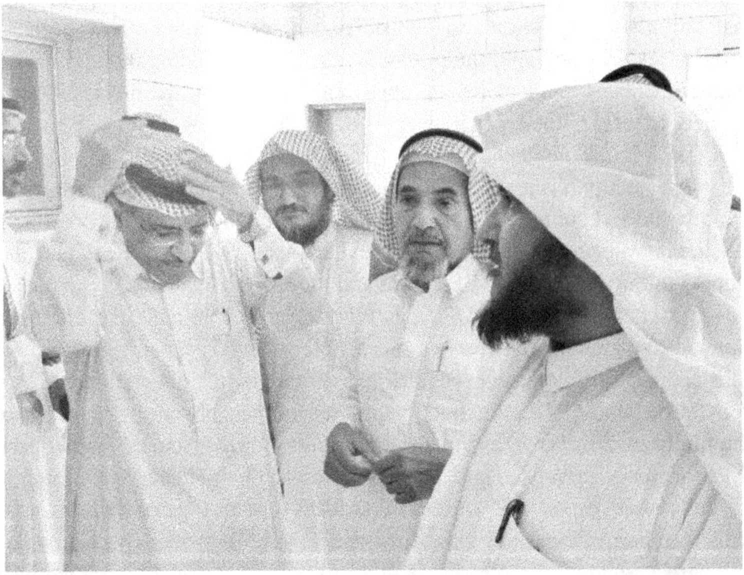

Figure 2 HASM founding members Muhammad al-Qahtani, Abd ar-Rahman al-Hamid, Abdallah al-Hamid and Abd al-Karim al-Khadr, 2013. Wikimedia Commons/Mosab Al-Abdulkareem.

a clear separation between the legislative, executive and judicial powers of the state, and the establishment of an elected legislative council. In addition to these structural reforms, an empowerment of civil society would provide a further guarantee for the protection of people's God-given rights.

The authors declared that, to reach these aims, HASM would resort to different peaceful means. They included publishing declarations and books about human rights and the Islamic political doctrine, organizing lectures, educating the people about their rights, contacting political figures and documenting human rights abuses, as well as supporting the victims and their families in their struggle. The founding declaration ended with a call to provide the HASM members with any available information about rights abuses, so that HASM would be able to stand up for them and support their cases:

> The signatories of this declaration ask everyone who is subject to documented violations or who knows of such violations to inform one of the signatories of this declaration, so that they can be recorded and brought to the attention of the Guardian of the Two Holy Places [i.e., the king] and the relevant authorities.[57]

The authors of HASM's founding declaration presented the outline of a new Islamic theory of civil society activism by combining international human rights language with Islamic arguments. They called for the protection of human rights and the implementation of political principles like pluralism, justice, political participation and a separation of powers, and they did so by referring these principles to Islamic concepts and arguing that they were obligations of Islam.

Very soon after its founding, HASM started to translate its announcements into actions. The association started to publish regular declarations via its website and organized weekly meetings in the private homes of its founding members, in which alternating members held lectures on topics ranging from theorical discussions about civil society to reports about concrete cases of rights violations. The audience usually consisted of a small number of HASM members and supporters. Some of these lectures were later published via a channel on YouTube.[58] HASM member Abdallah al-Hamid wrote and published books on Islamic political doctrine, the possible shape of an Islamic constitution and civil society activism. All these texts and lectures contributed to the development of a more and more complex theory, which provided the theoretical background of HASM's activism. Through the activities of others, like Muhammad al-Qahtani, who reached out to international human rights groups and journalists, the association achieved notable publicity in international media.[59]

From the beginning, HASM actively supported political prisoners and their families, and the plight of prisoners was an important topic in the association's publications. HASM's members actively sought out those affected by political oppression in Saudi Arabia, and people responded to the call in HASM's founding declaration and informed HASM's members of cases of rights violations. HASM meticulously documented the cases it learned about and helped the families of the victims of rights violations write formal complaints addressed to the relevant Saudi authorities. According to HASM's leader at the time, Fawzan al-Harbi (*Fawzān al-Ḥarbī*), as of October 2013 CE, HASM had contributed to bringing around 300 cases of violations to the attention of the Saudi Board of Grievances (*dīwān al-maẓālim*), which is responsible for handling such matters in the kingdom, as well as the prison authorities.[60]

When the families of political prisoners were inspired by the great demonstrations of the Arab Spring and organized their own small protests in front of the Ministry of Defence, HASM members publicly endorsed the protests and voiced their support for the prisoners and their relatives. There were dozens of such small protests in the kingdom between early 2011 and 2013 CE. Most of them were held in front of buildings belonging to the Interior Ministry, and the core demands usually revolved around the release of political prisoners and an end to human rights violations by the security forces and prison guards. These were not large protests, and usually the number of participants did not exceed fifty people, most of whom were family members of prisoners. Nevertheless, the fact that there were protests in a tightly controlled state like Saudi Arabia was remarkable. HASM founding member Muhammad al-Bajadi was an especially active advocate of protests and demonstrations as a means to voice dissent and discontent with regard to the treatment of prisoners.[61]

The late 2000s CE, when HASM's activities began, were generally a time of increased human rights awareness in Saudi Arabia. The kingdom had long been criticized for its human rights record by international human rights advocates, and human rights language had already influenced many of the demands of the opposition since the 1990s CE. It was already mentioned that the Committee for the Defence of Legitimate Rights, which was founded in 1993 CE, had presented itself as an Islamically inspired human rights organization. The Saudi government did not want to leave the topic to the opposition and, in the 2000s CE, it established two official human rights bodies, namely the Human Rights Commission (*Hayʾat ḥuqūq al-insān*) and the National Society for Human Rights (*al-Ǧamʿīya l-waṭanīya fi-ḥuqūq al-insān*). Both soon turned out to be mere tools for the government. Instead of independently investigating human rights abuses in the kingdom, they mainly focused on issues that were in the interest of the Saudi government, like the plight of the Palestinians under the Israeli occupation.[62] The authorities consistently refused to grant independent human rights organizations official licences. Therefore, activists interested in the issue began to form unlicensed organizations in the 2000s CE. HASM was only one of them. In December 2008 CE lawyer Waleed Abu al-Khair (*Walīd Abū l-Ḫair*) founded the Human Rights Monitor in Saudi Arabia (*Marṣad ḥuqūq al-insān fī s-Sūʿūdīya*) in the city of Jeddah.[63] In December 2011 CE, the Adala Centre for Human Rights (*Markaz al-ʿadāla li-ḥuqūq al-insān*) was founded in the east of the kingdom.[64] In April 2013 CE, four Riyadh-based activists founded the Union for Human Rights (*al-Ittiḥād li-ḥuqūq al-insān*).[65] Later, Saudi opposition activists began to establish human rights organizations in exile, like the Berlin-based European Saudi Organisation for Human Rights (*al-Munaẓẓama l-ūrūbīya s-suʿūdīya li-ḥuqūq al-insān*) or the London-based NGO ALQST.[66] Thus, HASM was only one of several human rights groups that were founded in Saudi Arabia in the late 2000s and early 2010s CE. However, in contrast to all the other groups, which solely focused on the practical side of civil society activism for basic and human rights, HASM combined practical activism with the formulation of a new theory of this kind of activism. In their texts, the members of HASM presented an Islamic theory of civil society activism, and in their daily work they translated it into practice.

Soon, HASM's members had to face persecution, arrests and trials, just like many other opposition activists and the founders and members of other unlicensed human rights groups in the kingdom. HASM co-founder Muhammad al-Bajadi was arrested in March 2011 CE, after he had participated in a small protest for the release of political prisoners in front of the Interior Ministry in Riyadh. After a lengthy trial he was sentenced to four years in prison by the Specialised Criminal Court in April 2012 CE. In March 2012 CE, the police arrested HASM co-founders Abdallah al-Hamid and Muhammad al-Qahtani for crimes like 'breaking allegiance to the ruler', 'questioning the integrity of the officials' and 'seeking to disrupt public security'. Shortly afterwards, their trial at the Specialised Criminal Court began. In December 2012 CE, HASM member Sulayman ar-Rashudi was arrested. Only a few days earlier he had delivered a public sermon in which he argued that the right to peaceful demonstrations was guaranteed by Islamic law, thereby directly contradicting the position of the official religious establishment that demonstrations were contrary to Islamic teachings.[67] In April 2013 CE, the authorities arrested HASM member Abd al-Karim al-Khadr (*ʿAbd al-Karīm al-Ḫaḍr*) and charged him with 'inciting civil disorder' and 'participating in the founding of an unlicensed organisation'. The crackdown continued, and by mid-2013 CE all major members of HASM had been arrested.[68]

A few months later, the trials began and they were soon criticized for not complying with international standards of fair judicial procedure. According to human rights NGOs like Amnesty International, the activists suffered several serious rights violations during the investigations of the security services and the court trials. Most of them were reportedly mistreated in police custody. In many cases, the families of the arrested individuals were not informed of the arrests or the whereabouts of their family members. The trials themselves were also criticized for the vague nature of the charges, inadequate access to legal counsel and the fact that many court sessions were held behind closed doors, without obvious legal justifications.[69]

During many of the court sessions, the trials against HASM's members appeared less like criminal trials and more like ideological battles between the opposition and the official establishment over the interpretation of religious and political concepts. This was especially evident during the trial against HASM co-founders Hamid and Muhammad al-Qahtani in 2013 CE. In the last session, the judge did not simply pass the sentence against the two HASM members, but he actively tried to delegitimize the religious and political ideas that motivated their activism by claiming that HASM's theory suffered from flaws in its theological and legal reasoning, and that it was very similar to al-Qaeda's ideology of armed jihad.[70] The accused HASM members countered the arguments of the judge and used the trials as a stage for presenting their ideas to a wider audience. From the beginning of the trials, HASM published reports about what happened inside the court rooms online. Videos and photos published on social media showed al-Hamid and al-Qahtani among their supporters before and after the trials. During the trials, both al-Hamid and al-Qahtani repeatedly read out long texts in which they argued why their activism was legitimate and not a crime. After the sentencing HASM published a long refutation of the judge's claims, in which HASM's members condemned the trial as political and insisted on the legitimacy of their activism.[71]

Leaving aside the question of who won the ideological battle, in the court room HASM and its members did not stand a chance against the security apparatus and a judiciary dependent on the government. One after the other, all founding members of HASM were sentenced to prison sentences ranging from four to fifteen years. In March 2013 CE, the court finally sentenced Abdallah al-Hamid and Muhammad al-Qahtani to eleven and ten years in prison, respectively, and ordered the disbanding of the association HASM. According to the court's decision, HASM was an illegal, unlicensed organization, and all its activities had to stop. All property owned by the association inside the kingdom was confiscated.[72] Around the time of the sentencing, several articles by Islamic scholars and journalists who sought to refute the ideas of HASM were published in official Saudi newspapers and on Saudi-sponsored websites.[73] They reinforced the attempts of the security services and the official religious establishment to delegitimize the ideas behind the activism of HASM's members.

In social media, HASM continued to attract an audience after most of its members had been arrested, even though this online support could not be translated into actual activism on the streets. In February 2013 CE, a group of online supporters and sympathizers attempted to organize protests in support of the members of the association who had to defend themselves in court. They coined the Twitter hashtag 'We are all HASM' (*kullunā ḥasm*) and called for silent gatherings at selected mosques after Friday prayers in order to show support for HASM's reformist calls.[74] Despite the online support that these calls generated, the organizers did not appear to have had any

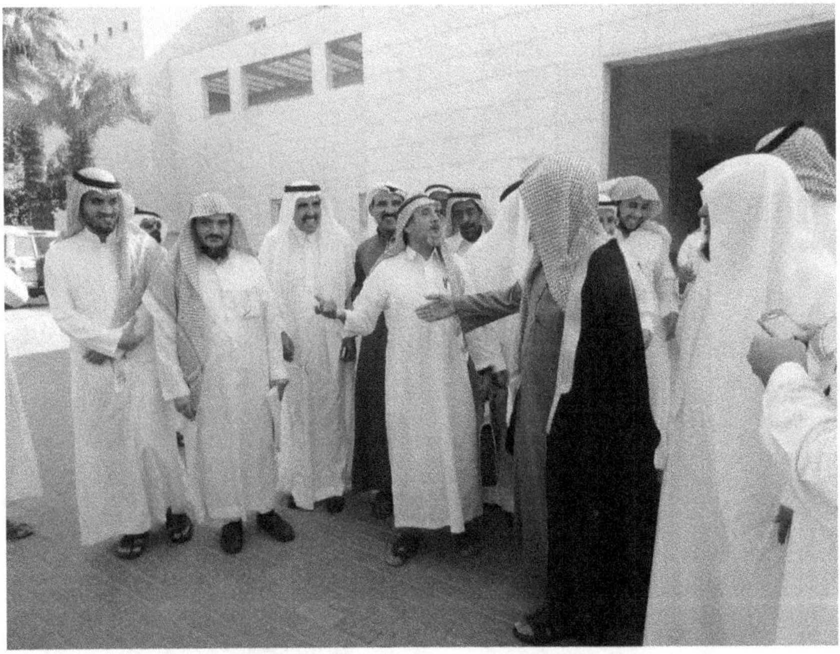

Figure 3 HASM member Abdallah al-Hamid (6th from left) together with other HASM members and supporters in front of the court, 2012. Wikimedia Commons/Sultan Alfifi.

success in actually motivating anyone to voice their support in the proposed way. It seems that, in light of the ongoing, indeed relentless, crackdown, no one was willing to expose themselves for the sake of the association, and the ideas of HASM alone were not enough to encourage actual activism.

By late 2013 CE, HASM had effectively ceased to exist as a result of the pressure of the security services and the judiciary. All founding members were either in prison or about to be sentenced to prison terms. Due to the lack of personnel outside of Saudi prisons, the frequency of HASM declarations and reports decreased until the association's official website finally stopped being updated in early 2014 CE. No new declarations have been published since, and there are no records of any public activities by HASM members since. In April 2020 CE, Abdallah al-Hamid, the main ideologue of the group, who had decidedly shaped the theory behind its activism, died while in Saudi custody. According to media reports, he had long suffered from health problems and had not received the necessary medical treatment. Al-Hamid reportedly had a stroke in his prison cell, fell into a coma and died a few hours later.[75] The news of his death triggered a wave of demonstrations of sympathy in international media and social media. At the time of writing, the other founding members of HASM remain in prison. Thus, on the ground in Saudi Arabia the Islamic civil rights movement, which had only just begun in the later 2000s CE, effectively ended in the mid-2010s CE.

2

Scholars, activists and intellectuals – HASM's social background

The Islamic civil rights movement developed against a specific social background, and this background naturally influenced the ideas and the activities of the movement. It has almost become a commonplace in the humanities to state that the environment in which ideas are formulated determines their eventual shape, the way they are presented and the appeal they have for different groups of people. Theories that were created in an institutionalized academic setting will always look very different from, say, concepts that develop in the context of formally uneducated, traditional rural communities. They will be presented in a different way, will allow different kinds of arguments and will recognize different individuals as figures of authority. The ideas will be accessible to different groups of people and might be perceived as convincing by different audiences. In light of this observation it is useful to look at the social context in which HASM and its ideas were created.

Paths to activism – Biographies of HASM's main members

At first glance, the founding members of HASM came from disparate social and professional backgrounds. Some were veteran opposition activists who had already participated in the first wave of Islamically inspired oppositional petitions in the 1990s CE; others were rather new to oppositional activism. Some were academics in non-Islamic fields like literature, economics or engineering, others had a civil society background and only a few were trained Islamic scholars or experts of Islamic law. In its founding declaration, HASM stressed the large share of civil society activists among its members. At the end of the declaration, it listed the names and professions of the founding members. Of the fourteen founding members, seven were described as civil society activists, three as academics in non-Islamic fields, two as Islamic scholars and one as a former judge. One founding member was not characterized by any specific profession. Figure 4 shows the backgrounds of HASM's founding members according to the founding declaration. While most of HASM's founding members were not trained Islamic scholars, all of them had gone through the Saudi Arabian education system, which places strong emphasis on Islamic subjects. In general, they all seemed to come from educated middle- to upper-class families.

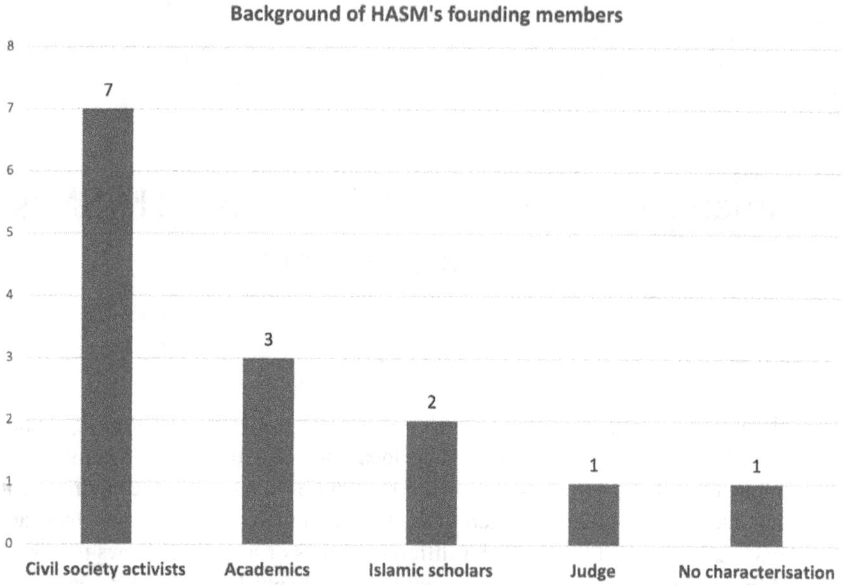

Figure 4 Background of HASM's founding members according to HASM's founding declaration.

The most prominent member of HASM was Abdallah al-Hamid (*ʿAbdallāh al-Ḥāmid*). He was born in 1950 CE in the central Arabian city of Burayda, which has long been known as a centre of conservative Islamic movements. There, he took his first religious courses in mosques and Islamic centres as a child. After graduating from secondary school in Burayda, he studied Arabic language at Imam Muhammad ibn Saud Islamic University in Riyadh. Later, he gained a doctorate in literary criticism from the renowned Al-Azhar University in Cairo. He worked as a lecturer for Arabic language and Islamic culture at Imam Muhammad ibn Saudi Islamic University and the College of Sharia and Islamic Studies in Burayda. In 1976 CE, he briefly taught Arabic to non-native speakers in Karachi in Pakistan. In 1981 CE he finally became Associate Professor and in 1988 CE Professor for contemporary Arabic literature at Imam Muhammad ibn Saud Islamic University in Riyadh. All in all, al-Hamid followed a classical academic career inside the Saudi Arabian university system. His political activism started during the wave of oppositional petitions in the early 1990s CE. Al-Hamid supported some of the petitions and was one of the founders of the short-lived civil society group Committee for the Defence of Legitimate Rights (*lağnat ad-difāʿ ʿan al-ḥuqūq aš-šarʿīya*) in 1993 CE. Since that time, al-Hamid was a central figure of the Islamo-reformist current in Saudi Arabia. He shaped many of the oppositional petitions of the early 2000s and after the Arab Spring in 2011 CE. From the beginning, he was the dominant ideological figure in HASM. His activism soon brought heavy personal costs. He was dismissed from his post at university and has been arrested several times since the 1990s CE.[1] In mid-April 2020 CE, al-Hamid died in Saudi detention. According to media

Figure 5 HASM member Abdallah al-Hamid, 2012. Wikimedia Commons/Sultan Alfifi.

reports, he had long suffered from health problems and did not receive the necessary treatment in prison.[2]

Like Abdallah al-Hamid, HASM founding member Muhammad al-Qahtani (*Muḥammad al-Qaḥṭānī*) had an academic background. He was born in 1965 CE and, after he had first studied at Saudi Arabian universities, he obtained a PhD in economics from Indiana University in the United States. He returned to Saudi Arabia and became a professor of economics at the Institute of Diplomatic Studies in Riyadh. In addition to his academic teaching, he hosted a TV show, in which he discussed economic issues. Al-Qahtani began to support the demands of the Islamo-reformist opposition during the second wave of reformist petitions in the 2000s CE. During that time, he began to help the victims of human rights abuses and their families in their interactions with the Saudi authorities, for example, by submitting formal complaints to the relevant Saudi authorities. He also gave several interviews to international media, thereby increasing the visibility of the movement abroad.[3]

Former judge Sulayman ar-Rashudi (*Sulaymān ar-Rašūdī*) was the 'grand seigneur' of HASM. He was born in 1937 CE and was the oldest of HASM's founding members. Ar-Rashudi had enjoyed a standard career in Saudi Arabia's judiciary, which is characterized by a strong influence of Wahhabi legal reasoning. He had studied at the faculty for sharia law at Imam Muhammad ibn Saud Islamic University in Riyadh and had been taught by some of the most prominent Wahhabi scholars of the country, including later Grand Mufti Abd al-Aziz ibn Baz (*ʿAbd al-ʿAzīz ibn Bāz*). In 1971 CE, he became a judge in Riyadh. Later, he worked as a judge in the United Arab Emirates and as a legal advisor in the Saudi Arabian Ministry of Agriculture. In 1976 CE, he was one of the first people in the kingdom to work as a lawyer. His political activism started during the wave of oppositional petitions of the early 1990s CE. Ar-Rashudi was one of the founding members of the Committee for the Defence of Legitimate Rights in 1993 CE, where he met Abdallah al-Hamid. Since that time, ar-Rashudi has been a central figure of the Islamo-reformist current, putting his knowledge of Saudi Arabia's legal system at the disposal of the movement's cause. He supported the victims of rights abuses and, like most HASM members, was arrested several times.[4]

Figure 6 HASM member Sulayman ar-Rashudi, 2012. Wikimedia Commons/Sultan al-Ajmi.

HASM founding member Abd al-Karim al-Khadr (*ʿAbd al-Karīm al-Ḫaḍr*) was another graduate of Saudi Arabia's Islamic universities. He was born in Riyadh in 1964 CE and studied Islamic law at Imam Muhammad ibn Saudi Islamic University in Riyadh, where he also attended lectures by prominent Wahhabi scholar and later Grand Mufti Abd al-Aziz ibn Baz. After his studies, he became a lecturer for Quranic Studies at the same university, until he was made Professor for Comparative Islamic Jurisprudence (*al-fiqh al-muqārin*) at the Faculty for Sharia Law at Al-Qassim University. In the 2000s CE, he participated in the second Islamo-reformist wave and was subsequently dismissed from his job at university. Like Sulayman ar-Rashudi, Abd al-Karim al-Khadr is a graduate of Islamic subjects and brings his skills as a trained religious scholar to the movement.[5]

HASM founding member Muhammad al-Bajadi (*Muḥammad al-Bağādī*) is one of the younger members of the association. In contrast to al-Hamid, ar-Rashudi and al-Khadr, he does not have a professional academic background. He was born in 1978 CE in the central Arabian city of Burayda. After he had studied law for a few semesters at Imam Muhammad ibn Saud Islamic University in Riyadh and King Abd al-Aziz University in the city of Jeddah in the west of the kingdom, he decided to leave university. He became a businessman and founded a logistics company. In the context of the second wave of oppositional activism in the 2000s CE, he began to participate in civil society activism for human rights and organized weekly meetings of like-minded individuals, who discussed the human rights situation in Saudi Arabia. Al-Bajadi was involved in exposing torture in prisons, and he supported the families of the victims of rights violations, for example, by organizing protests and publishing declarations. Since the late 2000s CE, he has been arrested several times.[6]

HASM's founding members also included a few additional individuals with a background in Saudi Arabia's higher education sector or the civil society movement for the release of political prisoners. Fawzan al-Harbi (*Fauzān al-Ḥarbī*) was an engineer and former employee at the King Abd al-Aziz City for Science and Technology in Riyadh before he co-founded HASM. Abd ar-Rahman al-Hamid (*'Abd ar-Raḥmān al-Ḥāmid*) is a brother of Abdallah al-Hamid and holds a PhD in Islamic economics from Umm al-Qura University in Mecca. Abd al-Aziz ash-Shubayli (*'Abd al-'Azīz aš-Šubaylī*) is another example of a HASM member with a civil society background. Before he joined HASM, he had supported the families of political prisoners in the 2000s CE and helped them submit formal complaints to the relevant Saudi authorities.[7]

As can be seen, most of HASM's founding members came from a similar social background, even if there were some differences in their personal histories. First of all, they were all men. Due to the marginalization of women in Saudi Arabia in general and in pious circles in particular, HASM's members obviously did not consider it appropriate to include women as active members of their association. Some female rights activists, like those campaigning for a lifting of the ban on women driving, unofficially supported HASM, but they did not actively seek to join it.[8] Second, all of HASM's founding members came from urban middle- to upper-middle-class families, which makes it something of an elite movement. Many had worked at Saudi universities or inside the Saudi government apparatus. There were no individuals from poor families or from rural areas among them. Third, all of them were educated men. The proportion of academics among them was extremely high. In fact, virtually all of the founding members had spent at least some time at Saudi Arabian universities. Many had obtained a doctorate. It can be said that all of them were products of the Saudi Arabian education system. In summary, HASM was essentially founded by a group of educated, middle-class, urban men.

The Islamic intellectual

Although the majority of HASM's members were not trained Islamic scholars, Saudi Arabia's religion-centred general education system had enabled them to make Islamic arguments and find Islamic justifications for their activism. It was already mentioned that some of the association's most influential and most prominent members had studied non-Islamic subjects and had not received any formal training as religious scholars. Abdallah al-Hamid was a literary scientist, Muhammad al-Qahtani had studied economics and Muhammad al-Bajadi was a businessman. Nonetheless, they criticized the positions of the official Wahhabi establishment and justified their demands in Islamic language. In their declarations and lectures, they skilfully moved in the territories of Islamic sciences, quoted verses from the Quran and explained what specific Islamic concepts actually meant according to their interpretation. The reason they could do this was Saudi Arabia's education system, which strongly emphasizes religious subjects. In 2004 CE Gilles Kepel observed that

> a third of the timetable at elementary schools consists of religious subjects, a quarter at middle school and between 15 and 35% at grammar school. At university, in the departments of social sciences, nearly half of all subjects are dedicated to religion.[9]

HASM's founding members were all educated men, who had gone through the Saudi education system. As a consequence, they were familiar with Quranic arguments and the basics of Islamic theology and Islamic law. Justifying their civil society activities through Islamic arguments seemed to come naturally to them. They were neither Islamic scholars nor simple laymen, but occupied a middle position between these two, that of the 'Islamic intellectual'.[10] They did not belong to the traditional class of religious scholars but were nevertheless able to speak their language and counter Islamic arguments with Islamic arguments. Since the Saudi Arabian education system had not provided them with sufficient training in other modes of argumentation, it was natural for them to use Islamic arguments in their texts.[11] The members of HASM had tried to make an asset out of their middle position between the official religious scholars on the one hand and laymen with knowledge of worldly things on the other hand. They claimed that in order to understand political questions, one needed to be educated in religious affairs as well as worldly affairs. In their eyes, bridging the gap between the religious establishment and non-religious sciences was the only way to solve existing political problems.[12]

The Islamic intellectual is not a specifically Saudi Arabian phenomenon, and Islamic intellectuals have decisively shaped new Islamic discourses in many countries of the Islamic world. Since the early twentieth century CE, many members of 'Islamist' movements, which called for bringing their societies and states into line with Islamic teachings, as they interpreted them, were not trained Islamic scholars but intellectuals with an education in other, non-religious fields. Modern, educated, middle-class professionals and university students have been a core constituency of movements like the Muslim Brotherhood in Egypt, the Islamically inspired opposition movement in Iran or contemporary Islamic parties and organizations from Morocco to Turkey, Pakistan and Indonesia. Many of their most important leaders were educated laymen, who had knowledge of worldly things but were also able to speak the language of Islam.[13] They were firmly rooted in modern reality, but also understood themselves as devout and educated Muslims, who were able to draw their own conclusions from the Islamic texts.

Islamic intellectuals often directly challenged the monopoly of the religious establishment. The members of the official religious institutions in countries like Egypt have been regularly criticized by Islamically educated intellectuals, who come from outside these establishments but nevertheless use the same Islamic language.[14] Influential Islamic movements like that of Islamic Modernism, which developed in Egypt at the end of the nineteenth century CE and strived to combine Islam with modern values like rationality, progress and democracy, had developed in circles of Islamic intellectuals, who were educated in Islamic affairs, but not part of the official Islamic institutions. It seems that, sometimes, these Islamic intellectuals, or 'heretical intellectuals', as they have also been called,[15] were more capable of finding new perspectives on Islamic teachings than the traditional keepers of Islamic heritage in the official religious institutions. While Islamic intellectuals usually remained committed to the implementation of the rulings of Islam, they were also more open to reconciling them with worldly needs than traditional religious scholars.[16]

In several countries, Islamic intellectuals were also responsible for major challenges to the ruling political forces, or at least for the formulation of a new contribution to political discourse. By bringing forward political demands and legitimizing them in Islamic language – as the Islamic civil rights movement did in Saudi Arabia – these movements questioned the legitimacy of the ruling order and presented their own counter-project. An illustrative example is the Islamically inspired opposition movement in Iran, which emerged in the 1990s CE and culminated in the election of the reformist Mohammad Khatami as president in 1997 CE. Khatami himself sometimes spoke of the 'religious intellectual', who had to replace the Islamic fanatics as well as the secular intellectuals. Opposition intellectuals in Iran in the 1990s CE endorsed rationality, modernity and human rights in Islamic language and criticized the ruling conservative political and religious establishment. Some of these ideas could also be found in the Green Movement, which protested against suspected election fraud in the 2009 CE presidential election in Iran.[17] Another example are Muslim Brotherhood-inspired movements in Tunisia or Egypt in the wake of the Arab Spring. Even though they were not the key forces behind the uprisings of the Arab Spring to begin with, Brotherhood-affiliated groups and movements, which were mostly led by Islamic intellectuals, soon joined the protests. Organizations like the An-Nahda party in Tunisia or the Egyptian Freedom and Justice Party played a major role in the aftermath of the revolutions. The arguments that they brought forward were often at odds with the arguments of important representatives of the official Islamic institutions, who supported the counter-revolutionary efforts. Thus, the political battle was also a battle for religious legitimacy.[18]

The Islamic civil rights movement is part of a trend of Islamic intellectuals, who have been shaping reformist Islamic discourses since the end of the nineteenth century CE, and it can be argued that their ideas could only develop against this social and intellectual background. The members of HASM did not argue within the Islamic discourse of the official Islamic scholarly institutions. They created another kind of Islamic discourse with its own rules, different from those of the official establishment. Like Islamic intellectuals in other countries, they strove to combine the best of two worlds, bringing together knowledge of the Islamic sources and the rules of Islamic argumentation as well as expertise in worldly sciences and subject areas. They had concrete political and social demands, which were informed by their preoccupation with the actual situation in Saudi Arabia, and they understood themselves as devout Muslims, emphasizing that any legitimate demand would have to be supported by Islamic arguments. In short, they were neither apolitical religious scholars nor areligious, secular worldly experts. In their writings, the members of the Islamic civil rights movement indeed merged Islamic language and references to Islamic sources with human rights language and knowledge of political and social circumstances. It was their middle position between the clergy and the laymen that allowed them to formulate their ideas and engage in their activism.

3

Summarizing HASM's theory

The members of HASM combined practical civil society activism with the creation of a new, complex theory that showed why this activism was legitimate and endorsed by Islam. This theory seemed to be shared by all of HASM's members and it drove their activism. In their texts, the members of HASM all seemed to speak of the same things and use the same language, arguing that Islam called for activism for basic rights and political reforms. First and foremost, the theory behind the activities of HASM is visible in the declarations that were published in the name of the association.[1] Between December 2011 CE and September 2017 CE, HASM also published videos of lectures by HASM members, in which they explained specific elements of their political and religious convictions. They featured prominent HASM members like Abdallah al-Hamid, Muhammad al-Qahtani, Sulayman ar-Rashudi and Abd al-Karim al-Khadr.[2] HASM's reports about the events during the court trials against its members also gave additional hints concerning the ideas and arguments that drive their activism.

The most comprehensive source of HASM's theory of civil society activism are the books of Abdallah al-Hamid, who can be considered the chief ideologue of the group. Since the mid-1990s CE, al-Hamid wrote at least twenty-five books about Islamic or political topics. Some of them were published by the Beirut-based publishing house Arab Scientific Publishers (*ad-Dār al-ʿarabīya li-l-ʿulūm*), while others were simply put on the internet for everyone to download and read. Al-Hamid's books cover a wide range of topics, including theoretical Islamic doctrine (*ʿaqīda*), Islamic political discourse, law and human rights, and civil society. In addition to these books, al-Hamid has written at least seven books of poetry. Many of HASM's declarations, including the association's founding declaration, cannot hide the fact that they were written or at least decisively influenced by al-Hamid, as the same arguments that appear in his books can also be found in these declarations. Taken together, al-Hamid's various books and HASM's declarations and lectures present a comprehensive theory of Islamic thought, politics and civil society activism, which has something to say about the problem of oppression, the principles of a new Islamic discourse focused on rights, the shape of the truly Islamic state and the role of civil society.

Breaking down the walls of oppression

According to HASM's founding declaration, the main reasons for the activities of its members were the continuous violations of human rights in Saudi Arabia and the general oppressive tendencies of the government. The fact that these violations had reached a scale that could not be justified and that could only be described as systematic necessitated the kind of activism that HASM propagated:

> The most important reason for the founding of the association is that human rights and basic freedoms, especially political ones, are subject to grave violations in the Kingdom of Saudi Arabia. These violations increased after the Gulf War, because the peoples' awareness of their rights increased. As their awareness of their rights increased, the government increased its violence and after the second Gulf War, it threw thousands of young people into prison.[3]

According to HASM, there were abominable human rights violations in Saudi Arabia. The government suppressed peaceful opposition, imprisoned dissidents, mistreated prisoners and neglected its duty to care for the well-being of the citizens of the kingdom. These violations were not isolated transgressions but linked to the oppressive political system. Where tyranny and political oppression ruled, rights violations naturally followed. HASM's members argued that, in order to understand the roots of these violations and fight for an end to them, one had to look at the oppressive political system and the way it legitimized the actions of the government. Once one had grasped where the strength of oppression came from, one could counter it and strive to improve the situation of the citizens who suffered under the heavy hand of the oppressor.

In several of his books, Abdallah al-Hamid argues that the dominant Islamic discourse is one of the key sources of strength of the oppressive political system. The official Islamic establishment in Saudi Arabia presents Islam in a way that justifies oppression and rights violations and legitimizes political tyranny. This is not only a problem in Saudi Arabia, and it is not limited to modern times. According to al-Hamid, since the times of ninth-century CE Islamic scholar Ahmad ibn Hanbal, the body of Islamic political thought has been dominated by scholars who justified oppression. Al-Hamid calls their discourse the 'Islamic jurisprudence of coercion' (*fiqh al-iḍṭirār*):

> The Islamic jurisprudence of coercion [*fiqh al-iḍṭirār*] spread and took roots in the education system and the academic system. [. . .] They considered oppression an evil without alternative. This current appeared in the generation of Imam Ahmad ibn Hanbal. After that, the despair of the Islamic scholars increased, and they considered oppression to be a natural aspect of the state and leadership, and preferred police-state security to justice.[4]

Due to the political circumstances of their times, Islamic scholars since the ninth century CE were oftentimes forced to accept that they were ruled by oppressive kings and caliphs. When writing about politics, they often seemed to assume that oppressive kingship was the natural form of government and that people had to obey their ruler, even if he was unjust. By resigning themselves to this political reality and aligning their Islamic legal theories with it, they consciously or unconsciously legitimized this form of rule and became the allies of the oppressive rulers. In one of his first texts, which was written in the mid-1990s CE, al-Hamid finds strong words to describe this link between such Islamic scholars and oppressive rulers:

> The most dangerous thing from which our Islamic community [*umma*] has been suffering over the centuries is the close alliance between the Islamic jurists of darkness [*fuqahāʾ aẓ-ẓalām*] and the rulers of oppression [*umarāʾ al-istibdād*].[5]

Al-Hamid adopts the idea, widespread among Salafists, that the message of Islam has been more and more distorted over the centuries. According to his analysis, the teachings of Islam were still implemented in an exemplary manner during the times of the prophet Muhammad and his four immediate successors, the Rightly Guided Caliphs. They had witnessed the revelation of the Quran and had tried to emulate the example of the prophet Muhammad in their political decisions. After the time of the Rightly Guided Caliphs, however, what the Islamic scholars understood to be Islam was further and further removed from the original Islamic message. Al-Hamid distinguishes several phases in the development of the Islamic discourse. During the time of the Umayyad caliphate (661–750 CE), Islamic scholars had already begun to marginalize Islamic principles like justice and political participation in favour of approaches that benefited the oppressive rulers of the Umayyad dynasty. However, there was still a group of dissident scholars who insisted on the implementation of these principles. Things grew worse after the Umayyad dynasty had been replaced by the Abbasid dynasty, which ruled the Islamic caliphate from 750 until 1258 CE. Under the pressure of the rulers, almost all independent Islamic voices were silenced and what al-Hamid calls the 'Abbasid form of Islamic doctrine' (*aṣ-ṣīyāġa l-ʿabbāsīya li-l-ʿaqīda*) became the dominant school of Islamic thought. It decisively influenced Islamic thought throughout the Abbasid era and until the times of the Ottoman rulers. The form of Islam that is being spread by the official religious establishment in countries like Saudi Arabia today is still based on it.[6]

Al-Hamid strongly criticizes the mainstream of Sunni Islamic thought, which has been shaped by the Abbasid form of Islamic doctrine, for its obsession with irrelevant theoretical issues and its political passivity. According to al-Hamid, Islamic scholars since Abbasid times have turned the priorities of Islam upside down. Instead of focusing on key issues, like how to build a just society, they buried themselves in speculation about secondary, theoretical issues. Instead of bringing the Muslim community together, they were responsible for relentless conflicts about petty questions. The writings of past Islamic scholars were full of ideological battles about questions such as whether the text of the Quran was eternal or had been created by God at a specific point in time. Scholars had declared each other unbelievers for petty reasons and had sown the seeds of political conflicts. As a consequence of these idle debates about questions that cannot be answered the message of Islam has been fragmented and has been deprived of its original clarity. Al-Hamid argues that, after centuries of these theoretical discussions, nothing seems to be clear in the teachings of Islam anymore. On any given questions, there appear to be several opinions, which all claim to be valid:

> The uncertainty is further increased by the fact that the contradiction is not limited to the spiritual part of Islamic doctrine, or to petty side questions or a number of secondary questions in the civil part [of Islamic doctrine]. It is there in big and many things. [. . .] Someone, who is looking for a legal opinion, finds both a particular opinion and its opposite, even with one Islamic scholar or jurist. He even finds two contradictory or incompatible opinions, not in one school, but even with one Islamic scholar and jurist.[7]

In addition to this increasing uncertainty about the principles of Islamic religion, the dominant discourse is characterized by its insistence on political passivity. Al-Hamid argues that, since Abbasid times, most Islamic scholars seem to agree that the Islamic sciences have to focus on such theoretical questions and abstain from anything remotely resembling politics. According to the 'Abbasid form of Islamic doctrine', one has to obey the ruler in political questions. It is not the function of Islamic sciences to give instructions about how the state should be organized. Instead, the Islamic scholar in his Abbasid form is politically passive. As a result of this restriction, the liberating potential of Islam was squandered. All over the Islamic world, Muslims were told that they should not resist the unjust policies of the oppressive ruler, but rather show patience in the face of his injustice.

The results of the dominance of the Abbasid form of Islamic doctrine for ordinary Muslims were devastating. As oppressive rule was unchallenged in many Islamic countries, and indeed justified by Islamic scholars, injustice spread, and the states of the Islamic world were helpless in the face of secularism, Westernization and the dominance of European and American powers:

> Therefore, we say: The Islamic legal scholars who preserve the Abbasid form of Islamic doctrine, education, politics and culture today in the era of Western imperialism [. . .] protect political backwardness with a religious discourse. [. . .] They open the gate for the winds of secularism, Westernism [*farangǎa*], Westernisation [*taġrīb*], globalisation and NATO dominance, like the ignorant scholars of the Ottoman state did before them.[8]

Al-Hamid concludes that the dominant Islamic discourse, which has been shaped by the 'Abbasid form of Islamic doctrine', is one of the most important reasons for the prevalence of oppression, injustice and political weakness in many Islamic countries.

Towards a new Islamic culture of rights

Abdallah al-Hamid argues that the dominant Islamic discourse needs an intellectual and cultural renewal. The mainstream Sunni doctrine, which emphasizes secondary, theoretical questions at the expense of key political issues and propagates political passivity, has to be replaced by a new, innovative Islamic discourse that can revitalize the political vigour of Islam. Muslims have to realize that the Islamic sharia does not only have a spiritual side, which regulates affairs of worship and belief, but also have a civil side, which includes political principles like justice. The way to achieve this is to return to the original texts of the Islamic sharia and re-read them, while keeping in mind how the instructions of Islam were implemented in the era of the prophet Muhammad and his immediate successors, the Rightly Guided Caliphs. In addition to this, the re-reading of the Islamic texts also has to be informed by a knowledge of the findings of modern science. In his book *So That the Quran Is Not a Carrier of Different Meanings* al-Hamid summarizes his approach by referring to the well-known metaphor of the so-called Verse of Light in the Quran, which compares the light of God to a light that emanates from an oil lamp inside a bottle, which stands in a niche in a wall:[9]

> [The aim is] re-formulating the Islamic doctrine [*ʿaqīda*], the stated aims of the sharia [*maqāṣid aš-šarīʿa*] and its spirit by returning to the lamp of the clear literal and deduced statements of the sharia in the bottle of the era of the Prophet and the Rightly Guided Caliphs and in the niche of the truths of the sciences, especially the social sciences, in order to focus on the elements which confront the modern challenges.[10]

Al-Hamid takes the Quranic metaphor and uses it to describe the kind of intellectual renewal he has in mind. Muslims need to re-read the Quran and the hadith. They have to follow the example of the prophet Muhammad and the Rightly Guided Caliphs with regard to the practical implementation of the rules that can be found in the Islamic texts. Finally, they have to bring their implementations in line with the findings of the sciences, for example concerning the social and political consequences of persistent injustice. In the end, the texts, their early implementation and modern science will unanimously tell Muslims that there is no sustainable alternative to a just political system.

According to al-Hamid, this is a Salafist approach and true Salafism means constant intellectual renewal. In one of his books, he calls his method 'middle path Salafism' (*as-salafīya l-wusṭā*).[11] Al-Hamid criticizes passive Salafist scholars, who simply imitate past religious authorities and accept their opinions without questioning them. The opinions of scholars from the past may be important points or reference for today's Muslims, but their opinions are not sacrosanct. In fact, they only constitute historical forms of Islam, which were influenced by their historical circumstances and the limited knowledge of their times. Past religious scholars were not infallible. Therefore, Salafism does not mean the imitation of religious authorities from the past, but rather a method of constant renewal in the framework of the established principles of Islam:

> The Salafist method [is] flexible. It is a framework which allows a real renewal that combines the preservation of the absolute principles [*aṯ-ṯawābiṯ al-qaṭʿīya*] with

> the renewal of the means, the detailed formulations, the branches, the application and the implementation. [. . .] Salafism is a method and an approach, not a specific school [*maḏhab*]. [. . .] Every Salafism is a temporary renewal, which constitutes a specific mixture of medicine, which focusses on a specific illness in a certain time and place.[12]

According to al-Hamid, the Islamic sharia lays down certain principles concerning the way Muslims should lead their everyday lives. For example, it calls on Muslims to work towards a just society. How the believers implement these principles is not laid down in detail in the sharia texts. They can freely choose the means of implementation that fit their circumstances and appear most appropriate to them. Nothing prevents Muslims from thinking about new ways to implement justice in modern times, irrespective of how it was understood a few hundred years ago. The principles are fixed and do not change, but the means of implementation vary from place to place and from era to era. Therefore, it is wrong to simply imitate Islamic scholars from the past and adopt their opinions without asking if they are appropriate today. Al-Hamid argues that independent reasoning (*iǧtihād*) is not only the task of learned scholars but the individual duty of all Muslims. Everyone has to test the arguments of others and criticize them freely in order to contribute to finding the best solution:

> Truth is known through argument [*dalīl*] and proof [*burhān*], not through the [fact that] it was said by this or that individual. [. . .] Therefore, the conscious legal scholars made it an obligation for every able Muslim to practice independent reasoning in affairs of his religion, especially in fundamental questions. He is not allowed to imitate others.[13]

According to al-Hamid, the Islamic discourse of renewal has to be built on practical ideas and firmly rooted in the affairs of the world, not in purely theoretical scholarly discussions. The aim is to return to an understanding of Islam that combines the spiritual part of the sharia, which regulates the Muslim's relationship to God, with the civil part of the sharia, which contains principles that enable Muslims to live a full and successful life. Al-Hamid argues that Islam is a very worldly religion. It does not only deal with the spiritual well-being of humans in the afterlife but also intends to help humans lead a good life in this world. Therefore, the practical findings of the sciences, which help people lead good and successful lives, belong to Islam, just like the texts of the Quran. The Islamic texts and the sciences do not contradict each other. On the contrary, they complement each other. In the end, the basic laws of nature and society and the rules laid down in the Islamic texts speak of the same things, because both come from God:

> The laws of God [*sunan allāh*] that are written in the book of the sharia do not contradict his laws that can be observed in the theatre of society and nature. Correct human thought in the sciences of society and nature does not contradict the transmitted clear statements of the sciences of the sharia. This great principle

was explained by Ibn Taymiya in his book 'Reason and Tradition' [*al-ʿAql wa-n-naql*].[14]

Al-Hamid refers to thirteenth-/fourteenth-century CE Islamic scholar Ibn Taymiya and adopts his idea that the findings of natural and social sciences and the statements of the Islamic texts cannot contradict each other. This means that the findings of the sciences can be used as arguments in an Islamic context. When one tries to understand a specific passage from the Quran, it can help to look at the findings of the sciences, because they can occasionally give a hint at a possible meaning of a verse. For example, both social sciences and certain passages from the Islamic texts indicate that only a just society is a stable society. Therefore, justice is a necessary quality in human societies. In worldly things, Muslims can, and indeed must, learn from other societies. They can benefit from the scientific advances of other people and implement them in their own countries. Everything that makes Muslim societies stronger and more successful, be it economically, politically or militarily, must be implemented.

Al-Hamid wants to contribute to the formulation of a new, practical Islamic culture, which re-focuses on the basic political principles of Islam and the protection of the people's political, economic and human rights. He argues that Muslims need to re-activate principles like freedom, pluralism, freedom of speech and political participation, which were part of the Islamic message in the times of the prophet Muhammad but were forgotten later on. Muslims need to rediscover that political, economic and human rights belong to the message of Islam. The founding declaration of HASM clearly stated that laying the foundation of such a new Islamic culture of rights was one of the main aims of the association. According to the declaration, the aims of HASM included:

1. Laying an Islamic foundation for a culture of political human rights, while considering the means of shura rule [*al-ḥukm aš-šūrī*, 'rule through consultation'] one of the pillars of the Islamic political doctrine, which – according to the sharia – cannot be abandoned or neglected. They include justice, freedom, ideological and political pluralism and tolerance. [. . .]
2. Laying an Islamic foundation for a culture of civil and economic rights, like equality, equal political opportunities, economic and social justice and fairness. [. . .]
3. Laying an Islamic foundation for a culture of human rights and the rights of the accused and the prisoners.[15]

According to al-Hamid, all these principles, which Muslims have to rediscover, are real Islamic principles and were implemented in Muslim societies in the past. For example, the principles of pluralism and tolerance can be observed in the way the fourth of the Rightly Guided Caliphs, Ali, treated the radical, heterodox group of the Kharijites. The Kharijites had seceded from the mainstream of Muslims. They were quick in declaring other Muslims infidels, if they did not follow their particular interpretation of Islam, and they did not recognize the leadership of Ali. Despite all that, Ali did not oppress them and did not force them to abandon their beliefs. He let them be and only fought against them after they had declared an open revolt against him and attacked his supporters.[16] Islam also guarantees many other rights. They include dignity, equality, the right to the protection of one's life and physical well-being, and the right to a just government and an independent judiciary. They also encompass the right to fair wages and working conditions, a fair distribution of wealth, the right to access to free media as well as to fair and humane treatment in prisons and courtrooms. According to al-Hamid, all these rights are guaranteed by the teachings of Islam. Muslims should rediscover them and build a new Islamic culture, which understands that these rights are an essential part of the message of Islam and that they need to be implemented in everyday life. Political, economic and human rights belong to the fundamental principles of Islam, and Muslims have to remember that 'Islam is the religion of rights, freedom, dignity and equality'.[17]

The shape of the Islamic state

According to Abdallah al-Hamid, the message of Islam contains political principles that need to be implemented in a Muslim state. Islam is not apolitical but has its own general ideas about how Muslims should organize their political affairs. The name that is often used by al-Hamid and other HASM members to designate a system of government that corresponds to the political principles of Islam is shura rule (*al-ḥukm aš-šūrī*, 'rule through consultation'). Shura stands for the right of the citizens to participate in political decision-making and to choose their leaders. Thus, the Islamic principle of shura rule is the antidote to classical forms of absolute rule and oppression, which are embodied by the examples of the Roman emperor (Caesar) and Persian king Khosraw. In a lecture published in November 2012 CE, al-Hamid summarizes this contradiction between Islamic shura and 'un-Islamic' oppression in one concise sentence:

> Shura rule [*al-ḥukm aš-šūrī*] is the defining feature that distinguishes between a rule that belongs to the way of Muhammad and a rule that belongs to the whim of Khosraw and Caesar.[18]

While Muslims have some leeway in the implementation of the political principles of Islam and must rely on individual reasoning (*iǧtihād*) to find the best and most appropriate means of their implementation, they are nevertheless bound by the principles of shura rule. According to al-Hamid's analysis, there are ten such principles:

1. Islam affirmed that the place of the Islamic community [*umma*] is above the ruler, not the other way around. [. . .]
2. The ruler is the authorised representative [*wakil*] of the Muslim community, and not its guardian. [. . .]
3. As long as the ruler is an authorised representative, he has to do what all authorised representatives do, namely abide by the rules of the authorisation and return to his employer in all important things. [. . .]

4. Rule in Islam is elected shura rule. The rule of the oppressor is not allowed and has no legitimacy. [. . .]
5. The ruler must not use violence, neither for reaching power, nor for clinging to it. He must not harass his opponents. [. . .]
6. The ruler is a salaried employee, and the rules of employment apply to him. [. . .]
7. The change of power and succession by the most competent person belong to the political rights in Islam. [. . .]
8. The judge is, like the ruler, an authorised representative of the Muslim community, not its guardian and not a representative of the ruler.
9. In the state of Islam, citizenship is the foundation for rights and obligations.
10. Jihad is against an aggression, not against un-belief without aggression. The foundation for the relationship between the Islamic state and the other states of the world is peaceful coexistence [*musālama*].[19]

All of these principles are basic rules that Islam has laid down with regard to the way Muslims should organize their societies, the relationship between them and their rulers and the relationship between their state and the world at large.

HASM argues that, according to the principles of Islam, the people are the real holders of power, sovereignty and political authority. HASM members like Abdallah al-Hamid and Abd al-Karim al-Khadr insist that the theory of some Islamic scholars who think that the rulers and the scholars are the guardians of the people, and that the latter have to obey the former, is wrong. The people do not need a guardian. They are their own guardian and political sovereignty belongs to them. The Quran is clearly addressed to all Muslims, not just the rulers or the scholars. All Muslims are called on to implement the principles of Islam. What is more, as a collective body, the Muslim community will always find the right solution and agree on the right things. The majority will never agree on something misguided. As a group, the Muslim community is 'rightly-guiding' (*mahdīya*).[20] After the death of the prophet Muhammad, only the community as a whole can be considered an infallible authority, because even if some go astray, the majority will always find truth. Al-Hamid argues that obedience to the majority decision of the Muslim community is, in fact, an Islamic obligation:

> Islam made obedience to the Muslim community [*umma*] a part of obedience to God, because it is the Muslim community that embodies the political consensus. They were authorised by God to protect the community and the state. Thus, they are blessed and, in their consensus, infallible, because, like it says in the authentic hadith: 'They do not agree on something misguided.'[21]

The people are the foundation of any state and all political power belongs to them. They have the right to decide the policies of their government. The ruler is never more than an authorized representative (*wakīl*) of the people and is bound by their decisions.

HASM's members argue that the relationship between the ruler and his subjects can be characterized as a social contract. By means of this contract, the people, who are the real holders of political sovereignty, make the ruler their representative, and in turn the ruler has to adhere to the rules of the contract. The Islamic principle of allegiance (*bay'a*) does not mean that the people have to obey the ruler in any case, but rather denotes this kind of contract:

> Rule in Islam is based on a contract between the state and society, which is called allegiance [*bay'a*] to the book of God and the customs of his prophet, peace be upon him. This also means that the ruler is an authorised representative [*wakīl*] of the community [*umma*] and that the representation requires that the ruler adheres to the institutional (meaning constitutional) tools and means which guarantee justice in property and administration, as well as compulsory collective shura rule (representative power).[22]

According to the social contract of allegiance, the ruler has clearly defined tasks and powers, and he is bound by the basic political principles of Islam. Whenever the ruler breaks his contractual obligations, the contract becomes void and the people are not obligated to obey him. In a lecture published in October 2012 CE, HASM member Abd al-Karim al-Khadr even argues that such a breach of duty on the part of the ruler can be considered an act of rebellion (*ḫurūǧ*). Just like the people can be accused of wrongful rebellion, if they resist a legitimate ruler, the ruler can be accused of rebellion against the people.[23] Whoever breaks the contract violates the basic political rules of Islam.

If the people are the true holders of political sovereignty, the Quran's call to obey 'those who have been entrusted with authority' (*ūlū l-amr*) cannot be understood to mean the rulers, but rather the notables, who represent the opinion and the will of the people. HASM strongly criticizes the opinion of some Salafist scholars who claim that Muslims have to blindly obey their rulers. They usually justify this by referring to the Quranic verse: 'Pay heed unto God, and pay heed unto the Messenger and unto those from among you who have been entrusted with authority.'[24] In several books and lectures, HASM members Abdallah al-Hamid and Abd al-Karim al-Khadr argue against this interpretation. They state that the term 'those who have been entrusted with authority' (*ūlū l-amr*) is a plural form and, therefore, cannot apply to the ruler or any specific individuals, but only to a group of people. As the people are the true owners of political sovereignty, the term can only mean the elected notables, who are trusted by the people and represent their will and their interests. Al-Hamid quotes the twentieth-century CE Egyptian reformists Muhammad Abduh and Muhammad Rashid Rida and enthusiastically adopts their idea that, today, an elected parliament is the best embodiment of the term 'those who have been entrusted with authority'. The members of parliament are chosen by the people and represent their wishes and opinions. They are trusted by the people and represent their interests. Therefore, the Quranic term applies to them, and they also correspond to the traditional concept of the 'people who loosen and bind' (*ahl al-ḥall wa-l-'aqd*), which has been used to describe notables and leaders:

> The council of the representatives of the Islamic community [*umma*] is the appropriate means today for the implementation of the concept of 'those who

> have been entrusted with authority' [*ūlū l-amr*] in the Quran and the concept of the 'people who loosen and bind' [*ahl al-ḥall wa-l-ʿaqd*] from tradition. They alone embody the consensus of the Islamic community.[25]

An elected parliament, or a council of representatives, is the best embodiment of the Quranic principle of 'those who have been entrusted with authority'. The members of such a council are trusted by the people who have chosen them. They are usually chosen because they are experts in different fields and represent the opinion of the people. They are the elected rulers and, therefore, they are owed obedience.

The members of HASM argue that, in the modern state, the political principles of Islam can only be implemented in the framework of a strong constitutional system. The checks and balances of a modern constitutional state create the right circumstances for the implementation of the Islamic principle of shura rule (*al-ḥukm aš-šūrī*, 'rule through consultation') and Islamic values like justice, freedom and pluralism:

> The shura system [*an-niẓām aš-šūrī*] includes organisations, procedures and branches, which are embodied by the constitutional system. The system of shura rule is the realisation or the sovereignty of the community [*umma*]. The constitution is the realisation of the system of shura rule. The constitution is the giver of competences and the preventer of violations.[26]

Only a strong constitution can establish a system of institutions which guarantee that there is no injustice and that the people's rights are protected. A constitution includes several elements, like the separation of the powers of the state, holding free and fair elections, an independent judiciary, a clear limitation of the responsibilities of the government, allowing the establishment of civil society organization and guaranteeing the protection of the citizens' rights. Taken together, these elements provide the framework for the implementation of the political principles of Islam. Therefore, states like Saudi Arabia need a constitution. The writing and passing of a constitution is the first step towards a fairer and more just state. However, HASM emphasizes that, despite the great importance of the constitutional system, a constitution alone does not make an Islamic state. In itself, a constitution is a neutral tool for the organization of the institutions of a state in a just and fair way. It is the principles that are implemented in the framework of the constitution that make it an Islamic constitution:

> Constitution is a general word. It can be secular, it can be Buddhist, it can be socialist, [. . .] and it can be Islamic, committed to the enjoining of virtue and the forbidding of vice.[27]

All real constitutions establish a framework for a just state, which gives the people a voice in the administration of their societies and guarantees the protection of their rights. The values that are implemented in this framework make it a secular, Buddhist, socialist or Islamic constitution. The constitution that HASM's members have in mind is an Islamic one. Consequently, it will have to include specific elements which are deemed Islamic and which distinguish it from other constitutions.

Civil society activism as Islamic obligation

The members of HASM argue that collective civil society activism for the people's rights and for a fairer political system is an Islamic obligation. In several passages of the Quran, God calls on Muslims to cooperate in matters of religion and in civil affairs. Many things can only be achieved when people unite their efforts. Spreading faith and justice is among these things. In Islamic doctrine, there are two concepts that describe this obligation to cooperate to strengthen the people's faith and to root out injustice, namely cooperating for fairness and piety (*at-ta'āwun 'alā l-birr wa-t-taqwā*) and enjoining virtue and forbidding vice (*al-amr bi-l-ma'rūf wa-n-nahy 'an al-munkar*). Both are Quranic obligations, and both have the aim of facilitating the implementation of the rules of Islam in the daily lives of Muslims, allowing them to enjoy full and successful lives. According to HASM's members, these activities, which the Quran demands, are nothing other than organized civil society activism, and they are exactly what HASM intended to do. Therefore, HASM's activities cannot be declared illegal:

> The founding of the association [HASM] is a legitimate activity in Islam, because it is one of the means of cooperating for fairness and piety [*at-ta'āwun 'alā l-birr wa-t-taqwā*] and cooperating for enjoining virtue and forbidding vice [*al-amr bi-l-ma'rūf wa-n-nahy 'an al-munkar*]. It is included in the words of the Almighty: 'That there might grow out of you a community who invite unto all that is good.' [Quran 3:104][28]

According to al-Hamid, the Islamic sharia calls on Muslims to dedicate themselves to building a better and fairer society, and this is what HASM's members are doing. Islam encourages civil society activism, because it can contribute to the building of just and stable societies, where everyone can indicate wrong developments and work to change them. When civil society organizations are outlawed and their members are persecuted, societies lose one of the most effective tools against injustice.

The means through which civil society organizations achieve the aim of bettering society are manifold, and one can learn from the experiences of civil society activists in other parts of the world. According to the members of HASM, history has already shown us that civil society activism can lead to positive developments and contribute to the elimination of injustice. One example are the peaceful revolutions that brought down communist regimes in the 1990s CE. All well-known means of civil society groups are legitimate in terms of Islam. They include the publication of books, organizing lectures, documenting rights violations, supporting victims, lobbying the leadership, informing the people as well as organizing strikes and demonstrations.

Demonstrations have been a particularly controversial subject in Islamic discourse since the beginning of the Arab Spring in 2011 CE. After the mass demonstrations had brought down the first dictators in Tunisia and Egypt, many members of the Wahhabi religious establishment in Saudi Arabia had declared demonstrations to be completely forbidden in Islam, because they supposedly only brought chaos and destruction.[29] Unsurprisingly, HASM did not agree. In November 2012 CE, HASM published a lecture by its member Sulayman ar-Rashudi in which he refuted the Islamic arguments of the official religious establishment. Ar-Rashudi started by declaring that, according to the rules of Islamic jurisprudence, in civil affairs things were generally allowed, except when there was a specific reason for forbidding them. Demonstrations naturally fall into the category of civil affairs and are, therefore, basically allowed. Ar-Rashudi argued that, contrary to what the Wahhabi establishment said, there was no reason for outlawing them. On the contrary, several arguments spoke for them. Demonstrations were an expression of free speech, which was a basic human right and belonged to the principles of Islam. Pointing out injustice was an Islamic obligation and fell into the category of enjoining virtue and forbidding vice. If the aim of demonstrations was to eliminate injustice, and if they were peaceful, they were therefore allowed:

> Demonstrations and protests are means. The principle of the sharia says that the judgement about the aims also applies to the means. If demonstrations are a peaceful means and if their aims are eliminating injustice and implementing truth and justice, they are allowed. [. . .] Calling for peaceful demonstrations to lift injustice and oppression, eliminate corruption and give the people their stolen rights and freedoms and their lost dignity belongs to the call to virtue and to enjoining virtue and forbidding vice, which God has made a sharia obligation. As long as this is the legitimate aim any means which is allowed and leads to it is legitimate, and indeed an obligation.[30]

Ar-Rashudi concluded that all ways of peaceful activism that civil society organizations usually engage in were allowed in sharia law and were, indeed, even obligations of Islam. It was simply wrong to declare them illegal.

In the right circumstances, civil society activism can even be considered a kind of jihad. In several of his books and lectures, Abdallah al-Hamid presents a complex theory of jihad, which recognizes that military jihad in defence of Muslim lands is an obligation but also elevates certain peaceful activities to a higher form of jihad than military activities. He argues that there are two kinds of jihad:

> So that we Arabs and Muslims revive and renew the concept of jihad, there is no alternative to a discourse which affirms that jihad is a twin: Military and war-jihad repels invaders and civil, peaceful jihad repels tyrants.[31]

According to al-Hamid, military jihad is legitimate, but it is only one kind of jihad. Military jihad means defending Muslim lands against an external aggression. It is by necessity defensive and can never be used to expand the lands of Islam or to force other people to accept Islam. Apart from defending fellow Muslims against an invader, there are several peaceful activities that fall into the category of jihad. In contrast to military jihad, which is a response to external aggression, they focus on internal injustice in the Muslim community. Al-Hamid emphasizes that not every civil society activism is jihad. Many things that are done by engaged citizens are commendable and fall into the category of enjoining virtue and forbidding vice, but they do not fulfil the conditions of jihad. In order to be counted as civil, peaceful jihad, an activity must aim at eliminating injustice and oppression by peaceful means, and it must contain an element of hardship and self-sacrifice. Only when someone courageously exposes themselves to danger for the betterment of society can their activities be considered jihad.

In an oppressive environment like Saudi Arabia, the kind of civil disobedience and civil society activism that the members of HASM propagate fulfils these conditions and, therefore, falls into the category of peaceful, civil jihad. Al-Hamid argues that, other than military jihad, which is a collective obligation that is fulfilled if a reasonable number of people has done it, civil jihad is an individual duty for every Muslim, no matter how many others have already engaged in it:

> Military jihad is a collective obligation [*farḍ kifāya*]. If a sufficient number of people do it, the others do not commit a sin [by not doing it]. Peaceful jihad is an individual obligation [*farḍ ʿain*], because as long as the citizens continue to cut the nails of tyranny, this is a safety valve. The participation of the people in demonstrations, protests, declarations, and in voting, nominating and being nominated in elections is a guarantee for their rights.[32]

All Muslims are called on to engage in peaceful jihad against tyranny and injustice, because the constant vigilance of this kind of activity is the best way to guarantee that tyranny does not take roots. Only through this kind of civil society activism can the return of tyranny and oppression be prevented. Al-Hamid argues that peaceful jihad comes before military jihad, because a stable and just society is the precondition for an efficient military defence. Only after the inner tyrant is defeated can a society defend against an external aggressor. Al-Hamid refers to several hadiths and states that, according to Islamic doctrine, peaceful jihad is also higher in rank than military jihad. Those who engage in peaceful jihad have to endure more hardship, and the benefits of peaceful jihad are much greater. Therefore, Muslims have to revive the concept of peaceful jihad, which has been forgotten or deliberately obscured in dominant Islamic discourse. Al-Hamid addresses young people who are enthusiastic about joining military jihad abroad and calls on them to engage in peaceful jihad at home instead:

> May the sheikhs, the young people and the grown men, who long for jihad on the way of God and ask God to grant them martyrdom, [. . .] while thinking that jihad can only be waged in Afghanistan, in the Philippines, in Bosnia or in Chechnya, that it can only be waged against the aggression of the unbelievers and that there is no other way to it than training in the use of cannons and machine guns and mounting armoured vehicles and tanks, wake up.[33]

> To the young people, who seek jihad and martyrdom outside of the Arabian Peninsula we say: Come to peaceful jihad in order to establish shura rule in the Arabian Peninsula. This is one thousand times more worth it than military jihad abroad.[34]

4

Heroes or heretics? – Reactions to HASM

The ideas and activism of HASM have provoked diverse comments and reactions inside and outside of Saudi Arabia. Many of their ideas have been adopted by other Islamically inspired Saudi Arabian oppositional activists, especially those in exile in Europe and North America. Saudi Arabian dissidents in London have praised the activities of HASM's members and have shown their solidarity with the movement. Inside Saudi Arabia, the trials against HASM's members were accompanied by a media campaign of decided critics of the association and its ideas, who attacked them in articles and on social media. On the international level, many human rights organizations have publicly shown their support for HASM. Among international human rights advocates, it seems to be undisputed that HASM is a human rights organization comparable to other human rights groups all around the world, and that it deserves unequivocal international support. All in all, there is a wide range of reactions to the association and its activities. The ideas of HASM have been the cause of much controversy in circles interested in the human rights situation in Saudi Arabia. There is, however, no consensus on what they actually mean and how they should be interpreted.

Reactions to HASM in Saudi Arabia

As was already mentioned, the members of HASM actively participated in the debates of the Saudi Arabian opposition during the 2000s and 2010s CE, and their ideas were praised and taken up by other Saudi Arabian dissidents. For example, Abdallah al-Hamid's concept of civil society activism as civil, peaceful jihad was adopted by writers like Muhammad al-Abd al-Karim, who repeatedly referred to it in his own writings.[1] In the early 2010s CE, some women's rights campaigners in Saudi Arabia publicly voiced their support for HASM. After the trials against HASM members had begun, activists like Manal Ash-Sharif, who had organized a number of women's rights protests, declared their solidarity with HASM and compared the trials against its members to the oppression of women's rights activists.[2] HASM was also in close contact with other human rights activists in Saudi Arabia, like Waleed Abu al-Khair (*Walīd Abū l-Ḫair*), founder of the Jeddah-based Human Rights Monitor in Saudi Arabia (*Marṣad ḥuqūq al-insān fī s-Sū'ūdīya*). He publicly showed his solidarity with HASM and coordinated some of his efforts with HASM.

As most oppositional activists inside the kingdom suffered under increasing government oppression from the early 2010s CE onwards, after this point much of the explicit support for HASM came from dissidents in exile. One prominent example is Saudi Arabian dissident Omar ibn Abd al-Aziz az-Zahrani (*ʿUmar ibn ʿAbd al-ʿAzīz az-Zahrānī*), who lives in Canada and regularly publishes videos, in which he ridicules the policies of the Saudi government. In one of his videos, which was published in 2014 CE, he recommends reading al-Hamid's book *The Word Is Stronger than the Bullet* to his viewers.[3] Another example is London-based Saudi Arabian dissident Sahar al-Faifi (*Saḥar al-Faifī*), who praised al-Hamid's ideas and activities in a 2019 CE article and called him 'the Saudi Nelson Mandela'.[4]

Saudi Arabian human rights groups in exile also repeatedly showed their solidarity with HASM and its members. In March 2018 CE, a number of human rights organizations in exile published a joint statement calling for the release of all members of HASM, who were in prison at the time.[5] In their publications, Saudi Arabian human rights groups in exile like London-based ALQST regularly demand the release of HASM members. In 2018 CE, ALQST even started a public campaign to nominate Saudi Arabian dissidents, including HASM members, for international human rights prizes in order to draw attention to the human rights situation in the kingdom.[6] As can be seen, among Saudi Arabian dissidents, there is clearly much support for the members of HASM and their ideas.

Supporters of the Saudi government and the official religious and judicial establishments did not share these positive views. They harshly criticized HASM's activities and tried to counter the group's ideas. During the trials against HASM's members in the 2010s CE, the prosecutors and the judges as well as commentators and scholars close to the official establishment attacked the association, accusing it of using illogical or wrong arguments and declaring the group's ideas dangerous. A good example was the trial against HASM members Abdallah al-Hamid and Muhammad al-Qahtani in March 2013 CE.[7] In his decision, the judge did not only explain why the accused were guilty, but he tried to delegitimize the ideas behind HASM's activism. He referred to many verses from the Quran and passages from the books of religious scholars and argued that, through their calls for demonstrations, the accused had violated the God-given right of the citizens to national security and stability. The thought of HASM was not so different from al-Qaeda's ideology, the judge claimed, because both called for martyrdom and jihad. Finally, he argued that the ideas brought forward by HASM's members were characterized by a lack of logical and doctrinal coherence and therefore false from a theological standpoint. In the eyes of the judge, al-Hamid and al-Qahtani took from different heterodox theological schools what they wanted without following a stringent line of reasoning:

> He who looks at the two accused finds that they are in a state of lacking doctrinal stability. Sometimes they tend towards the school of the Mutazila and its position concerning forbidding vice and enjoining virtue; sometimes they tend towards the school of the Kharijites and its allowing of rebellion against the ruler; sometimes they go to the school of the Murjiʾa and its splitting of monotheism [*tauḥīd*] into two halves, namely a spiritual half with prayer as its pillar, and a civil half with

> justice and shura rule [*al-ḥukm aš-šūrī*, 'rule through consultation'] as its pillar; and sometimes they go to the school of the Greek philosophers and their position concerning the social contract.[8]

All of the aforementioned historical schools are considered incompatible with Islam in the Wahhabi interpretation and have been attacked by Wahhabi scholars as deviant or even heretical. The judge was clearly trying to delegitimize the ideas behind the activism of al-Hamid and al-Qahtani, instead of just sentencing them for their actions. He argued that not only the defendants' activities but their very ideas were harmful and had to be combatted.[9]

This criticism of HASM's ideas was repeated by some commentators who attacked HASM and other protagonists of the Islamo-reformist current and argued that their ideas were wrong and dangerous. One common tactic of these critics was to sow doubt about the Islamic credentials of HASM's members. For example, in an essay titled 'Someone Asked Me about Dr. Abdallah al-Hamid', Wahhabi scholar and commentator Sulayman ibn Salih al-Kharrashi (*Sulaymān ibn Ṣāliḥ al-Ḫarrāšī*) argued that concepts like civil society, which were used by al-Hamid, were secular concepts that were not compatible with the Islamic sharia. In light of al-Hamid's criticism of Islamic doctrine and his infatuation for supposedly non-Islamic concepts, his theory could hardly be considered compatible with Islam.[10]

HASM did not only face intellectual criticism like this but was also confronted with a media campaign by supporters of the government. For example, after 2013 CE, internet users could read an article that was highly critical of HASM's activities on the Saudi-sponsored website assakina.com, which was used as an outlet for the government's counter-narratives about political and religious issues.[11] Several government-controlled media published articles about the alleged defections of HASM members and their criticism of the development the association had taken.[12] In summary, supporters of the Saudi government were highly critical of HASM and the ideas behind the group's activism. They accused the association of logical and argumentative mistakes and considered the ideas that were spread by HASM's members dangerous, describing them either as secular and 'un-Islamic' or as comparable to the ideology of violent Jihadism.

International reactions to HASM

The reactions of journalists, researchers and human rights advocates from outside Saudi Arabia to the ideas and activities of HASM were overwhelmingly positive. In articles and papers written in English, the members of HASM have been called 'political reformers',[13] 'Islamic liberals'[14] or 'neo-reformists'.[15] In the mind of the average English-speaking reader, all these labels carry predominantly positive connotations. They alone suggest that the activities of HASM's members are commendable and that they should receive the support of the European and North American audience. Respected international human rights NGOs usually call HASM an 'independent human rights organisation'. In doing to, they automatically suggest that HASM is comparable to other human rights organizations around the world, and that its members are committed to the same set of universal human rights. In 2014 CE, Amnesty International published a detailed special report on HASM, in which it praised the peaceful activism of HASM's members and called for their immediate and unconditional release from Saudi prisons.[16] The solidarity shown by prestigious international human rights organizations certainly strengthens the credibility of HASM and confers greater legitimacy to the association's actions, at least in the eyes of an international audience.

Some NGOs and think tanks have directly called on the international community or on specific states to put pressure on the Saudi government in support of HASM. Human rights NGOs regularly call for the release of political prisoners, including HASM members. An interesting example is the NGO Americans for Democracy & Human Rights in Bahrain, which published a report on HASM in 2017 CE. In it, HASM is praised for its peaceful human rights activism and the US government is called on to urge the Saudi authorities to release HASM's members from prison.[17]

After Abdallah al-Hamid had died in a Saudi prison in mid-April 2020 CE, there was a remarkable wave of demonstrations of sympathy in international media. Saudi opposition activists in exile, journalists and human rights advocates praised him as a 'human rights activist',[18] a 'prisoner of conscience'[19] and the 'sheikh of the rights activists' (*šaiḫ al-ḥuqūqīyīn*).[20] Many international human rights advocates, journalists and researchers seem to agree that the ideas and activities of HASM are commendable, and that the association and its members deserve the support of governments and ordinary people in Europe and North America.

In recent years, HASM's members have received several international prizes in connection with their peaceful activism, while they remained imprisoned in Saudi Arabia. This is at least partly a result of the public campaign of the London-based Saudi NGO ALQST to nominate Saudi Arabian dissidents for such prizes.[21] In 2018 CE, HASM members Abdallah al-Hamid and Muhammad al-Qahtani as well as Saudi Arabian human rights activist Waleed Abu al-Khair received the Swedish Right Livelihood Award. This award is sometimes called the 'alternative Nobel Prize', is awarded annually, and is intended to honour individuals who contribute to finding solutions to the most pressing social problems of mankind. The three Saudis received the prize for 'their visionary and courageous efforts guided by universal human rights principles, to reform the political system in Saudi Arabia'.[22] As all three laureates were imprisoned in Saudi Arabia, the founder of ALQST, Yahya Asiri, received the award on their behalf in December 2018.[23] In 2020 CE, the association HASM was awarded the Dutch Geuzenpenning prize for human rights. In a press statement, the foundation behind the prize referred to HASM's efforts to persuade the Saudi government to implement much-needed reforms. Again, Yahya Asiri received the award on behalf of HASM.[24] According to some news reports, HASM member Abdallah al-Hamid was even nominated for the actual Nobel Peace Prize in 2019 CE.[25]

The statements of support published by journalists, researchers and human rights advocates as well as the international prizes clearly show that HASM and the association's members are received very positively by the international audience. Non-Saudis who are interested in the group almost exclusively perceive it as a human rights organization whose aims are compatible with the worldview of European and North American advocates of human rights and democracy. HASM's members are seen as peaceful activists who want to protect human rights and encourage the development of a more democratic political system, and who are persecuted by the Saudi government for it. As such, they are seen as deserving the solidarity and support of European and North American leaders and activists.

Thus, as can be seen, the Islamic civil rights movement and its ideas have been received very differently by different people inside and outside Saudi Arabia. When looking at these different reactions, one is tempted to assume that the stark difference between those who support it and those who think it is dangerous can at least party be explained by superficial or biased interpretations of the movement's ideas. In the end, it is hardly conceivable that the critics, who liken their ideas to al-Qaeda's ideology of violent jihad, and the international supporters, who consider them representatives of a universal human rights ethos, are both right. If we really want to understand the theory and the activities of the Islamic civil rights movement and go beyond such simplistic labels, we need a thorough and detailed analysis of what its members were doing, writing and saying. The next few chapters will present such an analysis of the language, the arguments and the ideas of the Islamic civil rights movement.

5

The intellectual foundations of HASM

The theory of the Islamic civil rights movement was clearly inspired by a wide range of religious and scholarly sources, and it is based on ideas that can be found in these sources. In their texts, the members of HASM refer to the ideas of numerous authors and schools from the past and the present, some from an Islamic context, others belonging to European or North American schools of thought. In one of his books, HASM member Abdallah al-Hamid argues that it is only natural to build on the findings of past scholars and authors and criticize them, because this enables us to see further than they could:

> The form of knowledge of social thought in general, and political thought in particular, in theory and implementation, is a pyramidical pile, where the one who comes later stands on the shoulders of those who came before him, and he can see further than they could.[1]

The members of the Islamic civil rights movement refer to different authors and schools in different ways. Some are quoted much more often than others. Some are referred to in a positive way, while others are criticized. Some are described in great detail, while others are only mentioned in passing. Some sources and authors are obviously more important for their theory than others.

The many different sources and authors that the members of the movement refer to in their texts can be subdivided into seven groups:

- the primary sources of Islam, like the Quran and the hadith corpus, the collections of reports about the sayings and actions of the prophet Muhammad;
- 'classical' Islamic scholars and authors from the early days of Islam until *c.* 1750 CE; they include authoritative scholars from the formative period of Islamic thought until 1050 CE, like the founders of the four large schools of Sunni Islamic jurisprudence, as well as authors from the post-formative period of Islamic thought after 1050 CE;
- authors from the different reformist and revivalist Islamic movements of the eighteenth and nineteenth centuries CE, like the founder of Wahhabism, Muhammad ibn Abd al-Wahhab, or the protagonists of the movement of Islamic Modernism, Muhammad Abduh and Muhammad Rashid Rida;
- contemporary Islamic thinkers and authors from the twentieth and twenty-first centuries CE, like the Egyptian-Qatari Islamic scholar Yusuf al-Qaradawi;

- European and American philosophers and political thinkers, from ancient Greek philosopher Plato to twentieth-century CE British philosopher Bertrand Russell;
- contemporary academics and experts in fields other than Islamic sciences, like international law, human rights or political science; and
- International symbols of political activism, like Mahatma Gandhi or Nelson Mandela.

Of course, in reality these categories are not as clear-cut as this list might suggest. Like any categorization, it is a simplification of complex facts. Nevertheless, it is useful in the limited context of this analysis.

Simply counting how many times certain sources, authors and schools are mentioned in the texts already gives us a first impression of which sources are the most important for the members of the Islamic civil rights movement. Figures 7, 8 and 9 on pages 51, 52 and 53 show how often the different types of sources are referred to in selected books by members of the movement. The graphs show the absolute frequency with which sources and authors belonging to the different types are mentioned in each individual text, as well as their relative share compared to the other types. Figures 7 and 8 focus on selected texts by members of the Islamic civil rights movement that were written between the late 1990s and the early 2010s CE. Figure 9 shows the numbers for selected books written by authors of the broader Islamo-reformist current in the 2000s and 2010s CE. A detailed table of the different sources and authors that are being referred to and the frequency of references to them can be found in an online resource, which is accessible via www.bloomsburyonlineresources.com/peaceful-jihad.

As can be seen in the graphs, the absolute numbers as well as the relative shares of references vary slightly, depending on the focus of the texts, but some general observations can be made. First of all, in light of the high number of quotes from the Quran and the hadith in most of the analysed books, it is, once again, evident that references to the primary sources of Islam constitute an essential part of the argumentation of the Islamic civil rights movement. In most books of the movement, the primary sources of Islam are the largest or second-largest group of sources that are mentioned. For example, on the 166 pages of his book *Human Rights between the Light of Islam and the Darkness of Biting Kingship* (*Ḥuqūq al-insān baina nūr al-islām wa-ġabaš al-mulk al-ʿaḍūḍ*), Abdallah al-Hamid quotes 169 different passages from the Quran or the hadith. On average, this is more than one distinct verse or hadith per page. Matruk al-Falih's fifty-three-page paper 'Constitutional Reform in Saudi Arabia' (*al-Iṣlāḥ ad-dustūrī fī s-Suʿūdīya*) contains forty quotes from the Quran and the hadith, that is, 0.75 quotes per page.

Second, there are a lot of references to Islamic scholars, especially 'classical' ones from the time until *c*. 1750 CE. In seven of the ten analysed books by members of the Islamic civil rights movement, 'classical' Islamic scholars are the largest group of sources that are referred to in the texts. In al-Hamid's books *Middle Path Salafism* (*as-Salafīya l-wusṭā*), *So That the Quran Is Not a Carrier of Different Meanings* (*Likay lā yakūnu l-qurʾān ḥammāl auğuh*) and *The Islamic Constitution* (*ad-Dustūr al-islāmī*), almost three quarters of references are to 'classical' Islamic scholars. Authors that can be categorized as members of Islamic reformist and revivalist

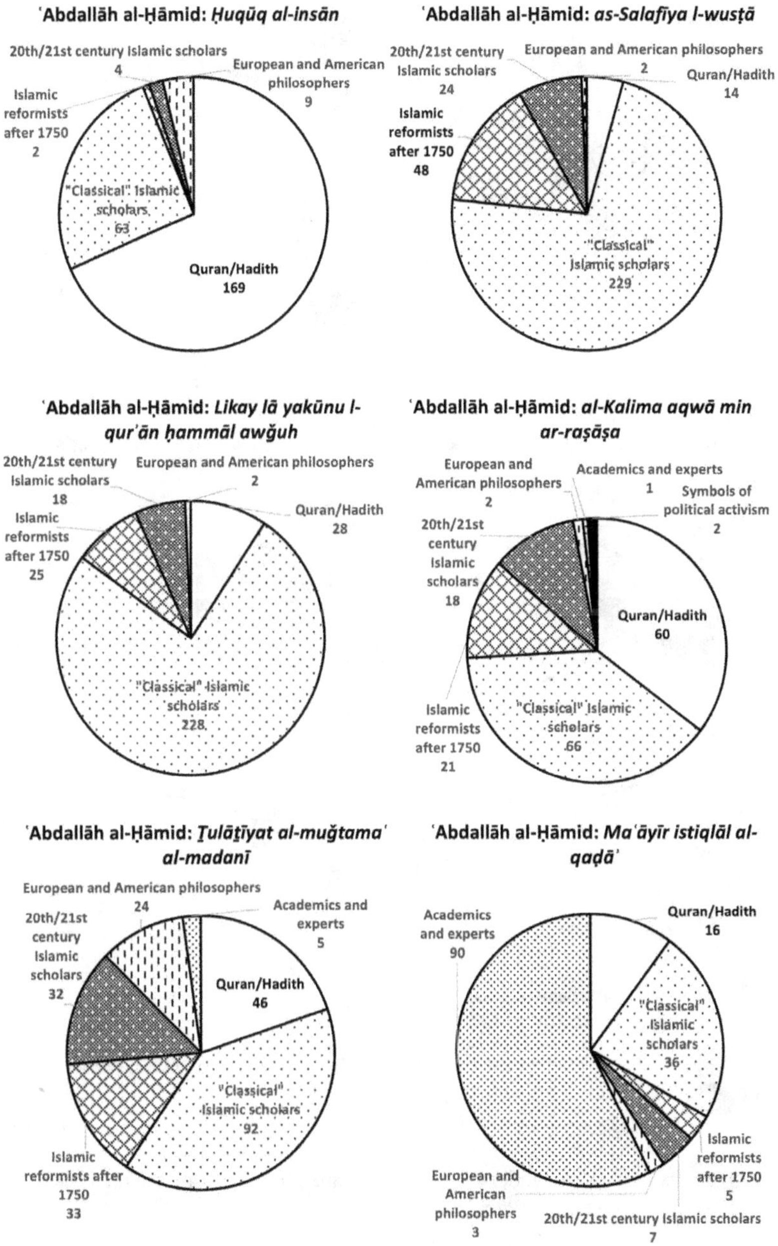

'Abdallāh al-Ḥāmid: *Ḥuqūq al-insān*
20th/21st century Islamic scholars 4
European and American philosophers 9
Islamic reformists after 1750 2
"Classical" Islamic scholars 63
Quran/Hadith 169
'Abdallāh al-Ḥāmid: *as-Salafīya l-wusṭā*
20th/21st century Islamic scholars 24
European and American philosophers 2
Quran/Hadith 14
Islamic reformists after 1750 48
"Classical" Islamic scholars 229
'Abdallāh al-Ḥāmid: *Likay lā yakūnu l-qur'ān ḥammāl awǧuh*
20th/21st century Islamic scholars 18
European and American philosophers 2
Quran/Hadith 28
Islamic reformists after 1750 25
"Classical" Islamic scholars 228
'Abdallāh al-Ḥāmid: *al-Kalima aqwā min ar-raṣāṣa*
European and American philosophers 2
Academics and experts 1
Symbols of political activism 2
20th/21st century Islamic scholars 18
Quran/Hadith 60
Islamic reformists after 1750 21
"Classical" Islamic scholars 66
'Abdallāh al-Ḥāmid: *Ṯulāṯīyat al-muǧtama' al-madanī*
European and American philosophers 24
Academics and experts 5
20th/21st century Islamic scholars 32
Quran/Hadith 46
"Classical" Islamic scholars 92
Islamic reformists after 1750 33
'Abdallāh al-Ḥāmid: *Ma'āyīr istiqlāl al-qaḍā'*
Academics and experts 90
Quran/Hadith 16
"Classical" Islamic scholars 36
Islamic reformists after 1750 5
European and American philosophers 3
20th/21st century Islamic scholars 7

Figure 7 Types of sources and how often they are referred to in selected texts of the Islamic civil rights movement (Part 1).

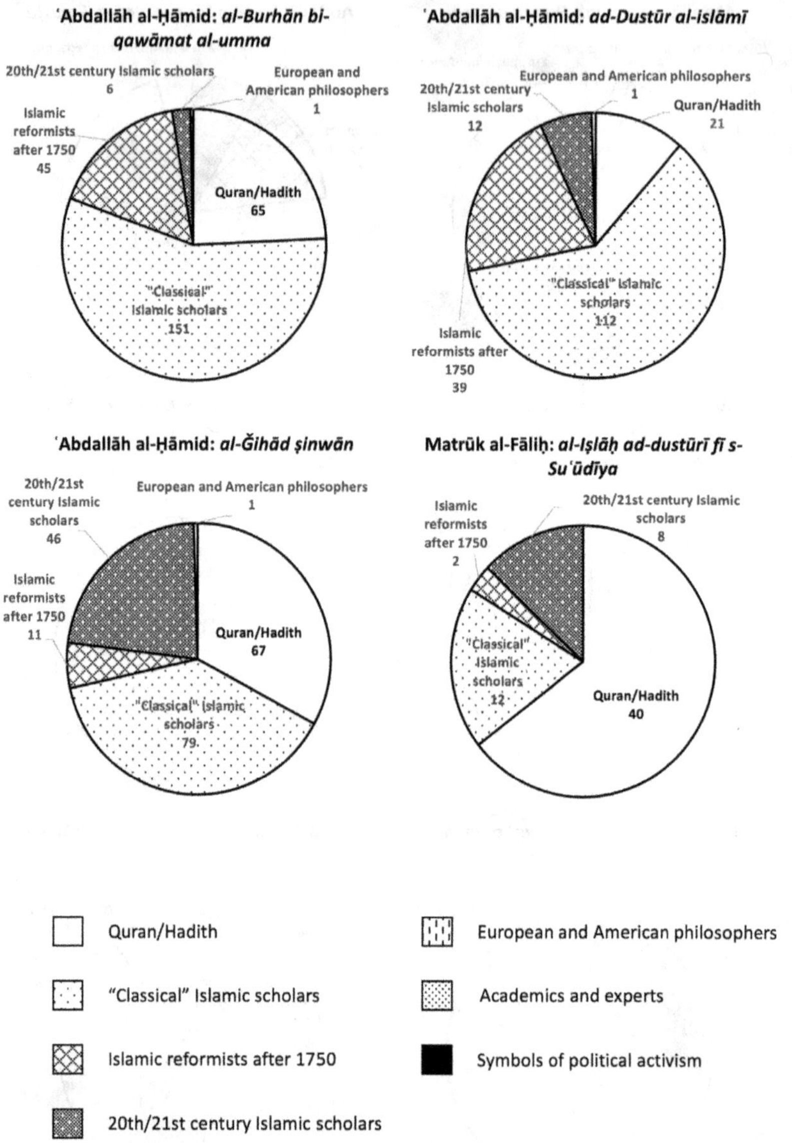

Figure 8 Types of sources and how often they are referred to in selected texts of the Islamic civil rights movement (Part 2).

movements of the eighteenth and nineteenth centuries CE, as well as contemporary Islamic scholars from the twentieth and twenty-first centuries CE, are also referred to on a regular basis, although usually not as frequently as the 'classical' scholars.

Third, references to European or American philosophers, as well as to contemporary academics and experts in other fields than Islamic sciences, are relatively rare. There are some mentions of authors belonging to these groups in most of the analysed books,

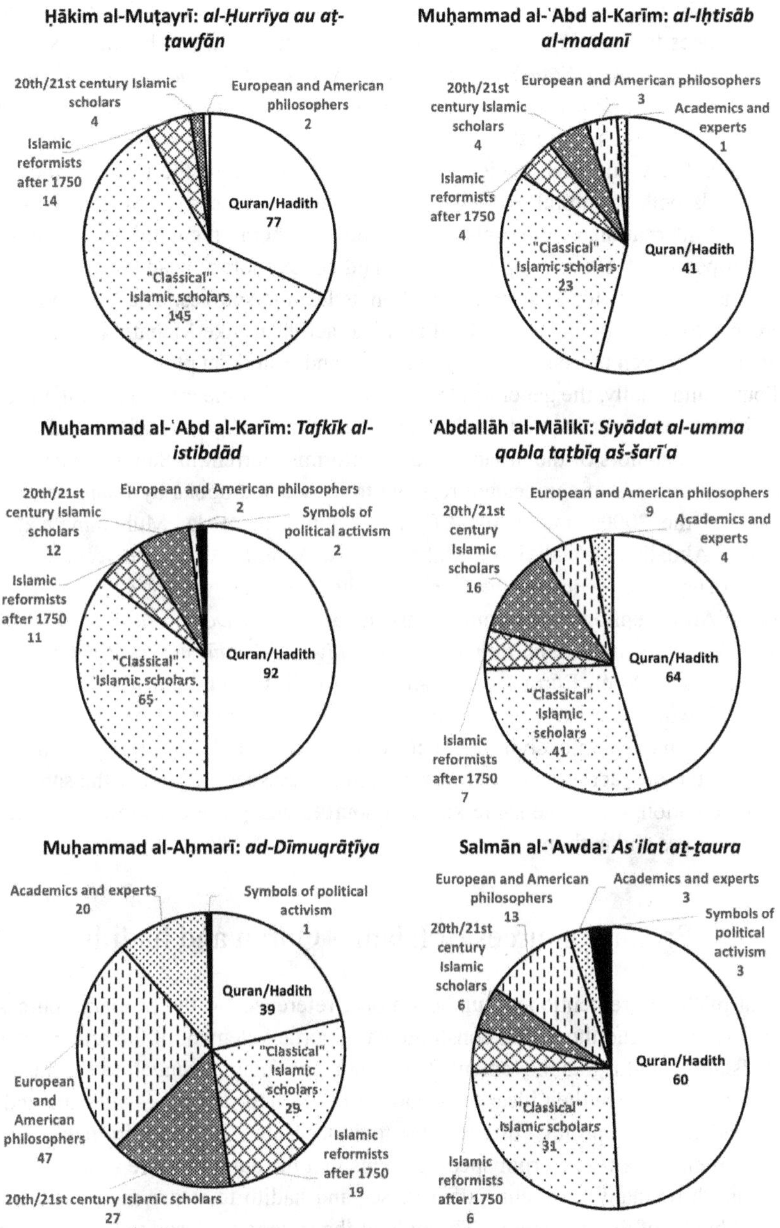
Ḥākim al-Muṭayrī: al-Ḥurrīya au aṭ-ṭawfān
20th/21st century Islamic scholars 4
European and American philosophers 2
Islamic reformists after 1750 14
Quran/Hadith 77
"Classical" Islamic scholars 145
Muḥammad al-ʿAbd al-Karīm: al-Iḥtisāb al-madanī
20th/21st century Islamic scholars 4
European and American philosophers 3
Academics and experts 1
Islamic reformists after 1750 4
"Classical" Islamic scholars 23
Quran/Hadith 41
Muḥammad al-ʿAbd al-Karīm: Tafkīk al-istibdād
20th/21st century Islamic scholars 12
European and American philosophers 2
Symbols of political activism 2
Islamic reformists after 1750 11
"Classical" Islamic scholars 65
Quran/Hadith 92
ʿAbdallāh al-Mālikī: Siyādat al-umma qabla taṭbīq aš-šarīʿa
European and American philosophers 9
20th/21st century Islamic scholars 16
Academics and experts 4
Quran/Hadith 64
"Classical" Islamic scholars 41
Islamic reformists after 1750 7
Muḥammad al-Aḥmarī: ad-Dīmuqrāṭīya
Academics and experts 20
Symbols of political activism 1
Quran/Hadith 39
"Classical" Islamic scholars 29
European and American philosophers 47
Islamic reformists after 1750 19
20th/21st century Islamic scholars 27
Salmān al-ʿAwda: Asʾilat aṯ-ṯaura
European and American philosophers 13
Academics and experts 3
Symbols of political activism 3
20th/21st century Islamic scholars 6
Quran/Hadith 60
"Classical" Islamic scholars 31
Islamic reformists after 1750 6

Figure 9 Types of sources and how often they are referred to in selected texts of the Islamo-reformist current in Saudi Arabia.

but they only rarely exceed single-digit numbers and are dwarfed in comparison to the references to Islamic sources and authors. An exception is Abdallah al-Hamid's book *The International Standards of the Independence of the Judiciary in the Melting Pot of the Islamic Sharia* (*Maʿāyīr istiqlāl al-qaḍāʾ ad-duwalīya fī būtaqa š-šarīʿa l-islāmīya*), in which more than half of the references are to experts in areas like international law and civil society. This is probably due to the topic of the book, which deals with structural and legal judicial independence and draws heavily on a number of international studies about the issue. In general, the numbers clearly show that European and American philosophers and contemporary academics and experts are not as important for their argumentation as Islamic sources. The same applies to references to international symbols of political activism, like Mahatma Gandhi, who are mentioned even more rarely than European and American philosophers.

Fourth and finally, the general selection of sources that the members of the Islamic civil rights movement mention in their texts does not change over time, and it is not unlike that of authors of the broader Islamo-reformist current in Saudi Arabia. Figure 9 shows what types of sources are referred to in selected books by Islamo-reformist authors of the 2000s and 2010s CE, like Salman al-Awda, Muhammad al-Abd al-Karim, Abdallah al-Maliki and Muhammad al-Ahmari. As can be seen, they, too, mainly focus on references to the Quran and the hadith, as well as 'classical' Islamic scholars. An exception is Muhammad al-Ahmari's book *Democracy: Its Roots and the Problem of Its Implementation* (*ad-Dīmuqrāṭīya: al-Ǧuḏūr wa-iškālīyat at-taṭbīq*), which draws more on European and American philosophers and political thinkers. In general, with regard to the types of sources that they refer to in their books, the members of the Islamic civil rights movement do not differ greatly from other authors of the broader Islamo-reformist current. They seem to follow the same rules of argumentation, quote the same kinds of sources and place the same emphasis on Islamic sources and authors.

Primary sources of Islam – Quran and hadith

In light of the aforementioned numbers alone, references to the primary sources of Islam, the Quran and the hadith constitute an important element of the argumentation of the Islamic civil rights movement. This is not surprising inasmuch as the members of the movement want their ideas to be compatible with the teachings of Islam, and the Quran and the hadith promise direct access to these teachings. Quotes from the primary sources often serve to underpin specific points that the authors make in their texts. It is striking how many different Quran verses and hadith texts are mentioned in the selected books of the movement. Throughout the sixteen analysed texts by members of the Islamic civil rights movement, and the Islamo-reformist current in general, the authors mention 365 different verses from the Quran. Many are mentioned only once in one or two of the analysed books. A detailed list showing the different verses and how often they are referred to in the various texts can be found in an online resource, which can be accessed via www.bloomsburyonlineresources.com/peaceful-jihad. In their references to passages from the hadith corpus, the members of the Islamic civil rights movement also show a remarkable eclecticism, and they refer to many different passages from the hadith. The authors obviously know the Quran and hadith very well and draw from the entire range of available passages in order to strengthen their arguments. However, some passages are mentioned more often and seem to be more important for their lines of argument.

An example for a verse from the Quran that is discussed in more detail in several of the analysed books is verse 104 of Sura 3 (*Āl ʿImrān*), which is used as an argument for the legitimacy of civil society activism on several occasions. Muhammad Asad translates it as follows:

> That there might grow out of you a community [of people] who invite unto all that is good, and enjoin the doing of what is right and forbid the doing of what is wrong: and it is they who shall attain a happy state![2]

The verse has been used by many Islamic scholars since the early days of Islam to argue that enjoining virtue and forbidding vice (*al-amr bi-l-maʿrūf wa-n-nahy ʿan al-munkar*), as the activity mentioned in the verse can be translated, is an Islamic obligation. The members of the Islamic civil rights movement follow this interpretation and add that this duty of Islam includes the kind of civil rights activism that HASM wants to encourage:

> The basis for the legitimacy of banding together to defend the public interest is the saying of the Almighty: 'That there might grow out of you a community [of people], who invite unto all that is good and enjoin the doing of what is right and forbid the doing of what is wrong: and it is they who shall attain a happy state.' There is no greater right thing than justice, and there is no greater wrong thing than injustice.[3]

Abdallah al-Hamid and other members of the movement argue that the Quranic invitation to enjoin virtue and forbid vice is addressed to all the people, not just a specific group or a government agency. In order to fulfil this obligation, people have to join together in groups and strive to eliminate injustice through peaceful civil society activism.[4] Thus, the verse becomes a justification for the founding of associations like HASM and the activities that groups like HASM are involved in.

Another example for an important verse is verse 38 of Sura 42 (*aš-Šūrā*), which is frequently referred to in the context of arguing for political participation. In Muhammad Asad's translation, the verse reads:

> [God's blessing shall be given] to those, who respond to the [call of] their Sustainer and are constant in prayer; and whose rule [in all matters of common concern] is consultation among themselves.[5]

At least since the times of the protagonists of the movement of Islamic Modernism in the late nineteenth century CE, the Quranic expression 'those whose rule is consultation among themselves' (*wa-amruhum šūrā bainahum*) has been seen as an endorsement of democratic forms of government. For authors like Abdallah al-Hamid, shura rule (*al-ḥūkm aš-šūrī*), or 'rule by consultation', is a byword for democratic rule and popular participation in political affairs; hence, their argumentation often refers to this verse. In one of his books, Abdallah al-Hamid explicitly adopts the interpretation of two of the most influential representatives of Islamic Modernism, Muhammad Abduh and Muhammad Rashid Rida:

> Muhammad Rashid Rida and Muhammad Abduh agreed on concluding from the verse about 'those who have been entrusted with authority' and the verse about shura (*aš-Šūrā* 38) that power belongs to the community and that the council of representatives embodies it.[6]

According to Muhammad Rashid Rida and Muhammad Abduh, the verse justifies democratic participation. Abdallah al-Hamid and other Saudi Islamo-reformists readily adopt this interpretation and use this verse as a strong argument for a democratic form of government.[7]

The two most important hadiths that the members of the Islamic civil rights movement refer to in their texts are probably the following two, which describe peaceful activities as jihad:

> [The prophet Muhammad said:] 'The best jihad is a word of justice in front of an unjust ruler or an unjust commander.'[8]
>
> [The prophet Muhammad said:] The lord of the martyrs is Hamza ibn Abd al-Muttalib and a man who comes to an unjust imam, commands him [to do good] and forbids him [to do wrong] and is killed by him.[9]

In both hadiths, peacefully pointing to the injustice of an unjust ruler is described not only as jihad but as the best form of jihad, which puts the person who is engaged in it on the same level as the uncle of the prophet Muhammad, Hamza ibn Abd al-Muttalib (*Ḥamza ibn 'Abd al-Muṭṭalib*), who was killed in battle in the seventh century CE. Both hadiths are well established in the classical canonical hadith collections and have been judged to be authentic and correct by hadith scholars.

The two hadiths are clearly one of their main arguments for their theory of civil society activism as peaceful jihad. In the discussion about the two hadiths in his book *The Word Is Stronger than the Bullet* (*al-Kalima aqwā min ar-raṣāṣa*), Abdallah al-Hamid shows that he is familiar with the hadith sciences. He lists five different versions of the first hadith and two versions of the second one, which can be found in the different classical hadith collections as well as the books of contemporary hadith scholars like Nasir ad-Din al-Albani (*Nāṣir ad-Dīn al-Albānī*). The versions differ with regard to single words, but the key message does not change. Al-Hamid also mentions that both hadiths have been confirmed as reliable by reputable scholars.[10] Here, as well as in other passages, the two hadiths serve as strong arguments for their claim that civil society activism is considered a kind of jihad, a form that even stands above military jihad.[11]

An interesting example for al-Hamid's display of his knowledge of the hadith sciences is his discussion of another hadith about jihad, which also seems to place peaceful activities on a higher level than military action. The hadith in question is the following saying of the prophet Muhammad, which was reported on the occasion of the return of the Muslim army from a military campaign:

> [The prophet Muhammad said:] We have returned from smaller jihad to greater jihad.[12]

The prophet Muhammad seems to say that, now the military campaign is over and the soldiers return to their ordinary, peaceful lives, they are waging a greater kind of jihad than when they were fighting the enemy. Abdallah al-Hamid mentions the hadith in his book *The Word Is Stronger than the Bullet* and immediately adds that it is not an authentic hadith, because, according to the hadith sciences, the reliability of its reporting is not beyond doubt. Therefore, it cannot be used as an argument, even though its message may be correct in the eyes of Abdallah al-Hamid:

> It is not confirmed that this is a prophetic hadith, which the Messenger, peace be upon him, said, when he returned from his attack in Tabuk. But it is a correct political hadith, if we mean by it peaceful, political jihad, even if it is not literally correct according to the hadith scholars.[13]

As can be seen, Abdallah al-Hamid scrupulously follows the rules of the hadith sciences when quoting hadiths, because only then will the hadiths truly strengthen his arguments in the eyes of the religiously educated audience he has in mind.

Another example for a hadith which is discussed in detail in several of the selected books is the following, stating that the consensus of the Muslim community will always be right:

> [The prophet Muhammad said:] My Islamic community does not agree on anything misguided. The hand of God is with the group.[14]

Over the centuries of Islamic thought, Islamic scholars have understood this hadith to mean that the consensus of the Muslim community will lead to correct conclusions. According to some, after the death of the prophet Muhammad, who was the last of the prophets, only the Muslim community as a whole can claim infallibility. While some may go wrong, the majority will always choose the right ideas. Authors like Abdallah al-Hamid adopt this interpretation and use it as an argument for a democratic form of government. Not the ruler, but the people have to be obeyed, because their consensus will always be right.[15] The theological idea that the Muslim community is infallible and will always find truth in its majority decision becomes a political argument for a democratic system of government. The right policies are found not by obeying the ruler but by asking the people and adhering to their decisions.[16]

As can be seen, the authors of the Islamic civil rights movement, and the Islamo-reformist current in general, make frequent use of quotes from the Quran and the hadith in their texts. The way they do it clearly shows that they are familiar with the primary sources of Islam and know how passages from these texts have been interpreted and categorized throughout the centuries. They do not only refer to a limited number of verses from the Quran and passages from the hadith but quote many different verses and hadiths. When they refer to a certain passage, they show that they know the rules of their interpretation according to the Islamic sciences and how the passage has been interpreted in the past. In their texts, quotes from the Quran and the hadith and explanations about how they should be interpreted usually play an important role in either refuting positions that they deem wrong or strengthening their own arguments. When they can show that certain points are underpinned by quotes from the primary sources of Islam, their theory is all the more plausible and convincing in terms of Islam.

'Classical' Islamic scholars

The texts by the Islamic civil rights movement, and the Islamo-reformist current in general, contain many references to 'classical' Islamic authors from the early days of Islam until the eighteenth century CE. In seven of the ten analysed books by the Islamic civil rights movement, and in one of the six additional books by members of the broader Islamo-reformist current, authors from this period are the largest group of sources referred to. In total, seventy-one different Islamic scholars, philosophers, theologians and Islamic legal experts from the time between the seventh and the eighteenth centuries CE are mentioned in the sixteen analysed books. A detailed list of all the authors who are referred to can be found in the online resource, which is accessible via www.bloomsburyonlineresources.com/peaceful-jihad. Evidently, discussing these past scholars and their ideas constitutes an important element of their argumentation.

The scholars that are mentioned include virtually all of the most influential authors who have shaped Islamic thought since the beginning of Islamic scholarly thinking. Among them are the founders of the four large schools of Sunni Islamic jurisprudence, Abu Hanifa (*Abū Ḥanīfa*, 699–767 CE), Malik ibn Anas (*Mālik ibn Anas*, 711–795 CE), Abu Abdallah Muhammad ash-Shafii (*Abū ʿAbdallāh Muḥammad aš-Šāfiʿī*, 767–820 CE) and Ahmad ibn Hanbal (*Aḥmad ibn Ḥanbal*, 780–855 CE), as well as later representatives of these school. The four founders are usually recognized as courageous intellectual reformers and 'pious predecessors', whose example is to be followed according to Salafist thought. In one passage, Abdallah al-Hamid calls them 'renewers' and 'free mujahidun':

> We have to separate the famous Abbasid, Mamluk and Ottoman pious predecessors into renewers and imitators. The renewers among them were free mujahidun, like the imams Abu Hanifa, Malik, ash-Shafii and Ahmad [ibn Hanbal].[17]

Of the four founders, Ahmad ibn Hanbal, founding figure of the Hanbali school, is mentioned most frequently in the texts of the movement. This is not surprising inasmuch as Wahhabism, which still dominates the official Islamic establishment in

Saudi Arabia, developed in the context of this school. In the view of Abdallah al-Hamid, Ahmad ibn Hanbal becomes an advocate of many ideas that he himself supports. According to him, he supported freedom of thought and criticized occupying oneself with secondary transcendental questions, as long as there are more important practical ones. In other words, he endorsed ideas that al-Hamid also argues for. Therefore, quoting him is an important part of al-Hamid's argumentation. While Ahmad ibn Hanbal is a crucial point of reference for Abdallah al-Hamid, he also makes the critical comment that the school of Hanbalism, which was created by Ahmad ibn Hanbal's disciples after his death and remains the dominant school of jurisprudence in Saudi Arabia, contains many contradictions.[18] Nevertheless, Ahmad ibn Hanbal himself is an important source of inspiration for the members of the Islamic civil rights movement.

In addition to the four founding figures of the large schools of Sunni Islamic jurisprudence, the members of the movement also quote a large number of other influential 'classical' scholars. An example is Islamic scholar, philosopher and mystic Abu Hamid al-Ghazali (*Abū Ḥāmid al-Ġazālī*, 1058–1111 CE), who is among the most frequently quoted 'classical' scholars in several of the analysed books. Abdallah al-Hamid recognizes him as a Salafist, who successfully resisted the infiltration of abstract Greek philosophy into Islamic thought.[19] In several texts, Al-Ghazali is quoted as someone who encourages everyone to practice individual reasoning (*iǧtihād*) instead of blindly following others,[20] who argues that holding the powerful accountable does not need their permission[21] and who insists on the importance of enjoining virtue and forbidding vice.[22] The quotes serve to underpin the statements of the authors of the Islamo-reformist current, who strongly argue for these ideas.

The same is true for their references to influential Islamic scholar and philosopher Fakhr ad-Din ar-Razi (*Faḫr ad-Dīn ar-Rāzī*, 1149–1209 CE). Ar-Razi is quoted several times in many of the analysed books. In more than one of his texts, Abdallah al-Hamid adopts ar-Razi's idea that 'those who have been entrusted with authority' (*ūlū l-amr*), who are owed obedience according to the Islamic texts, are the representatives of the people, who embody their consensus (*iǧmāʿ*). Thus, ar-Razi's interpretation of the term becomes a supporting argument for Abdallah al-Hamid's idea that political power belongs to the people and that the only individuals who are owed obedience are their elected representatives.[23]

Another example of a 'classical' Islamic scholar who is referred to frequently is Andalusian Islamic legal scholar Abu Ishaq ash-Shatibi (*Abū Isḥāq aš-Šāṭibī*, 1320–88 CE). In six of the ten analysed books by members of the Islamic civil rights movement, ash-Shatibi is among the five most frequently mentioned scholars. References to him almost exclusively concern his theory of the stated aims of the sharia (*maqāṣid aš-šarīʿa*), according to which the rules of Islam are there so that humans can reach specific aims in this world, like the protection of life and property. Authors like Abdallah al-Hamid praise this theory and use it in their own argumentation, for example, by stating that Islam requires people to follow the laws of nature and society in order to be successful in this world. Praying alone will not make Muslim states stronger.[24]

The scholar from the period before the eighteenth century CE who most influenced the movement is probably Ahmad ibn Taymiya (*Aḥmad ibn Taymīya*), who is generally a very important point of reference for many Salafists all over the Islamic world. He is among the five most frequently mentioned authors in fifteen of the sixteen selected books of the Islamic civil rights movement and the Islamo-reformist current. In Abdallah al-Hamid's book *So That the Quran Is Not a Carrier of Different Meanings*, Ahmad ibn Taymiya is mentioned forty-two times. He appears in the text even more often than quotes from the Quran or the hadith. Of the analysed texts, only Muhammad al-Ahmari's book *Democracy* does not include Ahmad ibn Taymiya among the five most frequently mentioned authors, but even here, he is referred to on four occasions. For Abdallah al-Hamid, Ahmad ibn Taymiya is the prime example of a courageous Salafist scholar who resisted political oppression. He frequently mentions him and his disciple Ibn Qayyim al-Jawziya (*Ibn Qayyim al-Ǧauzīya*, 1292–1350 CE) in the same breath as the extremely influential founding figures of the four large schools of Sunni Islamic jurisprudence.[25]

The members of the movement adopt several of Ahmad ibn Taymiya's ideas. In more than one of his books, Abdallah al-Hamid refers to Ahmad ibn Taymiya's theory that, after the death of the prophet Muhammad, only the Muslim community as a whole can be considered infallible. Therefore, the consensus of the community is to be obeyed.[26] Another idea that they adopt from Ahmad ibn Taymiya is his statement that there is no contradiction between reason (*ʿaql*) and tradition (*naql*), or between the truths of the sciences and the truths of the sharia, provided the sciences do not become mere abstract, impractical thinking.[27] One literal quote that appears in several of Abdallah al-Hamid's text is the following, stating that God judges states according to whether they are ruled justly, not according to the religion of its rulers:

> Ibn Taymiya said in the book 'Sharia politics': 'God treasures the just state, even if it is an unbeliever [*kāfira*] state, and He does not treasure the unjust state, even if it is a Muslim state.' [. . .] No state can rightfully be called Muslim, so long as it does not respect the two conditions of the oath of allegiance [*bayʿa*]: shura and justice.[28]

All these ideas are readily adopted by Abdallah al-Hamid and used as arguments in his own theory. Despite all these positive references, Abdallah al-Hamid also criticizes some aspects of Ibn Taymiya's thought. In his book *Middle Path Salafism*, he states that Ahmad ibn Taymiya was not able to completely ignore the spirit of conflict that reigned in his time, and he exaggerated when he declared his intellectual adversaries to be unbelievers.[29]

The way the members of the movement refer to another scholar, historiographer and philosopher, Ibn Khaldun (*Ibn Ḫaldūn*, 1332–1406 CE), shows that their inspirations are not limited to Islamic scholars and sources in the strict sense of the word. In the famous introduction to his monumental book of history titled *Book of Lessons* (*Kitāb al-ʿIbar*), Ibn Khaldun tried to explain the laws according to which human societies and states rise, develop and are destroyed. He is widely considered a rationalist scientist and a forerunner of modern sciences like sociology or historiography.[30] In the books of the Islamic civil rights movement, and the Islamo-reformist current in general, Ibn Khaldun is mentioned relatively often. In three of the sixteen analysed books, he is among the five most frequently mentioned authors. Members of the movement like Abdallah al-Hamid have a very high opinion of Ibn Khaldun. Abdallah al-Hamid considers him a representative of Salafism – which is a good thing in his view – and argues that he should be given the honorary title 'shaykh of Islam' (*šayḫ al-islām*), which is usually reserved for very influential scholars of Islamic sciences like Islamic jurisprudence, theology or Quran sciences:

> One can build on enlightened ideas of prominent personalities like ash-Shatibi, Ibn Taymiya, Ibn al-Qayyim, al-Ghazali and especially Ibn Khaldun, who should be called 'shaykh of Islam' in the science of political sociology.[31]

Ibn Khaldun's sober, rational way of thinking about social and political developments in this world clearly appeals to authors like Abdallah al-Hamid, who argue that studying the laws of nature and society is an Islamic obligation. Therefore, references to the renowned scholar Ibn Khaldun serve as effective arguments and underpin their claim that the kind of politics most in line with the sharia is one that keeps the natural laws of politics and societies in mind.

Not all the authors from the period between the seventh and the eighteenth centuries CE who are referenced in the selected books are regarded positively. Many of the Islamic scholars, especially from the era of the Abbasid caliphate and the Mamluk sultanate in Egypt, are sharply criticized for the opinions they held. The criticized opinions all concern the position of the ruler and the obligation of the people to obey him. Among the scholars who are criticized for these views are al-Fudayl ibn Iyad (*al-Fuḍail ibn ʿIyāḍ*, d. 803 CE), Sahl ibn Abdallah at-Tustari (*Sahl ibn ʿAbdallāh at-Tustarī*, 818–894 CE), Abu Jaafar Ahmad at-Tahawi (*Abū Ǧaʿfar Aḥmad aṭ-Ṭaḥāwī*, 843–933 CE), al-Hasan ibn Ali al-Barbahari (*al-Ḥasan ibn ʿAlī al-Barbahārī*, d. 941 CE) and Ibn Abi al-Izz (*Ibn Abī l-ʿIzz*, 1331–90 CE). According to Abdallah al-Hamid, all of them glorified the ruler and wrongfully obliged the people to blindly obey their rulers:

> They gave the ruler absolute power and considered shura [*šūrā*, 'consultation'] to be non-compulsory. They spread sayings that glorified the ruler, like the sayings of al-Fudayl ibn Iyad, al-Barbahari, Sahl ibn Abdallah at-Tustari, Ibn Abi al-Izz, the explainer of [at-Tahawi's book] '*aṭ-Ṭaḥāwīya*', and others like them. Then they made them a part of Islamic doctrine, so that no one would dare to question them.[32]

Likewise, Islamic scholar Abu al-Hasan al-Mawardi (*Abū l-Ḥasan al-Māwardī*, 972–1058 CE), who wrote a famous, very pragmatic treatise about the politics of the Muslim state titled *The Ordinances of Government* (*al-Aḥkām as-sulṭānīya*),[33] is criticized for his supposed glorification of the worldly ruler.[34] Authors like Abdallah al-Hamid mention the names of all these scholars and their opinions so that they can refute them and contrast them with their own theory, according to which the ruler has to obey the people and not the other way around.

Finally, the members of the movement also refer to some of the most influential Arabic-Islamic philosophers, while criticizing their opinions. Al-Kindi (*al-Kindī*, 801–

873 CE), al-Farabi (*al-Fārābī*, 872–959 CE) and Ibn Sina (*Ibn Sīnā*, 980–1037 CE) are all condemned for their excessive enthusiasm for foreign intellectual traditions, but they are praised for bringing some useful elements of these traditions into Arabic-Islamic thought. The following passage from Abdallah al-Hamid's book *Middle Path Salafism* is a good example of this approach:

> Our Abbasid predecessors lived in times of violent contact between civilisations, where the Arab people mixed with the Persian, Roman, Syrian, Coptic and Indian peoples. Everyone who accepted Islam did so with his cultural background and his national identity. [. . .] Just like the secular culture forces itself on us today, the foreign cultures forced themselves on the intellectuals yesterday. [. . .] In their mistakes, they were victims, but in their true statements, they were pioneers. Their mistakes were bridges, over which those who came after them crossed. [. . .] This was the role of al-Kindi, al-Farabi and Ibn Sina and others like them.[35]

The Arab philosopher who is most harshly criticized by authors like Abdallah al-Hamid is the Andalusian Ibn Rushd (*Ibn Rušd*, or Averroes, 1136–98 CE), who is known for his commentaries on the works of the Greek philosopher Aristotle. In his books, Abdallah al-Hamid describes Ibn Rushd as someone who did little more than adopt the school of Greek abstract rationalism, which has no practical benefit for the people and only squanders intellectual energies. In one of his books, he calls him a 'disciple in the prayer niche of Aristotle'.[36] Abdallah al-Hamid insists that the core of Greek philosophy is idle speculation about transcendental things, where human reason cannot reach certain knowledge. It has nothing to do with the practical reason that makes nations great. Therefore, Ibn Rushd understood neither the Islamic sharia nor practical reason. Al-Hamid concludes that his role in Arabic-Islamic thought was not positive:

> As for the role of Ibn Rushd in Islamic culture, it was not productive, because he did not go beyond the role of the explainer of the origin of Greek thought. [. . .] The writings of the likes of Ibn Rushd [. . .] were far removed from understanding the sharia, just like they were far removed from practical philosophy. This means they were also far removed from practical reason, through which the West rose, after Bacon and others like him let go of the guardianship of Aristotle and Plato.[37]

In the interpretation of Abdallah al-Hamid, Ibn Rushd becomes a representative of an abstract, impractical Greek rationalism, which has to be overcome, just like European and North American peoples overcame it when British philosopher Francis Bacon and others founded the school of scientific empiricism in the sixteenth century CE.

In summary, other than most references to Islamic scholars from the time before the eighteenth century CE, references to philosophers from this period are overwhelmingly critical. They mainly seem to serve to warn against an abstract form of rationalism, which has no connection to action and is therefore incompatible with Islam. The enthusiasm of Arabic philosophers for foreign cultures, like the Greek one, is compared to the situation today, when many pious Saudis feel that secularism is threatening their Islamic identity.

Islamic reformers and modernists of the eighteenth and nineteenth centuries CE

In light of the aforementioned numbers and the way the members of the Islamic civil rights movement refer to Islamic reformist and modernist authors from *c.* 1750 until the beginning of the twentieth century CE, they are clearly a major inspiration and point of reference for them. Figures 7, 8 and 9 on pages 51, 52 and 53 show that references to these reformist and modernist authors are very frequent in the books of the movement. In many of their writings, they constitute the second or third most frequently quoted group of sources, coming directly after references to the Quran and the hadith or 'classical' Islamic authors. Authors from this group are among the five most-mentioned authors in five of the sixteen selected books that were analysed.

The group of Islamic reformers and modernists includes a number of Islamic scholars and politicians from the eighteenth, nineteenth and early twentieth centuries CE who claimed that Muslim societies needed to reform the way they practised Islam and the way they were governed. In their eyes, the status quo was influenced by fallacious Islamic ideas and made Muslims susceptible to foreign hegemony. The authors differ, however, with regard to the concrete ideas they formulated. On the one hand, the Saudi Muhammad ibn Abd al-Wahhab, the founder of Wahhabism, concentrated on purifying Islamic doctrine and eliminating false practices, while supporting the absolute political rule of the Al Saud family. On the other hand, authors like the Egyptians Muhammad Abduh and Muhammad Rashid Rida stated that Muslim societies needed to adopt some of the innovations of European and American states, like democracy, in order to regain political strength and revive the innovative spirit of Islam. The members of the Islamic civil rights movement, and the Islamo-reformist current in general, mention several authors from this group and refer to them in different ways.

An interesting example for their complex views on some of these authors is their discussion of Muhammad ibn Abd al-Wahhab, the founder of Wahhabism. Wahhabism is still the dominant form of Islam in Saudi Arabia, and practically all the members of the movement have undergone a religious education that was shaped by Wahhabi doctrine. Still, their writings demonstrate a decidedly differentiated view of Muhammad ibn Abd al-Wahhab. On the one hand, Muhammad ibn Abd al-Wahhab is praised for purifying Islamic doctrine and initiating a successful movement for political independence, which culminated in the founding of a kingdom that claimed to be based on Islamic teachings. Abdallah al-Hamid also lauds the easily understood language of Wahhabism, which is free of the complexities of the scholarly discussions of the 'classical' Islamic discourse.[38] In one passage, he praises him as the representative of a 'desert Salafism'.[39] On the other hand, Muhammad ibn Abd al-Wahhab is criticized, because he allied himself with an absolute ruler and did not realize the importance of justice and political participation. Abdallah al-Hamid concludes that the teachings of Muhammad ibn Abd al-Wahhab were valuable, but only suitable for their time and place. Today, as Muslims are faced with new challenges, Wahhabism alone therefore cannot give all the answers:

> The final verdict depends on the extent of change towards reform and success, and in this regard, Wahhabism realised a lot. Muhammad ibn Abd al-Wahhab was standard-setting when he implemented the ideas of Ibn Taymiya and fought against spiritual violations of the Islamic doctrine. He was in fact standard-setting in the civil half of Islamic doctrine, when he realised that implementing just rule was an obligation of religion. [. . .] Ibn Abd al-Wahhab wanted to implement justice through the example of the just oppressor. Like other reformers after the Rightly Guided Caliphate, he did not value the relationship between justice, shura, pluralism, freedom and the spirit of knowledge. His renewal was only temporary and bound to a place. It fitted one era of the desert society of the Arabian Peninsula.[40]

As someone who grew up in the Wahhabi education system in Saudi Arabia, Abdallah al-Hamid recognizes Muhammad ibn Abd al-Wahhab's influence on Islamic thought. At the same time, he criticizes the structural alliance of the Wahhabi establishment with the Saudi political leadership and its religious justification of political oppression. He does not outrightly reject Muhammad ibn Abd al-Wahhab's thought, but he weakens its authority by criticizing certain elements of it and putting them into the context of the time and place of their conception. In Abdallah al-Hamid's texts, references to Muhammad ibn Abd al-Wahhab are mainly a tool for criticizing the political positions of the official religious establishment in Saudi Arabia.

In contrast to Muhammad ibn Abd al-Wahhab, other reformers and modernists are referred to in a positive way. The members of the Islamic civil rights movement see themselves in the tradition of a series of Islamic modernist and reformist thinkers, and they frequently refer to them in their texts. Most of these authors are members of the movement of Islamic Modernism or the Awakening (*an-nahḍa*), which was shaped by thinkers like Jamal ad-Din al-Afghani (*Ǧamāl ad-Dīn al-Afġānī*, 1839–97 CE), Muhammad Abduh (*Muḥammad ʿAbduh*, 1849–1905 CE) and Muhammad Rashid Rida (*Muḥammad Rašīd Riḍā*, 1865–1935 CE) in nineteenth-century CE Egypt. Others are Tunisian thinker and politician Khayr ad-Din at-Tunisi (*Ḫair ad-Dīn at-Tūnisī*, 1873–77 CE), Syrian Islamic scholar Abd ar-Rahman al-Kawakibi (*ʿAbd ar-Raḥmān al-Kawākibī*, 1849–1902 CE) and the Egyptian founder of the Muslim Brotherhood, Hasan al-Banna (*Ḥasan al-Bannā*, 1906–49 CE). All of them argued that Muslims needed a reform of their thinking and their politics, and all advocated adopting some practices from European and American states in order to combine the benefits of modernism with the values of Islam. In one passage of his book *Middle Path Salafism*, Abdallah al-Hamid mentions these thinkers as role models, whose message has to be continued:

> This requires a deepening and spreading in order to continue the discourse of the Awakening [*ḫiṭāb an-nahḍa*], which was started by its pioneers, like al-Afghani, Khayr ad-Din at-Tunisi, al-Kawakibi, Muhammad Abduh, [. . .] Muhammad Rashid Rida and Hasan al-Banna.[41]

Muhammad Abduh and Muhammad Rashid Rida are referred to relatively often in the books of Abdallah al-Hamid. Both are repeatedly praised as clear-minded Islamic thinkers who resisted oppression and laid the foundation for a modern Islamic doctrine which recognizes the importance of just rule. Abduh's and Rashid Rida's Quran commentary, the '*Tafsīr al-manār*', is quoted very often in the context of the interpretation of specific verses from the Quran. The members of HASM integrate some of the ideas of Abduh and Rashid Rida into their own theory. For example, an argument which Abdallah al-Hamid enthusiastically adopts is that an elected council of representatives is the modern embodiment of the Quranic term 'those who have been entrusted with authority', who are to be obeyed according to Islam. Therefore, according to Abduh and Rashid Rida, a democratic system is the form of government that is most in line with Islamic teachings today.[42] In addition, civil society associations are the legitimate embodiment of the Islamic obligation to enjoin virtue and forbid vice.[43] In summary:

> The two sheikhs Muhammad Abduh and Rashid Rida adopted the concept [of shura rule] in the 'Tafsīr al-manār' and the two sheikhs Muhammad Abduh and Muhammad Rashid Rida considered the social associations and the council of representatives the ideal structures and means for bringing the will of the community to light, because they embody the social authority of the community, or, to use a political term, they represent the power of the community.[44]

The Syrian Islamic scholar Abd ar-Rahman al-Kawakibi is frequently quoted for his explanations in his book *The Nature of Oppression and the Demise of Slavery* (*Ṭabā'i' al-istibdād wa-maṣāri' al-isti'bād*),[45] in which he argues that the oppressive rule of the Ottoman Sultan over the Arab people is not compatible with Islam. In the interpretation of Abdallah al-Hamid and other authors of the Islamo-reformist current, al-Kawakibi becomes a critic of oppression and an advocate of shura rule and civil society activism.[46] Hasan al-Banna, the founder of the Egyptian Muslim Brotherhood, is also mentioned occasionally in the texts of the movement. He is quoted as having said that an elected council of representatives, which embodies the consensus of the people, is what Islam requires today.[47]

Overall, the representatives of the movement of Islamic Modernism are clearly a major point of reference for the Islamic civil rights movement. They called for a new intellectual beginning and tried to combine Islamic concepts with selected elements they found in European and North American societies.[48] This innovative, eclectic and hybrid way of thinking obviously appeals to the members of the Islamic civil rights movement. Many elements of their theory, like the Islamic framing of democracy and the strong role of civil society, are clearly inspired by these authors. Therefore, it is not surprising that the members of the Islamic civil rights movement see themselves as a continuation of the movement of Islamic Modernism and frequently mention its protagonists as role models.

Contemporary Islamic authors

Islamic scholars from the twentieth and twenty-first centuries CE are also an important inspiration for the authors of the Islamic civil rights movement. As can be seen in Figures 7, 8 and 9 on pages 51, 52 and 53, contemporary Islamic scholars are the third or fourth most frequently mentioned group of sources in several of the analysed books. In most of them, only references to the Quran and hadith, 'classical' Islamic scholars and Islamic reformers of the eighteenth and nineteenth centuries CE are more frequent. Contemporary Islamic scholars are among the five most-mentioned authors in nine of the sixteen analysed books of the Islamic civil rights movement and the broader Islamo-reformist current. Thus, even looking at the absolute numbers alone one, one can hardly miss their importance for the argumentation of the movement.

The group of contemporary scholars includes a wide range of authors with different backgrounds, and they are referred to in different ways in the books of the Islamic civil rights movement. Some are praised as 'free Salafists' and presented as role models, like the Egyptian Muhammad al-Ghazali (*Muḥammad al-Ġazālī*, 1917–96 CE) or the Egyptian-Qatari Yusuf al-Qaradawi (*Yūsuf al-Qaraḍāwī*, b. 1926 CE). Others, like the Egyptian as-Sayyid Sabiq (*as-Saiyid Sābiq*, 1915–2000 CE), the Syrian Muhammad al-Buti (*Muḥammad al-Būṭī*, 1929–2013 CE) or the Syrian Muhammad Khayr Haykal (*Muḥammad Ḫair Haikal*, b. 1941 CE), are only mentioned in passing and in the context of a specific scholarly book about a particular topic of the Islamic sciences. In general, it is obvious that the authors of the Islamo-reformist current do not rely on historical Islamic scholars alone but are also aware of contemporary debates within the Islamic discourse.

One of the most important twentieth-century CE scholars for the authors of the Islamic civil rights movement is the controversial Egyptian Sayyid Qutb (*Saiyid Quṭb*, 1906–66 CE), who is generally considered an intellectual precursor of the ideology of Jihadism. He was a leading member of the Muslim Brotherhood and formulated a radical theory, according to which every society which did not uncompromisingly implement the teachings of Islam could not be considered Muslim. For him, the Islamic term 'ignorance' (*ǧāhilīya*), which had originally designated the time before the arrival of Islam, also applied to the situation of most societies with a Muslim majority today. For Qutb, Islam was all-encompassing and concerned all aspects of human life. According to him, the state, like everything else, should be ruled by the laws of Islam, which required government to be just. This did not rule out democratic forms of government, as long as it happened in the framework of Islam.[49] For his role in an assassination plot against the Egyptian president Gamal Abdel Nàsser, he was executed in 1966 CE.

Abdallah al-Hamid praises Sayyid Qutb as a representative of an active form of Salafism and a renewer, who resisted the secular oppression of Gamal Abdel Nasser. In al-Hamid's books, Qutb is presented as a courageous activist, who acted out of his religious belief that one had to resist unjust, 'un-Islamic' regimes.[50] Abdallah al-Hamid also quotes him on the importance of doing what the natural laws of society and politics require people to do. Only if Muslims realize that following these laws of nature is the only way to succeed in this world and, indeed, an obligation of Islam will they regain their strength and confront imperialism.[51] Abdallah al-Hamid does not discuss all elements of Sayyid Qutb's theory in detail. For example, Qutb's ideas concerning the status of un-Islamic 'ignorance' of contemporary Muslim states are not explicitly mentioned in his texts. Nevertheless, Sayyid Qutb appears to be a major inspiration and point of reference for him.

Authors like Abdallah al-Hamid also mention a number of other contemporary Islamic scholars who all argued for democratic forms of government. This includes scholars who are usually considered to be a part of the so-called centrist stream (*al-wasaṭīya*) in Egypt. This stream, which was shaped in the second half of the twentieth century CE by authors like Muhammad al-Ghazali and Yusuf al-Qaradawi, endorses many of the ideas that the Islamic civil rights movement argues for as well. Its members consider Islam an all-encompassing system of life, which has to be defended against European and American cultural imperialism and secularism. According to them, the Islamic sharia contains fixed elements, which are always true, and changeable elements, which allow Muslims to freely look for the solutions to their problems that best fit their circumstances. This requires constant innovation and allows for the adoption of some practices of other nations that are deemed useful. For example, according to them, democratic forms of government are an ideal modern form of the kind of political participation that Islam requires. Significantly, all of this has to happen inside the framework of the Islamic sharia, which remains the ultimate source of rules.[52]

As shown previously, all of these ideas also appear in the writings of the Islamic civil rights movement. Therefore, it is natural for them to refer to these renowned scholars in their books. In his writings, Abdallah al-Hamid quotes several passages from books by Muhammad al-Ghazali, in which the latter argues that the people should have the right to choose their rulers and should be the sole source of legislation.[53] Yusuf al-Qaradawi is praised as a clear-sighted 'Salafist' who is aware of the importance of the political principles of Islam. Authors like Abdallah al-Hamid adopt his view that demonstrations can be a form of jihad[54] and his conclusion that democracy is the best form of government today.[55] Apart from the thinkers of the 'centrist stream', the members of the movement also refer to other Islamic scholars who have expressed their approval of democracy. Two examples are the Tunisian Islamic scholar Muhammad at-Tahir ibn Ashur (*Muḥammad aṭ-Ṭāhir ibn ʿĀšūr*, 1879–1973 CE)[56] and the Tunisian scholar and politician Rashid al-Ghannoushi (*Rāšid al-Ġannūšī*, b. 1941 CE),[57] who is also the founder of the Tunisian Nahda Party. The members of the Islamic civil rights movement use references to all of these scholars as arguments for the legitimacy of democracy in terms of Islam.

The Islamic civil rights movement does not agree with all contemporary scholars who are mentioned in its texts. Among those who are criticized are the most prominent representatives of the official Wahhabi establishment in Saudi Arabia. This can be seen in this passage from one of Abdallah al-Hamid's books in which he criticizes the famous late Grand Mufti of Saudi Arabia Abd al-Aziz ibn Baz (*ʿAbd al-ʿAzīz ibn Bāz*, 1910–99 CE) and the influential Wahhabi scholar Muhammad ibn al-Uthaymin (*Muḥammad ibn al-ʿUṯaimīn*, 1925–2001 CE) for their refusal to recognize the right to make the mistakes of the ruler public:

> Imam Abd al-Aziz ibn Baz has said: 'Making the mistakes of the rulers public and mentioning them on the pulpit does not belong to the method of the predecessors,

> because it leads to chaos.' [. . .] The fact that this principle was propagated by righteous Islamic legal scholars like Ibn Baz and Ibn al-Uthaymin [. . .] shows that a scholar who is known for his superiority in the spiritual sciences does not necessarily have a good knowledge of political, administrative and civilisational affairs.[58]

Abdallah al-Hamid respectfully, but openly, criticizes two of the most esteemed members of the Wahhabi establishment in Saudi Arabia and accuses them of having expressed incorrect positions in matters of politics. The Wahhabi establishment and its alliance with the absolute rulers of the Al Saud family are one of the main targets of the criticism of the Islamic civil rights movement. Therefore, it is not surprising that the main representatives of this establishment are also criticized in their texts, albeit in a somewhat restrained way.

Finally, a current that is almost completely absent from the books of the Islamic civil rights movement is that of Jihadism. Jihadist authors are not quoted in their books, and when they are mentioned, they are only referred to indirectly as a negative consequence of oppression and injustice. An example for this position is a lecture by Abdallah al-Hamid, in which he tries to explain the phenomenon of Jihadism and convince the people to choose peaceful, civil jihad instead of military jihad abroad:

> How did someone like sheikh Usama ibn Laden come into being? There is no doubt that sheikh bin Laden was an honest man, who was encouraged to wage jihad in Afghanistan, the best jihad. Then, he returned to the country. There should have been a place and a role for people like him. [. . .] It was his right to participate in the building of his country and to establish a peaceful association, but oppression was on the lookout for him. If they had welcomed him, honoured him and recognised the role of people like him, . . . But they did not want to open up to peaceful activism. Bin Laden did not have any options and he was harassed everywhere. Finally, he exploded like a volcano.[59]

Abdallah al-Hamid seems to show understanding for the personal situation of bin Laden but always emphasizes that Jihadism is an adversary that has to be fought. For the members of the Islamo-reformist current, Jihadist authors are not quotable. They are, instead, a problem and an example of the negative consequences of oppression and injustice.

It is evident, as in the case of the 'classical' Islamic scholars and the representatives of reformist and modernist movements from the eighteenth and nineteenth centuries CE, that the members of the Islamic civil rights movement display an unabashed eclecticism when dealing with contemporary Islamic authors. They are obviously well informed about current debates in Islamic discourse and can easily quote from the books of some of the most important scholars of the twentieth and twenty-first centuries CE. When they refer to certain contemporary authors, they adopt what they see as convincing and criticize what they see as wrong. They do not adhere to a specific school, even if they show a noticeable preference for scholars with an affinity to the thought of the Muslim Brotherhood, like Yusuf al-Qaradawi or Rashid al-Ghannoushi, or other authors who are open to adopting practices like democracy in an Islamic setting. The representatives of the official Wahhabi establishment, as well as members of Jihadism, are criticized in their writings. All in all, their theory is clearly also anchored in the contemporary Islamic debate about politics and the state.

European and American political thinkers and philosophers

Although the authors of the Islamic civil rights movement and the broader Islamo-reformist current refer to some European and American philosophers in their books, references to this group of sources are relatively rare. As Figures 7, 8 and 9 on pages 51, 52 and 53 show, other types of sources, like the Quran and the hadith or 'classical' Islamic scholars, are much more common. Apart from Muhammad al-Ahmari's book *Democracy*, in which European and American philosophers constitute the most frequently referred to group of sources, the overwhelming majority of the analysed books only mentions them in passing or in the context of rather vague, general references. The authors of the movement do not discuss the theories of these philosophers in detail, like the ideas of some Islamic scholars. The general nature of references to these philosophers and thinkers suggests that the authors of the Islamic civil rights movement did not actually read the original texts but learned about them through references in other texts or introductions in Arabic. While mentioning these philosophers certainly seems to be important to them, not least because it shows the universal nature of some of the concepts that they endorse, their interest in them is evidently not as substantial as that in Islamic sources and authors.

The philosophers and thinkers that are mentioned in the texts of the Islamo-reformist current include ancient Greek philosophers like Plato (428–423 BC) and Aristotle (384–322 BC) as well as classical European political thinkers like the Frenchmen Montesquieu (1689–1755 CE) and Jean-Jacques Rousseau (1712–78 CE). Rousseau and the two Englishmen Thomas Hobbes (1588–1679 CE) and John Locke (1632–1704 CE) are referred to in several books as the founders of social contract theory, according to which the citizens of a state voluntarily surrender some of their freedoms to the state apparatus, which in turn guarantees their rights. Their ideas are often referred back to Islamic sources, like the following passage from a book by Abdallah al-Hamid shows:

> The constitutional state is contractual. This means that it embodies the 'mutual commitment of the people and the government', or a 'document between a people and a leader, between the one who leads and those who are led', like Rousseau mentioned in the book 'The social contract', and like Islam stated before him in the form of the concept of allegiance [*bay'a*].[60]

Others, like Montesquieu, the Frenchman Alexis de Tocqueville (1805–59 CE) and the German philosopher Georg Wilhelm Friedrich Hegel (1770–1831 CE), are mentioned as supporters of a strong role of civil society organizations in the state.[61] French philosopher Denis Diderot (1713–84 CE) is referred to as a critic of despotism.[62]

Others, like the US-American linguist and philosopher Noam Chomsky or the Brazilian philosopher Paolo Freire are only mentioned in passing. As can be seen, the mentioned European philosophers and political thinkers include many of the most influential representatives of classical European political thought.

In the argumentation of the Islamic civil rights movement, European thinkers are only secondary sources, which are used to confirm ideas and concepts that are primarily argued for in terms of Islam. The civil society that European political thinkers speak of is equated with the concept of enjoining virtue and forbidding vice (*al-amr bi-l-maʿrūf wa-n-nahy ʿan al-munkar*) from Islamic discourse. The social contract that philosophers like Rousseau argue for is presented as something that is practically identical with the oath of allegiance (*bayʿa*), which appears in Islamic texts. In the books of Abdallah al-Hamid and other authors of the movement, European philosophers like John Locke, Jean-Jacques Rousseau, Denis Diderot and Georg Wilhelm Friedrich Hegel become advocates of the system of 'shura rule':

> In the oppressive state, the vertical system of relationships, which rests on a class distinction between the lords and the slaves, rules. The relationship rests on oppression and force. In it, power is only stable through the military and police-state-like concept of security. [. . .] Because of these corruptive effects, it was rejected by thinkers of the West, like Locke, Rousseau, Diderot and Hegel, and they called for a civil society built on consultation [*al-muǧtamaʿ al-madanī š-šūrī*].[63]

Mentioning these thinkers serves mainly to show that the concepts that have been argued for in terms of Islam, like enjoining virtue and forbidding vice, allegiance or shura, are universal concepts, which also appear in the European tradition of thought. This is certainly important for the authors of the Islamic civil rights movement. In the end, however, it is clearly more important for them to show that these concepts are legitimate in Islam.

Contemporary academics and experts in fields other than Islamic sciences

Sometimes, the members of the Islamic civil rights movement, and the Islamo-reformist current in general, mention contemporary academics and experts in fields like legal science, human rights or political science in their texts, but in most books, these references are extremely rare. In fact, of the sixteen selected books that were analysed, nine completely abstain from mentioning them. In most others, references to contemporary academics in fields other than Islamic sciences hardly exceed low single-digit numbers. A noteworthy exception among the writings of the Islamic civil rights movement is Abdallah al-Hamid's book *The International Standards of the Independence of the Judiciary in the Melting Pot of the Islamic Sharia* (*Maʿāyīr istiqlāl al-qaḍāʾ fī būtaqa š-šarīʿa l-islāmīya*), in which more than half of all references relate to this group. From among the selected books of the broader Islamo-reformist current only one, Muhammad al-Ahmari's *Democracy*, refers to relatively many contemporary academics. In general, academics and scholars of legal or political sciences do not appear to be a major point of reference for the movement, but when the topic of a book is one where contemporary academics can support the arguments of members of the Islamo-reformist movement, they are not afraid to make extensive use of references to them.

In his book on the independence of the judiciary, Abdallah al-Hamid quotes and mentions several Arab, European and American experts of law and human rights. They include legal scholars from different Arab countries, like the Tunisian Ghazi al-Gharayra (*Ġāzī al-Ġarāyira*) and the Lebanese Khalid al-Qabbani (*Ḫālid al-Qabbānī*). Among them are also several American academics like Linn Hammergren, a development consultant for the United States Agency for International Development (USAID) and the World Bank; Margaret Popkin, a legal scholar and expert on human rights; and Edwin Rekosh, an academic from Columbia University in New York City focusing on civil society. Abdallah al-Hamid quotes entire passages from texts of these authors and refers to them in speaking about judicial independence and the factors that influence it across the world.[64]

The number of references to international academics is very much determined by which texts the authors have access to. If one looks at where the texts of all these academics who are mentioned in al-Hamid's book on judicial independence come from, one realizes that virtually all of them are parts of two large publications. The first is a collection of essays by different international scholars that was published in the context of the so-called Second Justice Conference in Cairo in February 2003 CE. The conference was organized by the independent Arab Center for the Independence of the Judiciary and the Legal Profession (ACIJLP) and the United Nations High Commissioner for Human Rights, bringing together legal scholars and civil society activists from different Arab countries.[65] Abdallah al-Hamid attended the conference and also held a lecture about the dire state of the judiciary in Saudi Arabia. The essays and lectures by the different attendees are one of the two sources that Abdallah al-Hamid relies on in his book.

The second is a handbook about judicial independence published in Arabic in 2003 CE by the American NGO International Foundation for Electoral Systems (IFES) and the United Nations Development Programme. It contains essays by many, mostly US-American legal scholars about the state of judicial independence in the different regions of the world. Abdallah al-Hamid evidently studied this handbook and extensively refers to specific essays from it in his book. Obviously, the fact that Abdallah al-Hamid had access to these two publications enabled him to quote from the texts of all these international legal scholars. Because he had the opportunity to hear and read all these texts in Arabic, al-Hamid realized that they included thoughts that he could use as arguments in his own writings.

Even if Abdallah al-Hamid quotes many international academics on the specialist issue of judicial independence, this does not mean that the Islamic foundation of his theory is softened. The principles and sources of Islam remain the main points of reference for his ideas. With regard to the technical question of judicial independence and its institutional and procedural guarantees Abdallah al-Hamid relies heavily on the aforementioned texts, quoting them extensively and adopting their main points. However, with regard to the key questions like how oppression is to be fought and what the future Muslim state and society should look like, the sources of Islam are the main inspiration. Nevertheless, the example of judicial independence shows how international academics from the global discourse about democracy and good governance occasionally are an additional source of inspiration in specific technical questions.

International symbols of political activism

Very rarely, the authors of the Islamic civil rights movement, and the Islamo-reformist current in general, refer to individuals who are neither Islamic scholars nor classical philosophers or contemporary academics, but can rather be called international symbols of political activism. They include Indian anti-colonial activist and politician Mahatma Gandhi, American civil rights activist Martin Luther King Jr., American Muslim civil rights activist Malcolm X and South African anti-apartheid politician Nelson Mandela. These individuals are mostly referred to in a general way, without a detailed discussion of their ideas or activities, as shown in the following passage from one of Abdallah al-Hamid's books about the virtue of appealing to the international public opinion:

> The international public opinion intervenes and, in the era of open media, the one who spills blood cannot continue his actions. This is the method of the school of peaceful change of Gandhi.[66]

The rare references to these symbols of political activism obviously have the function of adding another layer of argument, for example, by showing that the kind of peaceful activism that Islam calls for has also been practised in other regions of the world. They are not essential for the key points of their theory. With regard to their ideas and the way they argue for them, the members of the Islamic civil rights movement rely more on other sources, especially the primary sources of Islam and Islamic scholars from the early days of Islam until today.

Islam is the foundation – Summarizing the analysis of the references

Abdallah al-Hamid, Matruk al-Falih and other members of the Islamic civil rights movement all seem to share a preference for specific sources, which they rely on strongly in their texts. As could be seen, this preference is also discernible in the texts of other authors of the broader Islamo-reformist current in Saudi Arabia. Thus, in this regard, there does not seem to be a substantial difference between the broader current and the Islamic civil rights movement. Several conclusions can be drawn.

First, it is evident that Islamic sources are extremely important for the theory of the Islamic civil rights movement, and the broader Islamo-reformist current in general. This includes the primary sources of Islam and the texts of Islamic scholars from the early days of Islam until today. No other sources are referred to as often as Islamic sources, and no other sources seem to be as important for formulating their arguments. The authors of the movement quote extensively from the Quran and the hadith to show that a specific point is endorsed by the primary texts of Islam, and they refer to Islamic scholars from the eighth century until today to argue that a specific interpretation has already been mentioned by these reputable scholars.

Second, the authors of the movement know these Islamic sources very well and are able to critically assess them. They not only quote a limited number of Quran verses or passages from the hadith, but they draw from the entirety of the primary sources of Islam. Referring to specific questions from Islamic discourse, they are able to explain the positions of a wide range of Islamic scholars, from the founders of the four large schools of Islamic jurisprudence to contemporary Islamic authors like Yusuf al-Qaradawi. The members of the movement practice a remarkable eclecticism. They select different texts from different scholars, adopt ideas that they deem convincing and openly criticize what they see as false. They do not seem to be bound by any loyalties to any specific school.

The authors of the Islamic civil rights movement especially praise three groups of Islamic scholars, and they extensively rely on their ideas in their writings. The first are a number of 'classical' Islamic scholars, who created new theories about how to think about Islam, politics or the world. They include the four founders, Abu Hanifa, Malik ibn Anas, ash-Shafii and Ahmad ibn Hanbal, as well as the thirteenth-/fourteenth-century CE scholar Ahmad ibn Taymiya and later scholars like Abu Ishaq ash-Shatibi and Ibn Khaldun. The second group are the members of the nineteenth- and twentieth-century CE movement of Islamic Modernism, like Muhammad Abduh, Muhammad Rashid Rida, al-Kawakibi or Khayr ad-Din at-Tunisi. The third group are contemporary Islamic authors who tried to combine Islamic authenticity with political modernity and sometimes have links to the Muslim Brotherhood. Prominent examples are Yusuf al-Qaradawi and Muhammad al-Ghazali. Authors like Abdallah al-Hamid often mention them and their ideas in their texts. They describe all these scholars from the three groups as 'free Salafists' and courageous reformers, and they see themselves in their tradition. Other Islamic scholars, like many authors from the time of the Abbasid caliphate, the key figures of Arabic-Islamic philosophy or contemporary Wahhabi scholars, are criticized. For authors like Abdallah al-Hamid, they stand for political passivity, abstract and impractical thinking and religious justification for oppression. Criticizing them means criticizing the fallacious ideas that they represent in the eyes of the Islamic civil rights movement.

Third, other, non-Islamic sources are underrepresented in the writings of the Islamic civil rights movement. There are some references to European and American philosophers and political thinkers, like Jean-Jacques Rousseau, and to academics and researchers in fields like politics, law or civil society. However, they are only additional sources and are meant to strengthen specific points that have already been argued for in terms of Islam. The fact that Islam endorses specific principles, like an independent judiciary, comes first. References to international academics only seem to serve to show that these principles have also been implemented in other cultural contexts.

For a movement that states that it wants to protect human rights, it is also remarkable that there are virtually no references to international human rights documents. Of all analysed texts, only Abdallah al-Hamid's short treatise *The Founding of the Association HASM Is Legitimate, and Even a Sharia Obligation* and Matruk al-Falih's paper on 'Constitutional reform in Saudi Arabia' mention the Universal Declaration of Human Rights, the Cairo Declaration of Human Rights in Islam and the Arab Charter on Human Rights.[67] Evidently, it is more important for the members of the Islamic civil rights movement to show that the kind of human rights that they have in mind is supported by Islamic sources than showing that they belong to a universal notion of human rights.

Thus, Islamic sources, whether the Quran and hadith or Islamic scholars, are obviously much more important for the argumentation of the Islamic civil rights movement, and the broader Islamo-reformist current, than other sources. For most of them mentioning European and American thinkers, academics in non-Islamic fields, or the notion of universal values mainly seems to be an additional argument which strengthens a line of reasoning that is, in essence, Islamically inspired.

6

From words to proofs – The language and arguments of HASM

In their texts, the members of the Islamo-reformist current in general, and the Islamic civil rights movement in particular, wanted to convince their readers and listeners of their ideas by presenting arguments that the audience would find plausible. These arguments came from various different intellectual fields. In fact, the discourse of the Islamo-reformist current in general and the Islamic civil rights movement in particular can be described as a 'hybrid discourse', because it seemed to fuse Islamic arguments with human rights language, European and American political thought, and universal notions of democracy and political participation.[1] At the same time, they insisted on a Salafist foundation for their theory and they argued that their ideas were compatible with Wahhabi-Salafist Islam. They created their own version of Wahhabism. Thereby, they furthered the fragmentation of the official religious discourse in Saudi Arabia, which had originally been a tightly controlled product of the state establishment but had developed new strands and mutations that were highly critical of the state during the waves of opposition activism of the 1990s and 2000s CE.[2]

From the 1990s CE onwards, members of the Islamo-reformist current seemed to have developed new discoursive rules, which led them to appreciate Islamic arguments, like references to Wahhabi scholars, as well as human rights arguments. By producing their own rules of argumentation, they developed a theory which drew on Wahhabi arguments but was highly critical of the Wahhabi establishment and the political status quo. The theory of the Islamic civil rights movement can be considered a product of this hybrid discourse. The members of the movement used the new rules of argument of the Islamo-reformist current and adapted the language of the discourse so that they were able to create their theory and present it to their readers and listeners in a form that they would find convincing. In doing so, they relied on specific genres of texts, a specific vocabulary and specific arguments.

Poems, lectures, treatises – The genres of texts

In the 2000s and 2010s CE, the members of the Islamic civil rights movement produced and disseminated a large number of declarations, videos and books intended to convince the readers and listeners of their ideas. In their writings, they explicitly called on their colleagues and supporters to present their ideas in an easily understood language and in a form that appealed to a broad audience. Instead of writing academic texts filled with complicated specialist terms, the members of the movement wanted to reach out to the masses by bringing forward their ideas in a way that was plausible and attractive to ordinary people. Only then, they argued, the political reform movement could gain the support of the people and become successful:

> [The reform project] requires bringing together elitism [*nuḫbīya*] and populism [*šaʿbīya*] in the language and the content of the discourse. [. . .] The concepts and ideas will be presented in a simple and clear language, which is easy to understand for the people, but will also be scientific, precise, sober, calm and based on logical proof. It will rely on objectivism and convincing people.[3]

The ultimate aim of the texts that were produced and published by HASM's members was to convince the people of the plausibility of their ideas by presenting them in a way that is understood and seen as convincing.

In order to do so, the members of the association produced different kinds of texts, in which they explained their ideas and the motivation for their activism. The different types of texts had different characteristics and followed different rules, but their common aim was to demonstrate that what HASM was doing was justified. First of all, the association relied on the publication of declarations, reports and press releases. Between October 2009 CE, when HASM was founded, and July 2014 CE, the association regularly published declarations and press releases on its official website.[4] They contained explanations why HASM had been founded,[5] calls to release prisoners of conscience in Saudi prisons[6] and reports about new arrests of HASM members.[7] They also included reports by HASM members on the trials against the members of the association[8] and reactions to and refutations of the arguments and opinions of the prosecution and the judges in these trials.[9] The brief declarations and press releases, with their sometimes-informal register, were mainly used to spread HASM's views on what was happening in Saudi Arabia. They were an ideal outlet for short press statements and reports.

The second main type of text comprised videos of lectures and gatherings. Between December 2011 and September 2017 CE, HASM published a series of videos on the association's own YouTube channel.[10] Most of them were twenty to fifty minutes' long recordings of lectures by HASM members, in which they explained specific elements of their theory.[11] The lectures usually took place during weekly meetings of HASM members. In some of the videos, the camera shows part of the audience, which mostly consisted of known HASM members. Some videos show statements of HASM members in front of court buildings before or after the trial sessions.[12] In general, HASM's videos did not appear to have been produced by video experts. They were rather unremarkable with regard to their technical presentation. There were no flashy effects. The lecturers simply read out their texts, and the camera usually stayed on them without interruption.

Finally, the third type of texts produced by HASM's members was books, in which they presented their arguments in a detailed manner. HASM member Abdallah al-Hamid was a particularly productive author of books. Between the mid-1990s and the 2010s CE, he wrote and published at least twenty-five books about the theory behind his activism. As was mentioned earlier, some were published by the Beirut-based publishing house Arab Scientific Publishers (*ad-dār al-ʿarabīya li-l-ʿulūm*), while others were simply put online for free. While the declarations and lectures set certain limits to what could be said due to the limited space of a declaration or the limited time of a video, the books did not constrain the author in this regard. In his books, al-Hamid explains specific elements of his theory in detail, listing arguments for and against certain positions and quoting the Quran, Islamic scholars, as well as European and American thinkers and academics. Where the declarations were brief and focused on current events, the books provided sufficient space to elucidate the theoretical foundations of HASM's activities. The videos of the lectures assumed a middle position between the declarations and books in this regard, as they contained theoretical arguments as well as references to current events, but not in as much detail as the other two types of texts.

Interestingly, in keeping with the conventions of Islamic scholarly writing, the authors of the Islamic civil rights movement, and the Islamo-reformist current in general, also used poetry in their texts. Abdallah al-Hamid wrote seven books of political poetry, in which he presented his ideas in the form of poems, and even a stage play.[13] For example, in a 1991 CE poem, which uses a classical Arabic rhyme scheme and is titled 'After the Disasters of the Gulf: The Constitution . . . the Constitution, oh Guardian of the Two Holy Places', al-Hamid addressed then-king Fahd and tried to convince him of the necessity of giving the people a voice in political decisions through the means of shura (*šūrā*, 'consultation'):

> Oh, Guardian of the Two Holy Places, every disaster / is caused by an inadequate opinion.
> For the rulers there is no alternative to shura, even if / they possess outstanding minds.
> If an opinion could dispense with it in its excellence / the Chosen One [Muhammad] would not have been bound by it.
> No allegiance to Islam is complete without it / but [allegiance] is linked to shura.
> [. . .]
> This is Islam, it is free shura / nurturing neither oppressor nor oppressed.
> Is the opinion of free men enslaved / or submissive and then discovers what is hidden?
> There is no alternative to freedom / which Islam has commended even before shura.[14]

Al-Hamid, who used to be a professor of Arabic literature, had not only studied Arabic poetry but was also able to write poetry himself. Especially during the early days of his activism in the 1990s CE, he put his poetic skills at the service of his oppositional activities by writing poems which explained his ideas.

In addition to self-written poems, the books of authors of the Islamic civil rights movement also often included references to verses by other, classical and modern

Arabic poets. Usually, the quoted verses of poetry were intended to clarify arguments by adding a poetic way of expressing things. An illustrative example is this passage from al-Hamid's book *The Word Is Stronger than the Bullet*, which explains the virtues of self-sacrifice for the sake of a higher cause, first in al-Hamid's own, already poetic words, then through a quote from the Quran, and finally by quoting a verse of poetry by twentieth-century CE Syrian poet Omar Abu-Riche:

> Scientists who study insects have confirmed that ants and bees have a tendency of self-sacrifice for the sake of the group, which does not seem to appear in any other animal. It is the opposite of the other insects and animals, which are characterised by egoism and whose individuals prefer to flee, if they are in danger. The attacking enemy eats them one after the other, like sheep.
>
> What is the meaning of the saying of the Almighty: 'Your Lord inspired the bees' [Quran 16:68]?
>
> Is its meaning not the saying of the poet [Omar Abu-Riche]: 'Manhood requires that we extend our bodies as a bridge, so tell our comrades to cross.'[15]

In passages like this, the verses of poetry that are quoted are not decisive elements of the theoretical arguments, but they support the points being made by adding an additional, literary perspective. The quoted poems as well as the self-written works of poetry play a supportive role in so far as they reinforce the message conveyed in the books, lectures and declarations.

The authors of the Islamic civil rights movement, and the Islamo-reformist current in general, made an effort to produce texts of literary quality. Even when they were writing prose, their style was eloquent and sophisticated. This is especially obvious in the texts of Abdallah al-Hamid, who sometimes presented his arguments in elaborate rhymed prose, like in this passage from one of his books:

> How can a man be a Salafist today and not write with his fingers [*banān*] and speak with his tongue [*lisān*], in addition to joining the advocates of political reform in the publication of a declaration [*bayān*], and protesting and joining demonstrations in the square [*maydān*]?[16]

In this passage, al-Hamid attempts to make a point and he does so by applying the stylistic device of rhymed prose. The rhyming words are *banān* (fingers), *lisān* (tongue), *bayān* (declaration) and *maydān* (square). Occasional passages of rhymed prose are widespread in the Quran and in Islamic scholarly literature. Abdallah al-Hamid and other Islamo-reformist authors obviously adopted this specific stylistic device as a way to write prose texts of literary quality. They strove to formulate convincing arguments and presented them in a way that was appealing on a literary level. The literary quality of the texts was intended to enhance their powers of persuasion. Thus, whatever the genre of text, the members of the Islamo-reformist current put emphasis on the literary quality of their texts.

Names and labels

The names that a group is given by its members, its supporters and its opponents can tell us a lot about how the group sees itself and how it is perceived by others. This is also true in the case of the Islamic civil rights movement. The protagonists of the movement and the Islamo-reformist current in general have been given different names and labels by observers, supporters and critics, and they have been categorized in different ways. As was mentioned before, in European and North American media and academia, they have been called 'political reformers',[17] 'neo-reformists',[18] 'modernists',[19] 'Islamic liberals',[20] 'Salafi liberals'[21] or 'new Islamists'.[22] For an English-speaking audience, names like 'reformers', 'reformists', 'modernists' or 'liberals' usually carry positive connotations. Critics in Saudi Arabia have been calling them by different names, among them 'bearded liberals'[23] and 'people of enlightenment' (*tanwīriyūn*).[24] For Salafists, these terms do not have the same positive connotations as for a European or American audience. 'Liberal' often reminds Salafist readers of the supposed threat posed by the perceived invasion of immoral 'Western' customs to Islamic values. 'Enlightenment' is seen as a purely European intellectual phenomenon, which has nothing to do with Islam. Thus, while the names that foreign supporters and observers have given to the members of the movement usually suggest a connection to positive things like reform or liberalism, their critics use their own labels to discredit them.

The members of the Islamo-reformist current in general, and the Islamic civil rights movement in particular, have their own names and labels that they use when speaking about themselves and their supporters. Members of the larger current have used names like 'centrists' (*wasaṭiyūn*) or 'rationalists' (*ʿaqlāniyūn*), and some have even on occasion called themselves 'people of enlightenment' (*tanwīriyūn*) or 'liberal Islamists'.[25] However, it has to be noted that not all members of the Islamo-reformist current were comfortable with such names. The members of HASM have mostly been calling themselves 'reformists' (*iṣlāḥiyūn*). This name was already being used frequently by Islamically inspired Saudi Arabian opposition activists since the 1990s CE.[26]

In an Islamic context, 'reformist' means more than the rather neutral English translation of the term suggests. 'Reform' (*iṣlāḥ*) is a concept with a long history in Islamic thought. From early on, it was used by many to designate activities by Muslim individuals and societies for the good of mankind and to improve themselves and the world around them. 'Reform' is linked to the Quranic obligation to enjoin virtue and forbid vice (*al-amr bi-l-maʿrūf wa-n-nahy ʿan al-munkar*). The term featured prominently in the writings of the main protagonists of the current of Islamic Modernism in Egypt at the end of the nineteenth century CE, like Muhammad Abduh and Muhammad Rashid Rida.[27] Thus, when HASM's members call themselves 'reformists', all these elements are included in the meaning of the term.

Other names that the members of HASM have been using for themselves and their supporters are 'advocates of reform' (*duʿāt al-iṣlāḥ*),[28], 'advocates of shura rule' (*duʿāt al-ḥukm aš-šūrī*),[29] 'advocates of reform and civil society' (*duʿāt al-iṣlāḥ wa-l-muǧtamaʿ al-ahlī l-madanī*)[30] and 'comrades of the ship of peaceful jihad' (*rifāq safīnat al-ǧihād as-silmī*).[31] It is evident that when the protagonists of the Islamic civil rights movement speak about themselves, they usually use names and labels which emphasize their status as 'reformists', with all the connotations of the term, or point to central elements of their theory.

In general, the members of the Islamic civil rights movement see themselves as the continuation of a long history of Salafist reformist movements. In his writings, HASM member Abdallah al-Hamid frequently refers to dissident Islamic scholars and revolutionaries from the era of the Umayyad and the Abbasid caliphs, lauding their principled resistance to the political rulers and the Islamic mainstream of their times. These role models include Islamic scholar al-Hasan al-Basri (*al-Ḥasan al-Baṣrī*), who had supported the political rivals of the Umayyad caliph Yazid I. during the so-called Second Islamic Civil War from 680 until 692 CE. They also include Islamic jurist Said ibn Jubayr (*Sa'īd ibn Ǧubair*), who was a part of the so-called 'rebellion of the Quran reciters' (*ṯawrat al-qurrā'*) against Umayyad caliph al-Walid I. in 700 CE, and Islamic scholar Sufyan ath-Thawri (*Sufyān aṯ-Ṯaurī*, d. 778 CE), who had opposed the policies of Abbasid caliph al-Mahdi. Additional examples are Malik ibn Anas (*Mālik ibn Anas*) and Abu Hanifa (*Abū Ḥanīfa*), the founders of the Maliki and Hanafi Islamic schools of jurisprudence. Both had opposed the worldly rulers of their times and were persecuted for it. Abu Hanifa had even died in prison, after he had refused to become an employee of the Abbasid caliph Al-Mansur in 763 CE. According to al-Hamid, all these scholars had resisted injustice, and thus they serve as role models for the activities of HASM:

> The Umayyad Islamic jurists proved their political awareness and proved that Salafism is political reform, and that the method of the people of the sunna is not the method of patience in the face of the injustice and oppression of the ruler, but advising him to implement justice and shura [*šūrā*, 'consultation']. On this basis the first Islamic jurists resisted them, like al-Hasan al-Basri, [. . .] Sufyan ath-Thawri, [. . .] Said ibn Jubayr, Malik and Abu Hanifa did, who died in prison, because he refused [to be appointed] Chief Judge.[32]

By praising these scholars and their reported acts of resistance in this way, and by referring to them as inspirations for the activities of HASM today, al-Hamid constructs an intellectual pedigree, which makes HASM the direct successors of these scholars. Referring to these reputable scholars in this way implies that what HASM is doing is comparable to what they had done. They all resisted the injustice of the ruler and declared that Islam required a just political system. Al-Hamid often uses the term 'free Islamic jurists' (*al-fuqahā' al-aḥrār*) in speaking about dissident scholars from the past, and he sees them as representatives of an early activist strand of Salafism. The fact that al-Hamid describes himself and his associates as Salafists[33] further underlines the connection that he draws between HAMS's activism and the aforementioned scholars.

Apart from these examples from the first centuries of Islam, HASM's members also see themselves in the tradition of nineteenth-century CE Islamic Modernism. It included Islamic scholars like Afghan-born Jamal ad-Din al-Afghani (*Ǧamāl ad-Dīn al-Afġānī*), the Egyptians Muhammad Abduh (*Muḥammad ʿAbduh*) and Muhammad Rashid Rida (*Muḥammad Rašīd Riḍā*), the Syrian Abd ar-Rahman al-Kawakibi (*ʿAbd ar-Raḥmān al-Kawākibī*) and the Tunisian Khayr ad-Din at-Tunisi (*Ḫayr ad-Dīn at-Tūnisī*). While they came from different backgrounds and did not all agree on a concrete set of ideas, they were united by the wish to rediscover the innovative qualities of Islamic political thought and combine Islamic thinking with the findings of modern sciences. The members of this movement had vehemently called for political reforms and had endorsed democratic forms of government instead of the existing autocracies, which were instrumentalized by European colonial powers. Islamic Modernism has decisively shaped the Islamic debate of the twentieth century CE, and it has influenced many movements, including the Muslim Brotherhood. In one of his texts, al-Hamid states that he wants to continue the spirit of this movement:

> Today, in the era of Western imperialism, when we face the most violent, the greatest and the most dangerous challenge, we need to continue to build the civilisational form of Salafism, which was started by the prominent figures of the modern renaissance of Islam [*nahḍat al-islām al-ḥadīṯ*], whose lighthouse was ignited by the call for political reform of Jamal ad-Din al-Afghani, al-Kawakibi and Khayr ad-Din at-Tunisi. Some parts of it also appeared in the movement of the Muslim Brotherhood.[34]

Al-Hamid explicitly calls on Muslims to follow the intellectual example of the movement of Islamic Modernism. Again, this implies that this is exactly what HASM is doing. Thereby, HASM becomes a contemporary heir of the influential movement of Islamic Modernism.

In summary, the Islamic civil rights movement does not understand itself as a completely new movement in Islamic discourse. The members of HASM claim to be part of a long tradition of reformists who have been resisting the injustice of the rulers and calling for reforms on the basis of Islamic arguments since the earliest days of Islam. According to the interpretation of the members of HASM, the association is heir to all these respected dissidents, revolutionaries and visionaries, although they are not the only movement that can claim such an intellectual lineage. In the eyes of many supporters, this lineage also increases the legitimacy of the movement, because it indicates that the Islamic civil rights movement is simply continuing what these widely recognized, reputable scholars did in the past. Just as their actions were justified back in their days, the actions of the Islamic civil rights movement are justified today.

The political vocabulary

The words that the members of the Islamic civil rights movement use to designate political concepts like nation or constitution are drawn from the modern Arabic political vocabulary, and this vocabulary is relatively new. Before the nineteenth century CE, there existed a well-developed Arabic terminology for the political phenomena of the Arab and Islamic world, but the Arabic language lacked adequate terms for describing certain elements of the modern political systems, like elected legislative councils or constitutions. In the nineteenth century CE, various authors and scholars dedicated themselves to explaining the politics of Europe after the French Revolution to their Arab readers, and in doing so, they had to come up with new Arabic words to describe certain concepts that could not easily be translated into the existing Arabic political vocabulary. This development of new Arabic terms for modern political concepts was later continued and by the beginning of the twentieth century a whole new set of words had been created. For the most part, these new terms were based on existing Arabic words or roots, whose meaning was slightly changed or expanded by way of analogy.[35] However, their old meanings did not vanish completely. This resulted in some ambiguity, as these terms designated the new political concepts while simultaneously keeping the old meanings of the words and roots. As a consequence, one has to beware of simply equating Arabic terms with their English translations, because this would obscure the many connotations of these terms.[36]

An illustrative example is the Arabic word *umma*. Originally, *umma* had designated different tribes or peoples, or, more generally speaking, bodies of people that were characterized by a common linguistic, ethnical or religious bond. In the Islamic context, the term soon came to mean the community of all Muslims, in contrast to other *ummas*, like the Christian umma or the Jewish umma. When Arab authors started to study the new concept of the nation in the nineteenth century CE, the Arabic word *umma* eventually emerged as the most common term for it. From then on, *umma* also designated the nation state while keeping its older meanings.[37]

The word 'shura' (*šūrā*) is another example that shows the process of lexical innovation and the resulting ambiguity particularly well. Shura is deeply entrenched in the Islamic discourse, where it has always stood for the commendable act of a ruler asking other people for advice. According to classical Islamic thought, shura, that is rule by consultation, is something that a worldly ruler should do. Later, shura also came to designate advisory bodies who gave advice to the ruler. When Arab authors and scholars studied democratic systems in the nineteenth century CE, some, like Muhammad Abduh and Muhammad Rashid Rida, argued that shura and democracy were only slightly different forms of the same concept. Shura thus became something of a synonym for democracy, without losing its older, Islamic connotations.

These political terms are exactly the political language that the members of the Islamic civil rights movement use in their texts. When speaking about the community, they use the term *umma*, and when speaking about a democratic form of government, they often use the term *shura*. The connotations and ambiguities that have accumulated throughout the history of the use of these words are still present. Sometimes they deliberately exploit these ambiguities. An example is the ambiguous way they use the term 'human rights' (*ḥuqūq al-insān*). On the one hand, they argue that they are a human rights organization committed to universal human values, which are confirmed by all religions:

> When the word 'human rights' is used, not a few people think that it is a foreign concept, which was introduced into Islam, and that it is linked to secularism. [. . .]

> Human rights are not a secular concept, but the heavenly religions, and especially Islam, confirmed, endorsed and prescribed them.[38]

On the other hand, in HASM's founding declaration, the founding members stated that they wanted to lay the foundation for a specifically Islamic culture of human rights, which would not be influenced by the 'Western' view on the topic:

> One of the reasons for the founding of the association is that a number of international organisations is influenced by the Western view on human rights and does not display the Islamic view on human rights in an effective manner.[39]

The term 'human rights' (*ḥuqūq al-insān*) is a relatively new term in the Arabic language and asserted itself in the Arabic vocabulary only in the wake of the encounter with European and North American concepts of universal rights. To an Arabic speaker living in the nineteenth century CE, the composed expression 'human rights' did not necessarily mean the same thing as to someone interested in human rights today. In classical Islamic thought, rights (*ḥuqūq*) were a concept that was intrinsically linked to duties and concerned the relationship between God and his servants more than the relationship between human beings.[40] This meaning is still included in the term today, even as it has become the common translation for the English word 'human rights'. As a consequence, the Arabic expression 'human rights' is somewhat ambiguous and not as clear as the English translation would suggest. In the two quoted passages earlier, it can be seen how this ambiguity can be observed in the texts of the Islamic civil rights movement and how their authors sometimes seem to switch between meanings and connotations.

In addition to the sometimes ambiguous political vocabulary, the members of the movement also employ clearly Islamic language and imagery in their texts. One cannot deny that the language of their texts is inspired by Islam and Islamic imagery. An example that was already mentioned is al-Hamid's allusion to the Verse of Light in the Quran[41] in the following passage from his book *So That the Quran Is Not a Carrier of Different Meanings*:

> [The aim is] re-formulating the Islamic doctrine [*ʿaqīda*], the stated aims of the sharia [*maqāṣid aš-šarīʿa*] and its spirit by returning to the lamp of the clear literal and deduced statements of the sharia in the bottle of the era of the Prophet and the Rightly Guided Caliphs and in the niche of the truths of the sciences, especially the social sciences, in order to focus on the elements which confront the modern challenges.[42]

Al-Hamid takes the metaphor of the lamp in the bottle and the niche from the Verse of Light and poetically uses it to describe his approach to the renewal of the Islamic discourse. The metaphor from the verse is one of the best-known passages from the Quran, and virtually every Muslim reader will immediately recognize it. The title of the book in which the aforementioned passage can be found is also an allusion to a quote from the primary sources of Islam. 'So that the Quran is not a carrier of different meaning' is a slight variation of a saying which is ascribed to the fourth caliph, Ali ibn Abi Talib. According to some sources, Ali advised one of his envoys, who had the task of negotiating with the breakaway sect of the Kharijites, not to try to convince them by quoting verses from the Quran, because 'the Quran is a carrier of different meanings' (*fa-inna l-qur'ān huwa ḥammāl auǧuh*).[43] Without explicitly saying it, al-Hamid's title clearly refers to this hadith, and this reference is clearly recognizable to a reader who has been educated in Islamic affairs.

The way al-Hamid and other members of the Islamo-reformist current speak about oppression and democratic systems is also heavily influenced by Islamic language and imagery. For example, oppressive rule is frequently called 'biting kingship' (*mulk ʿaḍūḍ*).[44] This expression comes from a hadith, in which the prophet Muhammad predicts that the rule of the caliphate will be followed by the rule of 'biting kingship'.[45] The imagery used by the members of the Islamic civil rights movement is evidently influenced by Islamic sources.

Sometimes, the members of the movement use older words, which were used in classical Islamic sources, instead of others which are more common today, even if they designate the same thing. When speaking about European states and nations, they sometimes use the old Arabic word *ifranǧī* instead of the modern standard term *ūrubī*.[46] Etymologically, the word *ifranǧi* can be traced back to the medieval European kingdom of the Franks, which had dominated European politics in the early Middle Ages. In classical Arabic texts, the word is often used as a name for all inhabitants of Europe. Today, its use is more or less limited to conservative Islamic scholars who want to continue the diction of classical Islamic sources, like, it seems, the members of the Islamic civil rights movement do. The most striking example for their preference for older terms from an Islamic context is their frequent use of the term *kāfir* ('unbeliever') when speaking about non-Muslims. In several of their texts, they use the Quranic word *kāfir* to designate people of other faiths, although other terms like 'non-Muslim' (*ġayr al-muslim*) are used as well. In their writings, the designation *kāfir* does not necessarily carry the derogatory meaning that its English translation, 'unbeliever', does. Two examples from texts by Abdallah al-Hamid illustrate this:

> Other texts have clearly stated that Islam confirmed that the Muslim and the non-Muslim [*ġayr al-muslim*] are equal in all rights, which are based on citizenship. Therefore, an aggression against the unbelievers [*al-kuffār*] is like an aggression against the Muslims.[47]
>
> The legitimacy of jihad is limited to defending the state of justice and shura, because there is no difference between a local, Muslim oppressor and a foreign, unbeliever [*kāfir*] oppressor.[48]

In both passages, 'unbeliever' (*kāfir*) appears to be used as a neutral designation for non-Muslims. At least on the surface of the text, the people, who are called 'unbelievers' are not attacked for their being non-Muslims. On the contrary, the first passage emphasizes that Muslims and non-Muslims, or 'unbelievers', should have the same rights in a Muslim state. The second passage underlines that oppression is bad, no matter what the religion of the ruler is. Despite this positive context, the fact remains that al-Hamid chooses the term 'unbeliever' instead of more neutral words like 'non-Muslims', and he accepts all the connotations of the term which will come to the mind of his Arabic-speaking readers. The example of the use of 'unbeliever' shows how the members of the movement often pick old, established terms from an Islamic context instead of newer, more neutral terms, thus bringing a wide range of connotations from the Islamic discourse into their texts.

Thus, the members of the Islamic civil rights movement clearly show a strong preference for terms, images and metaphors with Islamic connotations. When using the political terminology that was created in the nineteenth century CE, they are aware of all the ambiguities of specific words that have accumulated over the time of their use in different, religious and non-religious, contexts. The imagery that they use is inspired by the primary sources of Islam, like the Quran and the hadiths. Often, they directly adopt specific expressions from these primary sources, like 'biting kingship' (*mulk ʿaḍūḍ*) or 'unbeliever' (*kāfir*). The images that they use to illustrate their points very often come from the pool of Islamic tradition. The authors of the movement obviously consider this language and imagery, which is based on Islamic sources, an element of a good and convincing literary style. Educated Muslim readers will understand these Islamic references and their connotations, and consequently the arguments of the Islamic civil rights movement may appear more plausible to them if their language is that of Islam.

Quran, logic and science – The arguments

In their declarations, lectures and books, the members of the Islamic civil rights movement use different sets of arguments to convince the audience that their ideas and actions are justified. Most of their texts are argumentative texts. They are meant to explain why what they are saying is plausible and why what they are doing is necessary. To achieve this, the authors and lecturers make use of different kinds of arguments, which are based on different sources and different scientific or intellectual fields. Generally speaking, five different types of arguments can be identified in the writings of the Islamic civil rights movement: references to Islamic sources, the rules of Islamic jurisprudence, the aims of the sharia, reason and logic, and finally the findings of the sciences.

Islamic sources

It has already been seen that in their argumentation, the members of the Islamic civil rights movement heavily rely on quoting and commenting on Islamic sources. When they try to make a point in their texts, they often cite verses from the Quran or passages from the hadith corpus to strengthen their arguments. An illustrative example is the following passage from HASM's founding declaration:

> Fourteen centuries before the appearance of the international laws which protect human rights and to which governments are committed, the Islamic sharia came

> to protect human dignity, safeguard the rights of man and end injustice. The Almighty God said: 'We have conferred dignity on the children of Adam' [Quran 17:70, translation M. Asad] and 'Whenever you judge between people, judge with justice' [Quran 4:58, translation M. Asad], and in the sacred hadith he said: 'O my servants, I have forbidden oppression for myself and have made it forbidden amongst you, so do not oppress one another'.[49]

Quotes from the primary sources of Islam often serve to strengthen specific arguments. The fact that the quoted statements appear in these sources and can be interpreted in a way that supports their points seems to be a plausible argument for them. In addition to the primary texts, the way they were understood by the first generations of Muslims also serves as a valid argument in their texts, as can be seen in this passage from a book by Abdallah al-Hamid:

> The best way is to understand [the Quranic and prophetic texts] through the bottle of the implementation of the prophet [Muhammad] and the Rightly Guided Caliphs, because it is the standard implementation of religion before the centuries of religious distortion.[50]

The members of the movement clearly state that with regard to the implementation of the religious texts, they want to imitate the first generations of Muslims. Therefore, reports about their actions and sayings are used as important arguments in their texts.

References to Islamic scholars from the early days of Islam until today also serve as strong arguments in their texts. Authors like Abdallah al-Hamid are obviously well informed about certain debates within Islamic discourse as well as the different positions and interpretations of Islamic scholars from the past. When discussing the interpretations of specific passages from the Quran or specific questions of the discourse of Islamic jurisprudence, they often refer to the opinions of various scholars from the history of Islamic discourse. This can be seen in the following passage, in which Abdallah al-Hamid argues that military jihad can be legitimate only when it is a response to aggression:

> The three Islamic legal scholars [Abu Hanifa, Malik ibn Anas and Ahmad ibn Hanbal] said that the reason for military jihad is aggression or fear of it, and later legal scholars agreed, the most famous of them being Ibn Taymiya. [. . .] The majority of legal scholars, and scholars of sharia politics in particular, share this opinion, like Muhammad Abduh, Muhammad Rashid Rida, Hasan al-Banna and Muhammad al-Ghazzali.[51]

Some of the mentioned scholars are classical Islamic scholars, like Abu Hanifa, Malik ibn Anas and Ahmad ibn Hanbal, while others are representatives of the nineteenth-century CE school of Islamic Modernism, like Muhammad Abduh and Muhammad Rashid Rida. The mere fact that a specific opinion was shared by all of them seems to count as a supporting argument.

In their dealings with all these Islamic scholars from the past, the members of the movement display a somewhat eclectic attitude, taking from different scholars what they deem useful, without outrightly committing to a specific school. In several passages, they explicitly state that they want to neutrally assess the ideas of the different scholars and schools, in each case deciding which points should be accepted and which should be rejected.[52] The members of the movement emphasize that they impartially analyse the ideas of different Islamic scholars, adopting correct arguments and rejecting wrong ones. Those that are deemed correct are then used as arguments in their own texts. Generally speaking, references to Islamic sources, be they primary sources of Islam or scholars and schools from the early days of Islam until today, constitute a major element of the argumentation of the members of the Islamic civil rights movement.

Rules of Islamic jurisprudence

The members of the movement are also versed in the rules of argumentation of classical Islamic jurisprudence and the Islamic sciences in general, and they use their knowledge in these areas in their arguments. On several occasions, they insist that arguments that claim to be grounded in Islam have to abide by the rules of Islamic reasoning. Only when the arguments of political reformers adhere to these rules will they be perceived as convincing by their audience:

> The advocates or shura rule will not possess popular credibility, as long as they do not possess religious credibility. They will not possess religious credibility, as long as their ideas are not grounded in Islamic jurisprudence [*fiqh*] through the four sciences: principles of Islamic jurisprudence [*uṣūl al-fiqh*], the aims of the sharia [*maqāṣid aš-šārīʿa*], theoretical Islamic doctrine [*ʿaqīda*] and sharia politics [*as-siyāsa š-šarʿīya*].[53]

References to the standards of argumentation of Islamic jurisprudence or Islamic doctrine feature prominently in several of the texts of the Islamic civil rights movement. When speaking about opinions they are critical of, they often refer to perceived methodical errors in their lines of argumentation.

An example is a lecture by HASM member Sulayman ar-Rashudi held in November 2012 CE, in which he argued that demonstrations are legitimate according to Islamic law. The former judge ar-Rashudi criticizes the opinion of the official Wahhabi establishment concerning the demonstrations of the Arab Spring and their claim that demonstrations are forbidden in Islamic law, because they allegedly lead to chaos and destruction. According to ar-Rashudi, this reading is wrong and based on a faulty line of Islamic legal reasoning. First of all, he argues that demonstrations fall into the category of questions of civil life rather than questions of worship, which are regulated in minute detail in the Islamic sources. According to the rules of Islamic jurisprudence, matters of civil life are generally allowed, except if there is a specific reason for forbidding them:

> A judgment about banning or allowing something is only possible on the basis of a sharia argument or a clear scientific proof. [. . .] The judgments of the sharia fall into two categories. The first category deals with everything related to questions of worship, the corporal punishments and everything which God has prescribed in religion and through which his servants serve him according to that which he has laid down in his book. [. . .] The second category deals with worldly affairs and questions of civil life. Here, the basis is permissibility, according to the principle of Islamic jurisprudence which states: The basis of things is permissibility [*al-aṣl fī l-ašyā' al-ibāḥa*]. Our question tonight, the question of demonstrations and protests in the Islamic sharia, completely falls into the second category.[54]

Because demonstrations fall into the category of things which are generally allowed, so ar-Rashudi's reasoning continues, they can be forbidden only if there are grave reasons to do so. Ar-Rashudi argues that there are no reasons for it. On the contrary, another principle which states that means like demonstrations are judged according to their aims can only lead to the conclusion that demonstrations for the lifting of injustice are legitimate:

> Demonstrations and protests are means. The principle of the sharia says that the judgement about the aims also applies to the means [*al-wasā'il lahā ḥukm al-ġāyāt*]. If demonstrations are a peaceful means and if their aims are eliminating injustice and implementing truth and justice, they are allowed. [. . .] Calling for peaceful demonstrations to lift injustice and oppression, eliminate corruption and give the people their stolen rights and freedoms and their lost dignity belongs to the call to virtue and to enjoining virtue and forbidding vice, which God has made a sharia obligation. As long as this is the legitimate aim, any means which is allowed and leads to it is legitimate, and indeed an obligation.[55]

These passages from the lecture by Sulayman ar-Rashudi show how the members of the movement apply Islamic legal reasoning in their texts and how they use it to argue their ideas. When a line of argumentation that deals with a question of Islamic jurisprudence complies with the rules of Islamic reasoning, it is considered plausible. Statements about compliance with these rules or alleged mistakes are therefore considered valid arguments and are, indeed, used to strengthen the persuasive power of their ideas.

Aims of the sharia

Apart from quotes from Islamic sources and references to the rules of Islamic legal reasoning, the members of the movement also frequently use references to the theory of the stated aims of the sharia (*maqāṣid aš-šarī'a*) as arguments. This theory, which was formulated by fourteenth-century CE Andalusian Islamic scholar Abu Ishaq ash-Shatibi (*Abū Isḥāq aš-Šāṭibī*), argues that God intends Muslims to reach specific aims by following the rules of Islam. According to the theory, once one has determined what the intention of God is, the knowledge of these aims can be used as arguments in

Islamic legal reasoning. Authors like Abdallah al-Hamid explicitly mention the theory of the stated aims of the sharia as a major inspiration for their arguments. Knowledge of the aims of the sharia can help determine whether something is in line with the spirit of the sharia, and any convincing argument should comply with this spirit.[56]

Al-Hamid argues that referring to the aims of the sharia is an important argument in any line of reasoning which is meant to be consistent in terms of Islam. According to ash-Shatibi's theory, the aims of the sharia are the protection of five basic interests of humans in this world, namely religion (*dīn*), life (*nafs*), progeny (*nasl*), the mind (*ʿaql*) and property (*māl*).[57] Therefore, everything which serves to promote one of these interests is considered legitimate, indeed even necessary, in Islamic reasoning:

> Everything which humanity agrees is necessary for the life of the people, be it affairs of livelihood or building cities and states, belongs to the sharia. Everything without which the lives of the people cannot function is counted among the fundamentals of religion [*uṣūl ad-dīn*], like ash-Shatibi has explained in [his book] '*al-Muwāfaqāt*'.[58]

Arguing that something is necessary for the protection of one of the basic interests of ash-Shatibi's theory is a strong supporting argument in the writings of the Islamic civil rights movement and indeed of Islamo-reformist authors in general. For example, as the following passage shows, Islamic scholar Salman al-Awda is also deeply influenced by a view of sharia reasoning that is based on ash-Shatibi's theory of the aims of the sharia:

> The view which is based on the aims of the sharia [*an-naẓar al-maqāṣidī*] looks at the highest, holistic interest in protecting the rights and freedoms, caring for justice, fighting corruption and adopting an interest in reform. If this is achieved through the way with the least costs and the least losses, this is closest to the soul of the sharia, its spirit and its general principles.[59]

The theory of the aims of the sharia is used by several authors to formulate arguments for the kind of civil society activism that the Islamic civil rights movement wants to inspire. In fact, this theory has become a major point of reference for many Islamic scholars and Islamically inspired political activists since the nineteenth century CE, when the protagonists of the Islamic Modernism movement revived it and introduced it into the reformist debate.[60] It has been observed that this theory has led to some pragmatic flexibility in the argumentation of several scholars and activists. If there are areas which are not precisely regulated by the primary texts of Islam, but where humans can identify the general intention of God, everything which fulfils this intention is legitimate, and everything which does not, or does no longer, is to be rejected. As a consequence, humans have some leeway in thinking about possible solutions to their worldly problems. Every human innovation that helps reach the aims of the sharia in this world is desirable. The members of the Islamic civil rights movement are evidently aware of these conclusions and use references to the aims of the sharia in several of their texts.

Reason and logic

Apart from religious sources and the established rules of Islamic argumentation, they also hold that human reason can lead to correct and convincing statements, and they use logical arguments in their writings. Abdallah al-Hamid repeatedly mentions that, in the affairs of this world, the God-given human intellect is able to find truth. Human intelligence and experience can understand the rules that govern nature and society, and when religious sources speak about worldly things, they only confirm what the human intellect can discover on his own:

> The affairs of the civil half [of the sharia], like organising life, culture and civilisation, come to the independent human minds [*ʿuqūl*] and they understand most of its interests and what harms it. God's law [*aš-šarʿ*] only comes to discover or confirm what the minds have discerned.[61]
>
> Man knows most interests in the civil half [of the sharia] through the innate nature [*fiṭra*] which God has given him, through the light of insight which He has granted him, and through that which experience and expertise have shown him.[62]

The heavenly gift of the human intellect enables humans to understand the world around them and make correct statements about the rules that govern it, without the need for an additional authority. However, the human mind can only make reliable statements about worldly affairs. Things like the rules of worship, which have been regulated in detail in the texts of Islam, cannot be understood by reference to the intellect alone. Here, humans need a revelation from God in order to understand the nature of things. As long as the human intellect stays in its domain, it can reach correct findings, and these rational findings are also true in terms of the sharia.

As can be seen in the following passage from one of Abdallah al-Hamid's books, he passionately adopts the idea of the thirteenth-/fourteenth-century CE Islamic scholar Ibn Taymiya that the rational truths of the sciences and the truths of religious revelation do not contradict each other. On the contrary, what is true in one field is also true in the other:

> The definitively rational [*al-maʿqūl al-qaṭʿī*] in terms of humans, civilisation or politics, be it sensory, empirical or proof-based, is automatically true in the sharia. Everything which is true in the sciences of man and nature harmonises with the sharia and is, therefore, legitimate [*mašrūʿ*] knowledge, like Ibn Taymiya said in the book 'Reason and Tradition'.[63]

The findings of human, rational sciences are also true in terms of Islam. Human reason is able to discover truths and make correct statements about the world. This especially applies to questions of politics and social interaction. For example, human reason tells everyone that a ruler has to be just. This is a self-evident truth, which every human being knows:

> Above all, the unjust ruler is exposed in front of his own conscience, because justice and truth are sown into the natural predisposition [*fiṭra*] and reason [*ʿaql*] of every human.[64]

The reason that al-Hamid and the other members of the Islamic civil rights movement have in mind is not an abstract, scholastic reason as allegedly propagated by the philosophers of ancient Greece and the Islamic theological school of the Mutazila (*muʿtazila*) but a practical, empirical reason. Al-Hamid contrasts the practical, empirical reason he recognizes in the primary sources of Islam with an impractical, abstract reason, which, according to him, was embodied by Greek philosophy and the theological school of the Mutazila.[65] As long as one relies on the former kind of reason and as long as it stays inside the domain of worldly questions, where it can reach valid conclusions, the human intellect is an important element in the argumentation of the Islamic civil rights movement.

Scientific findings

The final crucial source of arguments for their theory is references to modern sciences in general. They argue that the findings of modern political and social sciences need to be recognized and integrated into a political theory in order to ensure that it has a solid foundation. Modern sciences can tell us what we need to do to lead peaceful, just and successful lives in this world. A term which they frequently use in this context is 'laws of God' (*sunan allāh*). In the form which the members of the movement adopt it was coined by the Egyptian Muslim Brother Sayyid Qutb (*Saiyid Quṭb*). The 'laws of God' stand for the laws of nature and society, which regulate the course of things in this world. The success, stability and prosperity of nations and states are not determined by how pious they are but by whether they do what the laws of nature and society require them to do. If a nation wants to be successful, it has to listen to the requirements of these natural laws.[66]

Al-Hamid emphasizes that these laws do not make a difference between a pious, Muslim community and an immoral, non-Muslim community. If they do what these natural laws require, they will be successful and prosperous in this world. Therefore, it is worthwhile to study the history of past nations and the situation of contemporary states and thereby learn from their experiences. For example, one can thus conclude that civil jihad in the form of demonstrations and protests is a guarantee for justice and stability and that oppression necessarily leads to political weakness and suffering. The following passage by Abdallah al-Hamid illustrates this approach:

> This indicates that the greatest harm for the community comes from giving the rulers and the scholars authority over the community and considering the rulers and the scholars those who know best with regard to the interests of the community. [. . .] These are the sharia arguments in the laws of God [*sunan allāh*] that can be seen in the history of Islam since the times of the Umayyads. They are also arguments that can be seen in the history of the old nations, in the civilisation of the Pharaohs, of Babylon, of Ashur and of the Phoenicians, as well as the Chinese, the Indian and the Persian civilisation and the Greek, the Roman and the Saxon civilisations, and they are arguments that can be seen in the history of the modern European, American and other civilisations.[67]

Through the study of the experiences of all these nations, the historian and the political and social scientist can only conclude that oppression leads to stagnation, and that civil society activism leads to stable, prosperous societies. This, in turn, is an important argument in al-Hamid's text. As can be seen, al-Hamid and the other members of the Islamic civil rights movement consider these findings of history and social and political sciences weighty arguments, which they readily use in their writings.

In several passages, they also advise political reformists to combine insight gained by political and social sciences with insights from the primary sources of Islam. Al-Hamid complains that all too often Islamic scholars have no understanding of the political realities, while most political reformers lack knowledge of the principles of Islam. Only when scientific knowledge of political and social developments and familiarity with the Islamic sources are combined can one, as a reformer, formulate a coherent and convincing theory. The reformer has to possess knowledge of both the modern social sciences and Islamic sciences in order to reach correct conclusions on questions of political reform and present them in a convincing manner.[68]

Al-Hamid argues the natural and social sciences and the Islamic sciences complement each other. The truths of one help unveil the truths of the other and vice versa, because they are complementary:

> The clear statements from the sharia texts to not contradict what is true in the sciences of man and nature, because He who sent down the sharia is the same as He who created nature. [. . .] That which is not clear in the book [the Quran] and the sunna is referred to that which is clear in the sciences of humans and nature. And that which is unclear in the sciences of humans and nature is referred to that which is clear in the book and the sunna. This is a great principle, which Ibn Taymiya has laid out in [his book] 'Reason and Tradition'.[69]

Not only can the modern sciences help us understand specific passages in the religious texts, but the religious texts can also help us understand some natural or social phenomena in this world. Important truths, like the principle that societies are only stable if they are governed justly, are underpinned by both the Islamic sciences and the modern social sciences. In general, references to the findings of modern sciences, and especially the social and political sciences, as well as to the 'laws of God', which govern this world, are frequent and important arguments in the texts of the Islamic civil rights movement.

An interesting example of a specific science whose methods the members of the movement use to formulate arguments is the field of linguistics. The former professor of Arabic literature Abdallah al-Hamid refers to linguistic arguments in several of his books. Usually, these arguments are used in the context of his criticism of specific interpretations of the Islamic primary sources or of perceived mistakes in the Islamic theories of other thinkers and authors. Al-Hamid argues that, in the course of the history of Islamic thought, specific words that appear in the Quran changed their meanings. Terms like 'wisdom' (*ḥikma*), 'enjoining virtue and forbidding vice' (*al-amr bi-l-maʿrūf wa-n-nahy ʿan al-munkar*) and 'those who have been entrusted with authority' (*ūlū l-amr*) originally had a broad meaning, which was increasingly restricted by Islamic scholars over the centuries:

> In the Abbasid era, there was a great alienation of the meanings of terms. The term remained, but the people changed its meaning [*mafhūm*]. This is obvious in many terms, like patience [*ṣabr*], wisdom [*ḥikma*], enjoining virtue and forbidding vice [*al-amr bi-l-ma'rūf wa-n-nahy 'an al-munkar*] and learning the Quran and teaching it. [. . .] The same is true for the term 'those who have been entrusted with authority' [*ūlū l-amr*], whose comprehensive linguistic meaning as the people of opinion and insight and the notables of the Muslim community was restricted to [the meaning of] the Islamic legal scholars and the political leaders.[70]

According to al-Hamid, all these terms had a broad meaning in the Quran, but were given more specific and limited meanings by Islamic scholars. Patience came to mean political passivity, wisdom became the term for abstract philosophy, enjoining virtue and forbidding vice became a function of the government, and 'those who have been entrusted with authority' were understood to be the rulers and the religious scholars. In another passage, al-Hamid argues that the same semantic change happened to the term *fiqh*, which appears in the broad meaning of 'cleverness' or 'understanding' in the Quran, but later became the technical term for Islamic jurisprudence. Therefore, according to al-Hamid, it is wrong to exclusively understand *fiqh* as a reference to the Islamic legal science in every occurrence of the word in the Quran.[71]

For the sake of the linguistic purity of Islamic and political discourse, al-Hamid advises Muslims to stick to the broad meanings of terms, as they were used in the Quran, and always keep in mind that, in later usage, these terms often mean different things. According to al-Hamid, these semantic changes are also one of the reasons for the fallacious conclusions of some Islamic scholars who argued, for example, that when the Quran speaks of the people of authority it means the worldly rulers. Thus, linguistic arguments also feature prominently in the lines of reasoning of the members of the Islamic civil rights movement.

In summary, it is obvious that the members of the movement use a wide range of arguments to convince their readers and listeners that what they are saying and doing is right and correct. Their arguments include references to Islamic sources, the rules of classical Islamic legal reasoning, the conclusions of human reason, the findings of modern social sciences and linguistic analyses. What is striking is that even the arguments which do not appear to be directly linked to Islam are put into an Islamic framework. They emphasize that the insights of the natural and social sciences complement the Islamic sciences and advise reformers to combine Islamic and social sciences in their theories. In speaking about the natural laws of human society and the requirements that result from them, they usually use the terms 'laws of God' (*sunan allāh*) and 'aims of the sharia' (*maqāṣid aš-šarī'a*). This way, these laws are always understood as the rules that God has given the world. Studying them thus becomes a way of studying the laws and intentions of God. It becomes an act of worship. For the members of the Islamic civil rights movement, all of these different arguments appear to be ways of finding heavenly truths. They all lead to knowledge of what God has intended. Even when they apply historical or linguistic arguments they search for the truth of Islam. Islam remains the framework for all their intellectual and activist endeavours.

Identity, culture war and antisemitism

A surprising element of the theory of the Islamic civil rights movements is the occasional use of culture war rhetoric in their writings. In general, authors like Abdallah al-Hamid do not hide their conviction that Islam is not just the religious belief of Muslims, but that it is the defining element of their identity. According to Abdallah al-Hamid, Muslim peoples are defined by the fact that they are Muslim, and this distinguishes them from the peoples of Europe and North America, who are sometimes collectively referred to as 'NATO states':

> Islam is the civilisational identity of the umma. This is an important question, which one has to keep in mind. The idea of imitating NATO enlightenment comes from a naïve civilisational point of view because the result is a staggering wish to integrate the identity of the Muslim community until it becomes a part of NATO centralism. [. . .] The secular project did not come out of the identity of the Muslim community.[72]

Abdallah al-Hamid seems to contrast the Islamic identity of Muslims with the secular identity of Europeans and North Americans. In his eyes, blindly adopting the secular policies of European and North American states means giving up the Islamic identity of Muslims. Muslims need to protect their Islamic identity against any foreign civilizational threats and, today, these threats come from European and American imperialism, secularism and 'Westernization'. As long as the Muslim states are weak in terms of their political influence and stability, they cannot defend their Islamic identity against the advances of European and American culture:

> Forgetting civil jihad leads to a loss of honour and an exposure to civil strife, decline, psychological illness, the spreading of drugs and the exposure of Muslims to poverty, ignorance, oppression and illness. This makes them an environment which is ripe for the victorious values of Western imperialism. We have to start by protecting Muslims from imperialism, Westernism, secularism and foreign domination.[73]

In other passages by Abdallah al-Hamid, the culture war rhetoric becomes even more explicit, and the perceived political and civilizational threat of the 'West' is openly described as a deliberate 'Western' policy with the aim of weakening Islamic identity:

> It is clear that the long-term strategic aim of NATO imperialism through its possession of these weapons [of mass destruction] is creating a spirit of resignation and defeat in the minds and social values of us Arabs and Muslims, so that we

> think that Western civilisation and the immoral values which are part of it are our written destiny.[74]

Abdallah al-Hamid seems to see the Islamic identity of states with a Muslim majority under threat by a deliberate cultural and civilizational invasion by European and American powers, which threatens to replace the values of Islam with immoral secularism and serfdom to imperialist powers. He believes that Islamic civilization is under attack and that it has to be defended.

Abdallah al-Hamid also occasionally uses language carrying antisemitic connotations. In several passages, al-Hamid generally speaks of 'Zionist, American and European hegemony' [*al-haymana ṣ-ṣahyūnīya wa-l-amrīkīya wa-l-ūrubīya*],[75] 'Zionist, American and European dominance' [*at-tafawwuq aṣ-ṣahyūnī wa-l-amrīkī wa-l-ūrubī*][76] or 'Zionist and European imperialism' [*al-imbiryālīya ṣ-ṣahyūnīya wa-l-ifranǧīya*],[77] suggesting that Europeans, Americans and 'Zionists' are allies in their aggression against Muslims. Usually, the references to the 'Zionists' remain superficial and it appears that al-Hamid only wants to echo the language of other 'Islamists' who use similar language in their texts. However, in one passage from his book *Jihad Is a Twin*, al-Hamid discusses 'Zionism' in more detail and describes it as essentially aggressive and linked to imperialism:

> Zionist peace, which NATO imperialism propagates today, resembles the so-called Pax Romana in elder times, which is the peace of the dominant state and the subjugated state. [. . .] It is clear to the eyes that the Zionist occupation statelet is not a racist or a military state, but a criminal state, which threatens international peace and derives its crimes from racist beliefs. [. . .] Zionist thought is at its roots an aggressive thought.[78]

Here, al-Hamid uses explicitly anti-Zionist language and calls Israel a 'Zionist occupation statelet' [*duwailat al-iḥtilāl aṣ-ṣahyūnī*]. It appears that, although this kind of language is not very frequent in the texts of the Islamic civil rights movement, they occasionally do use expressions and arguments with antisemitic connotations.

Abdallah al-Hamid argues that, in order to mobilize the Islamic civilization for the sake of its own defence against secularism and 'Western' and 'Zionist' imperialism, Muslims have to adopt the universal values that can also be found in foreign thought, while eliminating its 'un-Islamic' elements. The political and technological success of European and North American states is due to the spirit of innovation and freedom that reigns in these countries. They do not necessarily have anything to do with the secular excesses that Abdallah al-Hamid seems to fear. According to him, freedom of opinion, scientific innovation, democratic rule and civil society activism are universal human values. People who believe they are products of a specific European way of thinking are wrong. Therefore, in order to regain their political power and their ability to defend against the civilizational challenge, Muslims have to adopt these universal values, while leaving aside all the specifically European values that are not compatible with Islam:

> Some members of the modern political and social Arab elite only think of the imitation of the European example, meaning the adoption of the three Western

> values of secularism, liberalism and capitalism. These three values are not in accordance with the Islamic sharia and they even contradict it in core points. [. . .] We have to ground the values of this concept on the melting pot of the Islamic sharia by liberating its human concepts from the illusions of the European special character.[79]

By separating the universal wheat from the Europe-specific chaff and combining the universal values with the Islamic values that constitute the identity of Muslims, they can reinvigorate the political discourse in Arab and Muslim countries and prevent being overwhelmed by 'Western' secular culture. In this civilizational fight, Muslims need to rediscover the true meanings of the Islamic sharia and revive their Islamic identity. In passages like these, Abdallah al-Hamid constructs two opposed identities. On one hand, he sees a presumedly homogeneous Islamic identity, which is that of all Muslims of the world. On the other hand, he sees an equally homogeneous 'Western' identity, which is characterized by secularism and liberalism, and dominates the societies of Europe and North America. Abdallah al-Hamid defines the inherent identity of Muslims by differentiating it from the big 'other', namely 'Western' secularism, which threatens it.

The members of the Islamic civil rights movement are not alone with this particular idea. The thought that Islam constitutes the identity of Muslim communities has been a key concept of different Islamic movements and thinkers since the late nineteenth century CE, especially among circles that are inspired by Salafism or by exclusivist forms of the thinking of the Muslim Brotherhood. Many have argued that Islam, rather than other qualities like language, ethnicity or class, is the defining feature of communities with a Muslim majority and that it is the characteristic that makes them what they are. Salafists, Wahhabis, the Muslim Brotherhood and others have emphasized the need to look for an 'authentic' model of society that harmonizes with the supposed Islamic identity of Muslim peoples, instead of simply importing laws and systems that are perceived to be foreign to them. The fear of an 'intellectual invasion' (*ġazw fikrī*) by 'Western' values has been a popular element of these theories.[80] It has been shown that all these ideas ultimately rest on a constructed contradiction between two seemingly homogeneous cultural identities, which are defined by their opposition to each other. On one side, the advocates of a 'Muslim identity' see the pure Islamic identity of Muslim peoples, and on the other side, they see the secular identity of 'the West', which applies to the people living in Europe and North America. Islamic identity is defined as the opposite of the secular, 'Western' identity. The 'West' is constructed as the 'other' of Islam, which, through its 'otherness', defines what Islam really is, namely an all-encompassing identity that stands against the secular 'Western' identity.[81]

In their search for 'Islamic authenticity', many twentieth-and twenty-first-century authors have resorted to the argumentative tool of 'authentication' (*taʾṣīl*), by referring everything to 'authentic' Islam and considering Islam the only yardstick of legitimacy. According to this basic idea, only if something can be shown to be compatible with the authentic Islamic identity of Muslims, it can be considered legitimate.[82] Paradoxically, 'authentication' has also been used to assimilate and 'Islamize' some values or practices from a European and American context. The search for Islamic authenticity can mean the simultaneous act of distancing oneself from 'the West' and adopting some of its institutions and structures. The way the Islamic civil rights movement speaks about adopting European innovations without the alleged secular exaggerations of European culture by basing them on the Islamic sharia is a good example of this approach.

Abdallah al-Hamid and other members of the Islamic civil rights movement seem to abide by the view that there is an 'Islamic identity' and that it has to be defended in a cultural war, where the main adversary is 'Western' culture. One can assume that the fear of a 'cultural invasion' is relatively widespread among religious-minded Saudis who are critical of the religious establishment and the political status quo. As this is the group from which not only HASM's members but also the target audience of their texts come, it is natural for them to integrate this idea into their theory. In the end, the references to this fear in their texts underline the urgency of creating a new reformist discourse in order to save the Islamic identity and independence of Muslims. For them, mentioning this threat is an argument for an urgent renewal of the way Muslims think about politics, and it is all the more convincing because it builds on the pre-existing feeling among many members of the target audience that this threat is real.

Ambiguous translations – Comparing Arabic and English texts by HASM

Civil society groups in Saudi Arabia have been criticized for their use of ambiguous language in their English texts since the mid-1990s CE. A famous example is the Committee for the Defence of Legitimate Rights (abb. CDLR, *lağnat ad-difāʿ ʿan al-ḥuqūq aš-šarʿīya*), which was founded in 1993 CE and published a number Arabic and English texts until the late 1990s CE. A closer look revealed that the English texts and the Arabic texts spoke of different things. To an international, English-speaking audience, the group presented itself as a human rights organization committed to universal human rights. Their Arabic texts, which were addressed to a domestic audience, emphasized Islamic themes, discussed whether Muslims who obeyed the Saudi king were real Muslims and avoided any mention of human rights, instead speaking of 'legitimate rights' or 'sharia rights' (*al-ḥuqūq aš-šarʿīya*).[83] Evidently, CDLR used different language and different arguments for different statements depending on whether they spoke to a domestic, Arabic-speaking audience or an international, English-speaking audience.

HASM also published a few English declarations in addition to the large corpus of Arabic texts. Compared to the many Arabic books, lectures and declarations, these English texts are very few. Only thirty-nine declarations and press releases in English were published on HASM's official website between February 2010 and September 2013 CE.[84] Mostly, these English declarations were translations of Arabic ones. It is unknown who exactly translated them. The English declarations broadly covered the same topics as the Arabic declarations. They informed about the arrests of HASM members,[85] contained calls for the release of political prisoners in Saudi Arabia[86] and urged journalists and observers to attend the trial sessions of HASM members like Abdallah al-Hamid and Muhammad al-Qahtani.[87] An English translation of an open letter to Saudi authorities concerning complaints about human rights violations was also published on the website.[88] It seems that HASM translated selected declarations, which the members of the association thought would be interesting for English-speaking journalists, researchers and human rights advocates. For HASM, the English declarations were a way of establishing contact with potential supporters abroad as well as conveying their version of events and their self-portrayal as a human rights group to the world.

A comparison between the Arabic founding declaration of HASM and an English translation of the declaration, which was published on HASM's website, clearly shows that, like CDLR, HASM wrote about different things in a different way when addressing an Arabic-speaking or an English-speaking audience. In February 2010 CE, four months after the publication of the original founding declaration of HASM in October 2009 CE, the association uploaded an English translation of the declaration on their website. In mid-June 2020 CE, it had been accessed over 5,200 times, according to the website.[89] The English founding declaration was clearly intended as a way to present the association and its aims to an interested, non-Arabic-speaking audience.

The English translation differs from the Arabic original in many respects. It is much shorter than the Arabic version and omits large parts of the original which reference Islamic sources or concepts. Quotes from the Quran and the hadith, of which there are nine in the Arabic original, are completely absent from the English version. Despite the fact that quotes from the primary sources of Islam are important arguments for their theory, not one quote was included in the English translation. The translation also leaves out important passages from the Arabic original which speak of the roots of human rights violations in the dominant Islamic discourse and the fact that the violations are justified by the Islamic establishment.[90] The English version only includes the statement that there are systemic human rights violations in the kingdom, without mentioning the dimension of their Islamic justification, which appears so prominently in the Arabic original. Other passages that refer to Islamic concepts like civil jihad and enjoining virtue and forbidding vice are absent from the English translation as well.[91] The translation also omits specific references that indicate the role of European and North American states in the perpetuation of human rights violations, like this passage from the Arabic original:

> One of the reasons for the founding of the association is the discovery of a suspicious complicity of most Western states, who brag about campaigning for human rights, when there are differences with some governments, and then the oil of the Gulf silences them.[92]

The most substantial difference between the Arabic original of the founding declaration and its English translation is the context in which the concept of human rights is mentioned. The English translation contains the general reference to the 1948 CE Universal Declaration of Human Rights that can also be found in the original, but completely omits other passages which speak about the need to establish a specifically

Islamic culture of human rights. For example, the following passage from the original is absent from the translation:

> One of the reasons for the founding of the declaration is that a number of international organisations is influenced by the Western view on human rights and does not display the Islamic view on human rights in an effective manner.[93]

In several passages, the English translation contains the core statements of the Arabic original, but somewhat distorts them by omitting any references to Islam or Islamic concepts. One example is the following presentation of the aim of the association, first in the English translation from HASM's website, then in its Arabic original:

> Promoting human rights awareness to become a corner stone in our culture, and emphasising other important values such as justice, rights, political and ideological plurality, tolerance, and civilised dialogues.[94]

> Laying the foundation for an Islamic culture of human rights, which considers the means of shura rule [*al-ḥukm aš-šūrī*, 'rule through consultation'] one of the pillars of the Islamic political doctrine [*al-ʿaqīda s-siyāsīya*], which – according to the sharia – cannot be abandoned or neglected. They include justice, freedom, ideological and political pluralism, tolerance and confining all conflicts to peaceful means.[95]

On the one hand, the English translation on HASM's website suggests that what HASM has in mind is the set of universal human rights as they were codified in international human rights documents. On the other hand, the Arabic original clearly states that the aim is a specifically Islamic culture of human rights, which complies with the principles of the Islamic sharia and is not directly influenced by a European and North American view on human rights.

In its English texts, HASM focuses more on portraying itself as a human rights organization than on explaining its complex theory of political reform and civil society activism, which is based on Islamic language and arguments. English texts like the previously discussed translation of the founding declaration omit all references to Islamic sources, like the Quran, and avoid Islamic concepts like peaceful jihad. They speak of the necessity of reforming the political system in order to put an end to the human rights violations but leave out their position concerning the need to reform the Islamic discourse. While the Arabic texts occasionally speak of the negative role of the foreign policy of European and North American states and the threat of 'Western' cultural imperialism for the Islamic identity of Muslims, one does not find similar arguments in the English texts. Finally, HASM's English texts suggest that the kind of human rights they have in mind is the same as advocated by international human rights organizations. The Arabic texts give a different impression, inasmuch as they explicitly state that HASM wants to establish a specifically Islamic culture of human rights, which is not influenced by the 'Western' view on the issue.

It is evident that HASM adjusted the content of their texts as well as their language and arguments to the intended audience. Texts that were addressed to a domestic, Islamically educated, Arabic-speaking audience featured references to Islamic sources, Islamic legal reasoning and language inspired by Islamic themes. Texts that were addressed to an English-speaking audience with an interest in the issue of human rights mostly used human rights language and avoided Islamic references. In the process of this translation and adaptation for an international audience, essential elements of their theory were lost or omitted. It seems that, in the few English texts that were produced by HASM, they focused on advertising their cause to the world at the expense of a true, in-depth explanation of the theory behind their activism.

7

Ideas and concepts – The building blocks of HASM's theory

The theory behind the activism of the Islamic civil rights movement is based on a set of terms and related underlying concepts that, in a sense, constitute the building blocks of their ideas. One might say that the language, the imagery and the arguments that they use as well as the sources that they refer to determine the architectural shape of their theory. The building material of which it is made consists of different fundamental concepts and abstract notions that, as a whole, make the formulation of their ideas and their demands possible. In their writings, they rely on concepts like shura (*šūrā*, 'consultation'), enjoining virtue and forbidding vice (*al-amr bi-l-maʿrūf wa-n-nahy ʿan al-munkar*) and jihad, which they interpret in a specific way. These concepts and their interpretations are combined so that they complement each other and form their complex theory of peaceful jihad.

Naturally, these concepts have not been invented by the authors of the Islamic civil rights movement, but they come out of the centuries-old Arabic-Islamic discourse. They all have a long history of scholarly debates behind them, and today's authors draw on the contributions and interpretations of many thinkers who preceded them. They carry complex connotations that the authors and the supporters of the movement associate with them. Words like 'jihad' already come with a history of interpretations and their meanings have changed over time and from one environment to another. For a Sunni Islamic scholar of the eighth century CE, 'jihad' probably referred to a completely different concept than for an Islamically inspired civil society activist today. It is also very different from what a contemporary English-speaking academic writer understands as 'struggle', the most common translation of 'jihad'. By using these terms and making them their own, the members of the Islamic civil rights movement join the great ongoing debate about the meaning of these concepts and make a contribution to it. In doing so, they inevitably refer to past interpretations and existing connotations and add their own ideas about what oppression, the sharia, Salafism or jihad can mean.

Oppression and the distortion of Islam – Defining the problem

The members of the Islamic civil rights movement have a clear idea of what the complex problem they want to tackle through their own theory and their activism looks like, and they openly speak about it in their writings. HASM's founding declaration begins by stating that the reason for the founding of the association is oppression and the prevalence of human rights abuses in Saudi Arabia:

> Firstly, one of the most important reasons for the founding of the association is that human rights and basic freedoms, especially political ones, are subject to grave violations in the Kingdom of Saudi Arabia. [. . .] Oppression, torture, the violation of human rights and restrictions on freedoms are not only a great injustice, but they also do not guarantee security and stability. Only justice and political reform, which confirms the power of the umma and its sovereignty over the government, guarantee security, stability and prosperity.[1]

The rights abuses are not isolated incidents but systemic, and they are linked to the lack of political rights in Saudi Arabia, as HASM member Muhammad al-Qahtani mentions in one of his lectures. The violations of rights are linked to the injustice of the political system:

> By the way, we focus on physical violations against the individual, like arbitrary arrest, torture, forced disappearance and deprivation of rights. But in reality, if you look at the system of rights, it is broader than these physical and psychological violations. What emerges from all these things is the deprivation of political rights. Why do these arbitrary arrests spread so much in our country? It is linked to the political system. Why are there no such violations in democratic countries?[2]

This view is also shared by Islamo-reformist authors who do not belong to the Islamic civil rights movement. For example, Hakim al-Mutayri, who has influenced HASM, also finds harsh words when he speaks about the problem of oppression in the introduction of his 2009 CE book *The Liberation of Man and the Exposure of the Tyrants*:

> Today, the Muslims, and the Arabs in particular, experience [. . .] the worst form of servitude to something else than God. Today, this servitude appears in the fact that most peoples are subject to and practically completely subdued by the tyrants. [. . .] Approximately 300 million Arabs from the Gulf to the Atlantic Ocean live as slaves without chains under the dominance of regimes, which are the worst political regimes in the world and the most unjust and most corrupt.[3]

Abdallah al-Hamid agrees and argues that, as a result of this prevalent oppression, Muslim countries were weakened on the political and the cultural level, and they could no longer resist the onslaught of European and American imperialism and their hegemonial claims:

> The Muslims suffered defeats in the era of European imperialism [*al-imbiryālīya l-ifranǧīya*] since the last days of the Ottoman state, as they ignored the nature of the imperial European challenge and aggression. [. . .] Why did the Muslims

> suffer defeat against European imperialism? Because inner tyranny destroyed the scientific and civilisational factors of the power of the community, and because of the lack of a culture of peaceful jihad, which protects the society from resignation and the state from destruction.[4]

The citizens of many Arab and Muslim countries suffer from systematic rights abuses and oppressive political systems, and this, in turn, has weakened them politically and has made them easy victims of imperial powers and foreign cultural influences.

According to the members of the Islamic civil rights movement, oppression and injustice have been persistent phenomena in Muslim countries, because unjust tyrants have been able to rely on Islamic establishment figures to legitimize their actions. They complain that the official Islamic establishment in Saudi Arabia has acted as an ally of the oppressive political system instead of advocating the true teachings of Islam. This has led to disenchantment with Islam among many young Saudis who believe the establishment's claim that what the rulers are doing is indeed in line with Islam. HASM argues that this fatal complicity between oppressive rulers and Islamic scholars goes back well into the history of the Islamic caliphate. For centuries, many influential Islamic scholars have been justifying the oppressive practices of the worldly rulers in Islamic language, and this discourse of legitimization has become the mainstream in many countries. Authors like Abdallah al-Hamid argue that, after the times of the prophet Muhammad and the Rightly Guided Caliphs, especially during the Umayyad and Abbasid caliphates, the message of Islam was gradually distorted. Islamic scholars were influenced by the environment of oppression and seemed to forget many of the main principles of Islam.[5] As a result of this development, many authors and scholars of the Arabic-Islamic discourse after the seventh century CE have been propagating submission to worldly rulers, no matter how oppressive they are, and this approach has become part of the Islamic mainstream. According to the members of the movement, the true teachings of Islam have nothing to do with these opinions. They are the products of a contamination of the Islamic discourse by other cultural influences, which have penetrated the debate about Islam.

These harmful influences that have distorted Islamic thought are manifold and are called by different names in the books of the movement. They include the 'desert-like spirit' (*ar-rūḥ aṣ-ṣaḥrāwīya*), which incites people to take up arms without thinking; and the political culture of classical despotism, which is often referred to by mentioning the examples of Persian king Khosraw, Roman ruler Caesar and pharaoh of Egypt. In the following passage from a book by Abdallah al-Hamid, he describes how the marriage between these two currents has influenced the mainstream of Islamic thought:

> The desert-like spirit [*ar-rūḥ aṣ-ṣaḥrāwīya*], which the Arabs brought from the Arabian Peninsula, and the pharaonic spirit, which was taken from the cities of Khosraw, Caesar and Pharaoh, participated in this [denying of political rights]. This marriage between Pharaoh and the desert produced the political crisis, which corrupted the political education, and brought forward two currents which are not able to produce anything successful:

> The first group: The Islamic legal scholars of the desert-like political activity of enjoining virtue and forbidding vice, who throw themselves at reforming the state with the weapon in their hands without intellectual preparation. [. . .]
>
> The second group: The Islamic legal scholars of misery, who surrender to oppression and pharaonism.[6]

In other passages, Abdallah al-Hamid speaks of additional influences and currents like 'monkism' (*rahbānīya*), which is the politically passive withdrawal from all worldly affairs; mystic Sufism; or 'sophistry' (*sūfisṭāʾīya*), the fruitless scholarly debates of some academic circles.[7] All these influences distracted Muslims from the political message of Islam and led them to submit to oppressive regimes and accept the violation of their rights. As a result, the political message of Islam and its call to engage in peaceful activism for justice were forgotten. Instead, Islamic scholars contented themselves with studying the spiritual half of Islam.[8] Schools and currents started to fight with others about banalities, and a closed school mentality (*maḏhabīya*) led the scholars to waste their energies on vain debates instead of focusing on the true meaning of the Islamic sources:

> The school mentality [maḏhabīya] wastes tremendous energies and does not discover the truth, namely that shura rule and its branches, like justice, freedom and pluralism, belong to the core of Islamic doctrine and that they come before these fights between the schools. The people have led bloody social struggles for them, [. . .] and they have not produced any report of truth about justice and shura.[9]

Authors like Abdallah al-Hamid argue that this constant bickering between the representatives of different schools of Islamic thought has to end and that Muslims have to re-focus on what Islam is really about. This requires purifying Islamic discourse and eliminating everything which has been attached to it over the course of the centuries. Abdallah al-Hamid summarizes this intellectual aim as follows:

> [We need] extraordinary efforts that remove the interpretations and distortions that have contaminated political Islamic reasoning and restore its theories and means to the clear message which God Almighty has sent down through the sharia, as well as the truth which God Almighty has laid down in natural things through the truths of the sciences of man and nature.[10]

All in all, the aim of the members of the Islamic civil rights movement in the area of Islamic thought amounts to nothing less but a complete re-reading of Islamic tradition and returning to the allegedly pure, unadulterated message of Islam.

In summary, the problem that the members of the Islamic civil rights movement identify is twofold. According to their analysis, the people in Saudi Arabia and, indeed, in many other Arab and Islamic countries, suffer from oppression and human rights abuses. This has not only made life hard for many ordinary citizens, but it has also weakened Muslim countries on the political and cultural levels, and they have become easy targets for European and American imperialism. But these violations are only the symptoms of a deeper problem, which lies in Islamic discourse. The members of the movement argue that, for centuries, Islamic scholars have been justifying oppression in religious language and have legitimized it in terms of Islam. They insist that the political message of Islam has been distorted over the centuries and that it needs to be restored through intellectual and civil society activism. Islamic discourse since Umayyad and Abbasid times has to be re-read and purified. The foreign influences of Persian, Roman and Egyptian despotism, as well as spiritual withdrawal, have to be eliminated. The people, the leaders and the Islamic scholars need to be reminded of the true content of the teachings of Islam, as they were implemented by the first generations of Muslims. In this regard, the members of the Islamic civil rights movement argue like true Salafists. Thus, while the issue of human rights seems to be the immediate reason for their activism, in their eyes the real problem lies in the Islamic discourse.

The view of authors like Abdallah al-Hamid on the problems that affect Arab and Islamic states and Islamic discourse in general is not new. There have always been Islamic authors who criticized the state of Islamic discourse. Calls for a renewal of Islamic thought have also been common in the history of thinking about Islam. For many Islamic thinkers with different backgrounds, like the Islamic Modernists Muhammad Abduh and Muhammad Rashid Rida, the radical Egyptian Muslim Brother Sayyid Qutb and contemporary Islamic scholars with connections to the Muslim Brotherhood, like Yusuf al-Qaradawi, these calls have been motivated, at least partly, by the fear of a European and American cultural invasion. Many reformist-minded Islamic scholars seem to share the thought that the Islamic identity of Muslim peoples has to be defended against secularism and 'Western' cultural hegemony and that this requires a renewal of Islamic discourse.[11]

The idea that Islamic thought has to be divided into a golden age, which encompasses the time of the prophet Muhammad and the Rightly Guided Caliphs, and an age of persistent decadence after that is also reasonably widespread among many Muslim movements, even if it is not the opinion of the mainstream. Salafists, who explicitly want to return to Islam as it was supposedly lived by the first generations of Muslims, are particularly ardent supporters of this argument.[12] The allegation that there was a clear mismatch between the requirements of Islam and the political practice of despotic political leaders since Umayyad times is almost a commonplace in Islamic thought. Salafists are not the only ones who criticize Islamic discourse. Contemporary philosophers and intellectuals from the Middle East and North Africa, like the Moroccan Muhammad Abid al-Jabri (*Muḥammad ʿĀbid al-Ǧābirī*) and the Egyptians Fuad Zakaria (*Fuʾād Zakarīyā*) and Nasr Hamid Abu Zayd (*Naṣr Ḥāmid Abū Zaid*), have also dealt extensively with the dire state of the political and social discourse in many Arab countries and have been involved in a comprehensive self-criticism of Arab reason since 1960 CE.

As can be seen, the different ideas that the members of the Islamic civil rights movement mention with regard to the problem of Islamic discourse are all reasonably widespread among Islamic intellectuals and especially those with an affinity for Salafism. Authors like Abdallah al-Hamid seem to adopt these views, which are perceived by many to be convincing accounts of reality. In their writings, they take these ideas as a foundation for their own view of the problem at hand. It can be assumed that, to most of their readers, these views are not entirely new either, and that the theory of the Islamic civil rights movement is perceived to be all the more convincing, because it contains these assumptions, which the readers already share.

Islamic doctrine and the sharia

The members of the Islamic civil rights movement insist that any solution to the problems of oppression and injustice must come from the Islamic sharia, and in their texts, they display a complex understanding of what the sharia and Islamic doctrine look like on a theological level. Authors like Abdallah al-Hamid argue that Islam is an all-encompassing system that has something to say about every aspect of life and the world. No area of life lies outside the scope of the norms of Islam, and Islam has different sets of rules, principles or recommendations for everything ranging from prayer to social interaction. Because Islam includes norms for everything, it has to be understood as a comprehensive system with many parts, which complement each other. Therefore, it is useless to solely focus on single parts of the sharia, like the rules of worship or the punishments that Islam prescribes for specific offences. One can only grasp the meaning of the Islamic sharia if one keeps its holistic picture in mind. Only when its parts intertwine can the aims that God has intended be realized:

> One cannot understand the texts of the sharia without grasping its holistic system. It is not possible, because grasping the holistic system of everything comes before knowing the functions of its parts and it inspires the grasping of the relationship between the units. [. . .] Every part has a function, be it small or big, and in his laws, which govern the lives of humans, God has given them importance according to their role in realising good things for humans in this world and the afterlife.[13]

According to Abdallah al-Hamid, the main parts of the sharia are its two halves: the spiritual half, which includes rules of worship and what to believe in; and the civil half, which regulates how believers should lead their lives in this world. The spiritual half, which centres around prayer and belief, aims at happiness in the afterlife, while the civil half, whose main principle is justice, serves to enable the believers to lead happy, successful lives in this world. Because the sharia is a comprehensive, holistic system, both halves have to be observed:

> There is no alternative to continuing to establish an Islamic discourse which balances between the two halves of Islam, the spiritual and the civil half.[14]

Islam, comprising both halves, is a spiritual as well as a worldly religion. Each side is complemented by the other. The spirituality of Muslims is enriched by their actions in this world, and their worldly actions are inspired by their spirituality. Islam expresses itself in worldly deeds.[15]

The sharia is a comprehensive system, and if one of its parts is neglected, all other parts suffer as well. According to Abdallah al-Hamid, this is exactly what happened in Islamic discourse after the time of the Rightly Guided Caliphs in the seventh century CE. The Islamic scholars, and, indeed, most ordinary Muslims, started to focus on the spiritual half of the sharia at the expense of the civil norms of Islam. Instead of following the rules of Islam with regard to the form of government and the requirements of justice, they only dealt with spiritual questions, like how to pray:

> For a long time, religious thinking has been preferring the scholar of the transcendental [*al-ġayb*] to the scholar of empiricism/martyrdom [*aš-šahāda*]. It forgot practical knowledge, which solves the problems of man on earth, and moved towards abstract knowledge, in which immersing oneself does not lead to action.[16]

Abdallah al-Hamid and others argue that, in the civil half of the sharia, Islam requires practical thought, which has both feet on the ground of worldly affairs. In one of his books, he states that 'The right Islamic doctrine is that we do righteous work'.[17] Muslims have to engage with the world and change it, not withdraw into the spiritual. One is almost reminded of Karl Marx's famous line from his 'Thesis on Feuerbach': 'The philosophers have only interpreted the world in various ways; the point is to change it.'[18] In any case, the members of the Islamic civil rights movement clearly believe that the Islamic sharia is only implemented as intended, if its spiritual side and its practical, worldly side are both observed.

In their texts, the members of the movement, and of the Islamo-reformist current in general, argue that the norms of the sharia can be divided into fixed rules, which always have to be followed, and changeable rules, which differ from place to place and from era to era. Some rules of the sharia, like the basic dogmas of Islam or rules of worship, are eternal and apply regardless of when or where Muslims live. No matter where a Muslim lives, he or she will always have to believe in the prophet Muhammad and pray in a specific way to be a Muslim. Other parts of the sharia are not as rigid, and here what is required can vary from one place to another or from one century to another. Therefore, when reading the texts of past reformers, one has to distinguish between the absolute, eternal truths they mention, and the opinions, which can only claim to apply to a certain place or time:

> In the renewal of every reformer, there is a combination of two elements, when he renews something: Something standard-setting and absolute, which is the foundation for reform in every time and place and which consists of the clear statements of Islam and the truths of wisdom; and something relative and temporary, which deals with a current problem. The mixture of renewal consists of these two elements.[19]

In the texts of past Islamic scholars, one always has to consider whether specific statements concern fixed truths, which are still true today, or only temporary interpretations and norms, which might no longer apply.

But the distinction between the fixed and the changeable does not only apply to the opinions of past scholars. It is a quality of the norms of the sharia in general. Abdallah al-Hamid argues that we can discard certain ideas of past scholars, which were right for their time and place, because what is right for a certain community in specific areas of life changes over time and is different for different communities. The norms of Islam recognize the changes of time and place, and they give humans a certain freedom for finding their own solutions to their problems. Societies change, and therefore, some rules also have to change, provided they are always in line with the teachings of the Quran and the hadith:

> That which is changeable necessarily changes because it is linked to the social movement of humans. Therefore, the people need a changeable form of religion, which is in sync with the movement of cultural, social and civilisational change. [. . .] When the questions, problems and circumstances change, the answers and solutions by necessity also have to change. The solutions are only legitimate, if they return to the pharmacy of the Quran and the sunna [that is, the hadith].[20]

The changeable norms especially include many areas of civil life in this world. The fact that the rules are changeable does not mean that they are arbitrary or that Muslims are not bound by any norms. General norms of civil life, like justice, always apply, but how Muslims implement them in their societies is left to the believers, as long as they always follow the teachings of the primary sources of Islam. Thus, in their view, the Islamic sharia gives Muslims some leeway with regard to the rules they follow. Humans have a role to play in the formulating of the norms of Islam. This free space is exactly what enables Muslims to renew Islamic discourse, as the members of the Islamic civil rights movement are trying to do.

In large parts, the concept of the sharia and Islamic doctrine that the members of the Islamic civil rights movement refer to in their texts is the same as that of the Sunni mainstream. According to the majority of scholars of Sunni Islamic discourse, the sharia is the totality of all norms that can be derived from the sources of Islam. It encompasses norms of belief (*aḥkām al-iʿtiqād*), which specify what to believe in; ethical norms (*aḥkām ḫulqīya*), which deal with moral questions; and binding norms concerning the actions of Muslims (*aḥkām ʿamalīya*). The latter can be divided into norms of worship (*ʿibādāt*), like how and when to pray; and norms of social interaction (*muʿāmalāt*), which concern various things from rules of marriage and commerce to rules concerning the organization of communities. Within this system, Islam has many different norms for specific areas of life, but not all norms are laws in the strict sense of the English word. In many areas, Islam lays down moral recommendations or basic principles without confronting the believer with a system of strict legal regulations. In addition, while the norms of worship are considered to be fixed and eternal, some of the norms of social interaction are changeable and allow the believers to adapt the rules to their requirements while still adhering to a set of basic principles. In addition, the Sunni mainstream explicitly leaves a free space, where Muslims can develop new norms to satisfy their special legal needs, when the primary sources of Islam do not contain specific rules for a certain area or activity.[21]

In general, what the members of the Islamic civil rights movement have in mind when they speak about the sharia corresponds with the concept of the sharia in the Sunni mainstream. Their insistence that the sharia has two halves, namely a spiritual one and a civil one, which both have to be observed, may not be a part of the official Sunni doctrine, but it is not completely incompatible with the mainstream's view on the sharia. In fact, this idea has already been voiced by a minority of 'classical' Islamic schools, like the movement of the Murjia (*al-murǧiʾa*), which originated in the eighth century CE.[22] Some of the writings of nineteenth-century CE Egyptian Islamic scholar Muhammad Abduh indicate that he leant towards this idea as well.[23] The free space that this concept of the sharia leaves for Muslims has also inspired other reformist-minded Islamic scholars and activists. For example, the representatives of the 'centrist stream' in Egypt, like Muhammad al-Ghazali, Muhammad Salim al-Awwa and Yusuf al-Qaradawi, have insisted that Islam requires Muslims to think of new solutions and thus justifies innovation and renewal in worldly things.[24]

While the members of the Islamic civil rights movement concur with the general view on the sharia in most of these details, their idea that Islam is an all-encompassing system in the sense that it contains rules of religion as well as precise political rules is not shared by all Muslims. However, the theory that the state has to abide by the rules of Islam and that Islam has concrete norms concerning the form of the state grew especially popular among many Islamic-minded circles after it had been endorsed by twentieth-century CE scholars like the Pakistani Abu al-Ala Mawdudi (*Abū l-Aʿlā Mawdūdī*, 1903–79 CE), founder of the organization Jamaat-e-Islami, and the Egyptian Hasan al-Banna, the founder of the Muslim Brotherhood. Both thinkers founded 'Islamist' organizations in their respective countries, whose aims were to bring the politics of their states more in line with Islamic teachings. Hasan al-Banna's saying that Islam is 'religion and state' (*dīn wa-daula*) has been a major slogan of Islamically inspired movements like that of the Muslim Brotherhood.[25] With regard to the idea that Islam is an all-encompassing system, which regulates everything up to the form of the state, the members of the Islamic civil rights movement are deeply rooted in the tradition of these activist thinkers and the thought of the Muslim Brotherhood.

The 'laws of God' in nature and society

Two important interrelated concepts that frequently appear in the writings of the Islamic civil rights movement, and of the Islamo-reformist current in general, are the 'laws of God' (*sunan allāh*) in nature and society, and innate human nature (*fiṭra*). Both terms are linked to the idea that God has given the world specific natural laws, which determine the development of nature, humans and societies. Because these laws come from God, the creator, they are divine truths, and everything they tell us to do can be considered divine orders. When describing what the 'laws of God' are, Abdallah al-Hamid frequently refers either to thirteenth-/fourteenth-century CE Islamic scholar Ahmad ibn Taymiya or to twentieth-century Islamic thinker Sayyid Qutb, as in this passage from his book *The Word Is Stronger than the Bullet*:

> The natural laws of God [*sunan allāh*] are, as Sayyid Qutb has said, 'the laws which govern the life of man, according to the will of God, and which have become general laws, which do not differ, so that what happened in the past also happens in the present, if the situation of the contemporaries is like the situation of those who preceded them.' Doing what is required by the political laws of God is the way of returning the Muslim community to its strength and unity.[26]

The 'laws of God' are, in essence, the natural laws which determine the course of things in this world. God, the creator, does not directly intervene in every single development in the world, but, in his creation, he has given the world universal rules which define what happens if certain preconditions are met. If a society wants to be successful in this world, it is not enough to hope for divine intervention, but they simply have to do what the natural laws of this world require them to do in order to reach their aim. Because they come from God, these laws cannot contradict the message that God has sent down in the books of religion. The message of God in the texts of Islam complements his message that can be found in the laws of nature, and vice versa:

> The 'laws of God' which can be read in the book of the sharia do not contradict his laws which can be seen on the stage of society and nature. Correct human thought in social and natural sciences does not contradict the clear, transmitted statements of the sharia sciences.[27]

One consequence of this view is that studying the laws of nature and society becomes one way of finding divine truth. The natural and social sciences produce insights that help understand the texts of Islam and the intent of God.[28] Authors like Abdallah al-Hamid argue that God wants Muslims to do scientific research on how nature and society develop and adhere to the rules that can be deduced from the findings of the sciences. When one studies these laws of nature, one quickly encounters certain basic norms and values that the rules of nature seem to endorse. For example, the social sciences can tell us that societies that are ruled justly are stable and prosperous societies.

In order to discover these universal values and laws, one does not necessarily need elaborate scientific research, since every human has a basic understanding of them. Here, the second concept, that of innate human nature (*fiṭra*), enters the stage. Abdallah al-Hamid and others argue that basic values which bring success and stability in this world are known to every human being, because God has implanted them into human nature:

> By innate nature [*fiṭra*] and experience, sane minds in civil nations come to know that shura rule is the condition for any government; that civil society organisations are the guarantee for shura rule; that a society that is actively practicing demonstrations, protests and declarations is a guarantee for the rights and freedoms of the people; and that the atmosphere of freedom is the environment in which societies grow. These things are known by every nation, community and state, Muslim or non-Muslims.[29]

> Above all, the unjust ruler is exposed in front of his own conscience, because justice and truth are sown into the innate nature [*fiṭra*] and reason [*ʿaql*] of every human.[30]

Through their natural predisposition, all humans know that justice, fairness and equality are necessary for societies to prosper. People only have to listen to what their conscience tells them, and they will discover these basic values. They are not culture-specific, but they are universal and known to all humans, because they are part of human nature and accessible to human reason.

Abdallah al-Hamid warns against rejecting anything that comes from Europe and America, simply because it is foreign. Sometimes, concepts that reach Muslim communities from there, like the values of civil society, are really universal concepts.[31] Because all humans share one innate nature, the insights of other cultures are sometimes worth adopting, even if some translation might be needed. In the end, we all share a common universal, human disposition. According to Abdallah al-Hamid, the insights of innate human nature are not only compatible with Islam, but they constitute an essential part of the sharia. Islam wants the believers to listen to the voice of their innate nature. That which our natural rational predisposition tells us to do is also an obligation of the sharia:

> Everything which is natural in our predisposition [*mā huwa fiṭrī fī l-ǧibilla*] is a holy right and belongs to human rights, because Islam, like any heavenly religion, is a religion of innate nature [*fiṭra*].[32]

That which our conscience tells us to do belongs to the instructions of Islam, because God also transmitted his commandments by way of innate nature. When the sharia texts speak about things like justice and equality, which we also know by nature, they only confirm what we know anyway. The civil half of the sharia is known by all people through their natural predisposition. Strictly speaking, its norms are not specifically Islamic norms but universal norms, and the Islamic texts only remind the believers of them.[33] Nevertheless, the 'laws of God' (*sunan allāh*) in nature and society and innate human nature (*fiṭra*) must be considered sources of divine truth and the findings of our studies of nature and society belong to the norms of the sharia. This is the theoretical concept behind the use of the two terms 'laws of God' and 'innate human nature' in the writings of the Islamic civil rights movement.

Both the idea that the findings of the natural sciences complement the sharia texts and the idea that God has instilled certain principles into innate human nature have been discussed in detail in the history of Islamic discourse. An example which is also mentioned by authors like Abdallah al-Hamid is Ahmad ibn Taymiya, who wrote a famous book titled *Reason and Tradition* (*al-ʿAql wa-n-naql*). In it he argues that the correct findings of rational sciences and the sharia sciences cannot contradict each other, because both speak about truths that were created by God. In fact, throughout the history of Islam, many authors who wrote about Islamic subjects also composed books about other scientific topics, like astronomy, physics or biology. For many of them, there was no dichotomy between Islamic sciences and natural sciences. Rather, studying the phenomena of the cosmos, which had been created by God, was a way of finding divine truth.[34]

The term 'innate nature' (*fiṭra*) is also one that comes out of the heart of Islamic discourse. It appears in the Quran and in several hadiths, and it has been hotly debated during the centuries of the history of Islamic thought. All in all, it was always a contested concept. Nevertheless, the view that all human beings have a natural inclination towards certain principles and values, and maybe even the message of Islam, was shared by several authoritative Islamic scholars.[35] A famous literary example is the book *Hayy ibn Yaqzan* (*Ḥayy ibn Yaqẓān*) by the twelfth-century CE Andalusian Ibn Tufayl (*Ibn Ṭufail*), which tells the story of a boy who grows up alone on an isolated island and reaches the knowledge that there is a God by studying the natural phenomena around him. The thought that human beings have a natural inclination towards the basic principles of Islam is also reasonably widespread among supporters of Islamically inspired political movements today, like the Muslim Brotherhood.[36] All these ideas come naturally to the members of the Islamic civil right movement in Saudi Arabia, and they readily adopt these concepts and integrate them into their own theory.

Re-defining Salafism

The members of the Islamic civil rights movement describe themselves as Salafists, and their writings show that they have a very specific idea of what this means. For them, Salafism, which etymologically comes from following the 'pious predecessors' (*as-salaf aṣ-ṣāliḥ*), clearly has positive connotations. They call many of the past scholars that they refer to as Salafists, and the methods they want to apply to solve the problems they see in Saudi Arabia are also described as Salafist. HASM member Abdallah al-Hamid has written an entire book entitled *Middle path Salafism* (*as-Salafiya l-wusṭā*) about the subject. In it, he discusses in detail what Salafism means for him and other members of the Islamic civil rights movement. He admits that Salafism is a somewhat ambiguous term with different meanings. For him, Salafism does not mean blindly following the 'pious predecessors' and imitating them. Rather, it means renewing the Islamic discourse while always having an eye on the Islamic texts and the way they were implemented by the prophet Muhammad and the first four caliphs. He argues that Salafism is a method. It means basing the interpretation of the primary texts of Islam on the implementation of these texts by the first generations of Muslims and the findings of the sciences, which inform us about the divine truths that God has placed in nature. In his book *Middle path Salafism*, Abdallah al-Hamid concisely summarizes this concept with reference to the Quranic metaphor of the Verse of Light,[37] which compares the light of God to the light of a lamp inside a bottle which stands in a niche:

> Salafism is calling for understanding the lamp of the Quran and the sunna through the clearness of the bottle of the implementation of the prophet [Muhammad] and

> the Rightly Guided Caliphs and the niche of the truths of the sciences of man and nature.[38]

Instead of understanding Salafism as a school of thought or a political movement, Abdallah al-Hamid presents it as a method for approaching the texts of Islam. Everyone who lets his interpretation of the Quran and the hadith be guided by the implementation of the first generations of Muslims and the truths of the sciences is a Salafist.

Abdallah al-Hamid argues that, throughout the history of Islamic thought, there have been many different forms of Salafism, whose adherents all used this method. Somewhat confusingly, in his interpretation many influential thinkers of Islam since the eighth century CE, who probably never thought of themselves as Salafists, are counted as such. This includes the eighth-/ninth-century CE founders of the four large schools of Sunni jurisprudence, Abu Hanifa, Malik ibn Anas, ash-Shafii and Ahmad ibn Hanbal, as well as eleventh-/twelfth-century CE polymath Abu Hamid al-Ghazali, thirteenth-/fourteenth-century CE Islamic scholar Ahmad ibn Taymiya and fourteenth-century CE historiographer Ibn Khaldun. It also includes the founder of Wahhabism, eighteenth-century CE Islamic scholar Muhammad ibn Abd al-Wahhab; representatives of nineteenth-century CE Islamic Modernism like Muhammad Abduh and Muhammad Rashid Rida; and key figures of the twentieth-century CE movement of the Muslim Brotherhood, like Hasan al-Banna and Sayyid Qutb. Essentially, all the scholars that Abdallah al-Hamid approvingly refers to in his books are seen as Salafists:

> Salafism agrees on the method of argumentation, but it has many forms and approaches. [. . .] The currents of Salafism were different according to the requirements of the societies, the mentalities of the individuals, the geography and the social climate. It was a movement for intellectual reform for Abu Hanifa, Malik, ash-Shafii and Ibn Taymiya, a movement for rejecting intrusions for Ahmad ibn Hanbal, a movement for contradicting Greek philosophy for [Abu Hamid] al-Ghazali, a movement for the founding of social thought for Ibn Khaldun, a movement for discovering the absolute, holistic aims of the sharia for ash-Shatibi in [his book] '*al-Muwāfaqāt*' and for [Waliullah] ad-Dihlawi in his book '*Huğğat allāh al-bāliga*', [. . .] and a movement of enlightenment and liberation of identity from stagnation and Westernisation for Muhammad Abduh, Muhammad Rashid Rida, [Abu al-Ala] Mawdudi, [Abd ar-Rahman] al-Kawakibi, Hasan al-Banna and Sayyid Qutb. It was a movement for political independence of identity for Muhammad ibn Abd al-Wahhab, [. . .] and a movement for calling for the values of civil society organisations as well as the guarantees for just rule and a constitution for all the movements which started since al-Kawakibi, Khayr ad-Din at-Tunisi, [Jamal ad-Din] al-Afghani and others.[39]

According to Abdallah al-Hamid, all of these different thinkers were Salafists, because they all used the aforementioned method. The forms of Salafism that they established were different because they all used this method to solve different problems and confront different challenges. The aforementioned authors all reacted to the circumstances of their times, and their forms of Salafism were therefore very different from each other. Abdallah al-Hamid frequently speaks of different Salafisms, in the plural form of the word. In his interpretation, Salafism becomes a changeable and flexible current, which encompasses very different theories and is only held together by a common approach to the interpretation of the Islamic texts.

Because of this flexibility, Salafism is the perfect method for a constant renewal of the Islamic discourse, which always remains faithful to the principles of Islam:

> The Salafi method is flexible. It is a framework that allows a real renewal because it combines the preservation of the absolutely fixed principles [*aṯ-ṯawābit al-qaṭʿīya*] with the renewal of the means, the formulation, the branches, the movement and the implementation. [. . .] Salafism is a method and an approach, not a specific school [*maḏhab*] from Umayyad, Abbasid, Mamluk or Ottoman times. Every Salafism is a temporary renewal, which constitutes a specific mixture of medicine, which focusses on a specific illness in its time and place.[40]

Because every specific historical form of Salafism has to be understood as a response to the challenges and circumstances of its time, the theories of past Salafists are suitable largely only for the specific environment they lived in. Abdallah al-Hamid argues that it is wrong to assume that simply following these past Salafist scholars will produce useful Salafist solutions today. The point of reference for any real Salafist theory is not the thoughts of past Salafist scholars from the times of the Umayyad and Abbasid caliphates, the Mamluk sultanate or the Ottoman Empire. The real reference point of the Salafist method is the sayings and actions of the prophet Muhammad and his companions until the end of the Rightly Guided Caliphate:

> The Umayyad, Abbasid, Mamluk and Ottoman Salafism are not the authority, but they are movements, forms and solutions, which are counted as belonging to Salafism. [. . .] The standard of Salafism is neither what Ahmad ibn Hanbal or al-Ashari said, nor what Ibn Taymiya and al-Ghazali said, or what Muhammad ibn Abd al-Wahhab and Sayyid Qutb said. The standard is that which God, the Messenger [of God, Muhammad,] and his companions said.[41]

According to Abdallah al-Hamid, the compass for every Salafist renewal has to be the implementation of Islam during the time of the first generations of Muslims. Instead of quoting later Salafist scholars, one has to refer everything back to the first generations and flexibly create one's own Salafist solutions for today's problems. Today, Salafists have to create their own, new Salafism.

Unsurprisingly, according to Abdallah al-Hamid, the Salafism that Muslims need today is an activist form which endorses civil society activism for justice and a fair political system:

> How can a man be a Salafist today and not write with his fingers and speak with his tongue, in addition to joining the advocates of political reform in the publication

> of a declaration, and protesting and demonstrating in the square, when he sees the great bad deeds in the Arab state, which is oppressive on the inside, and oppressed on the outside?[42]

Abdallah al-Hamid's own form of Salafism, which is meant to solve the problems of oppressed Muslims today, supports political activism and protesting. He warns against understanding Salafism as a politically passive, quietist immersion in spiritual questions or as a movement for the building of isolated pious communities, which withdraw from the world around them. Instead, his Salafism means political activism and an open engagement with the problems of the day.

In Islamic discourse, Salafism (*salafīya*) has always been a contested concept. Although its etymology is clear (as was mentioned, it comes from the 'pious predecessors', *as-salaf aṣ-ṣāliḥ*), its meaning is ambiguous. It has been used by different movements to legitimize different sets of ideas, and at different times, different groups of people described themselves as Salafists. In general, it can be stated that the term Salafism is an invention of the early twentieth century CE and was not part of Islamic discourse before that. Henri Lauzière has shown that it was not before the 1920s CE that Muslims started to speak of an Islamic movement called Salafism. While Islamic scholars before that had occasionally used the term *salafī* in their texts, it clearly did not refer to a well-defined school or movement with clear ideas and beliefs. Rather, before the twentieth century CE, adhering to 'Salafist ideas' mostly meant following the theology of the Hanbali school with regard to the interpretation of God's names and attributes, which was commonly called following the 'school of the forefathers' (*maḏhab as-salaf*). It did not refer to any specific ideas outside this narrow theological question, let alone an all-encompassing religious movement. This was also how scholars like Ahmad ibn Taymiya or Muhammad ibn Abd al-Wahhab used the term.[43]

It was long believed in the field of Islamic studies that the protagonists of Islamic Modernism, like Jamal ad-Din al-Afghani, Muhammad Abduh and Muhammad Rashid Rida, who wanted to combine Islam and modernity, were the first to identify as Salafists in the late nineteenth century CE.[44] Henri Lauzière has shown that this is a deeply entrenched social misconstruction. In fact, the protagonists of Islamic Modernism never referred to themselves as Salafists and this label was first used in French orientalist texts, which, falsely, spoke of them as Salafists.[45] Nevertheless, in the 1930s CE the term Salafism gradually entered the conceptual vocabulary of Muslims and Muslim reformers began to identify as members of a movement called Salafism. On the one hand, modernist reformers, like the Moroccan Allal al-Fasi, understood Salafism as a fusion of Islamic authenticity and the benefits of modernity.[46] On the other hand, others began to understand Salafism as a name for a movement that, above all, strove to purify Islamic discourse and was closely linked to the ideas of Wahhabism. Slowly, the meaning of Salafism was expanded beyond the original meaning of a specific theological position, until it included more and more questions outside the area of theology. In the early twentieth century CE, those calling themselves Salafists could easily hold modernist positions, because Salafism did not yet stand for a comprehensive ideological system of beliefs that was critical of modern ideas. By the 1950s CE, this had changed. Gradually, Salafism became a term for a comprehensive system of beliefs which put the quest for purity at the centre of all thought. As a consequence, Salafists found it increasingly difficult to adopt moderate positions with regard to questions that had not been part of the concept of Salafism before. Those with modernist inclinations slowly abandoned the label Salafist and were more attracted to other movements, like the Muslim Brotherhood.

In the 1960s CE, Wahhabi scholars themselves also adopted the term Salafist. They were attracted by the connotations of purity and authenticity that the term carried. Because of the considerable resources that the Saudi government poured into the spreading of the image of the kingdom as the hub of 'pure Islam', the influence of Wahhabism in the battle for the meaning of Salafism grew. Soon, Wahhabi Islam had acquired the prerogative of defining Salafism and was exporting it into the world. Later, the term was also used by other Sunni fundamentalist groups all over the Muslim world, who shared a strong dislike of 'classical' Islamic theology, Shia Muslims, Sufi mysticism, secularism and 'Westernization'. Like many Wahhabis, they claimed to be the successors of a long line of Salafist, reformist thinkers. Saudi oppositional movements, who criticized the ideas of the Wahhabi establishment, like the movement of 'Rejectionism' or the Sahwa movement also described themselves as 'Salafists'.[47] Finally, the creators of the ideology of Jihadism, like the Palestinian Abdallah Azzam, the Jordanian Abu Muhammad al-Maqdisi and the Saudis Osama ibn Laden and Yusuf al-Uyayri, also claimed the label Salafism for themselves, and Jihadist organizations all over the world have been using the term in their writings.[48]

Contemporary Salafism is a fragmented discourse. All Salafist movements share the belief that Islamic discourse has to be purified and that one has to return to Islam as it was allegedly practised by the first generations of Muslims, and all of them claim to stand in a long tradition of Islamic scholars, which includes thirteenth-/fourteenth-century CE scholar Ahmad ibn Taymiya. However, contemporary Salafist movements are very different from each other with regard to their concrete ideas and the means they espouse. In academic texts, Salafist movements are usually subdivided into three analytical categories:[49] 'Quietist Salafists' focus on personal piety and missionary work and abstain from politics. 'Political Salafists' try to shape the politics of their countries and bring them into line with Salafi teachings through political and social activism, for example, by founding Salafist political parties. Finally, 'Salafi-Jihadists' argue that Muslims have to wage armed jihad against the 'enemies of Islam' in order to really fulfil their Islamic obligations. In addition to these different Salafist movements, other Islamic scholars who are not usually considered Salafists, like the influential Egyptian-Qatari Yusuf al-Qaradawi, also occasionally comment on the meaning of Salafism and make the term an element of their own theories.[50] As can be seen, there is much disagreement among Islamic scholars and activists over what it actually means to be a Salafist.

Through their writings, the members of the Islamic civil rights movement participate in this great debate about the meaning of Salafism. It is not surprising that the concept is attractive for them. The members of the movement of Islamic Modernism, who have been called Salafist in the past, are a major inspiration to them. At the same time, the members of the Islamic civil rights movement are products of Saudi Arabia's Wahhabi education system, which also claims to be inspired by Salafism. Therefore, it is only natural for them to understand their own reformist theory as a part of the Salafist current.

In their texts, the members of the Islamic civil rights movement construct their own version of Salafism. Their negative view on the mainstream Sunni discourse after the Rightly Guided Caliphs and their argument that Muslims need to return to the 'pure' message of Islam are shared by the majority of contemporary Salafists. Like many other Salafists, al-Hamid and the other members of the movement construct an intellectual pedigree of 'Salafist' Islamic scholars, which especially includes thirteenth-/fourteenth-century CE Islamic scholar Ahmad ibn Taymiya and in whose tradition they see themselves. In these respects, the version of Salafism propagated by the Islamic civil rights movement agrees with many other contemporary interpretations of the concept. Other elements are more controversial. For example, they criticize the apolitical attitude of 'quietist' Salafists and accuse them of being the accomplices of political oppression. Other contemporary Salafists also do not necessarily share their enthusiasm for renewal and the modern sciences, which is clearly inspired by Islamic Modernism.

All in all, the school of Salafism that their version is closest to is that of activist 'political' Salafism in Kuwait, which was decisively shaped by Hakim al-Mutayri, or of similar movements in Egypt, which saw the founding of a Salafist political party, the Nur Party (*ḥizb an-nur*), in 2011 CE. As was mentioned earlier, in one of his books, al-Hamid mentions al-Mutayri as a major inspiration for his theory. The available texts suggest that, for the members of the Islamic civil rights movement, Salafism is less a theological school than a political movement. They want to peacefully influence the politics of Saudi Arabia and bring the state's policies into line with Islam. They do not discuss theological viewpoints, like the interpretation of the attributes of God, at all, but focus entirely on politics, civil society and the theoretical foundations for political and social activism. The renewal that they call for is above all a renewal of Islamic political discourse.

It has been said that Salafism 'arose historically and, therefore, can be changed in the course of history'.[51] Like all concepts, Salafism is changeable, and its meaning is fluid. In the context of the theory of the Islamic civil rights movement, it may be an exceptionally illustrative example of how the meaning of certain terms changes over time and how the contributions of single authors and movements can play a decisive role in these changes. The Islamic civil rights movement participates in the debate about what Salafism means. They are a part of it. They assimilate the term, claim it for themselves and construct a meaning that is convincing to them, along with an intellectual pedigree reaching back to the early days of Islam. Through their writings and actions, which they argue are inspired by Salafism, they contribute to the changing and the fragmentation of the concept of Salafism, producing a new meaning of the term.

The liberating power of Islam

One of the key points of the writings of the Islamic civil rights movement, and of the broader Islamo-reformist current in general, is that the citizens of Saudi Arabia have the right to political freedom. In many of their texts, they argue that any unjustified restriction of the people's freedom must be eliminated. Political systems that deny the people's freedom are considered illegitimate. According to their texts, freedom is a basic value of Islam. In fact, they explicitly understand Islam as a liberating system of beliefs. They argue that any form of worldly servitude is rejected by the Islamic sources, because Islam demands that the people are free to make their own decisions. The message of Islam is one of liberation. The following passages from several books of the Islamo-reformist current all seem to agree on this point:

> Islam considers it idolatry for a human to renounce his freedom. [. . .] The people who serve God become free from others in their worship of God. [. . .] The people are not separated into free men and slaves, but all people are slaves of God. They are, therefore, free and equal to their free human brothers.[52]
>
> The core of the Muhammadan message is liberation.[53]
>
> In our time, we need to understand Islam as a discourse of the liberation of the people in their lives, their minds and their thoughts.[54]
>
> Islam came to liberate the whole of humanity from all forms of servitude to anyone else but God. It made monotheism the slogan of liberation: 'There is no God but God', and there are no kings, no Caesars, no Khosraws, no Pharaohs and no giants.[55]

It is obvious that Abdallah al-Hamid, Muhammad al-Ahmari, Muhammad al-Abd al-Karim and Hakim al-Mutayri, the authors of these lines, share the view that Islam demands freedom from servitude to worldly rulers, and especially oppressive ones, like the Roman ruler Caesar, the Persian king Khosraw or the Egyptian pharaoh. Only free humans can truly embrace the message of Islam because the believers have to choose Islam of their own free will and without compulsion.[56] Thus, freedom is the foundation of Islam and its precondition. Only free humans can choose to believe.

Not only is the whole of Islam based on freedom, but important Islamic principles like shura rule (*al-ḥukm aš-šūrī*, 'rule through consultation') also require that the people are free. Abdallah al-Hamid argues that Islam makes shura rule an obligation for Muslim states. But shura always means that those who take part in it are free equals, who can think for themselves and are not bound by ties of servitude to others:

> When Islam made shura [*šūrā*] a political system, it based it on the fact that it is stabilised by an educational system. This means that, when it calls for shura, it calls for the consultation of free equals to every ruler who rules through shura. It is not the consultation of slaves and scoundrels, who serve any cruel tyrant. It is the consultation of those who are able to think for themselves [*mufakkirūn mujtahidūn*], not of imitators.[57]

In the interpretation of Abdallah al-Hamid and others, Islam's endorsement of freedom gains a revolutionary dimension. If Islam requires people to be free of the worldly oppression of the likes of Caesar, Khosraw and Pharaoh, it deprives every political system which does not guarantee the freedom and equality of the people of its legitimacy. Only governments which care for their citizens' freedom are legitimate in terms of Islam.

According to the Islamo-reformist current in Saudi Arabia, freedom is evidently a central principle of Islam, but if one looks at what this freedom actually means, things become a bit less clear. In several passages, they imply that the freedom that they have in mind is not limitless. It is rather defined by the Islamic framework. It is a freedom for Islam, which is bound by the rules that God has set down in the religious texts and in nature. Therefore, this Islamic freedom is different from 'secular freedom', which they equate with limitless freedom:

> The concept of freedom in Islam resembles the secular concept in one regard, and it is different from it in another regard. It resembles it to the extent that the freedom of a man ends where the freedoms of the others begin. It is different from it in another regard, namely that freedom in Islam is linked to innate nature [*fiṭra*]. Islam, and all non-distorted heavenly religions, are religions of innate nature. Everything that is good according to innate nature, like marriage, virtuousness and integrity, is good in Islam. Everything that is bad according to innate human nature is bad in Islam.[58]

> The freedom that Islam imagines is represented by the human being who is freed from the power of man for the sake of the power of the Lord of men. In his freedom, he only wants to defend his worshipped [God].[59]

The freedom that Islam demands is not limitless, like the freedom that secularism allegedly endorses. It is a qualified freedom and bound by specific norms. It is a freedom which is defined by what our human nature and our conscience tell us. It is a freedom for serving God. Freedom in Islam is a freedom for Islam. The aforementioned passages indicate that in speaking about freedom they insist on something that can be called a 'sharia caveat'. Freedom is desirable, as long as it stays inside the framework of the divine norms of Islam.[60]

It must be mentioned that not all the authors of the Islamo-reformist current share this particular belief, even if most of them do. Of the sixteen analysed texts of the Islamo-reformist current, two, namely Abdallah al-Maliki's *The Sovereignty of the Umma before the Implementation of the Sharia* (*Siyādat al-umma qabla taṭbīq aš-šarīʿa*) and Muhammad al-Ahmari's *Democracy*, seem to argue that the freedom of the people even comes before the implementation of the norms of the sharia.[61] However, within the Islamo-reformist discourse in Saudi Arabia, they seem to be the minority. Most authors of the Islamo-reformist current, and, indeed, all members of the Islamic civil rights movement, agree that the people's freedom must not stand above the authority of the Islamic sharia.

The members of the Islamic civil rights movement, and of the Islamo-reformist current in general, are not the first Islamic thinkers who have found revolutionary implications in Islam's strong endorsement of freedom. This idea can especially be found in the texts of many Islamically inspired political thinkers of the twentieth and twenty-first centuries CE. For example, influential contemporary Sunni authors like the Sudanese Islamic scholar and politician Hasan at-Turabi (*Hasan at-Turābī*, 1932–2016 CE), the Tunisian Islamic scholar and politician Rachid al-Ghannouchi (*Rāšid al-Ġannūšī*, b. 1941 CE), and the Egyptian-Qatari Islamic scholar Yusuf al-Qaradawi have emphasized the importance of freedom in Islam. All of them have argued that Islam demands that all humans are free from servitude to other humans, because only then can they truly serve God.[62] Iranian Shia authors have also argued that the liberating power of Islam carries in itself a revolutionary element. An example is Ayatollah Murtaza Mutahhari (1920–79 CE), who greatly influenced the ideas of the Islamic Revolution in Iran in 1979 CE. Like the aforementioned authors, he argued that Islam demands freedom, but that this kind of freedom is different from the limitless freedom that is allegedly being practised in Europe and America. Freedom in Islam aims at bringing forward the human side and keeping the animal desires in check. In Islam, freedom is the freedom to follow the instructions of God.[63]

As can be seen, the idea that Islam requires freedom from all worldly servitude in order to truly serve God is part of the common intellectual vocabulary of Islamically inspired political authors of the twentieth century CE. Several contemporary Islamic scholars have argued that this strong Islamic emphasis on freedom carries a revolutionary dynamic, directed against systems of political oppression. It appears to be a commonly held belief among religious-minded political thinkers in the Islamic world that Islam endorses freedom and revolt against oppression. When the members of the Islamic civil rights movement and the broader Islamo-reformist current use this idea in their own texts, they simply rely on this existing vocabulary and seize a widespread concept that many seem to find convincing.

The Islamic constitution

In their writings, the members of the Islamic civil rights movement argue that the modern Islamic state has to be ruled by a constitution (*dustūr*), and, again, they have a very precise idea of what this concept means. The idea that Saudi Arabia, which is ruled by an absolute monarch, needs to be turned into a constitutional state appears very often in the books, declarations and lectures of the movement. Indeed, they frequently refer to themselves as the 'advocates of constitutional reform' (*du'āt al-iṣlāḥ ad-dustūrī*), and some of them have written lengthy texts that deal with the issue of constitutional reform.[64] They argue that a constitution is the only means of guaranteeing that a state is just and that it is prevented from sliding into oppression. According to HASM member Matruk al-Falih, a constitution consists of a set of neutral tools and procedures that act as structural safeguards against unjust and oppressive actions by single individuals or institutions of the state. The constitution is the checks and balances that guarantee that the interests of all are protected:

> In order to guarantee the realisation of justice and the elimination of oppression, we need tools and structures. [. . .] These means, tools, structures, procedures and elements which enable us to achieve justice and eliminate oppression, and

which guarantee human rights and freedom are provided and encompassed by the constitution. The constitution in this meaning is neither unbelief [*kufr*] nor belief [*īmān*], but it is the neutral tools, structures, procedures and elements for the leading of an Islamic civil life.[65]

Al-Falih argues that it is wrong to ask whether constitutional reform in itself is compatible or incompatible with Islam. A constitution has to be understood as a set of neutral tools that can serve to promote values that Islam calls for, like justice. Therefore, it is something that Muslims can and should benefit from.[66]

The constitution regulates the relationship between the state and the people, and it guarantees that everyone is treated justly. The way it does this is through a series of institutional, structural or procedural measures which ensure that there are checks and balances. In one of his books, Abdallah al-Hamid lists nine principles that must be part of an 'Islamic constitution':

If we say 'Islamic constitutional system', we mean roughly ten points:

1 – The sovereignty of the community [*umma*] requires that the allegiance of the community to the ruler according to the book [the Quran] and the sunna is a social contract, based on equal rights and obligations and his recognition of the community's sovereignty over him. [. . .]

[2 –] One of the means of the sovereignty of the community over the ruler is the establishment of an elected council of representatives [*maǧlis nuwwāb muntaḫab*], which draws up the plans for the educational, political and financial sector, adopts the laws [*nuẓum*] and means [*wasā'il*] which guarantee the implementation of the sharia and supervises the government. [. . .]

[3 –] One of the means of the sovereignty of the community over the rulers is the definition of the role [of the rulers] as being 'executive'.

[4 –] One of the means of the sovereignty of the community over the rulers is the independence of the judiciary. [. . .]

[5 –] One of the means of the sovereignty of the community over the rulers is the separation of the three powers of the state.

[6 –] One of the means of the sovereignty of the community over the rulers is the establishment of political parties and the transfer of power, because this prevents the people from seeking refuge in bloody change.

[7 –] One of the means of the sovereignty of the community over the rulers is freedom of opinion, expression and assembly. [. . .]

[8 –] One of the means of the sovereignty of the community over the rulers is the establishment of civil society associations without government oversight.

[9 –] One of the means of the sovereignty of the community over the rulers is the organisation of elections and referendums.[67]

All these individual measures complement each other. The separation of the three powers of the state – the legislative, the executive and the judicial branches – logically entails that the judiciary is independent, and that the role of the executive branch is to implement the legal acts that the legislative branch passes. Regular elections for the council of representatives entail the peaceful transfer of power, if the majority changes. Both the free election of a council of representatives and the strong role of civil society require that the people enjoy freedom of opinion and expression. As a whole, all these measures form the constitution, which creates a political system in which power always lies with the people and no ruler can oppress them. Thereby, it is an effective means of safeguarding the rights of all citizens and guaranteeing that they are ruled justly.

According to the members of the Islamic civil rights movement, the general institutional measures of a constitution are neutral tools, which are neither Islamic nor secular. Nevertheless, different constitutions reflect different social values. The aforementioned general measures that can be found in all real constitutions will work, irrespective of the religion and values of the citizens and the rulers. However, different constitutions have different characters, because they are also expressions of the basic rules and values that different societies agree on:

> The shura system [*an-niẓām aš-šūrī*, 'system of consultation'] in every community embodies their belief [*'aqīda*], their values and their deeply rooted religious and social customs. When a developed non-Muslim state, be it secular, Buddhist or communist, establishes a constitution, its constitution is called a secular, Buddhist or communist constitution, and it realises justice and shura, which are the foundation of political, social and economic stability and flourishing in life in this world. [. . .] If a Muslim community establishes the shura system on the foundation of the sharia, they combine the good of this world and the afterlife. [. . .] Their constitution is called Islamic.[68]

Because constitutions embody the basic beliefs of the societies that have adopted them, they have different characters and express different values, even if all real constitutions contain the same general institutional guarantees. What distinguishes a specifically Islamic constitution from secular, Buddhist or communist constitutions is that, in addition to the general institutional measures, it includes references to the norms of the sharia and also aims at the salvation of the citizens in the afterlife. Measures like the separation of the three branches of government, elections for a legislative council of representatives and the independence of the judiciary all enable humans to lead a good life in this world. This is important for a state with an Islamic constitution. But in addition to this, it also seeks to enable its citizens to find salvation in the afterlife according to the teachings of Islam.

Of course, the Islamic constitution does not only focus on the afterlife, but it must also ensure that, in worldly questions, the norms of the sharia are observed. The core of a specifically Islamic constitution seems to be that the Islamic sharia remains the framework for all things that happen in the state. The following passage from a book by Abdallah al-Hamid illustrates this thought:

> In order for the constitution to be an Islamic one, we stipulate two conditions:
>
> The first: The constitution is not Islamic, if it does not put the obedience to 'those who have been entrusted with authority' into the framework of obedience to God and his Messenger. [. . .] The power of the community has to be put into the framework of the absolute statements of the sharia, so that the constitution is the embodiment of the power of a community which adheres to the sharia. [. . .] Every law which the state enacts, and which is not sharia-compliant [*ġayr šarʿī*] is not constitutional. [. . .]
>
> The second condition: Adhering to the absolute statements of the Islamic sharia in education, the judiciary and family affairs in particular, as well as in social affairs in general.[69]

Abdallah al-Hamid obviously has a kind of 'sharia caveat' in mind when he speaks about the specifically Islamic constitution. In the framework of such a constitution, political power belongs to the people, and their freedom is guaranteed by constitutional safeguards, as long as all decisions are in line with the norms of the sharia.[70] The function of the Islamic constitution seems to be to ensure that the sharia is the highest authority in the state. This way, the political principles of Islam are implemented, the people are enabled to find happiness in this world and the next, and the Muslim society can defend against the advances of secularism. Therefore, the Islamic civil rights movement passionately calls for establishing an Islamic constitution in Saudi Arabia, which is different from European or American constitutions. What is needed, accordingly, is

> an Islamic constitution, a constitution built on the teachings of Islam. We do not want positivist Western constitutions, but we want a constitution built on the teachings of Islam.[71]

The members of the Islamic civil rights movement call for an Islamic constitution and make this one of their main demands. They firmly believe that such a constitution, which guarantees that the politics of the state are in line with the teachings of Islam, solves the problems of injustice and oppression in Muslim countries.

The concept of the constitution (*dustūr*) in the modern meaning of the term is relatively new in the Arabic political vocabulary. It is one of the results of a series of lexical innovations in the Arabic language in the wake of the encounter with modern European political systems in the nineteenth century CE. As authors who wrote in Arabic wanted to explain political systems like that of post-revolutionary France, they had to find Arabic words that could describe certain elements of these systems. In time, the word *dustūr*, which had originally been a Persian honorary title for high officials and had later acquired the general meaning of 'rule', became the standard translation of the term constitution.[72] Today, the term *dustūr* is well established in the Arabic language and designates a constitution in the sense of the basic laws of states that lay down the fundamental principles of how politics and administration work in these states. Virtually all Arab and Muslim countries have constitutions.

Today, the benefits of constitutional systems are acknowledged by the overwhelming majority of people in Arabic-speaking countries, and many countries with a Muslim majority have constitutions which have an Islamic character. Many Islamically inspired thinkers and politicians, like the members of the Egyptian 'centrist stream', have praised the positive effects of a constitution on the political situation of a country. Contemporary authors like the Egyptians Muhammad Salim al-Awwa (*Muḥammad Salīm al-ʿAwwā*, b. 1942 CE) and Muhammad Ammara (*Muḥammad ʿAmmāra*, 1931–2020 CE) have emphasized that modern constitutions are the ideal embodiment of Islamic political principles like shura, justice, freedom and equality.[73] Frequently, the Charter of Medina, a contract drawn up after the arrival of the prophet Muhammad in Medina, which regulated the rights and obligations of all inhabitants of the city, is described as the first constitution in Islamic history.[74] The existing constitutions in several Muslim countries include provisions that explicitly refer to the teachings of Islam or the norms of the sharia and therefore give the state a decidedly Islamic character. For example, the constitution of the Islamic Republic of Iran stipulates that the Islamic sharia is the framework for all legislation and that all laws must conform with Islamic criteria.[75] The constitution of the Arab Republic of Egypt also includes articles declaring that the Islamic sharia is the main source of legislation. These articles have existed since the times of Egyptian president Hosni Mubarak (*Ḥusnī Mubārak*, 1928–2020 CE) and have survived revolutions, coups and amendments.[76]

Thus, when the members of the Islamic civil rights movement call for an Islamic constitution which includes structural safeguards against oppression and enshrines the values of the Islamic sharia, they echo the beliefs of many Islamically inspired authors and activists in the Islamic world. Thinkers and activists in other countries have also been voicing their support for such kinds of constitutions, and the existing constitutions of several Muslim countries indicate that it is possible to give a state a constitution with a specifically Islamic character. In the eyes of the members of the Islamic civil rights movement, turning Saudi Arabia into a constitutional state would only mean that the country would finally catch up with other Muslim countries that are already governed by constitutions.

Shura and democracy

The political system that the members of the Islamic civil rights movement call for is characterized, above all, by the concept of shura (*šūrā*), which can be roughly translated as 'consultation'. Shura rule (*al-ḥukm aš-šūrī*) is one of their main political demands. In their books, lectures and declarations, they vehemently argue that shura is one of the most important political principles that Islam has laid down and that it is an Islamic obligation. In the founding declaration of the association HASM, its members state that one of their main aims is to spread the idea that shura is a basic political principle of Islam:

> The association strives to accomplish the following: Laying the foundation for an Islamic culture of political human rights, which considers the means of shura rule [*al-ḥukm aš-šūrī*] one of the pillars of the political doctrine of Islam, which – according to the sharia – must not be abandoned or neglected.[77]

Shura is an Islamic obligation and belongs to the fundamental values of Islamic doctrine. Its great importance even means that, if it is not properly implemented in a state, this state cannot be considered an Islamic state:

> Every state that does not implement representative shura is not considered Islamic, even if its people are Muslims. It means that it rules by something other than what God has sent down.[78]

According to the members of the Islamic civil rights movement, the obligation of shura is so deeply ingrained in Islamic doctrine that not fully implementing it amounts to ignoring the revelation of Islam. The extent to which shura is realized in the state determines whether it can be called Islamic or not.

However, shura is not an end in itself. Authors like Abdallah al-Hamid argue that Islam endorses shura for a reason, namely because it is an effective means to prevent oppression and promote justice. In fact, in their eyes, justice and shura are interdependent. Without shura, there is no justice.[79] Thus, in addition to being an obligation of Islam, shura prevents developments that Islam warns against, and it promotes values that Islam endorses, like justice. It belongs to the fundamental basic principles of Islam and is intrinsically linked to other fundamental parts of the Islamic sharia.

In the interpretation of the members of the Islamic civil rights movement, shura means binding political participation of the people in choosing their leaders and deciding the policies of the state. Shura means that the people are the source of political power, and that they can decide who their leaders are, which laws and regulations the state enforces on the inside and how it deals with other states and transnational challenges on the outside. Only when the leaders are bound by the decisions of the people, the system of government is in line with the concept of shura. Shura means that the power belongs to the people, and that the ruler is their representative and bound by their opinion.[80] It is not optional but an obligation. In order to bring the opinion of the people to light, the people have used different tools of shura throughout human history. In the time of the prophet Muhammad and the Rightly Guided Caliphs, the rulers convened councils of notables, when they needed to consult public opinion. Today, in the era of large states, which extend over vast territories and have a population of millions of people, the best way to implement shura is an elected council of representatives, or a parliament:

> One cannot guarantee the shura of the community [*šūrā l-umma*] in states except through its delegates, representatives and notables, who are followed [by the people]. Therefore, the establishment of a council of representatives of the community [*mağlis li-nuwwāb al-umma*] belongs to the great obligations of any Islamic state.[81]

The members of the Islamic civil rights argue that Islam requires that major political decisions have to be taken by a council of elected representatives of the people, which has legislative powers. The ruler has to implement their decisions. They are trusted by the people and embody the public opinion. Therefore, they are the best modern tool to implement the concept of shura in the modern Islamic state. Islam calls for democracy.

Authors like Abdallah al-Hamid argue that shura, or democracy, is a universal human practice, which nevertheless takes distinct forms in different societies. According to them, shura was practised by all civilizations, and democratic forms of participation can be found across the world. Instead of believing everything that past Islamic scholars said about politics, Muslims should return to this universal practice, which was also confirmed by Islam. This idea is shared by representatives of the broader Islamo-reformist current in Saudi Arabia as well as by members of the Islamic civil rights movement:

> Democracy is one of the most successful attempts of man to administrate society and organise his relationships. [. . .] One of the takeaways of this text is that what is called democracy today is not an Athenian or Greek invention, even if it was consolidated by their experience. [. . .] This democratic experience is a human custom, which the world has tried in many regions since the oldest records of human voting and electing in nations.[82]

> So, democracy is the fruit of human experience and it has multiple forms. [. . .] There is no doubt that the democratic system is much better than the oppressive system. One of the most beautiful aspects of it is the realisation of an amount of justice, consent and voluntary transfer of power, like it can be seen in most countries of the world.[83]

> The people can only be saved from backwardness and stagnation by a renewal of the religious discourse and the uncovering of the deviation which developed in the Umayyad and Abbasid environment, which twisted the necks [. . .] of the implementation of the means of shura rule (democracy) by civilised nations since the times of the Greeks and the Romans.[84]

The Islamo-reformist authors Muhammad al-Ahmari and Salman al-Awda as well as HASM member Abdallah al-Hamid seem to agree that democracy, or shura, is a universal human practice and that Muslims should, again, adopt it today.

According to Abdallah al-Hamid, shura, or democracy, is in fact a neutral tool that can be implemented in different ways, some of which are compatible with the teachings of Islam, while others are more in line with the ideologies of secularism or socialism. In an interesting passage from one of his books, Abdallah al-Hamid distinguishes between 'Western democracy' and democracy as a universal human practice. While he believes the former to be intrinsically linked to secularism, the latter is a neutral tool, which can be implemented in Islamic or non-Islamic settings:

> Western democracy is one of the principles of secularism and a branch of an ideology. You cannot break the relationship between the branch and its tree. This Western democracy can only be accepted by nations that have no roots, [. . .] because it naturally leads to secularism. As for democracy as a human tool to implement the principles of social and political leadership, it does not contradict

> any communist, Buddhist or Islamic doctrine, but it is in harmony with them, because it is like the clothes to the body. It is one of the guarantees of justice and the sovereignty of the community over its rulers and one of the political moral virtues. There is nothing that speaks against adopting it, if we are careful, limit it by using a specifying expression and say: Islamic democracy.[85]

While the tools of democracy, or shura, are universal, the concrete forms they take in different societies are defined by the ideological background in which they are implemented. In the end, the democracy that Abdallah al-Hamid, and probably the other members of the Islamic civil rights movement, want to establish is not the so-called 'Western' one, which is supposedly linked to a secular worldview, but a specifically Islamic one. The shura that they call for is an 'Islamic democracy', where democratic tools are implemented in an Islamic framework. Abdallah al-Hamid does not explain in detail what this 'Islamic democracy' actually looks like; however, judging by what he says about other concepts, like the constitution (*dustūr*), the reader gets the impression that his idea of democracy is limited by a 'sharia caveat'. Democratic processes and their results are legitimate, as long as they are in line with the norms of the Islamic sharia. With this precondition in mind, Muslims can and should adopt democratic practices and built a state that is ruled by shura or by an 'Islamic democracy'.

The term 'shura' (*šūrā*), which features so prominently in the theory of the Islamic civil rights movement, has been interpreted differently by different authors throughout the centuries of Islamic thought. It is a Quranic term and appears in verse 38 of Sura 42 (*aš-Šūrā*), which says:

> [God's blessing shall be given] to those, who respond to the [call of] their Sustainer and are constant in prayer; and whose rule [in all matters of common concern] is consultation among themselves [*wa-amruhum šūrā bainahum*].[86]

Shura is obviously something that God wants the believers to practice. What it actually means has been hotly debated since Muslims started to think about how they should interpret the text of the Quran. In pre-Islamic times, Arab tribal leaders usually consulted the notables of their tribe, when they had to take major decisions. This practice continued after the death of the prophet Muhammad, and the election of the first four caliphs, the Rightly Guided Caliphs, is seen by many Muslims as a result of the practice of shura. Thus, the persistent use of shura can be described as a phenomenon of cultural continuity that reaches back into pre-Islamic times. However, soon there were differences of opinion between Islamic scholars about the details of the implementation of shura in their societies. Controversial questions concerned who the leader actually had to consult and whether he was bound by their opinion or not.[87]

During the nineteenth century CE, the term 'shura' acquired new importance, as it was given a new meaning in the writings of the protagonists of the movement of Islamic Modernism. In their attempts to combine Islamic authenticity with the accomplishments of modernity, authors like the Egyptians Muhammad Abduh and Muhammad Rashid Rida re-defined shura and equated it with the tools and institutions of democracies. They argued that modern representative democracies were the best embodiment of the concept of shura. Simply put, 'democracy' and 'shura' were two words that referred to the same basic underlying concept. However, because both terms still designated two distinct ideas and because Islamic Modernism also insisted on an authentically Islamic solution to modern problems, their discussion of shura was not unambiguous. When they spoke about shura in an Islamic setting, they meant something slightly different from what shura meant in a European context.[88] Nevertheless, Abduh's and Rashid Rida's interpretation of shura strongly influenced many Islamically inspired thinkers and activists after the nineteenth century CE and shaped the way they looked at democratic systems of government.

A large part of Islamic authors who wrote about politics in the twentieth and twenty-first centuries CE argued that at least some forms of democratic participation were required by Islam. Many authors, from Egyptian Muslim Brotherhood members to Iranian revolutionary thinkers, seem to share a set of interdependent ideas that lead them to conclude that the political doctrine of Islam demands that societies be governed by democratic systems. This conviction is built on specific interpretations of key terms, the most important of which is shura. It is widely accepted that shura means democratic forms of political participation, that it is compulsory and that it is a way to implement the Islamic call to make the people the real holders of political power. Although not all the authors agree on what a political system built on shura actually looks like – with some arguing that shura equals democracy, and others insisting that it is an own system that only resembles democracy in some respects – many have been inspired by the concept of shura to acknowledge the value of democracy.[89]

Statements endorsing democracy can be found in the writings of many different Islamic authors. Even the controversial member of the Muslim Brotherhood Sayyid Qutb, who described contemporary political systems in the Islamic world as un-Islamic, expressed his support of democracy, albeit within the strict limits of the Islamic sharia.[90] Many contemporary authors who are often referred to in the writings of the Islamic civil rights movement argue that shura means democracy and that it is an obligation of Islam. For example, the famous Egyptian-Qatari Islamic scholar Yusuf al-Qaradawi passionately endorsed shura and democracy in his 2007 CE book *Religion and Politics* (*ad-Dīn wa-s-siyāsa*).[91] The Sudanese Islamic scholar and politician Hasan at-Turabi also argued that the truly Islamic state can only be one that implements compulsory shura through an elected council of representatives which determines the policies of the state.[92] In Tunisia, the influential Islamic scholar and politician Rachid al-Ghannouchi has endorsed an active participation in democratic processes, because, according to him, this is the meaning of the Quranic term of shura today.[93] Other examples of authors who have argued that Islam calls for democracy are the Egyptian Islamic scholar Muhammad Khalaf Allah (*Muḥammad Ḫalaf Allāh*, 1916–97 CE),[94] the Pakistani lawyer and Islamic author S. M. Zafar (b. 1930 CE)[95] and the Omani journalist and Islamic author Sadek Sulaiman (*Sādiq Sulaymān*, b. 1933 CE).[96]

A positive view of democracy and the idea that it is compatible, and maybe even congruent, with the concept of shura is not limited to Sunni thinkers. Important Shia thinkers who have influenced Iranian revolutionary thought, such as Ali Shariati and Ayatollah Murtaza Mutahhari, have argued that Islam requires democracy and majority rule.[97] Islamically inspired opposition intellectuals in Iran since the 1990s CE have also insisted that a 'republican theology', which combines Islam with modernity, can only conclude that a truly Islamic state has to be democratic. The people are the legitimate holders of political power, and their will is to be respected. Therefore, the government must never impose its will on the people, especially if it claims to be an Islamic government.[98]

Finally, the idea that the Quranic term 'shura' equals democracy and that democracy is therefore an Islamic obligation can also be found in the party platforms of Islamically inspired parties in the contemporary Islamic world. For example, in the first parliamentary elections after the fall of President Hosni Mubarak in Egypt, both the Freedom and Justice Party (*ḥizb al-ḥurrīya wa-l-ʿadāla*), which had strong ties to the Muslim Brotherhood, and the Salafist Nur Party (*ḥizb an-nūr*) endorsed democracy in their electoral programmes.[99] The programme of the Freedom and Justice Party was particularly explicit about it and drew a clear connection between shura and democracy, as can be seen in this passage:

> The party believes that shura (democracy) is a fundamental principle on which the state with all its institutions rests. It is not merely a political principle which defines the forms of political relationships, but it is an approach and a general method for the administration of the different areas of life in the state. [. . .] The shura that we believe in, that we strive to realise and that we want to base the system of rule on is not a fixed form, but it means the embedding of the principle of a transfer of power and the right of the people to decide their affairs, choose their representatives and leaders, supervise them and hold them accountable.[100]

Like the Freedom and Justice Party after the fall of Mubarak, other political parties whose worldview is to a large extent defined by their interpretations of the message of Islam participate in democratic elections and justify this participation with the argument that democracy is the modern form of shura. As can be seen, the emphasis on the concept of shura, the idea that it is compatible with modern democracy and the thought that Islam therefore requires the state to be democratic is widespread among Islamically inspired political thinkers across the Islamic world.

The members of the Islamic civil rights movement are evidently not alone with their ideas concerning shura and democracy. The arguments and interpretations they mention in their texts are shared by a large segment of so-called Islamist thinkers and activists, whose political worldview is informed by their interpretations of specific Islamic concepts. Equating shura with democracy has almost become a mainstream idea among Islamically inspired activists who want their states to be democratic ones, provided this happens in accordance with the norms of the Islamic sharia. The members of the Islamic civil rights movement, and of the broader Islamo-reformist current in general, adopt these ideas, and in doing so can rely on the detailed arguments that have already been made in the writings of other supporters of these concepts. All that the members of the Islamic civil rights movement have to do is adopt the concept of shura and integrate it into their own theory.

The people and their rulers – Allegiance and authority

When they speak about the shape of the ideal Islamic state, the members of the Islamic civil rights movement rely on a group of interrelated terms and concepts that concern the relationship between the people and their rulers. They argue that the teachings of Islam include principles concerning the role of the government and the subjects, and that the Islamic sharia contains norms that regulate their rights and obligations. The terms and concepts that they use to describe this relationship cannot be looked at in isolation. They are interrelated and refer to each other. In their eyes, the relationship between the citizens and the rulers has to be defined by a correct understanding of the underlying concepts of sovereignty or guardianship (*siyāda*/*qawāma*), allegiance (*bayʿa*), authorized representation (*wakāla*) and the role of 'those who have been entrusted with authority' (*ūlū l-amr*). The texts by authors of the Islamic civil rights movement indicate that they have a very clear understanding of what these concepts mean for them and how they complement each other. Only when these interrelated concepts are understood correctly and are implemented in the state, the relationship between the people and their rulers will be in line with the teachings of Islam.

To begin with, authors like Abdallah al-Hamid are adamant in their opinion that political sovereignty (*siyāda* or *qawāma*) belongs to the people and not to the ruler. The people do not need a guardian who watches over them and determines what is best for them. They are their own guardian and the source of political power:

> The community [*umma*] is its own guardian [*walīya amrihā*] and sovereignty [*siyāda*] and guardianship [*qawāma*] over the state in general, and the government in particular, belong to it. The community is the keeper of the sharia, not the rulers. [. . .] The ruler is not the authority for resolving a conflict, but the community is the authority of the state.[101]

One of the main arguments for the sovereignty of the people is that the Quran usually addresses the entire Islamic community when speaking about political decisions.[102] Everyone is called on to implement the principles of Islam. Therefore, according to Abdallah al-Hamid, political sovereignty belongs to the people. That the people are the true holders of sovereignty means that they choose their leaders and decide the policies of the state. It is simply wrong to assume that the worldly rulers are the legitimate holders of political power and that they are owed unconditional obedience. The true keeper of the Islamic state is the Muslim community. Political power belongs to the people.

Abdallah al-Hamid argues that it is not the ruler who is owed obedience according to the teachings of Islam. Instead, the people are to be obeyed in political affairs. They are the keepers of the state, and it is their responsibility to ensure that the norms of the Islamic sharia are implemented. According to Abdallah al-Hamid, the ideal relationship between the people and their rulers can be described by the term 'allegiance' (*bayʿa*). However, allegiance does not mean that the people have to blindly obey the ruler. On the contrary, allegiance means a social contract between the people and the ruler, which is based on mutual rights and obligations. The people voluntarily promise to support the ruler, as long as he adheres to the decisions of the people. The legitimate ruler is not an absolute monarch or a despot, but an authorized representative (*wakīl*) of the people. The following passage from Abdallah al-Hamid's book *The Word Is Stronger than the Bullet* illustrates this point:

> Rule is based on a social contract, a voluntary shura contract of allegiance between the community and the ruler, in which the ruler acknowledges the power of the community and that he is its authorised representative [*wakīl*]. There is no validity and no legitimacy in an absolute, unilateral system of power, which is based on subduing and a forced allegiance of coercion.[103]

The same concept of allegiance can be found in books by authors of the broader Islamo-reformist current, for instance, in texts by Abdallah al-Maliki and Hakim al-Mutayri:

> The contract of allegiance [*ʿaqd al-bayʿa*] is like all other contracts. According to the Islamic legal scholars, it resembles the contract of authorised representation [*wakāla*] or lease [*iğāra*], whereby the community is the basis and the one who is chosen as a ruler for it is its authorised representative.[104]

The relationship between the community and the imam [that is, the ruler] rests on the foundation of a contract between two parties, in which the community is the basis and the imam is its authorised representative [*wakīl*] for the administration of its affairs.[105]

Allegiance is a social contract between the people and the ruler that assigns rights and obligations to both sides. Whosoever neglects his obligations breaks the contract. In a lecture that was published in October 2012 CE, HASM member Abd al-Karim al-Khadr argues that both parties have to abide by the terms of the contract of allegiance. If one party breaks the contract, this party is guilty of rebellion against the other. This means that not only the people can rebel against the ruler, but that the ruler can be accused of rebellion against the people as well, if he does not adhere to the rules of the contract:

> When we look at this accusation [of rebellion], which is usually made against individuals, we find that this accusation is often only limited. There is another side to this accusation, namely the rebellion of the ruler against the community. The relationship between the ruler and the community is a contractual relationship, which is called the sharia allegiance [*al-bayʿa š-šarʿīya*] in the Islamic sharia. Whoever breaks the sharia allegiance, be it the ruler, while the community still abides by it, or be it the community, while the ruler still abides by it, rebels against the other.[106]

Therefore, if the ruler breaks the contract by not listening to the people, they are not obliged to obey him, and the contract of allegiance is void. Sovereignty and political power do not belong to the ruler but to the people, who enter into a social contract with the ruler. As long as both sides adhere to the terms of this contract of allegiance, the contract is valid. If, however, one side fails to meet the necessary requirements of the contract, the other side is no longer obliged to obey. If a faction of the people rebels against a just ruler who is accepted by the majority and follows their decisions, they are wrong, just like a ruler is wrong who claims all political power for himself.

In modern political practice, the principle of the power of the people is implemented in the form of the institution of elected representatives of the people, who are trusted by them and who take political decisions in the state. Much of the debate about political authority in the modern Islamic state revolves around the interpretation of two technical terms for the people who are owed obedience in political affairs: the Quranic expression 'those who have been entrusted with authority' (*ūlū l-amr*) and the traditional Arabic-Islamic term 'the people who loosen and bind' (*ahl al-ḥall wa-l-ʿaqd*). Authors like Abdallah al-Hamid argue that past interpretations of these two terms which claimed that they designated the despotic rulers of Arab states are wrong. Scholars who have been equating 'those who have been entrusted with authority' with the worldly rulers ignore that the term appears in plural form in the Quran, and not in the singular form, which could refer to a ruler. In addition, they have been confusing the term with the Arabic word for guardianship over underage children, *wilāyat al-amr*, and have been drawing an inaccurate comparison between this kind of guardianship and the rights of the ruler vis-à-vis the people.[107]

Instead of assuming that 'those who have been entrusted with authority' are the rulers, one has to understand them as the trusted notables of a society, who have been labelled the 'people who loosen and bind' in Arabic-Islamic discourse. Abdallah al-Hamid argues that when the Quran speaks about 'those who have been entrusted with authority', it means a group of people who are the leaders of a community by virtue of their expertise, their social standing and their integrity. In his books he strives to show that this is not a novel opinion, but, indeed, the opinion of many Islamic scholars since the earliest times of Islam. Abdallah al-Hamid argues that respectable Islamic scholars like thirteenth-/fourteenth-century CE Islamic scholar Ahmad ibn Taymiya and twelfth-/thirteenth-century CE Islamic scholar Fakhr ad-Din ar-Razi agreed that 'those who have been entrusted with authority' are the 'people who loosen and bind' and that both mean the trusted notables of the community.[108] In one passage, Abdallah al-Hamid lists the true features of 'those who have been entrusted with authority':

> The [. . .] features of 'those who have been entrusted with authority': [. . .]
>
> 1. People of opinion, cleverness and vision, as well as knowledge and leadership; this is the original meaning.
> 2. People of altruism, consultation [*šūrā*] and loyalty to the community; this is an additional meaning.
> 3. People of special courage; this is an additional meaning.
> 4. People of integrity and righteousness in their actions; this is an additional meaning.[109]

In light of these features, an oppressive ruler can hardly be equated with the Quranic term. Instead, both 'those who have been entrusted with authority' and 'the people who loosen and bind' mean the notables and the natural leaders of a community, who are trusted because of their knowledge, their experience and their good character. They are to be obeyed in political affairs.[110]

Abdallah al-Hamid argues that in today's large, organized states, which are faced with complex problems, the 'people who loosen and bind' are a diverse group of experts with knowledge in different fields. Every field of knowledge has its own experts, and they are all included in the meaning of the term:

> The 'people who loosen and bind' are named after the knot that needs untying. [. . .] If it concerns a matter that is explicitly mentioned in the sharia, there is no problem with them being the Islamic legal scholars. If it concerns a matter of individual reasoning that is only known by the Islamic legal scholars, they are also the people who loosen and bind it. If it concerns a matter of individual reasoning that is only known by economists, the people who loosen and bind are the economists. If it is an educational problem, they are the people of education. They are also the construction engineers in their area of expertise, the technicians in technics, the physicians in matters of medicine and nutrition, or the people of politics, administration and society in political, administrative or social matters. Every group of people with expertise in a branch of knowledge is considered the people who loosen and bind in this area of expertise.[111]

All these experts belong to the group of trusted notables, who are the modern embodiment of the term 'those who are entrusted with authority'. It is wrong to claim that the term only means a specific group, like the closest associates of the ruler or the Islamic scholars. Instead, it stands for a diverse group of trusted specialists, who can contribute valuable insights in their respective areas of expertise and help the state solve specific problems in these areas.

In the modern Islamic state, which is based on an Islamic constitution, all these experts are gathered in two important institutions of the state, namely the elected council of representatives and civil society. Both the legislative council of representatives and the organizations of civil society bring together experts who are trusted by the people and who represent their opinions. They are the 'people who have been entrusted with authority', and the 'people who loosen and bind'. It is they who are to be obeyed:

> In the modern Islamic state, the best implementation of the concept of 'those who have been entrusted with authority' takes the shape of two basic institutions [*qālibān asāsīyān*]:
>
> The first institution: The council of representatives is the most important of them and directly linked to the concept. It is the apparatus which lays down the broad political plans of the state in domestic and foreign politics. [. . .] It enacts the laws which are applicable in the state. It comprises the important members of the people from civil society who are followed by the people and who are characterised as being the people of knowledge, cleverness, altruism, advice for the community, courage and integrity. [. . .]
>
> The second institution: The organisations of civil society are the collection of the opinion of the community and the summary of its thinking in one area. In this

case, 'those who have been entrusted with authority' are the associations, groups, leagues and forums as well as other organisations.[112]

In the modern Islamic state, the two terms 'those who have been entrusted with authority' and 'the people who loosen and bind' do not mean the ruler, his associates or a specific group of religious scholars, but the members of the elected council of representatives and civil society. Both consist of experts in various fields who are trusted by the people and who represent their opinions in the relevant field.

Like all theoretical concepts that the members of the Islamic civil rights movement use in their writings, the concepts concerning the relationship between the people and their ruler are not new to Islamic discourse. Indeed, they already have a long history of intellectual debates behind them. The concept of allegiance (*bayʿa*) is a case in point. In the 'classical' Islamic discourse before the nineteenth century CE, allegiance was primarily a name for the recognition of the authority of a person, but especially the caliph, by a group of powerful people. According to Islamic legal doctrine, allegiance also demanded certain things of the ruler, who had to remain faithful to the norms of the Islamic sharia. There was some disagreement about how many people had to participate in the act of allegiance and who these people were, but in general, the concept of allegiance was relatively stable. In the mainstream Islamic discourse of the time, the concept of authorized representation (*wakāla*) had nothing to do with allegiance. It was rather a technical term in commercial practice, which designated the relationship between an employing trader and his representative in a transaction. In general, at least since the eighth century CE, the mainstream of Sunni Islamic thought gave more attention to the rights of the despotic rulers than the rights of their subjects. Obedience to the worldly rulers was considered to be an Islamic obligation by many Islamic scholars. When discussing texts from this period, the Moroccan philosopher Muhammad Abid Al-Jabri sees 'a tendency growing steadily in Islamic writings throughout the centuries: one which gives priority to "the right of the ruler over the ruled", which entails "obedience" at the expense of justice'.[113] The tendency to consider it an obligation of Islam to obey the worldly ruler, regardless of his injustice, continued to influence Islamic scholars well into the twentieth century CE. For example, Wahhabi doctrine also states that ordinary Muslims have to obey their rulers and the religious scholars, and that this obedience is required by Islam.[114]

At the same time, there were always Islamic scholars who argued that the people, and not the ruler, were the real holders of power in Islam. The idea that allegiance did not mean the blind obedience to the ruler but rather a social contract between the rulers and their subjects can already be found in the writings of thirteenth-/fourteenth-century CE Islamic scholar Ahmad ibn Taymiya,[115] who is quoted very often in the books of authors like Abdallah al-Hamid. In the twentieth and twenty-first centuries CE, the view that the true meaning of allegiance is a social contract with mutual rights and obligations almost entered the Sunni mainstream, and it has appeared prominently in the books of Islamic scholars like Hasan al-Banna. For many contemporary Islamic thinkers, historical events like the election of the first caliph after the death of the prophet Muhammad are early examples of a political practice that identifies allegiance with a contract between the ruler and his subjects.[116]

Hence, with regard to the power of the umma and the interpretation of allegiance as a social contract, the members of the Islamic civil rights movement can easily rely on the contributions of past and contemporary Islamic writers who stood against the 'classical' mainstream.

The same can be said about the twin concepts of 'those who have been entrusted with authority' (*ūlū l-amr*) and the 'people who loosen and bind' (*ahl al-ḥall wa-l-ʿaqd*). Before the nineteenth century CE, the Quranic term 'those who have been entrusted with authority' was mostly seen as a name for the worldly rulers. For many Islamic scholars, the Quranic verse which includes this term was an argument for the obligation to obey worldly rulers. The term 'people who loosen and bind' was usually understood to refer to the powerful men in the capital of a Muslim state, who, together with prominent scholars, formed the political elite of the state. In early Wahhabi doctrine, the 'people who loosen and bind' were an important group whose task it was to confirm the accession of a new ruler to the throne. This interpretation was also adopted by Wahhabism. However, neither Muhammad ibn Abd al-Wahhab, the founder of the Wahhabi movement, nor later Wahhabi scholars produced a clear definition of who actually belonged to the group. In practice, since the first Saudi state on the Arabian Peninsula, new Saudi rulers were formally confirmed by the royal family and the most important religious scholars. Wahhabi thought has been especially adamant in its belief that the correct interpretation of 'those who have been entrusted with authority' is that they are the worldly rulers, who are, therefore, owed uncompromising obedience.[117]

Both terms acquired new meanings through their re-interpretation by the protagonists of the movement of Islamic Modernism in the nineteenth century CE. As they tried to describe European political systems to their Arabic-speaking audience, authors like the nineteenth-century CE Tunisian Khayr ad-Din at-Tunisi used the term 'people who loosen and bind' to describe the social and political elites of European countries and, later, the members of certain elected bodies.[118] Finally, the influential nineteenth-century CE Egyptian Islamic scholars Muhammad Abduh and Muhammad Rashid Rida argued that both 'those who have been entrusted with authority' and 'the people who loosen and bind' mean the same group of people. They are the trusted experts, intellectuals and leaders of a society, who are chosen by the people, represent their opinion and are to be obeyed in political affairs. This opinion has inspired many Islamically inspired political thinkers in the twentieth and twenty-first centuries CE,[119] among them sympathizers of the Muslim Brotherhood. When they refer to the two terms 'those who have been entrusted with authority' and 'the people who loosen and bind', the members of the Islamic civil rights movement obviously adopt the widespread interpretation of Muhammad Abduh and Muhammad Rashid Rida.

Thus, as in the case of other fundamental concepts that the members of the Islamic civil rights movement use in their theory, their ideas concerning the relationship between the people and their rulers obviously come from contemporary Islamic discourse. When they speak about sovereignty, allegiance or the people of authority, they mostly adopt ideas that have already been discussed in Islamic discourse and that are reasonably widespread in contemporary Islamic circles. As the mentioned examples show, their main inspiration seems to come from the authors of the nineteenth-century CE movement of Islamic Modernism and from contemporary Islamic political thinkers who argue for a state that is Islamic and modern at the same time. The influence of the school of thought linked to the Muslim Brotherhood is also obvious. The concepts discussed earlier show very clearly that, in terms of the underlying theoretical concepts, the members of the Islamic civil rights movement are part of 'Islamist' discourse, which includes Islamically inspired political actors like the Muslim Brotherhood and other thinkers and parties with a similar mindset. They also share their intellectual forefathers, namely the nineteenth-century CE movement of Islamic Modernism, and agree with them on many issues regarding the shape of the modern state and the role of Islam in it. They participate in this pan-Islamic discourse and readily make use of its concepts and arguments.

Individual reasoning and consensus

According to the Islamic civil rights movement, the members of the elected council of representatives and civil society represent the opinions of the people, and they do so by virtue of two additional concepts that are at work here, namely individual reasoning (*iğtihād*) and consensus (*iğmāʿ*). When the members of the council of representatives are confronted with a problem and devise a political solution for it, they practice individual reasoning. Originally, the term designated a rigorously regulated tool for Islamic legal scholars, which enabled them to give rulings in matters where the primary sources of Islam did not contain explicit rules. When there were no clear instructions in the Quran or the hadith, the legal scholar could devise his own ruling, provided it stayed inside the framework of the rules of the sharia. In the political theory of the Islamo-reformist current, the term individual reasoning also applies to the process of political decision-making. In worldly matters, the primary sources of Islam only contain general principles. When the representatives of the people take them and implement them according to their needs, they practice individual reasoning. Every expert does this in his area of expertise. When a legal expert, a social scientist or an agricultural expert seeks to find feasible solutions to contemporary problems, they rely on individual reasoning.[120] For the state to be successful, it has to give all experts the opportunity to practise individual reasoning in their relevant field.

If everything works as it should in the modern Islamic state, the individual reasoning of the trusted experts in the council of representatives will produce consensus (*iğmāʿ*). Because the members of the council of representatives are elected by the people, they represent popular opinion. If they take a decision by majority, it can be assumed that this particular decision is supported by the majority of the people. The members of the elected council of representatives embody the consensus of the people. In one of his books, Abdallah al-Hamid argues that there are two kinds of consensus. Special consensus is the consensus of the scholars of a particular field, while general consensus is the name for the public opinion that appears in the decisions of the council of representatives:

> The scholars of the fundamentals [of Islamic jurisprudence] have spoken of two issues with regard to the argument of the consensus, namely general consensus

> and special consensus. General consensus is the consensus of the community in general affairs of politics, economics, administration and trade. [. . .] This consensus is usually found through the notables, who are trusted by the groups of the people and chosen to represent them. [. . .] They embody the principle of the 'people who loosen and bind', as Muhammad Abduh, Muhammad Rashid Rida, Hasan al-Banna and Muhammad Diya ar-Rayyis have concluded. The special consensus is the consensus of those who practice individual reasoning in any science or any area of expertise, like the consensus of the Islamic legal scholars, the consensus of the hadith scholars, the consensus of the scholars of the fundamentals of Islamic jurisprudence, the consensus of the grammarians, the consensus of the political scientists, the consensus of the physicians and the consensus of the economists. [. . .]
>
> The consensus of the community is the whole point. It is one of the principles of sharia politics. The hadith clearly speaks about the authority of the majority of the community in the saying [of the prophet Muhammad], peace be upon him: 'Follow the greatest majority.'[121]

Abdallah al-Hamid refers to the influential nineteenth- and twentieth-century CE scholars Muhammad Abduh (1849–1905 CE), Muhammad Rashid Rida (1865–1935 CE), Hasan al-Banna (1906–49 CE) and Muhammad ar-Rayyis (1912–77 CE), arguing that they were right to place great emphasis on the consensus of the trusted representatives of the people. Because the elected members of the council of representatives embody public opinion, their consensus will always agree with the consensus of the people. The council of representatives is where the general consensus of the people comes to light.

This consensus is important, not only because it enhances the legitimacy of the political decisions, but also because general consensus is a sure way of finding truth. Authors like Abdallah al-Hamid argue that the general consensus of the people is always right. The community is owed obedience, because, after the death of the last prophet, Muhammad, only the community as a whole can be considered a reliable authority. Therefore, the task of preserving and developing the norms of the sharia is not given to a specific group of people, but to the entire Muslim community:

> Islam defines the obedience to the ruler in the framework of obedience to the community [*umma*] because the community is authorised to preserve the sharia. Islam made obedience to the community a part of obedience to God, because it is the community who embodies the political consensus. It was authorised by God to protect the community and the state. Therefore, it is blessed and, in its consensus, infallible [*maʿṣūma*], because, as it says in the authentic hadith: 'It does not agree on anything misguided.'[122]
>
> The community is rightly-guiding [*mahdīya*]. Even if some go astray, most will not.[123]

According to Abdallah al-Hamid, the majority decision of the Muslim community will always be right. After the prophets, only the people as a collective body can be trusted to always produce correct results and make the right decisions. Remarkably, the members of the Islamic civil rights movement seem to ascribe an almost holy infallibility to the general consensus of the people. Therefore, making the people the ultimate authority of all political decisions in the state by installing an elected council of representatives is also a way to guarantee that all substantial decisions are taken in accordance with the norms of Islam. The majority is always right. As a result, a democratic system also becomes a tool to find heavenly truth.

The concepts individual reasoning (*iǧtihād*) and consensus (*iǧmāʿ*), which are important building blocks of the theory of the Islamic civil rights movement, also stem from Islamic discourse and have a long history of scholarly debate and various interpretations. In the context of Islamic jurisprudence after the eighth century CE, individual reasoning was a structured way of finding solutions to legal problems, used when scholars could not rely on detailed rules in the primary sources of Islam. 'Consensus' was also a term of Islamic jurisprudence and designated the third fundamental source of the rules of the Islamic sharia, after the Quran and the hadith. When the learned experts agreed on a specific point, it could be assumed that it was correct, and it could consequently be used in Islamic legal reasoning.

While both individual reasoning and consensus had mostly been technical terms that were relevant for the narrow discipline of Islamic legal reasoning in 'classical' Islamic thought, their meanings were profoundly expanded after the seventeenth century CE. Movements that strove to bring about a renewal of Islamic discourse, like the Wahhabi movement of Muhammad ibn Abd al-Wahhab, often relied on the concept of individual reasoning to break the dominance of long-established traditions. They argued that, instead of imitating the wrong traditions of their forefathers, they had to apply their own reasoning in order to re-create the original spirit of Islam. In the nineteenth and twentieth centuries CE, Islamic Modernist authors like the Egyptian Muhammad Abduh and the Indian Muhammad Iqbal expanded the meaning of individual reasoning and consensus beyond the area of religious thinking. They linked the two terms to the democratic system of shura rule and argued that the terms explained how the norms of the Islamic sharia were to be implemented in the modern Islamic state. According to Abduh and Iqbal, the modern Islamic state needed to establish an elected council of representatives, whose members would practice individual reasoning in order to solve today's problems. They would embody the consensus of the people, whom they represent. In their theories, a collective democratic body became the institutionalization of individual reasoning and consensus in the modern state. Individual reasoning was the name given to the attempts of modern Muslims to solve the problems of modernity within the framework of Islam.[124]

This broad interpretation of the two terms has become a widespread idea among many twentieth- and twenty-first-century CE Islamic authors who think about how best to combine Islam and the benefits of modernity. It can be found in the writings of the Egyptian-Qatari Islamic scholar Yusuf al-Qaradawi,[125] the Sudanese Islamic scholar and politician Hasan at-Turabi[126] and the Tunisian Islamic scholar and politician Rashid al-Ghannouchi,[127] all of whom also argue that Islam calls for democracy. Indeed, the idea that the Islamic concept of shura stands for democracy is obviously closely linked to this interpretation of individual reasoning and consensus. It is also present in the books of contemporary Egyptian scholars and activists, like the founder of the Egyptian Wasat party, Abu al-Ala Madi (*Abū l-A'lā Māḍī*, b. 1958 CE),[128] and in the programmes of Islamically inspired parties, for example, in Morocco.[129] It seems that it has become somewhat of a consensus among Islamically inspired political thinkers in several Muslim countries. The members of the Islamic civil rights movement obviously adopt this interpretation and use it in their own theory in order to give democratic decision-making an Islamic foundation.

Freedom of thought and difference of opinion

In their writings, the members of the Islamic civil rights movement often emphasize the importance of freedom of opinion, and their view on this concept is framed by a few basic ideas that link it to Islam. In his books, Abdallah al-Hamid repeatedly argues that freedom of opinion and pluralism are protected in Islam, and that they even belong to the fundamental values of Islamic doctrine. In his book *Middle path Salafism*, he is especially explicit about this point, as the following passages show:

> Fighting for defending the freedom of individual reasoning with regard to opinion and expression is part of Islamic doctrine [*'aqīda*].[130]
>
> The principle of freedom, pluralism and tolerance belongs to the pillars of Islamic doctrine [*'aqīda*].[131]

According to Abdallah al-Hamid, Islam demands that the people are allowed to form their own opinion and express it. What is more, this is not merely a right but an obligation. God equipped humans with reason. Every man and woman is able to think for himself or herself and has all the necessary intellectual abilities to try to make sense of the world. This includes the revelation of Islam. Abdallah al-Hamid argues that everyone has the obligation to try to understand the rulings of Islam according to his or her abilities. Interpreting religion is not the remit of religious scholars alone. Everyone must think for himself and it is even forbidden to blindly follow a scholar without testing his arguments first. Individual reasoning (*iğtihād*) is a duty for everyone:

> It is the right of every individual or group to understand the revelation according to their abilities and it is their right to make mistakes and innovate, without exaggerations, extremism or declaring others unbelievers [*takfīr*].[132]
>
> Truth is known through argument [*dalīl*] and proof [*burhān*], not through the saying of this or that individual. [. . .] Therefore, the clever scholars of Islamic jurisprudence made it an obligation for every able Muslim to perform individual reasoning [*iğtihād*] in affairs of his religion, and especially in fundamental questions. He is not allowed to imitate others.[133]

Interpreting the teachings of Islam is an obligation for everyone and not just a group of clerics or scholars. The believers even have the right to make mistakes in their individual attempts to understand Islam, as long as they do not resort to extremist arguments.

Abdallah al-Hamid argues that the veracity of an opinion should be determined by a neutral testing of arguments and proofs, and that Islam calls for a free exchange of opinions. No one should accept an opinion, if the underlying arguments do not convince him or her. Abdallah al-Hamid emphasizes that one has to critically assess the opinions of past Islamic scholars and schools instead of following them because of their perceived reputation and authority. An eclectic approach, which takes from different schools what is convincing and leaves what is not, is better than blind partisanship. Abdallah al-Hamid criticizes the widespread 'school mentality' (*maḏhabīya* or *tamaḏhub*), which defends all the positions of representatives of one's own school, simply because they belong to the same school. What counts is individual reasoning and not the perceived authority of a school. Only a free exchange of rational arguments which is dominated by pluralism is able to produce correct results and to eliminate falsehoods.[134]

Such an open exchange of arguments necessarily leads to differences of opinion. According to Abdallah al-Hamid, this is not a problem, because Islam allows, and even endorses, the existence of differences of opinion:

> As long as Islam allows individual reasoning [*iǧtihād*], it allows difference of opinion [*iḫtilāf*].[135]

Abdallah al-Hamid seems to argue that, because Islam calls on everyone to think for themselves, differences of opinion naturally follow, and that they are a good thing. However, he does not discuss this particular point in detail. This leaves some questions unanswered, for instance how far these differences of opinion are allowed to extend. It is unclear whether Islam's endorsement of differences of opinion also includes differences about fundamental principles of Islam, or whether Islam sets certain limits to this open debate. Nevertheless, according to Abdallah al-Hamid, differences of opinion are allowed and even encouraged in Islam.

The authors of the Islamic civil rights movement, and of the broader Islamo-reformist current in general, often refer to practical examples from the early times of Islam to illustrate that differences of opinion were allowed back then. One prominent example is the way the fourth caliph Ali ibn Abi Talib treated the breakaway sect of the Kharijites in the seventh century CE. The Kharijites had refused to acknowledge the leadership of Ali and had later revolted against him. Abdallah al-Hamid and others argue that Ali fought against them only after they had attacked him and his representatives. As long as they only disagreed with his leadership, he left them alone:

> One of the signs of the exaggeration [of the Kharijites] was that they considered everyone who violated the Quran by a wrongful act or opinion someone who committed a grave sin, and for them, someone who committed a grave sin was an unbeliever [*kāfir*], like Ibn Taymiya mentions in his fatwas. Building on this principle, they declared [the caliphs] Uthman and Ali unbelievers, just like they declared the people of the so-called Battle of the Camel [between Ali and a rebellious faction] and the arbitration, and everyone who accepted the arbitration

> unbelievers. [. . .] How did Ali treat them? He said to them: 'You have three [rights] with us, as long as you are friendly: We will not exclude you from the mosques of God, so that you mention His name in them. We will not exclude you from the spoils of war, as long as your hands are with our hands, and we will not fight against you until you attack us.' This was mentioned by at-Tabari in his history. [. . .] Everyone who only interprets [Islam differently] has not left Islam, and they did not suppress them or deprive them of their civil rights.[136]

The example of Ali's treatment of the Kharijites is complex, because, in the eyes of Abdallah al-Hamid, it illustrates both the wrong and the correct view on freedom of opinion in Islam. The Kharijites embody the wrong view. For them, only those who flawlessly adhere to the rules of Islam as they understand them are real Muslims. Anyone who endorses ideas or developments that they deem un-Islamic, in contrast, loses the benefit of being Muslims, no matter what they actually believe in. This leads to the extreme position that even the two Rightly Guided Caliphs Uthman and Ali were considered unbelievers. In addition to this, they also accused anyone who supported the arbitration that was meant to end the armed conflict between Ali and the Umayyad dynasty during the so-called First Fitna between 656 and 661 CE of unbelief. Ali's treatment of these radicals embodies the correct view on freedom of opinion. Although they opposed him, he let them be and continued to consider them equal citizens of the state. He only took up arms against them, after they had started a violent rebellion against him. According to Abdallah al-Hamid, this is what freedom of opinion means in Islam.

The concept of freedom of opinion has been an important part of the Islamic debate in the twentieth and twenty-first century CE, and the ideas that the members of the Islamic civil rights movement adopt have already been discussed by other contemporary Islamic scholars. Today, the concept of difference of opinion (*iḫtilāf*) is used by many Islamic thinkers to argue for a pluralist spirit in the teachings of Islam. Influential Islamically inspired theoreticians and politicians like the Egyptian Muhammad Salim al-Awwa, the Sudanese Hasan at-Turabi and the Tunisian Rashid al-Ghannouchi have recognized that Islamic societies are pluralistic and that difference of opinion is a good thing.[137] The idea that individual reasoning (*iğtihād*) is an obligation for everyone, and that it means that every Muslim has to form his own opinion about the teachings of Islam instead of blindly following a scholar or a school, is also relatively widespread in twentieth- and twenty-first-century CE Islamic thought. Prominent examples of Islamic authors who have taken this view are the Indian Muhammad Iqbal and the Egyptians Muhammad ar-Rayyis[138] and Muhammad Ammara.[139]

However, there is no consensus on how far this freedom of thought is allowed to go. In general, the mainstream of Sunni Islamic thought has been arguing that Islam demands consensus (*iğmāʿ*) in the fundamentals of Islam (*uṣūl*) and pluralism in questions of details (*furūʿ*).[140] Therefore, the fundamental doctrines of Islam are exempted from the call to produce a plurality of opinions. They have to be accepted by every Muslim; otherwise, the person in question cannot convincingly argue that he or she is a Muslim. What exactly is included in these fundamental doctrines, however, is open for debate. Islamic authors like the Egyptians Muhammad Ammara and Muhammad Salim al-Awwa, and the Egyptian-Qatari Yusuf al-Qaradawi, have all argued, with varying nuances, that Islam sets specific limits to freedom of opinion. According to them, pluralism is something to be cherished, but only within the limits of the norms of the sharia and the rules of common decency. Questioning the truth of the fundamental doctrines of Islam, or leaving Islam altogether, cannot be justified by reference to freedom of opinion.[141] Thus, as in the case of many other concepts that the members of the Islamic civil rights movement use in their texts, their understanding of freedom of thought and difference of opinion is evidently influenced by the ideas of twentieth-century CE authors from countries like Egypt, Sudan and Tunisia.

Citizenship and the community

According to the Islamic civil rights movement, the people are the true holders of power in the modern Islamic state, and the words they use to speak about them also refer to complex underlying concepts. The two terms that are used to designate the people are citizenship (*muwāṭana*) and community (*umma*). Abdallah al-Hamid argues that citizenship is the foundation of all the rights that the people should enjoy and one of the principles that should be implemented in the modern Islamic state. Equal rights are given to all citizens:

> Citizenship [*muwāṭana*] is the foundation of rights. In its framework the values of pluralism, dialogue, tolerance, majority, shura and coexistence are formed.[142]

All citizens of the state have the same rights and obligations. Their ethnic, social or religious background makes no difference. In the state that truly implements the teachings of Islam non-Muslims enjoy the same rights as Muslims. Abdallah al-Hamid argues that this approach can also be seen in the political practice during the time of the prophet Muhammad. The prophet considered Jews and Christians who lived in territory controlled by Muslims equal citizens, and he acted against them only after they had attacked him. According to Abdallah al-Hamid, this approach had also inspired the so-called Charter of Medina (*ṣaḥīfat al-madīna*), a document that was drawn up after the prophet Muhammad had come to Medina and that guaranteed the rights and obligations of all inhabitants of the city:

> At the beginning, one has to note that Islam focuses on humanity [*insānīya*] as the source of rights and obligations and the concept of human dignity. It made this the core of citizenship [*muwāṭana*]. [. . .] In the era of the prophet [Muhammad] the Jews and the Christians were a part of the concept of the community [*umma*]. [. . .] The basis for being awarded rights in Islam is the humanity of everyone who lives in the motherland. Non-Muslims are awarded the same rights, as long as they do not fight a war.[143]

Dignity is conferred to all humans, and all citizens are equal. All belong to the community (*umma*).

At first sight, Abdallah al-Hamid's inclusive concept of community seems to contradict the widespread use of the word in contemporary Islamic literature, where it usually refers to the Muslim community alone. However, a closer look reveals that the members of the Islamo-reformist current use a multilayered concept of community. Community can refer to national belonging as well as religious belonging. The following passage from a book by the Islamo-reformist author Abdallah al-Maliki illustrates this point:

> [In the era of the prophet Muhammad] the Jews were given the right to follow their religion. They were a religious community [*umma*] with its specific religious and cultural characteristics, which was different from the Muslim community. However, at the same time they were a community that belonged of the political community in a broad meaning, namely the community of the state. This means there was distinctiveness in the religious community and integration in the political community.[144]

Community can refer both to the specific group of adherents of a certain religion (in this sense, there is a Muslim community and a Jewish community) and to the all-encompassing group of the citizens of the state (in this sense, the Muslims and the Jews form one large community). The concept of community that al-Maliki presents here is compatible with the use of the term by Abdallah al-Hamid. There is something called a Muslim community, and it is different from other communities that follow other religions. However, when we speak of the citizens of a state, everyone is a part of the large political community and enjoys the same rights.

The terms 'citizenship' (*muwāṭana*) and 'community' (*umma*) have different backgrounds and intellectual histories. 'Citizen' and 'citizenship' are relatively new Arabic terms that were created in the nineteenth century CE to designate the thing that European languages called 'citoyen' or 'citizen'. Before that time, the term had not existed in Arabic.[145] In contrast to citizenship, community has a much longer history in the Arabic-Islamic discourse. It appears in several passages of the Quran, where it usually designates groups of people who are bound together by a common religion. In later texts, it almost always designates the Muslim community as distinct from other religious communities. In Islamic political thought until the nineteenth century CE, non-Muslims who lived in Muslim states were usually called the 'people of protection' (*ahl aḏ-ḏimma*). In principle, non-Muslim communities, like Christians and Jews, were guaranteed the protection of the Muslim leadership of the state, but in return they had to pay specific taxes, such as the jizya tax (*ǧizya*), and they had to accept that the state was run in accordance with Islamic rules. During the nineteenth century CE, the meaning of the term 'community' (*umma*) changed. After a phase of lexical innovation, it became the Arabic equivalent of the English word 'nation' and the strictly nationalist idea behind it. However, the old idea of the Muslim community did not vanish and was still present in the term. This led to some degree of ambiguity. For example, when the protagonists of the movement of Islamic Modernism, like Jamal ad-Din al-Afghani and Muhammad Abduh, used the word in their texts, they were obviously aware of the different connotations that the word carried.[146]

Today, the majority of Islamically inspired political thinkers have accepted the legitimacy of the modern nation state. However, there is, and was always, a certain tension between the notion of national belonging and the notion of Islamic belonging. For example, the founder of the Egyptian Muslim Brotherhood, Hasan al-Banna, both called for a just treatment of all compatriots (*muwāṭinūn*) in the Egyptian state, including non-Muslims, and argued that non-Muslim communities were to be treated differently, namely as 'people of protection' (*ahl aḏ-ḏimma*), by the Muslim majority. In his texts, both concepts of belonging appear side by side.[147] Sayyid Qutb, another influential member of the Muslim Brotherhood, adopted a less ambiguous and much more restrictive stance, calling for the exclusion of non-Muslims from most benefits of the Muslim state, thereby privileging religious belonging over national belonging.[148]

The case of the influential Egyptian-Qatari Islamic scholar Yusuf al-Qaradawi shows that opinions can change over time. In his 1977 CE book *Non-Muslims in Islamic Society* (*Ġayr al-muslimīn fī l-muǧtamaʿ al-islāmī*), he adopted al-Banna's opinion and argued that, while everyone was a citizen (*muwāṭin*) of the state, non-Muslims had to be treated as 'people of protection' (*ahl aḏ-ḏimma*). This meant that they had to pay the jizya tax and had to acknowledge that the state was run according to Islamic law.[149] In his 2010 CE book *The Homeland and Citizenship* (*al-Waṭan wa-l-muwāṭana*), he took a more pragmatic approach and preferred the inclusive concept of citizenship to the concept of the 'people of protection'. All people had to enjoy the same rights, and it was no longer appropriate to refer to non-Muslims as 'people of protection'.[150]

Prominent contemporary Islamic writers like the Egyptians Muhammad Ammara, Muhammad Salim al-Awwa, Tariq al-Bishri (*Ṭāriq al-Bišrī*) and Fahmi Huwaydi (*Fahmī Huwaidī*) all agree that, while the contract of protection for non-Muslims in the Muslim state was valuable in the past, the modern Islamic state no longer needs it. Instead, the equal rights of all citizens, Muslims and non-Muslims alike, are guaranteed by the constitution and functioning state institutions.[151] A similar argument can be found in the writings of the Tunisian Islamic scholar and politician Rashid al-Ghannouchi.[152] For many of the aforementioned scholars who argue that Islam calls for equal rights for all citizens, the Charter of Medina (*ṣaḥīfat al-madīna*) is an important point of reference.[153] The view that it embodied the principle of equal citizenship appears to be relatively widespread among Islamic thinkers who want to combine Islam with political modernity.

Thus, the concepts of citizenship (*muwāṭana*) and community (*umma*), again, show that the lively inner-Islamic debate about Islam and modernity is an important inspiration for the Islamic civil rights movement. Its members adopt many of the ideas and arguments that have been brought forward in the contemporary debate. In addition, the example of citizenship and community shows that many of the ambiguities of this debate are also present in their writings.

Civil society activism

The Islamic civil rights movement sees itself as a movement of civil society, and its idea of civil society activism rests on two interrelated Islamic concepts. The first is enjoining virtue and forbidding vice (*al-amr bi-l-maʿrūf wa-n-nahy ʿan al-munkar*), which is also called ihtisab (*iḥtisāb*) or hisba (*ḥisba*), and the second is cooperating for righteousness and piety (*at-taʿāwun ʿalā l-birr wa-t-taqwā*). The Quran mentions both and calls on the believers to implement them in their lives.

Abdallah al-Hamid argues that both enjoining virtue and forbidding vice as well as cooperating for righteousness and piety are Islamic obligations, and that they mean that Muslims have to support their fellow human beings in need:

> The principle of supporting the downtrodden is a principle with many implementations and means, which are absent from many Arab countries. The Islamic sharia affirmed the principle of cooperating for righteousness and piety [*at-taʿāwun ʿalā l-birr wa-t-taqwā*] in general and the principle of hisba [*ḥisba*] in particular.[154]

Abdallah al-Hamid argues that, despite the fact that the Quran made it an obligation for Muslims to encourage the implementation of righteousness and virtue in their societies, Muslims have largely been ignoring these duties, with catastrophic results.

The aim of enjoining virtue and forbidding vice as well as cooperating for righteousness and piety is to support people in need, eliminate injustice and promote justice and human rights. To achieve this, Muslims have to strive to bring their societies into line with Islamic teachings and encourage the implementation of Islamic principles, like justice. Both concepts are tools to make societies more Islamic. Because many of the norms of Islam concern the way societies are governed, both enjoining virtue and forbidding vice – or ihtisab – and cooperating for righteousness and piety are inevitably political acts:

> A word of truth, justice and good [. . .] is enjoining virtue and forbidding vice [*al-amr bi-l-maʿrūf wa-n-nahy ʿan al-munkar*]. There is no grater virtue than justice and there is no greater vice than injustice.[155]
>
> Ihtisab of power belongs to enjoining virtue and forbidding vice and it focuses on enjoining political virtue and forbidding political vice. The most important kind of political virtue is the establishment of justice, enjoining it and calling for it in writing and speech and by presenting opinions.[156]

In the eyes of HASM members Abdallah al-Hamid and Matruk al-Falih, striving to implement justice in society at large and make the political system fairer clearly belongs to enjoining virtue and forbidding vice. It is included in the great Quranic obligation to promote the values of Islam in society.

According to the members of the Islamic civil rights movement, enjoining virtue and forbidding vice is an obligation for all Muslims. No group of individuals can rightfully claim to have the sole right of performing it. No one has to ask for permission before they enjoin virtue and forbid vice. It is an obligation for everyone:

> Ihtisab of power in the area of politics does not need permission, like some Islamic legal scholars, like Ibn Taymiya, Abu Hamid al-Ghazzali and others have stated,

> because practicing ihtisab is a right of the individual and the group. It even goes beyond a right and becomes an obligation for everyone who has the ability to do it.[157]

Abdallah al-Hamid and Matruk al-Falih are adamant that working towards a better society that implements the norms of the Islamic sharia and its principles is the remit of all people and not just the ruler or a specific group of individuals. This obligation cannot be taken away by anyone and no one can claim that it is the sole right of a specific group, such as the government or the Islamic scholars. The Quran speaks to everyone when it demands that Muslims enjoin virtue and forbid vice.

However, since it is impossible for single individuals to tackle all instances of injustice and bring about justice in their society, people need to join together and form groups. Enjoining virtue and forbidding vice, and cooperating for righteousness and piety, require that the people establish groups and associations. HASM's founding declaration summarizes this thought as follows:

> Helping the oppressed in civilised societies with many inhabitants is nothing that single individuals who are occupied with their affairs in life can accomplish. No matter what his power, an individual cannot accomplish supplications and support, because his efforts are limited. Therefore, cooperation between individuals in matters that concern them has become a necessity of the sharia, [. . .] like God Almighty said: 'And that there might grow out of you a community [of people] who invite unto all that is good, and enjoin the doing of what is right and forbid the doing of what is wrong: and it is they, they who shall attain a happy state!' Those who enjoin virtue and forbid vice are made into a group, because this obligation can only be accomplished in a group. That without which an obligation is not accomplished, is itself an obligation.[158]

This line of argumentation is often used by members of the Islamic civil rights movement to argue that what they are doing is legitimate. Because enjoining virtue and forbidding vice is an Islamic obligation for everyone, and because it can only be done in groups, Islam requires that people establish civil society associations, like HASM. Civil society activism for rights and justice is a duty of Islam.[159]

Abdallah al-Hamid argues that Muslims should not reject the concept of civil society, simply because it appears to be a European and American concept. While it is true that the term 'civil society' was coined in Europe, the concept is not specifically 'Western', but a universal human concept. It is relevant for all societies of the world, and it was endorsed by Islam:

> The concept of civil society, which allowed the West to rise, is the way to progress in every time and place. The term civil society is a Western term. [. . .] As for the concept, it is a human, worldwide, civilisational concept, which was known by the people before Islam and which was endorsed by Islam.[160]

According to Abdallah al-Hamid, enjoining virtue and forbidding vice as well as cooperating for righteousness and piety are simply the terms that the Quran uses to endorse the universal human concept of civil society, which is known by all people of the world. Civil society activism, like the one that HASM wants to encourage, is legitimate, because it is justified by these two great obligations of Islam, and because it refers to a universal human concept.

The concept of enjoining virtue and forbidding vice, which the members of the Islamic civil rights movement use to argue for the legitimacy of civil society activism, is a contested term in Islamic discourse. It was already mentioned that both enjoining virtue and forbidding vice as well as cooperating for righteousness and piety appear in the Quran. Throughout the history of Islamic thought, most Islamic scholars agreed that they were obligations of Islam. However, the meaning of these two terms has been fiercely debated.

In the mainstream of Sunni Islamic thought until the nineteenth century CE the prevailing view was that there were different kinds of enjoining virtue and forbidding vice, or ihtisab, and that different kinds of people were responsible for them. Ihtisab of the hand, or actively intervening in public life to eliminate sinful activities, was the remit of the ruler and his representatives. Ihtisab of the tongue, or pointing out sinful activities, was the responsibility of the Islamic scholars. Ihtisab has also been an important element of Wahhabi thought. Since the time of Muhammad ibn Abd al-Wahhab, Wahhabi scholars and supporters saw it as their task to actively eliminate supposedly 'un-Islamic' elements in public spaces, and this was justified by reference to ihtisab. Since 1976 CE, the official government body that monitors the implementation of Wahhabi rules has been called 'Committee for enjoining virtue and forbidding vice' (*hay'at al-amr bi-l-ma'rūf wa-n-nahy 'an al-munkar*).

However, this institutionalized view on enjoining virtue and forbidding vice was, and is, not the only interpretation of the term. In the thirteenth/fourteenth-century CE Islamic scholar Ibn Taymiya already argued that the obligation of enjoining virtue and forbidding vice meant that all Muslims had to get involved in political affairs and work towards bringing their society in accordance with Islamic rules and principles.[161] The view that enjoining virtue and forbidding vice was an obligation for everyone, and that it meant that all Muslims had to cooperate to make their societies more just, was also endorsed by the influential nineteenth-/twentieth-century CE Islamic Modernist thinker Muhammad Abduh. Later, organizations like the Muslim Brotherhood were inspired by the same thought, and they argued that the obligation to enjoin virtue and forbid vice required grassroots activism in local communities and on a national level in order to encourage the people to follow the norms of Islam. The idea that the Quranic principle of enjoining virtue and forbidding vice means that Muslims have to be active on the political scene in order to bring their states into line with Islamic teachings has since become a crucial part of the vocabulary of Islamically inspired movements.[162] For some, it even acquired a potential for revolutionary mobilization. In the 1970s CE, Ayatollah Murtaza Mutahhari, who greatly influenced the Islamic Revolution of 1979 CE, argued that enjoining virtue and forbidding vice could also mean rebelling against the corruption of society.[163] During the Arab Spring after 2011 CE, Islamic scholars like the Egyptian-Qatari Yusuf al-Qaradawi used the concepts of ihtisab and cooperating for righteousness and piety to argue for the legitimacy of demonstrations against injustice and oppression.[164]

Thus, today many Islamically inspired political thinkers and activists, be they Sunni or Shia, share the conviction that ihtisab is an obligation for all Muslims, and that it is a call for political engagement in order to work towards a better society. It is obvious that the members of the Islamic civil rights movement share the instincts of all these twentieth- and twenty-first-century CE authors who understand enjoining virtue and forbidding vice as an obligation to participate in civil society activism. The view of the Wahhabi establishment and other Salafists that enjoining virtue and forbidding vice is the sole right of the ruler is firmly rejected by them. Instead of making ihtisab the responsibility of a government body, they see it as an Islamic call for political activism.

Islamic human rights

The Islamic civil rights movement presents itself as a movement that defends and promotes human rights (*ḥuqūq al-insān*). In HASM's founding declaration, its founding members declare that 'human rights and basic freedoms [. . .] are subject to grave violations in the Kingdom of Saudi Arabia'[165] and that it is one of the aims of the association to 'lay the foundation for an Islamic culture of political human rights'.[166] They evidently show a determined commitment to human rights.

However, it is not always clear what is included in their understanding of human rights. Detailed, authoritative lists or examples are nowhere to be found in the writings of the movement. Nevertheless, certain passages, like the following from a book by Abdallah al-Hamid, indicate the general principles that inform their understanding of human rights:

> One can define the basic rights of the citizens as being roughly ten: [1.] justice, [2.] equality, [3.] shura (popular participation in political decisions), [4.] freedom, [5.] pluralism, [6.] dignity, [7.] committing to the peaceful spirit and the solution of conflicts through dialogue, [8.] learning, [9.] security, [10.] ruling according to the opinion of the majority while guaranteeing the rights of the minority, [11.] enjoining virtue and forbidding vice, [12.] cooperating for righteousness and piety, [13.] harmony, and all other human rights which man knows by nature and which the sharia endorsed, before the modern states called for them.[167]

Most of the rights and principles that are mentioned here concern the form of government and the institutions of the state. They can all be classified as political rights. Many of them, like shura (*šūrā*), enjoining virtue and forbidding vice (*al-amr bi-l-maʿrūf wa-n-nahy ʿan al-munkar*), and cooperating for righteousness and piety (*at-taʿāwun ʿalā l-birr wa-t-taqwā*) refer to complex Islamic concepts that have already been discussed in detail. Political rights and civil liberties are obviously important parts of their understanding of human rights.

Something that they repeatedly insist on is that human rights are universal and independent from ideological or religious belief. Abdallah al-Hamid and others argue that human rights are known by all humans by virtue of their natural disposition or their innate nature. All people in all periods of history have known that man should enjoy dignity, freedom and basic rights. This is something that nature and their rational minds tell them. All that religions like Islam do is remind the people of these values and endorse them:

> Everything that is natural in our predisposition [*mā huwa fiṭrī fī l-ǧibilla*] is a holy right and belongs to human rights, because Islam, like any heavenly religion, is a religion of innate nature [*fiṭra*].[168]

Thus, human rights are universal, because all humans essentially know them, irrespective of their religious or cultural background. When Islam and other religions speak about human rights, they only remind their believers of values that they know anyway.

However, this does not mean that human rights have nothing to do with religion, and that they are, in essence, a secular concept. Human rights are a gift from God and protecting and promoting them are important obligations of Islam. Therefore, it is wrong to reject them on the assumption that they are foreign to Islam:

> When the word 'human rights' is used, not a few people think that it is a foreign concept, which was entered into Islam, and that it is linked to secularism [. . .] The truth is that human rights are not a secular concept, but the heavenly religions, and especially Islam, affirmed, endorsed and prescribed them.[169]

It was already shown that, for the members of the Islamic civil rights movement, Islam is the religion of innate human nature. Therefore, it makes sense for them to argue that human rights are known by all humans through their natural disposition, and that, at the same time, Islam endorsed them and made their protection an obligation of the Islamic sharia. Human rights are thus argued to be both universal and endorsed by Islam.

On the one hand, in texts like those mentioned earlier, the members of the Islamic civil rights movement argue that human rights are universal; on the other hand, other texts suggest that they are aiming for a specifically 'Islamic' form of human rights, which is different from 'Western' human rights. This call for specifically Islamic human rights can already be found in HASM's founding declaration:

> One of the reasons for the founding of the association is that a number of international organisations is influenced by the Western view on human rights and does not display the Islamic view on human rights [*an-naẓarīya l-islāmīya li-ḥuqūq al-insān*] in an effective manner.[170]

According to the Islamic civil rights movement, there is evidently a difference between the 'Western' view on human rights and the 'Islamic' view on human rights. The members of the movement explicitly say that they only want to promote the latter view and that they reject the former. The nature of this difference can be seen in passages like the following from one of Abdallah al-Hamid's books:

> The concept of human rights in Islam differs from the secular concept. In Western countries [*al-farangǎa*], their parliaments declare permissible what they like and what their attitude sees as permissible. They declare adultery [*zinā*], homosexuality [*liwāṭ*], the drinking of alcohol [*šurb al-ḫumūr*] and usury [*ribā*] permissible and these things are part of their understanding of freedom. [. . .] Truth is relative in the secular doctrine and what one people see as bad, the other see as good. Truth in Islam, on the other hand, is absolute. Everything which innate nature [fiṭra] declares detestable is detestable and forbidden, and everything which innate nature declares good is good and allowed.[171]

Abdallah al-Hamid strongly contrasts the supposedly natural 'Islamic' view on human rights with the supposedly unnatural 'Western' view. He argues that the 'Western' view allows things that are clearly forbidden according to the 'Islamic' view. In Abdallah al-Hamid's analysis, the 'Western' form of human rights is nothing short of radical moral relativism. Everything is allowed, and the people are free to do whatever they want, including violating the rules of religion and decency.

Adultery, homosexuality, the drinking of alcohol and usury are all considered grave sins according to many Islamic scholars from Saudi Arabia. Therefore, they cannot be allowed in the 'Islamic' understanding of human rights that the members of the Islamic civil rights movement want to promote. The same applies to equal rights for men and women, which are enshrined in international human rights documents such as the UN's 1948 CE Universal Declaration of Human Rights. Several texts by members of the Islamic civil rights movement suggest that they insist on different rights for men and women. The following two passages from texts by Abdallah al-Hamid and Matruk al-Falih illustrate this:

> The man of opinion [. . .] has to be in accordance with the rules of the sharia. This is the meaning of showing obedience to God and obedience to the Messenger. For example, there is no value in an opinion which says that suspicious mixing of men and women is not harmful in this age, that the woman has to be freed from the hijab, that she should be allowed to travel without a male guardian or that it is not bad if she is found in a closed room with a stranger.[172]
>
> Equality in principle between the people does not suspend the distinction between men and women because of the difference in their physical and mental composition. Therefore, there is a difference in some rights and obligations, like the Quran indicates in questions of inheritance, testimony and divorce.[173]

Abdallah al-Hamid and Matruk al-Falih obviously believe that women should not be allowed to travel without the consent of a male guardian, that women should inherit less than men, that their testimony in court should be worth less than a man's and that women should not have the same rights with regard to divorce. While these opinions are clearly not compatible with human rights, as codified in the Universal Declaration, they seem to be in line with the view of the Islamic civil rights movement on human rights.

The concept of human rights that the members of the Islamic civil rights movement use in their writings seems to be defined more by their strict interpretation of the norms of the Islamic sharia than international human rights documents. Their commitment to human rights is qualified by yet another 'sharia caveat'. Human rights are to be protected and promoted, but only if they are in line with the rules that are allegedly derived from innate human nature and the norms of the Islamic sharia. The specifically 'Islamic' character of 'Islamic' human rights seems to be that their limits are defined by the sharia. This ultimately clashes with the claim that human rights are universal and independent from religious or ideological convictions. In the end, the contradiction between the commitment to the universality of human rights and the call for a specifically 'Islamic' form of human rights is solved by giving up the claim to universality. According to the Islamic civil rights movement, 'Islamic' human rights are linked to human nature and universal, but this universality is exclusively defined by their interpretation of Islam.

The inner-Islamic debate about the relationship between Islam and human rights, in which the members of the Islamic civil rights movement participate, is immensely complex. Since the beginning of the twentieth century CE, the debate in Muslim countries went through several phases. Until the Second World War, the concept of human rights was met with distrust by the majority of Muslims, because it was mostly perceived to be a product of hypocritical imperialist colonial powers, who did not abide by their own human rights rules when dealing with the inhabitants of their colonies. After the Second World War, newly independent Muslim states began to actively participate in the human rights debate and they supported international human rights documents. For example, the 1948 CE Universal Declaration of Human Rights was adopted by the UN's General Assembly with the support of several countries with Muslim majorities. Saudi Arabia abstained. In the 1960s CE, the attitude of many Muslim intellectuals and politicians towards human rights changed again. Since then, there has been a tendency to create independent Islamic or Arab charters of human rights, which differ from earlier, universalist approaches. This trend culminated in the drawing up of separate documents like the 1990 CE Cairo Declaration on Human Rights in Islam, which was adopted by the Organisation of Islamic Cooperation, or the 1994 CE Arab Charter on Human Rights, which was finally adopted by the Arab League in 2004 CE. Both documents make strong references to the Islamic sharia as a framework for human rights.[174] The Kingdom of Saudi Arabia was among the strongest backers of own 'Islamic' human rights documents since the 1970s CE, and, according to some, wanted to exploit the term human right to legitimize Saudi politics and social values.[175]

Indeed, since the middle of the twentieth century CE, there has been a lively debate in Muslim countries about the relationship between Islam and human rights. This debate is part of the global discussion about the compatibility of human rights with different regional mindsets, which basically revolves around the contradiction between universalism, which argues that human rights are fixed and valid all over the world, and cultural relativism, which insists that the differences in cultural backgrounds must lead to some differences in the human rights that are valid in different societies.[176] It is hard to categorize all contributions to the inner-Islamic debate about human rights, and in academic literature there have been numerous attempts to summarize and classify the different contributions to it. Usually, these classifications make use of ambiguous labels and speak of 'Islamist', 'fundamentalist', 'secularist' or 'reformist' positions in Islamic human rights discourse, with different definitions and assessments of the compatibility of these views on human rights with universal human rights.[177] I argue that many of these categorizations tell us more about the personal views of the authors who drew them up than about the actual shape of the Islamic human rights debate.

In my view, the categorization of Mahmoud Bassiouni is most useful for achieving an overview of the diverse positions and opinions within contemporary Islamic human rights discourse. Bassiouni manages without ambiguous ideological labels like 'Islamist' or 'liberal' and instead focuses on the actual arguments that are made regarding human rights. He distinguishes between four argumentative strategies which have been used in the debate. They are called 'rejection' (Ablehnung), 'incompatibility' (Unvereinbarkeit), 'assimilation' (Aneignung) and 'harmonization' (Angleichung). According to him, the adherents of 'rejection' outrightly reject the concept of human rights, because the rules of Islam are considered superior. The supporters of 'incompatibility' argue that Islam and human rights are incompatible and that, therefore, Islam has to be rejected. Those using the argument of 'assimilation' attempt to appropriate human rights and believe that they must only be complied with, if they are in line with the norms of the sharia. They are those who argue for the need to adopt specifically 'Islamic' human rights charters, which emphasize cultural differences at the expense of the claim that these rights are universal. Finally, the supporters of 'harmonization' argue that there are no incompatibilities between Islam and universal human rights, because both speak of the same things, thus overcoming the contradiction between universalism and cultural relativism.[178] The debate is still ongoing, and all four argumentative strategies continue to be used by Muslims in this discussion.

As can be seen, the concept of human rights is being fiercely debated by Muslims across the Islamic world. The ambiguities that appear in the writings of the Islamic civil rights movement in Saudi Arabia are exactly the same as those that drive this extensive debate. Like they, Muslims in other parts of the Islamic world fluctuate between endorsing the universal character of human rights and insisting on a specifically 'Islamic' version of them. Through their writings, the members of the Islamic civil rights movement participate in this debate. In the classification of Mahmoud Bassiouni, the movement clearly falls into the category of 'assimilation' (Aneignung). On the one hand, they believe that the concept of human rights is meaningful in Islam and that human rights are universal. On the other hand, they insist that human rights have to be based on the foundation of their conservative interpretation of the Islamic sharia and that the rules of Islam have the last word on what human rights are. In short, 'Islamic human rights' are different from 'Western' or 'secular' interpretations of human rights. Gender equality is an area where this is especially obvious. In the end, compatibility with their conservative interpretation of the social rules of Islam seems to be more important for them than the universal nature of human rights.

Peaceful, civil jihad

One of the most interesting and novel concepts that the members of the Islamic civil rights movement use in their texts is that of political, civil, peaceful jihad. In declarations by the association HASM and in books and lectures by its members, it is frequently argued that peaceful civil society resistance to tyranny and injustice is a kind of jihad, which can be called 'civil jihad' (*ǧihād madanī*), 'peaceful jihad' (*ǧihād silmī*) or 'political jihad' (*ǧihād siyāsī*). These terms seem to be interchangeable and refer to the same concept. The basic idea is that peaceful activities like demonstrations, protests, lectures and lobbying can be considered civil, political jihad, if their aim is the common good of the community and if they are accompanied by an element of hardship and risk for those engaged in it. Peaceful jihad means actively resisting injustice and oppression as well as making personal sacrifices for the sake of the common good:

> Political jihad is a peaceful jihad. Its means are the pen and the tongue as well as standing together at demonstrations, strikes and protests. No revolvers or machine guns are fired and the people who wage it do not lift a whip or a stick. [. . .] It is in most cases an interior jihad. [. . .] Interior jihad aims at resistance against the inner breakdown of the community and its deviation from the right path, because the absence of the spirit of shura leads to oppression and oppression leads to servitude and subjugation.[179]

The aim of peaceful, civil jihad is to improve the political situation of the society one is living in and work towards the implementation of freedom, justice, real political participation and human rights. In fact, in HASM's founding declaration, its members argued that peaceful jihad is a guarantee for justice. If it is properly done, it necessarily leads to a freer and fairer society:

> One of the aims of the association is spreading the culture of peaceful, civil jihad, which is considered an authentic Islamic culture, because it is the guaranteed way to reach the state of justice, shura and human rights, no matter how long the path, how dense the sand of the desert and how winding its wadis.[180]

Peaceful jihad is the best way to eliminate injustice and to encourage fairness and freedom in a society. Without people who wage peaceful jihad, societies can easily slide into oppression, and injustice becomes a permanent phenomenon. Peaceful jihad makes communities freer, fairer and stronger, because it points to problems in the state and in the fabric of society, and it offers solutions.

The means of peaceful jihad include demonstrations, protests, strikes, collecting information on violations, writing books and declarations, holding lectures, educating the people and presenting reports and recommendations to those in power. All of these are classic means of civil society activism. However, not every civil society activity can be considered peaceful jihad. Some of the things that civil society organizations do are certainly legitimate and commendable, but they are not jihad. Many of them can be understood as implementations of the principle of enjoining virtue and forbidding vice (*al-amr bi-l-maʿrūf wa-n-nahy ʿan al-munkar*), or ihtisab (*iḥtisāb*), which has already been discussed. Both ihtisab and peaceful jihad stand for activities of individuals or groups that aim at the common good of society. The difference is that, for an activity to qualify as jihad, it has to involve an element of hardship and danger for those doing it. If someone is risking their life and well-being by selflessly promoting a cause, they are waging jihad. Simply protesting something may be ihtisab, but it is not civil jihad. However, if someone protests against something despite government threats to crack down on protesters, this activity qualifies as jihad:

> The word of good, truth and justice and the other peaceful means come in two kinds:
>
> The lower kind, the rank of ihtisab: In this case, a word of truth, justice and good is enjoining virtue and forbidding vice, and there is no greater virtue than justice and no greater vice than injustice, like sheikh Muhammad Abduh has said. But it is not jihad, because the element of hardship, danger and adventure is missing. It belongs to the lower rank.
>
> The higher kind, the rank of jihad: [. . .] In this case, the word is an adventure and it means danger. [. . .] In this case, the word and the other peaceful means become jihad. This means they belong to the higher rank.[181]

Thus, if an individual or a group takes peaceful actions for the sake of the common good of society and if these actions are associated with hardship and danger for these individuals or this group, they are waging peaceful, civil, political jihad. In these special circumstances, civil society activism such as that HASM wants to promote becomes jihad.

Peaceful, civil jihad is not the only form of jihad. In their writings, the members of the Islamic civil rights movement argue that there are different forms of jihad in Islam, and military jihad also belongs to them. According to their theory, jihad generally comes in two kinds, namely military war-jihad (*ǧihād ʿaskarī ḥarbī*) and peaceful, civil jihad (*ǧihād madanī silmī*). In one of his books, Abdallah al-Hamid speaks of the 'twin' of jihad:

> So that we Arabs and Muslims can rise, there is no alternative to renewing the concept of jihad, and there is no alternative to a discourse which confirms that jihad is a twin: military war-jihad [*ʿaskarī ḥarbī*] repels invaders and civil, peaceful jihad [*madanī silmī*] repels tyrants.[182]

Under the right circumstances, military jihad is an obligation for Muslims, just like peaceful jihad. In some situations, it can be an Islamic duty to take up arms and fight against an enemy. However, according to Abdallah al-Hamid, military jihad is only legitimate in cases of defensive fighting against an aggressor. In several of his books, he argues that military jihad can never serve to justify an attack on non-Muslims or an attempt to expand the territory of a Muslim state by military means. According to his understanding, war is allowed in Islam only if there is an aggression that has to be repelled. Only a defensive war is a legitimate war. If Muslims are attacked anywhere, it is a collective duty of all Muslims to support them in their fight against the aggressor. Thus, fighting a war can be a form of jihad, but only if the aim is to defend against an attacker.[183]

In addition to military action, Abdallah al-Hamid also mentions other civilizational activities that can be civil jihad, given the right circumstances. Spreading new interpretations of specific Islamic concepts, like jihad, educating the people about them and countering false interpretations can be considered cultural jihad (*ğihād ṯaqāfī*).[184] Industrial activities that aim at strengthening the capabilities of the Muslim community in the area of civil and military engineering can be industrial jihad (*ğihād ṣināʿī*).[185] If someone selflessly works towards strengthening the state's economy and enabling the state to provide a fair distribution of wealth, he or she is waging economic jihad (*ğihād iqtiṣādī*).[186] Scientific research and technical development can also be a kind of jihad, namely jihad of technical innovation (*ğihād al-iḫtirāʿ at-tiqnī*).[187] In Abdallah al-Hamid's interpretation of the term 'jihad', all these activities can be considered different forms of civil jihad, if they aim at the common good of the community and if they are accompanied by hardship and the risk of personal danger.

According to Abdallah al-Hamid, the different forms of jihad can be categorized into different ranks. The highest rank of jihad (*al-ğihād al-aʿlā*) includes peaceful, civil jihad to eliminate injustice and oppression as well as defensive military jihad to repel an attacker. Both activities mean that those engaged in them expose themselves to grave danger for the sake of the community. If someone brings sacrifices for the common good of the community but does not necessarily have to fear for their own safety, this is middle jihad (*al-ğihād al-awsaṭ*). Finally, actions that do not necessarily have an impact on society at large but change the personal environment of an individual can be lower jihad (*al-ğihād al-adnā*), if the individual in question has good reasons why he cannot wage other forms of jihad. They include things like caring for one's parents, if there is no one else to support them, or leaving public service jobs to protest against an unjust regime.[188] It is evident that Abdallah al-Hamid adopts a broad interpretation of the concept of jihad. Many different activities can be jihad, but they are not all on the same level. Only when someone puts themselves in danger for the sake of eliminating injustice or repelling an attacker their activities can be counted as higher jihad. Other forms of jihad may be commendable, but they do not reach the highest rank. The greater the hardship and the danger to oneself, the higher the rank of jihad.

Abdallah al-Hamid and other members of the Islamic civil rights movement argue that peaceful, civil jihad against injustice and oppression is the highest form of jihad and an obligation for all Muslims. It does not simply belong to the level of higher jihad, but its rank is even higher than that of military jihad, which is also a higher jihad. Military jihad is needed only in specific situations, namely if there is an attack by an external aggressor, and it is limited in time. It is the exception. Peaceful, civil jihad is a permanent activity. If people stop being engaged in it, the state is at risk of sliding into injustice and oppression. The benefits of peaceful, civil jihad are greater and more sustainable than those of military jihad. Successful civil jihad leads to the prospering of society. It produces freedom, justice and prosperity for the entire community, while military jihad only repels a specific external threat. Military jihad is an obligation only for able-bodied men, whereas peaceful, civil jihad also allows for the involvement of women and old people. Thus, peaceful jihad is more valuable and more important than military jihad in every regard.

Peaceful jihad is the highest form of jihad and an individual duty for everyone. It is an obligation for every Muslim (*farḍ ʿain*), no matter how many people are already engaged in it, whereas military jihad is only a collective obligation, which is considered fulfilled if a sufficient number of people have joined it (*farḍ kifāya*):

> Military jihad is a collective obligation [*farḍ kifāya*]. If a sufficient number of people do it, the others do not commit a sin [by not doing it]. Peaceful jihad is an individual obligation [*farḍ ʿain*], because as long as the citizens continue to cut the nails of tyranny, this is a safety valve. The participation of the people in demonstrations, protests, declarations, and in voting, nominating and being nominated in elections is a guarantee for their rights.[189]

Islam calls on all Muslims to wage peaceful, civil jihad. It is an obligation for everyone, and no one has the right to prevent people from doing it. Abdallah al-Hamid argues that people do not need permission to wage peaceful, civil jihad, because God has called on everyone to do it:

> Civil jihad, and especially political jihad, which demands shura rule, is an open jihad for everyone who is able to do it. There is nothing in the divine sharia, let alone human nature, which limits enjoining good and forbidding evil to one group alone.[190]
>
> The peaceful mujahid enjoins and forbids the ruler without humiliation or submissiveness, because God has authorised him directly [*allāh ḫawwalahu mubāšaratan*] to enjoin virtue and forbid vice. He is strong through this authorisation from the Lord [*at-taḫwīl ar-rabbānī*]. This is something which a healthy predisposition and righteous nature tell him.[191]

God has directly authorized all Muslims to wage peaceful, civil jihad, and he has made it an obligation for them. Peaceful, civil jihad is an individual obligation, which no one can shirk. According to Abdallah al-Hamid, all this again confirms that civil jihad is the highest form of jihad and that those who are engaged in it reach the highest rank of mujahidun. People who die while waging peaceful, civil jihad, for example, by being killed during a protest or dying while being unjustly imprisoned, reach the highest level of martyrdom. Those involved in peaceful jihad need more strength and perseverance than people involved in military jihad. The benefits of peaceful jihad for the community are greater because it enables the citizens to lead free and prosperous lives. Finally, two passages from the hadith clearly endorse peaceful jihad as the highest form of jihad:

> Why do we describe political jihad as the greatest civil jihad?
>
> Firstly, because Islam laid down a great principle, which confirms that the word is stronger than the bullet. In the authentic hadith it says: ‘The lord of the martyrs is Hamza ibn Abd al-Muttalib and a man who comes to an unjust imam [i.e., ruler], commands him [to do good] and forbids him [to do wrong] and is

> killed by him.' This hadith, which puts the speaker of the word on the same level as [revered 7th century CE Muslim military leader] Hamza, clearly indicates that the speaker of a word in a meeting is of the rank of the lord of the martyrs and not that of an ordinary martyr, if he is killed. [. . .]
>
> Secondly, in the textual arguments, it also says: 'The best jihad is a word of justice in front of an unjust ruler.' This clear text indicates that political jihad is the best form of jihad.[192]

There is no greater jihad than participating in peaceful, political, civil activities like demonstrations, protests and lobbying for the sake of justice and freedom, and doing so in spite of the hardship and personal danger that it brings. Thus, according to the complex theory of jihad that Abdallah al-Hamid, HASM's main ideologue, presents in his books and lectures, peaceful, civil jihad for basic rights and political reforms is an obligation for all Muslims and the highest form of jihad.[193]

Like many other concepts that are being discussed in the texts of the Islamic civil rights movement, the concept of jihad has been fiercely debated in Islamic discourse since Muslims started to think about the meaning of the divine revelation. Etymologically, jihad designates an effort to achieve a certain aim. The word appears frequently in the Quran. In 'classical' Islamic thought until the nineteenth century CE, jihad was mostly understood as military action, even if some traditions like Sufism also adopted other, more spiritual interpretations of the term.[194] While some Islamic scholars argued that it could refer to the struggle against one's own flaws or for the moral betterment of society, most books that dealt with the subject focused on military jihad. There was some disagreement about whether jihad was limited to defence against an aggression or also a legitimate tool to expand the territories of Islam by conquering non-Muslim states. Most Islamic scholars from the formative and post-formative period of the Islamic sciences leaned towards the latter opinion. In the eighteenth century CE Muhammad ibn Abd al-Wahhab, the founder of Wahhabism, also endorsed a military interpretation of the term 'jihad'. He justified the conquests that led to the rise of the first Saudi state by describing them as jihad for the spreading of pure Islam, that is, the Wahhabi interpretation of Islamic teachings. Fighting against people who practised Islam in a way that was deemed incompatible with this strict interpretation was considered compulsory jihad. Generally, in the Sunni mainstream, military jihad was considered an individual obligation (*farḍ ʿain*) for the people living in the immediate territory where the fighting was taking place. For the rest, it was a collective obligation (*farḍ kifāya*), meaning they were not obliged to join the fight if enough other people already had. So, until the nineteenth century CE jihad was overwhelmingly understood to designate military action, and military jihad remains an important point of reference for some today.[195]

The most radical contemporary theory of military jihad is the ideology of Jihadism, which developed in the late twentieth century CE. Its supporters were decidedly influenced by the twentieth-century CE Egyptian Islamic author Sayyid Qutb, who had endorsed jihad as a means to spread Islam. This meant explaining the teachings of Islam (*bayān*) as well as taking actions to expand its reach (*ḥaraka*). The action did not necessarily involve the use of violence, but military action was definitely included in his understanding of jihad. Qutb espoused a worldview that was based on a clear distinction between pure Islam and the rest. Ultimately, every system that was not in line with his strict interpretation of Islam was considered unbelief (*kufr*). The aim of jihad was to destroy unjust and un-Islamic political systems and expand the influence of the correct view on the teachings of Islam.[196] Qutb's radical view on jihad was rejected by the mainstream of the Muslim Brotherhood,[197] but it was further developed by Islamic scholars and fighters during the Afghan war of the 1980s CE, as thousands of Muslims travelled to Afghanistan to join the fight of the Afghan mujahideen against the Soviet invaders. There, the doctrine of Jihadism was heavily influenced by the Palestinian Islamic scholar Abdallah Azzam (*ʿAbdallāh ʿAzzām*, 1941–89 CE), who had joined the Muslim Brotherhood in Jordan and had later spent a few years in Saudi Arabia as a university teacher. In 1985 CE, he had published a fatwa titled 'The Defence of the Lands of Muslims. The Most Important Individual Duty' (*ad-Difāʿ ʿan arāḍī l-muslimīn. Ahamm furūḍ al-aʿyān*), in which he argued that the fight against the Soviet invaders in Afghanistan was a jihad and that Muslims everywhere had to join it. Azzam's theory of jihad was very similar to that of 'classical' Islamic scholars. The new element was that he considered it an individual obligation (*farḍ ʿain*) of all Muslims to come to the aid of the Muslim inhabitants who were attacked in Afghanistan. Jihad was no longer a collective obligation for the people who did not live in the immediate area of the fighting, but an individual obligation for everyone.[198]

In Afghanistan, a group of Arab fighters around Usama bin Laden soon developed another, more radical theory, namely that of 'Global Jihad'. It was based on Azzam's ideas but greatly expanded the scope of military jihad. The military jihad that Abdallah Azzam had in mind mostly relied on classical guerrilla tactics to fight the attacker. It insisted on a distinction between military targets and civilian targets, and restricted military action to the battlefield. The doctrine of 'Global Jihad' changed all this. For bin Laden, suicide attacks were a legitimate means of attack, and it was allowed to deliberately attack civilians and people outside of the immediate combat zone. Above all, bin Laden and the supporters of 'Global Jihad' no longer wanted to restrict the fighting to actions against a specific military force in a specific military theatre. For them, the adversary was a global coalition of enemies of Islam, who had to be fought all around the world. Terrorist attacks in European or American states were therefore simply a part of this global war between the enemies and the followers of Islam.[199] Since the 1990s CE, this doctrine of 'Global Jihad' has been the ideological foundation of the operations of Jihadist terrorist organizations like al-Qaeda or Islamic State.

The Jihadists' conviction that jihad only refers to military action is certainly the minority view among Muslims today, and many contemporary Islamic scholars and authors have focused on non-military, peaceful forms of jihad. Since the nineteenth and twentieth centuries CE, Islamic scholars and intellectuals have been increasingly understanding jihad not primarily as offensive war against unbelievers but rather as political participation in their own Muslim societies, and the members of the Islamic civil rights movement are obviously inspired by them. The nineteenth-century CE protagonists of the movement of Islamic Modernism, Muhammad Abduh and Muhammad Rashid Rida, still thought of jihad in military terms, but restricted it to cases of defence against an external aggression. According to their theory, this also involved resistance to colonial oppression in Muslim countries.[200] Inspired by Abduh and Rida, the founder of the Egyptian Muslim Brotherhood, Hasan al-Banna, created his own theory of jihad in the early twentieth century CE. According to him, struggling against injustice and striving to improve the conditions of the Muslim community through grassroots activism could be jihad.[201] The Pakistani Abu al-Ala Mawdudi, who founded the Islamic organization and political party Jamaat-e-Islami in 1941 CE, argued that jihad could also mean active political participation in the political system of the state.[202]

Peaceful, non-military forms of jihad remained the focus of many contemporary Islamic scholars, authors and politicians in the twentieth and twenty-first centuries. An interesting example is a speech by the Tunisian president Habib Bourguiba (*al-Ḥabīb Būruqayba*, 1903–2000 CE) in February 1960 CE, in which he proclaimed that the state's measures for economic development were nothing less than jihad. According to Bourguiba, they were even a great jihad and more important than the fight for liberation from French colonial rule, which had only been a small jihad. He argued that, because the fight against underdevelopment was a jihad, certain Islamic ritual obligations, like fasting during the month of Ramadan, were temporarily suspended.[203] Thus, for him, working towards economic development was a higher form of jihad than military action.

In the 1970s CE, Muslim activists in South Africa who were part of the anti-apartheid resistance began to understand their struggle as jihad. They endorsed both peaceful and non-peaceful means of resistance and some adopted a broad interpretation of martyrdom, arguing that also non-Muslims who were killed in the course of the struggle were martyrs.[204]

In the 1970s CE the influential Indian Islamic scholar Abu al-Hasan Ali an-Nadwi (1914–99 CE) focused on another form of peaceful jihad. He wrote a book titled *The Political Interpretation of Islam* (*at-Tafsīr as-siyāsī li-l-islām*), in which he argued that the most important jihad in those days was explaining true Islam to the people and restoring their trust in Islamic teachings. An-Nadwi made the case for an intellectual renewal of Islamic thought, and, in the circumstances of his time, this renewal could be called jihad.[205]

The Egyptian Islamic scholar and member of the Muslim Brotherhood Ali Jarisha (*ʿAlī Ǧarīša*, 1935–2011 CE) also argued for a broad interpretation of the concept of jihad. In his doctoral thesis, which was later published as a book titled *The Highest Islamic Legitimacy* (*al-Mašrūʿīya l-islāmīya l-ʿulyā*), Jarisha focused on the importance of the 'jihad of the word' (*ǧihād al-kalima*). For him, it meant pointing out injustice and resisting tyranny in a peaceful way. For Jarisha, this kind of jihad was an individual obligation (*farḍ ʿain*) for the intellectual elite, and a collective obligation (*farḍ kifāya*) for the rest. Active resistance against injustice by other, non-peaceful means was only the last resort, after the 'jihad of the word' had failed.[206]

Finally, in the 2000s CE, the Egyptian-Qatari Islamic scholar Yusuf al-Qaradawi described specific forms of charity work and civil society activism as 'civil jihad' (*ǧihād madanī*). According to al-Qaradawi he invented the term 'civil jihad' in the 2000s CE to designate the peaceful civil society activities of Palestinians who attempted to improve their situation under the Israeli occupation in Jerusalem.[207] Indeed, there are no indications that the term was used by an Islamic scholar or author before that. In his monumental 2009 CE book *The Islamic Legal Theory on Jihad* (*Fiqh al-ǧihād*), al-Qaradawi mentions 'civil jihad' as one of four kinds of jihad. The others are military jihad (*ǧihād ʿaskarī*); spiritual jihad (*ǧihād rūḥī*), which means fighting one's own evil inclinations; and missionary jihad (*ǧihād daʿwī*), which includes the spreading of the message of Islam. According to al-Qaradawi, civil jihad can take various forms, but it is always peaceful and aims at improving the general situation of the community:

> Here, we mean: The jihad that provides answers to the different needs of society, solves its different problems, meets its material and moral needs and allows it to rise in all other areas, so that it can take its rightful place. It includes different areas: the scientific and cultural area, the social area, the economic area, the educational area, the health and medical area, the environmental area and the civilisational area in general. [. . .] The obligation of this jihad means that we show effort and bear strain to teach the ignorant, give work to the unemployed, train the worker, feed the hungry, clothe the naked, give shelter to the homeless and treat the sick, as well as give everyone in need what he needs.[208]

Demonstrations and political activism are not explicitly mentioned in al-Qaradawi's explanations. In his theory of jihad, 'civil jihad' seems to designate charity work more than peaceful resistance. 'Civil jihad' means making an effort for the common good of the community despite the difficulties and the hardship that can come with it. Peaceful resistance and demonstrations do not seem to automatically fall into this category. In fact, in other texts by al-Qaradawi that explicitly deal with protests, the term 'civil jihad' is absent. Demonstrations like the ones of the Arab Spring have not been called civil jihad by him.[209] Nonetheless, the term 'civil jihad' certainly plays a role in the texts of Yusuf al-Qaradawi. He seems to have been the creator of the term and his interpretation of it influenced other Islamic thinkers, like the Tunisian Rashid al-Ghannoushi.[210] However, his concept of civil jihad seems to focus more on economic and social development than on peaceful resistance and political civil society activism.

It is obvious that many contemporary Islamic scholars have understood peaceful activities as jihad. However, none of them presented a theory of peaceful, civil jihad comparable to that of the Islamic civil rights movement. Authors like Abdallah al-Hamid are clearly inspired by some of the mentioned authors. They seem to have adopted their activist spirit, for which it is natural to argue that it is the obligation of Muslims to participate in public life and to actively improve the situation of the societies they live in. They also agree with many Islamic scholars and activists who state that the obligation of jihad includes many different kinds of peaceful actions for the sake of the common good. However, their theory of peaceful, civil jihad appears to be entirely their own.

A comparably coherent concept of jihad, according to which civil society activism against injustice is the highest form of jihad, cannot be found in the Islamic discourse before them. It may be true that Yusuf al-Qaradawi was the creator of the term 'civil jihad', and Abdallah al-Hamid hints at this in one passage of his book *The Word Is*

Stronger than the Bullet.[211] However, al-Qaradawi's theory of jihad does not provide the same theoretical foundation for civil society activism as the theory of the Islamic civil rights movement. Abdallah al-Hamid seems to have taken al-Qaradawi's term and the spirit that is present in the writings of Islamic scholars like the ones that were mentioned earlier, using them to create his own concept of peaceful, civil jihad. In

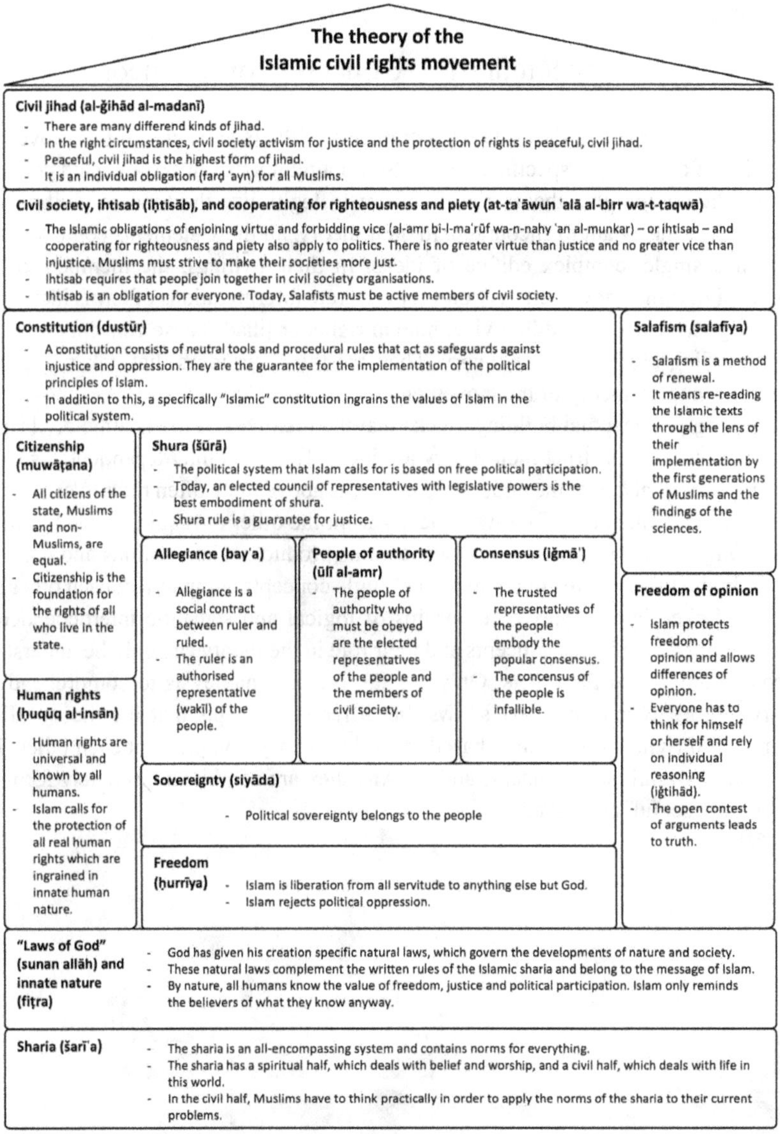
The theory of the Islamic civil rights movement
Civil jihad (al-ǧihād al-madanī)
- There are many differend kinds of jihad.
- In the right circumstances, civil society activism for justice and the protection of rights is peaceful, civil jihad.
- Peaceful, civil jihad is the highest form of jihad.
- It is an individual obligation (farḍ 'ayn) for all Muslims.
Civil society, ihtisab (iḥtisāb), and cooperating for righteousness and piety (at-ta'āwun 'alā al-birr wa-t-taqwā)
- The Islamic obligations of enjoining virtue and forbidding vice (al-amr bi-l-ma'rūf wa-n-nahy 'an al-munkar) – or ihtisab – and cooperating for righteousness and piety also apply to politics. There is no greater virtue than justice and no greater vice than injustice. Muslims must strive to make their societies more just.
- Ihtisab requires that people join together in civil society organisations.
- Ihtisab is an obligation for everyone. Today, Salafists must be active members of civil society.
Constitution (dustūr)
- A constitution consists of neutral tools and procedural rules that act as safeguards against injustice and oppression. They are the guarantee for the implementation of the political principles of Islam.
- In addition to this, a specifically "Islamic" constitution ingrains the values of Islam in the political system.
Salafism (salafīya)
- Salafism is a method of renewal.
- It means re-reading the Islamic texts through the lens of their implementation by the first generations of Muslims and the findings of the sciences.
Citizenship (muwāṭana)
- All citizens of the state, Muslims and non-Muslims, are equal.
- Citizenship is the foundation for the rights of all who live in the state.
Shura (šūrā)
- The political system that Islam calls for is based on free political participation.
- Today, an elected council of representatives with legislative powers is the best embodiment of shura.
- Shura rule is a guarantee for justice.
Allegiance (bay'a)
- Allegiance is a social contract between ruler and ruled.
- The ruler is an authorised representative (wakīl) of the people.
People of authority (ūlī al-amr)
- The people of authority who must be obeyed are the elected representatives of the people and the members of civil society.
Consensus (iǧmā')
- The trusted representatives of the people embody the popular consensus.
- The concensus of the people is infallible.
Freedom of opinion
- Islam protects freedom of opinion and allows differences of opinion.
- Everyone has to think for himself or herself and rely on individual reasoning (iǧtihād).
- The open contest of arguments leads to truth.
Human rights (ḥuqūq al-insān)
- Human rights are universal and known by all humans.
- Islam calls for the protection of all real human rights which are ingrained in innate human nature.
Sovereignty (siyāda)
- Political sovereignty belongs to the people
Freedom (ḥurrīya)
- Islam is liberation from all servitude to anything else but God.
- Islam rejects political oppression.
"Laws of God" (sunan allāh) and innate nature (fiṭra)
- God has given his creation specific natural laws, which govern the developments of nature and society.
- These natural laws complement the written rules of the Islamic sharia and belong to the message of Islam.
- By nature, all humans know the value of freedom, justice and political participation. Islam only reminds the believers of what they know anyway.
Sharia (šarī'a)
- The sharia is an all-encompassing system and contains norms for everything.
- The sharia has a spiritual half, which deals with belief and worship, and a civil half, which deals with life in this world.
- In the civil half, Muslims have to think practically in order to apply the norms of the sharia to their current problems.

Figure 10 Visual representation of the interrelated theoretical concepts (or building blocks) of the theory of the Islamic civil rights movement.

connection with other concepts like human rights and shura, this concept provided the theoretical foundation for the kind of civil society activism and civil disobedience that HASM strove to encourage during the five years of its existence. While Abdallah al-Hamid seems to rely strongly on other scholars and authors when he speaks about other concepts, the concept of peaceful, civil jihad seems to be his own creation. This part of the theory of the members of the Islamic civil rights movement seems to be the product of their own original thinking.

Interconnectedness – Concepts form a theory

The last few pages have shown that the members of the Islamic civil rights movement use a specific language, specific arguments and a number of interconnected concepts to formulate a complex theory that is meant to legitimize the kind of civil society activism that they want to encourage. In their theory, all these elements come together to form a single, complex edifice of ideas. In their writings, the members of the Islamic civil rights movement rely on very concrete interpretations of terms like shura, enjoining virtue and forbidding vice, human rights or jihad. These concepts form the basic building blocks of their theory. They are the basic ideas that, taken together, form the complex theory of the movement.

The single conceptual building blocks that the members of the Islamic civil rights movement use to construct their theory are interrelated and interdependent. As could be seen in the analysis of the underlying concepts above, they often refer to each other. One is based on the other, follows logically from the other or requires others to make sense. Only the combination of all the elements produces a harmonious and coherent theory. In the theory of the movement, the single concepts complement each other and they are linked by complex relationships of logical and semantic interdependence. The true meaning of these concepts and their role in the theory can only be understood in combination with the others. Only the full picture enables us to comprehend the theory. Figure 10 on page 161 shows the different concepts that the theory of the Islamic civil rights movement is based on and how they complement each other. The combination of all these concepts and the way they are combined ultimately form the theory of peaceful, civil jihad.

8

The limits of HASM's theory

The enthusiasm of the members of the Islamic civil rights movement for civil society activism, a constitution, a democratic form of government, freedom of speech and human rights is ultimately qualified by their insistence that all these ideas have to be in line with their particular interpretation of the rules of Islam. In Chapter 7 it has already become clear that, despite their claim to support universal human rights, their interpretation of human rights is characterized by a 'sharia caveat', which stipulates that only human rights compatible with their interpretation of Islam are real human rights. It is also obvious that, while they endorse democracy and a constitution in principle, they also insist that the Islamic sharia has to mark the limits of democratic decision-making and that the constitution they want to introduce is a specifically 'Islamic' one. Here, too, a 'sharia caveat' seems to come into play. In her discussion of 'alternative' Islamic human rights declarations like the Cairo Declaration on Human Rights in Islam of 1990 CE, Anna Würth has shown that this 'sharia caveat' is a common characteristic of many of these declarations and that it potentially leads to contradictions with other, universal concepts of human rights. However, the actual extent of these contradictions depends on the underlying interpretation of the Islamic sharia. The more rigid the interpretation of the sharia, the higher the chance that the 'Islamic human rights' that are based on it are incompatible with universal human rights as codified in international documents, like the UN's Universal Declaration of Human Rights. The more open the interpretation of the sharia, the higher the likelihood that it can integrate the concept of universal human rights without sacrificing either some of these rights or the claim that they are supported by Islam.[1] Indeed, this logic also applies to 'Islamic interpretations' of many other concepts, like democracy or politics in general. The more rigid the underlying interpretation of the sharia, the higher the likelihood that a particular interpretation of democracy that is based on it imposes heavy limits on democratic decision-making that openly contradict how the concept is being understood elsewhere.

Despite their openness to seemingly foreign concepts like civil society and democracy, the members of the Islamic civil rights movement ultimately endorse a very rigid, 'Salafist' interpretation of Islam, and this leads them to impose limits on politics and basic rights. Here, the limits of their theory come to light.

The limits of their concept of Islam

The Islam of the Islamic civil rights movement is a decidedly Salafist Islam, and it is hostile to large parts of the diverse history of Islamic thought. In recent years, authors like Shahab Ahmed and Thomas Bauer have shown that until the nineteenth century CE, the majority of Muslims turned to many different cultural techniques in their quest to understand the message of Islam. They did not only rely on reading the Quran or books of Islamic theology and jurisprudence. For many divine truth also revealed itself in poetry, philosophy, mysticism, the natural sciences or even activities that were considered sinful in Islamic jurisprudence, like wine drinking. The fact that these different activities and the knowledge they produced sometimes contradicted the truths of other discourses about Islam, like Islamic jurisprudence, did not seem to bother many Muslims, who continued to understand their being-Muslim as an explorative and creative engagement with the Islamic revelation. Contradictions and ambiguities were accepted, and sometimes even celebrated. Many accepted the simultaneous existence of competing interpretations of certain passages from the Quran without having to commit to one version. Differences of opinion were considered a blessing. Many Muslims saw no problem in writing poems about wine drinking and the sensual beauty of young men, while simultaneously accepting the authority of Islamic jurisprudence, which considered the drinking of alcohol and licentiousness sins. They obviously found a way to integrate these contradictions into their Muslim lives.[2]

While the majority of Muslims up until the nineteenth century CE obviously accepted that Islamic meaning could be found in different, divergent discourses, many 'Islamist' reformist movements since the nineteenth century CE have been trying to reduce Islam to one unambiguous discourse and eliminate all others. According to them, there is only one Islamic truth and it can only be accessed through theology and Islamic jurisprudence. Instead of studying the explorative experiments of mystics, poets, scientists and ordinary Muslims before the nineteenth century CE, only a reading of the primary texts of Islam and their literal interpretation are seen as giving access to divine truth. Salafist movements are particularly hostile to the complex, multifaceted Islamic discourse after the seventh century CE. Salafism wants to de-historize Islam and return to the seemingly clear and unadulterated version of it that was allegedly practised by the first generations of Muslims. They want to do away with the many complicated attempts of Muslims to find truth in mysticism, philosophy or poetry, and instead focus on the Islamic texts and their theological and legal dimensions. Only theology and jurisprudence count and there is only one truth.[3]

In this great pan-Islamic debate about how to find Islamic truth, the Islamic civil rights movement obviously shares the Salafists' aversion to the diverse and ambiguous positions that were created during the long history of Islamic thought. The members of the movement claim that they can reach unambiguous truth if they adhere to the primary texts of Islam and their implementation by the earliest generations of Muslims. What counts is the text and its implementation by the prophet and the Rightly Guided Caliphs, not Islamic discourse after them. The following passage from a book by HASM members Abdallah al-Hamid illustrates this:

> It is maybe best to understand [the texts of the Quran and the hadith] through the bottle of the implementation of the prophet [Muhammad] and the Rightly Guided Caliphs, because it is the standard implementation of religion before the centuries of religious distortion.[4]

Members of the Islamic civil rights movement, like Abdallah al-Hamid, argue that the message of Islam was distorted after the time of the Rightly Guided Caliphs. The Islamic discourse during the times of the Abbasid caliphs or the Mamluk and Ottoman sultans, which was characterized by a great openness to diverging ways of finding Islamic meaning according to Shahab Ahmed and Thomas Bauer, is outrightly rejected by them. They criticize the 'Abbasid form of the Islamic doctrine' for its lack of coherence and the many contradictions that are present in books from this time. They do not contain the pure and clear truths of Islam:

> What helps [. . .] is to remember that the Arabic-Islamic culture which we find in the mothers of the books of tradition and their children is not the pure, exact Islamic culture. It is rather the Abbasid, Mamluk and Ottoman form of Islamic doctrine and Islamic culture, which deviates into far-fetched, merely probable or outrightly false interpretations. [. . .] Islamic thought as a whole became vague and lacked stability and standards. It became fragmented and contradictory and lacked unity and harmony, because in the shadow of the fragility of the scientific background the text became an open text, which accepted many wrong and far-fetched interpretations.[5]

In order to return to the pure message of Islam, Muslims have to discard the long history of Islamic thought and return to the unadulterated Islamic texts and their correct interpretations that can be found in the Islamic sciences and Islamic jurisprudence. Only this way can Muslims really find out the truth about Islam. Alternative interpretations are simply wrong. Even if the members of the Islamic civil rights movement sometimes argue that the findings of modern sciences are a relevant source of truth, these findings always seem to be interpreted through the lens of Islam. In their texts, references to the sciences mainly serve to strengthen arguments that are primarily based on Islamic reasoning. Occasionally, they simply project *a priori* judgements onto nature, for example, when they claim that homosexuality is inherently unnatural.[6] In the end, there is only one truth and there is only one way to find it, namely Islamic reasoning.

The members of the Islamic civil rights movement are obviously not in favour of the ambiguity-rich history of Islam. Like many other Salafists, they want to eliminate the influence of the contributions of Islamic scholars since the end of the Rightly Guided Caliphate and call for a return to the perceived purity and clearness of the implementation of Islam before that. They are convinced that they can access the divine truth of Islam by re-reading the Quran and the hadith and looking at it through their implementation by the first generations of Muslims. According to them, taking the first generations as guides means returning to the pure message of Islam, which has been distorted by the Islamic discourse with all its competing, and sometimes contradictory, ways of speaking about Islam. The theory of the Islamic civil rights movement is clearly based on the Salafists' simplified and reduced view of Islam, which believes in an easy access to divine truth, if one simply discards the complex contributions of the Islamic discourse after the seventh century CE.

The members of the Islamic civil rights movement also seem to believe that Islam is not only a religion in the classical sense of the word but an all-encompassing identity, which permeates all aspects of thought. It was already mentioned that they insist that only an idea that is being argued for in terms of Islam – meaning in terms of a decidedly restricted theological and juridical discourse about Islam – is legitimate. Human rights are not to be protected, because they are the subject of international documents and charters, but because the legal rules of Islam call for their protection. It does not suffice to argue that a democratic system is more likely to lead to a just and stable society, but they strive to convince their audience that it is legitimate in terms of Islam. According to their fundamental understanding of Islam, it is an all-encompassing identity and the sole source of legitimacy and authenticity.[7] At the same time, it is a fundamentally theological and juridical discourse, which does not recognize alternative ways of finding Islamic meaning, and it is a Salafist discourse, which insists that Islamic discourse needs to be purified by removing these alternative ways, which can lead to ambiguity. This combination of mistrust of the diversity of Islamic discourse and insistence on the all-encompassing nature of Islam makes every thought subject to a potential 'sharia caveat'. If the Islamic sharia is the sole source of truth and legitimacy, and if strict Salafist theology and jurisprudence are the only way to speak about Islam, then everything is limited by the strict Salafist interpretation of Islam. As will be seen in the next chapter, this is especially visible in the area of politics.

The limits of 'Islamic politics'

The Islamic civil rights movement insists that only Islam determines political legitimacy. This is a relatively new idea in Islamic thought. Until the nineteenth century CE, the majority of Muslims thought about politics in different, divergent ways, which were not necessarily religious. There were always different discourses about politics in the Islamic world, and Muslims derived political instructions from several different intellectual and literary disciplines, which sometimes contradicted each other. Important premodern examples are panegyric poetry (*madīḥ*) about the necessary qualities of the ruler; 'classical' Arabic philosophy, which was largely inspired by Greek thought; and 'classical' Arabic historiography, as well as guidebooks for the heirs of rulers about the lessons of history. All these discourses were sources of political meaning for Muslims and they turned to them when they were looking for answers to political questions. Before the nineteenth century CE, Islam was not the only legitimate discourse about politics.[8]

The idea that other non-religious discourses about politics are irrelevant and that Islam alone determines political legitimacy was made popular only in the nineteenth and twentieth centuries CE. It was created by Islamic thinkers like the Indian Abu al-Ala Mawdudi and the Egyptian Sayyid Qutb, who argued that Islam was a religion and determined the shape of the state ('*dīn wa-daula*'). For them, there was only one legitimate discourse about politics, namely Islam. Suddenly, Islamic theology and jurisprudence had a monopoly on political thinking. Something was only legitimate if it could be shown to be justified in Islam.[9] The majority of Muslims before the nineteenth century CE would probably have laughed at the idea, but it has grown particularly popular among Islamically inspired political thinkers in the twentieth century. Many contemporary Islamic authors, who endorse it, have been insisting that the Islamic sharia – or their interpretation of it – has to mark the limits of legitimate politics. A prominent example is the Egyptian-Qatari Yusuf al-Qaradawi, who, in the 1990s CE, endorsed democracy and freedom of speech, but only within the limits of a strict interpretation of the norms of the Islamic sharia.[10] The scope of legitimate politics is thus defined by the limits of the Islamic sharia and 'Islamic politics' is considered the only legitimate form of politics.[11]

Despite their openness in some areas, the theory of the members of the Islamic civil rights movement clearly shows signs of such restricting claims and they set strict limits to politics. The multilayered and ambiguous political discourse of 'classical' Islamic thought, which found political meaning in several distinct sources, both religious and non-religious, is heavily criticized by the Islamic civil rights movement. It was already mentioned that Abdallah al-Hamid attacks the 'classical' Islamic discourse, or the 'Abbasid form of Islamic doctrine' (*aṣ-ṣiyāġa l-ʿabbāsīya li-l-ʿaqīda*) as he calls it. According to him, after the time of the Rightly Guided Caliphs, Muslims neglected the real political commandments of Islam and succumbed to un-Islamic political tyranny:

> The Abbasid discourse [*aṣ-ṣiyāġa l-ʿabbāsīya*] with its desertlike, pharaonic, sufi and sophistic trends, which have petrified the understanding of Islam in the spiritual half of the Islamic doctrine and have marginalised the political and civilisational half of the Islamic doctrine, has to be rejected.[12]

Abdallah al-Hamid wants to bring back the civil half of the Islamic doctrine and implement the political norms that are part of it. Other political discourses, like that of 'pharaonic' classical despotism, apolitical mystical withdrawal or 'sophistic' philosophy, are not considered legitimate. The study of history mainly serves to clarify the teachings of Islam. What counts is Islamic political doctrine. Thus, the only way to create a legitimate political order is by implementing the political rules of the civil half of Islamic doctrine.[13]

The members of the Islamic civil rights movement insist that the only legitimate form of democracy is an 'Islamic democracy'. In one of his books, Abdallah al-Hamid argues that democracy is a universal human practice and culturally neutral. Depending on the beliefs of the people who implement it, it can be secular, communist, Buddhist or Islamic. What counts is how it is put into practice:

> Western democracy is one of the principles of secularism and a branch of an ideology. You cannot break the relationship between the branch and its tree. This Western democracy can only be accepted by nations which have no roots, [. . .]

> because it naturally leads to secularism. As for democracy as a human tool in order to implement the principles of social and political leadership, it does not contradict any communist, Buddhist or Islamic doctrine, but it is in harmony with them, because it is like the clothes to the body. It is one of the guarantees of justice and the sovereignty of the community over its rulers and one of the political moral virtues. There is nothing which speaks against adopting it, if we are careful and limit it by using a specifying expression and say: Islamic democracy.[14]

Of course, the members of the Islamic civil rights movement want to implement a specifically Islamic democracy in Saudi Arabia. It is a democracy that is kept in check by the rules of the Islamic sharia and protects the 'Islamic identity' of Muslims. Thus, while the members of the movement obviously share the enthusiasm of many Islamically inspired movements for democracy, they insist that it has to be an 'Islamic democracy'. According to them, democracy belongs to the principles of Islamic politics, as long as it adheres to the rules of the Islamic sharia.

The members of the Islamic civil rights movement clearly show a tendency to restrict the options of legitimate politics by referring politics to the Islamic sharia. It was already mentioned that they view Islam as an all-encompassing system of values and norms, which includes rules for everything, including politics. What is legitimate in politics is determined by these rules. Islamic politics means adhering to the eternal rules of the Islamic sharia, which define the limits of political action. The following passage from a book by Abdallah al-Hamid about the 'Islamic constitution' illustrates this thought. The constitution can only be called Islamic, if it guarantees that the Islamic sharia marks the limits of political action:

> In order for the constitution to be an Islamic one, we stipulate two conditions:
>
> The first: The constitution is not Islamic, if it does not put the obedience to 'those who have been entrusted with authority' in the framework of obedience to God and his Messenger. [. . .] The power of the community has to be put into the framework of the absolute statements of the sharia, so that the constitution is the embodiment of the power of a community which adheres to the sharia. [. . .] Every law which the state enacts, and which is not sharia-compliant [*ġair šarʿī*] is not constitutional. [. . .]
>
> The second condition: Adhering to the absolute statements of the Islamic sharia in education, the judiciary and family affairs in particular, as well as in social affairs in general.[15]

Islamic politics means abiding by the rules of the Islamic sharia. The sharia determines in which areas the people may decide things for themselves. What makes the state Islamic is the guarantee that nothing can be decided against the sharia. The only legitimate discourse about politics is that of Islam. There is no politics against the rules of Islam. How restrictive this limitation is in practice depends on the interpretation of these rules. However, even with the most lenient interpretation, the fact remains that the highest political authority is the Islamic sharia. For the members of the Islamic civil rights movement, the ultimate yardstick of political legitimacy is Islam.

Chapter 7 has already shown the effects of this on the concept of human rights adopted by the Islamic civil rights movement. On the one hand, they argue that human rights are universal. On the other hand, they repeatedly insist that they want to protect only 'Islamic human rights' and that these 'Islamic human rights' are essentially different from 'Western human rights'. They argue that, whereas 'Western human rights' allow practices like homosexuality, these things cannot be considered protected under 'Islamic human rights'.[16] They also argue that 'Islamic human rights' do not necessarily include gender equality, because the 'natural differences' in the rights of men and women with regard to inheritance, testimony in court or divorce are not suspended.[17] Here, it can be seen that the members of the movement share a very conservative and rigid interpretation of the rules of Islam, which outlaws homosexuality and stipulates different rights for men and women in many areas. Because they believe that Islam is the sole source of political legitimacy, everything must ultimately comply with their conservative interpretation of the rules of Islam. As a result, the politics they have in mind are always potentially limited by their conservative views on social issues, and in some areas, like human rights or politics in general, they set very narrow limits to what is legitimate. The people are the holders of political power, but their decisions are limited by the Salafist interpretation of the rules of Islam. In the end, the view of the Islamic civil rights movement on human rights and democracy is essentially different from the view of supporters of universal human rights and liberal democracy.

Conclusion

The members of the Islamic civil rights movement are neither 'Jihadist' supporters of a violent political overthrow, which the Saudi government accuses them of being, nor 'liberal' advocates of universal human rights, which some of their supporters believe them to be. They are Islamic intellectuals who have created their own complex Islamic theory of politics and civil society activism, which is not truly grasped by either of these labels. In their writings, authors like Abdallah al-Hamid present elaborate justifications for their activism and argue that what they are doing is legitimate and, indeed, an obligation of Islam. They believe that Islam calls for the protection of the basic rights and freedoms of all citizens, that the modern Islamic state has to be democratic and that Islam requires the believers to resist injustice and oppression through peaceful, civil jihad. According to their theory, all these ideas are part of a contemporary, activist form of Salafism, which is able to rediscover the dynamism of Islam and inform a kind of politics that is in line with the Islamic teachings.

The Islamic civil rights movement is the product of the lively Islamically inspired Sunni oppositional debate in Saudi Arabia. Its main organization, the association HASM, developed in the context of the so-called Islamo-reformist current, which has been challenging the official religious-political discourse since the 1990s CE. As part of the broader Islamo-reformist current in Saudi Arabia, the members of the Islamic civil rights movement cannot hide the fact that they are ideological successors of the so-called Sahwa movement. Like the Sahwa, the Islamic civil rights movement combines the rigid theology and jurisprudence of Wahhabism with the Muslim Brotherhood's ideas on social and political activism. Like other intellectuals and activists of the Islamo-reformist current they fuse Islamic language with seemingly foreign concepts like democracy and civil society, and they use knowledge in Islamic affairs as well as knowledge in other scientific fields. They are inspired by Islam and by their knowledge of worldly things. HASM was not the only non-governmental organization of the 2000s and 2010s CE in Saudi Arabia that focused on the issue of civil rights. However, what sets HASM apart from these other organizations and other members of the broader Islamo-reformist current is the fact that they combined original Islamic political thinking with practical civil society activism. They invented the idea of peaceful, civil jihad for basic rights, and they directly applied it by waging peaceful jihad themselves. This is the main reason why HASM is not just another short-lived civil society organization in Saudi Arabia or one of many groups of the diverse Islamo-reformist current, but the main organization of a new movement, the Islamic civil rights movement.

The theory of the Islamic civil rights movement has been called a 'hybrid'[1] or 'post-Islamist'[2] theory because it allegedly fuses Islamic thought with the global discourse on human rights and democracy. However, in its core, it is above all an Islamic theory. Islam is the main frame of reference for them. Their texts breathe Islam. In their books, videos and declarations they use old Islamic diction and imagery. The arguments that they use come from the tradition of Islam. When they want to convincingly show that something is plausible or true, they quote Islamic sources or refer to the rules of Islamic legal reasoning. In their texts, they almost exclusively refer to Islamic sources, from the primary sources of Islam to 'classical' Islamic scholars and contemporary Islamic authors. Sometimes, they show a degree of pragmatic openness to worldly sciences, for example, when they emphasize that, in worldly affairs, Muslims can choose the tools of implementation that they see fit. Reason and the findings of the natural or social sciences are occasionally used as arguments in their texts, but they are understood in terms of Islam. Authors like Abdallah al-Hamid argue that what the Islamic revelation tells us to do, and what the natural laws tell us to do, cannot contradict each other. Because God is the creator of both the Quran and the laws of nature, they speak of the same truth. Studying the laws of nature and society thus becomes a means to confirm Islamic knowledge.

The theory of the Islamic civil rights movement rests on a set of interconnected concepts that originate in Islamic discourse. The members of the movement argue that shura (*šūrā*, 'consultation') means consulting the 'people of authority' (*ūlū l-amr*), or the 'people who loosen and bind' (*ahl al-ḥall wa-l-ʿaqd*), who are chosen by the people and represent their consensus (*iğmāʿ*). The people are the true holders of political sovereignty (*siyāda*), and the ruler is only their authorized representative (*wakīl*). The people have to enjoin virtue and forbid vice (*al-amr bi-l-maʿrūf wa-n-nahy ʿan al-munkar*) and wage peaceful, civil jihad (*ğihād madanī silmī*) for basic rights and political reforms. Most of these interpretations of Islamic concepts are reasonably widespread in contemporary Islamic political thought. The members of the movement adopt these ideas and integrate them into their own theory. Their most novel contribution is their concept of peaceful, civil jihad. It seems to be the invention of HASM member Abdallah al-Hamid, and a similar theory of jihad cannot be found in the writings of other Islamic authors from the past or the present. The members of the movement take all these concepts and combine them into one coherent Islamic theory of politics and civil society activism. They use Islamic language and concepts to call for reforms and help the oppressed. They mobilize Islamic discourse in Saudi Arabia for the sake of the downtrodden and for what they consider a just political system.

In their texts, the members of the Islamic civil rights movement show great intellectual openness in many areas. In this regard, they are very similar to other Islamically inspired movements that have been trying to fuse Islam with modernity. They are not afraid to adopt seemingly alien concepts that they deem useful and legitimate, like civil society and democracy, and integrate them into their Islamic theory, arguing that Islam requires Muslims to flexibly adapt some rules to their respective circumstances. In principle, this approach, which is not exactly new in Islamic political discourse, allows for the pragmatic and dynamic adoption of innovations and gives Muslims a role to play in rulemaking.

However, this openness ultimately turns out to be limited. The members of the movement insist that Islam is the sole source of political legitimacy and that only political decisions based on Islamic arguments are justified. Their underlying conception of the norms of Islam is also rather rigid and conservative. Like all Salafists, they believe that Islamic discourse has to be purified and that Muslims have to return to the supposedly unadulterated Islamic truth that can only be found in the theological and juridical discourse of the first generations of Muslims. The diverse approaches of Islamic tradition to Islamic truth are rejected. In the end, they follow a very rigid interpretation of the rules of Islam, and because Islam is the sole source of legitimacy for them, this interpretation influences many aspects of their theory. An example is their concept of innate nature (*fiṭra*). On the one hand, they argue that studying nature is a way of finding divine truth. On the other hand, their view on nature is obviously shaped by *a priori* moral judgements, which are informed by a particular interpretation of the teachings of Islam. According to Abdallah al-Hamid, all humans know certain values, like justice, by nature. But he also insists that homosexuality is against innate human nature and that natural physical differences between men and women must lead to different rights. What really belongs to the values of innate human nature is defined by a specific interpretation of the Islamic sharia, which not all humans on the planet share. Another example is their concept of human rights. On the one hand, they claim to believe in universal human rights. On the other hand, they insist that they only care for 'Islamic human rights', which are different from 'Western human rights', for example, insofar as they do not endorse the same protection of the rights of homosexuals or gender equality.

Everything appears to be subject to a 'sharia caveat', which stipulates that concepts like human rights, democracy or a constitution are only valid as long as they comply with the Islamic sharia. This potentially, but not necessarily, leads to contradictions between 'Islamic human rights' or 'Islamic democracy' and universal human rights or the concept of liberal democracy. Whether there really are contradictions ultimately depends on the underlying interpretation of the Islamic sharia, which is the yardstick of legitimacy according to the 'sharia caveat'. In the case of the Islamic civil rights movement, it is obvious that their basic understanding of the Islamic sharia indeed leads to severe limits on human rights and political decision-making. Despite their initial insistence on the universal value of human rights and democracy, the members of the Islamic civil rights movement ultimately seem to sacrifice their universal claim for the sake of compatibility with their very conservative interpretation of the rules of Islam.

In many areas the ideas of the Islamic civil rights movement are similar to those of comparable Islamic movements, like the Muslim Brotherhood, the Islamically inspired opposition in Iran or Islamic groups and parties from Tunisia to Indonesia. They adopt the idea, widespread in these circles, that Islam calls for democracy, the protection of rights and civil society activism. However, in contrast to many of these other movements, they see themselves primarily as Salafists and insist on a Salafist theological foundation of their theory. Indeed, they share many characteristics with other Salafist movements, among them the wish to return to the allegedly pure Islam of the first generations of Muslims and their very conservative stance on social issues. Like other Salafists they consider Islam a comprehensive lifestyle, which regulates everything, and the true identity of Muslims. They echo many common themes of

Salafist and 'Islamist' theories, including the feeling that Muslim identity is under threat by a secular cultural invasion. However, unlike quietist Salafists, who abstain from politics, and Salafi-Jihadis, who emphasize the obligation of armed jihad, the members of the Islamic civil rights movement focus on peaceful political activism. They are part of the political and modernist strand of Salafism, which includes political movements and parties in countries like Kuwait and Egypt. They call for political activism and for adopting some modern innovations while insisting on a Salafist foundation. In the end, their movement is a modern strand of Salafism. Salafism, and its specifically Saudi form, Wahhabism, were never clearly defined schools of thought and there were always ideological battles over their meaning. The members of the Islamic civil rights movement take part in the ongoing Salafist debate and present their own re-definition of the term, which combines the rigid worldview of Salafism with political activism and the spirit of modernity. They are a Salafist mutation. They are modernist Salafists.

Despite its inner contradictions, the theory of the Islamic civil rights movement remains a powerful contribution to ongoing debates in the Islamic world and beyond. It presents a possible answer to the question of how Muslims can lead a politically meaningful life in terms of Islam. It contributes to the lively inner-Islamic discussion about what Islamic concepts like jihad or Salafism can mean for Muslims today. And it is part of the wide-reaching, indeed global, debate about the meaning of human rights and democracy in a complex, globalized world. The Islamic civil rights movement in Saudi Arabia is a modernist Salafist contribution to all these discussions. It emerged from an ever-changing, mutating Salafist discourse. It is also part of a diverse trend of Islamic intellectuals in many countries, who have been attempting to fuse Islamic reasoning and identity with modernity, democracy and the discourse of human rights. This trend is not homogeneous, and statements about the Islamic civil rights movement are not necessarily applicable to other movements of Islamic intellectuals, for example, in Tunisia, Egypt, Iran or Indonesia. However, like other Islamically inspired activists, the members of the movement believed that they could be devout Muslims and support modern ideas about the state and how it should treat its citizens. Like other Islamic intellectuals, they competed with traditional conservative 'Islamists', violent jihadists, politically passive Islamic scholars, and the supporters of authoritarian regimes for the hearts and minds of the people. Although the story of the Islamic civil rights movement seems to have ended after the trials against its members, their imprisonment and the death of the movement's main ideologue, Abdallah al-Hamid, their ideas live on in these debates. It might well be that their Salafist theory of civil rights jihad will inspire others, who are confronted with similar questions, and that their ideas will mutate and evolve further as they are adopted and adapted by others.

Appendix A

Arabic original of HASM's founding declaration

The following is the original Arabic text of the founding declaration of HASM. It was published on 12 October 2009 CE on HASM's website. The founding declaration is a concise programmatic text, which gives an insight into the theory and the aims of the association HASM and the language they are presented in. Appendix B contains an English translation of the original text.

Source: HASM, *al-Iʿlān at-tàsīsī*, published on acpra .or g, 12 October 2009, accessible via http://www.acpra.org/news.php?action=view&id=1 (accessed 11 June 2020).

جمعية الحقوق المدنية والسياسية
في المملكة العربية السعودية
(الإعلان التأسيسي)

الرياض الاثنين 1430/10/23 (2009/10/12)

بســــم الله الرحمن الرحيم
الحمد لله رب العالمين القائم بالقسط والصلاة والسلام على أشرف الانبياء والمرسلين وعلى آله وصحبه واتباعه الذين أقاموا معالم العدل والشورى الى يوم الدين

أما بعد فان الشريعة الإسلامية جاءت بحفظ كرامة الإنسان وصيانة حقوقه ونهت عن الظلم، قبل أربعة عشر قرنا من ظهور القوانين الدولية التي كفلت حقوق الإنسان والتزمت بها الحكومات، كما قال تعالى (وَلَقَدْ كَرَّمْنَا بَنِي آدَمَ) وقال (وَإِذَا حَكَمْتُم بَيْنَ النَّاسِ أَن تَحْكُمُوا بِالْعَدْلِ) وكما قال في الحديث القدسي "يا عبادي إني حرمت الظلم على نفسي وجعلته بينكم محرما فلا تظالموا" (رواه مسلم والترمذي وابن ماجه وصححه الألباني، عن أبي ذر - رضي الله عنه -عن رسول الله صلى الله عليه وسلم)

أ=(ديباجة)
لماذا جمعية للحقوق المدنية والسياسية؟:
أولا: أهم دواعي إنشاء الجمعية أن حقوق الإنسان والحريات الأساسية ولا سيما السياسية -في المملكة العربية السعودية- تتعرض لانتهاكات خطيرة، وقد ازدادت هذه الانتهاكات منذ حرب الخليج، لازدياد وعي الناس بحقوقهم، وعندما ازداد وعيهم بحقوقهم زادت الحكومة بطشا على بطش، فساقت آلاف الشباب إلى السجون، بعد حرب الخليج الثانية، فعندما قمع العمل السلمي الذي تجلى بمذكرة النصيحة وخطاب المطالب وانشاء لجنة الدفاع عن الحقوق الشرعية ظهرت تفجيرات الرياض والخبر وعندما تفردت الحكومة دون تفويض ومشاركة من المجتمع بالسياسة والقرارات المصيرية على المستوى الداخلي والخارجي جاءت أحداث الحادي عشر من سبتمبر وتبعاتها.

واستمر بعض الافراد المتنفذين في النظام السياسي بالاستفراد بالمجتمع، ومواصلة الوصاية عليه، وتحويل القنوات الرسمية إلى جوقات، تزيف على الناس أسباب العنف الحقيقية ومكوناته الأساسية، وصارت تعالج قضايا العنف والإرهاب علاجا بوليسيا وتتجاهل العلاج السياسي، والعلاج أمر بديهي بسيط لا يحتاج الى كثير من الاستراتيجيات والتخطيط وهو أن تسمح للفئات المكتوية بالاحتقان السياسي وغيرها من مكونات المجتمع بإنشاء أحزاب وتجمعات سياسية، وممارسة نشاطها علنا، تحت شعاع الشمس والهواء.

فالقمع والتعذيب وانتهاك حقوق الانسان ومصادرة الحريات فضلا عن كونها ظلما كبيرا لا تضمن الامن والاستقرار وانما الذي يضمن الامن والاستقرار والازدهار هو العدل والاصلاح السياسي الذي يقر بسلطان الأمة وقوامتها على الحكومة، فقمع دعاة التغيير السلمي يرفع أسهم دعاة التغيير بالعنف.

ومن البديهي أن حرمان الناس من التعبير العلني السلمي يؤدي إلى لجوئهم إلى تأسيس تنظيمات سرية عنيفة.

ومن المعروف أن حركات العنف تولدت في السجون التي اشتهرت بالتعذيب الشديد، وزنازين التعذيب هي التي تمد حركات العنف بالكوادر، وهي بالإضافة إلى مصادرة الحقوق المدنية والسياسية تزيد الاحتقان، ومن ثم ينتج التمرد والاحقاد والتوتر، و الدوران في دوامة العنف والعنف المضاد

تكاثر الشكاوى من انتهاكات حقوق الإنسان، في السنوات الثلاث الأخيرة. وعلى الرغم من أن عهد الملك عبد الله بدأ بداية مبشرة بالإصلاح، من خلال إطلاق عدد من السجناء السياسيين، وأن الناس استبشرت بمناداته بضرب هامة الظلم بسيف العدل، وتفاءلت ببعض الخطوات كإنشاء هيئة حقوق الإنسان إلا أن هذه الإصلاحات تعثرت، وعادت أوضاع حقوق الإنسان إلى ما كانت عليه من انتهاكات بسبب ازدياد هيمنة وزارة الداخلية على شئون العباد والبلاد.

ورغم ضعف الأنظمة التي أصدرتها الدولة، في مجال حقوق الإنسان والمتهم والمسجون فإنها لم تلتزم بها، وقد كتب عدد من دعاة العدل والشورى وحقوق الإنسان؛ خطابات وبيانات سرية وعلنية، ولكن وزارة الداخلية اتخذت محاربة الإرهاب ذريعة للقضاء على جميع الأفكار التي تبرهن على أن أسباب الإرهاب الأساسية إنما هي سياسية، وتبرهن على أن علاجه الأساسي إنما هو سياسي. وقد تكاثر في الآونة الاخيرة الحديث عن انتهاكات خطيرة وصارخة لحقوق الانسان عامة والمتهم والسجين خاصة، وتداول الناس تقارير عديدة.

من هذه التقارير بيان المعتصمات في القصيم بتاريخ 2 رجب 1428 هـ الذي أعلن فيه أنهن أرسلن تقريرا-قبله- الى مساعد وزير الداخلية عما واجهه ذووهن من تعذيب جسدي ونفسي، كالضرب المبرح والتجويع والتسهير، واستخدام العصى الكهربائية وادخال رؤوسهم في حاوية النفايات، وإهانتهم بترديد أقوال نابية ومهينة وغيرها من صنوف العذاب. وهذا التقرير وأمثاله-إن صحت معلوماته - يوضح المعاملة القاسية، ويكشف بشاعة التعذيب في سجون المباحث العامة، التي يقال إنها وصلت الى انتهاك العرض والتهديد بإحضار المحارم وتقييد السجين وسحبه بالسيارة في فناء السجن حتى يكره على الاعتراف بتهم ملفقة لم يرتكبها.

وقد ورد في بعض التقارير أن بعض المحققين تجاوز كافة الحدود بسب الذات الإلهية وإهانة الرسول صلى الله عليه وسلم.

وقد أشارت بعض التقارير إلى أن الكثير من الذين تعرضوا لأصناف التعذيب القاسي كالتهديد بانتهاك العرض، أو الأفعال الأخلاقية المشينة يعانون من رهبة شديدة منعت الكثير منهم عن الحديث والكشف عن ما لحق بهم من أذى وتعذيب، و هذا يدل على أن ما ورد في التقرير من فظائع ما هو الا غيض من فيض.

ولا دخان من غير نار. ولكن السرية تحول دون كشف الاستار، والخوف يلجم الحناجر عن الشكوى، وأحيانا يتحرج المنتهكة حقوقهم من الافصاح، بسبب الحرج الاجتماعي، ورغم هذا وذاك فلم نسمع أن لجنة قضائية شكلت للتحقيق في هذه الانتهاكات

وقد واصلت الحكومة تضييقها على التجمع المدني الأهلي، ووأدت مشروع الجمعيات الأهلية، التي هي صمام أمان مستقبل البلاد وتجنيب البلاد خطر العنف والعنف المضاد. لأن إبقاء المجتمع بلا تجمعات مدنية أهلية فعالة، أتاح لوزارة الداخلية الإجهاز على البقية الباقية من حقوق المواطنين، وإشاعة الخوف والكئابة وسائر الأمراض النفسية الناتجة عن الكبت والقمع وقد أثبتت تقارير الدولة نفسها أن ستين بالمئة من الشعب السعودي يعانون من "الرهاب" (انظر جريدة الرياض 24/7/2009م)، إنها العلاقة الجدلية بين (الرهاب) و(الإرهاب) إذن.

ثانيا: ومن أهم دواعي إنشاء الجمعية؛ أن الدولة تقدم انتهاكات حقوق الإنسان السياسية بخطاب ديني محرف ظاهره تطبيق الشريعة، يزين للناس الجور والجبر وانتهاك حقوق الإنسان، ، و كثير من الناس لا يدرون أن

الإسلام بريء من كل ممارسة لوأد قوامة الأمة على الحكومة، وقمع الحرية والتعددية والعدالة وشورى نواب الأمة والتسامح، ولعل في الباب الأول من (شرح الديباجة) ما يوضح البون الواسع بين قواعد حقوق الإنسان على العموم والسياسية على الخصوص في الإسلام، وبين دعاوى الحكومة تطبيق الشريعة: دستورنا الإسلام.

ثالثا: ومن دواعي إنشاء الجمعية؛ أن العديد من المنظمات الدولية متأثر بالنظرة الغربية لحقوق الإنسان، ولم تبرز بشكل فعال النظرية الإسلامية لحقوق الإنسان.

رابعا: ومن أهم دواعي إنشاء الجمعية؛ أن ضعف وعي المواطنين بحقوقهم، يعرضهم إلى مزيد من الانتهاك والإحباط، وإذا كان سقراط قد حدد بداية وعي الإنسان بذاته، بشعار "اعرف نفسك"، فإن شعار الوعي بالذات الجمعية هو "اعرف حقوقك".

خامسا: ومن دواعي إنشاء الجمعية؛ أن كثيرا من المنظمات الدولية؛ التي تتحدث عن انتهاكات حقوق الإنسان في البلدان العربية، تتوجه إلى القضايا الفردية، فتوجه الأنظار إلى الاعتقال التعسفي، والمراقبة القضائية، والاختفاء والتعذيب. وهذه الأمور على أهميتها، تبقى اختزالية وتتناول قضايا تم حسمها في الغرب. وهي تهمل التوازن الضروري بين الحقوق المدنية والسياسية من جهة والحقوق الاقتصادية والاجتماعية والثقافية من جهة ثانية، فهي لا تصدر تقارير عن انتهاكات الحقوق السياسية والمدنية العامة، كعدم وجود برلمان، وعدم الفصل بين السلطات وعدم استقلال القضاء ، وعدم وجود جمعيات أهلية فضلا عن عدم وجود أحزاب سياسية، واختلال المساواة في توزيع الثروة، والطبقية السياسية، وعدم تداول السلطة.

سادسا: ومن دواعي إنشاء الجمعية؛ أن انتهاكات حقوق الإنسان والمتهم والسجين، تقدمها الدولة أيضا تحت عنوان تطبيق الشريعة، ولأن تشريع المحاكمات الصورية والسرية والقاسية كلها تجري في الظلام تحت لافتة الحكم بما أنزل الله ؛ ولأن التعذيب يبرر تحت عنوان حفظ الأمن، وجلاء الحقيقة، ولا بد من كشف بدع تشريع التعذيب والمحاكمات السرية، كما أشار الباب الثالث من (شرح الديباجة) المرفق.

سابعا: ومن دواعي إنشاء الجمعية؛ أن القضاء السعودي في نظامه المعلن -فضلا عن تطبيقاته - يجسد إخلالا صريحا مكشوفا، بالمعايير التي قررتها الشريعة الإسلامية قبل أربعة عشر قرنا من تواصي المنظمات الدولية بالمعايير الدولية لاستقلال القضاء ونزاهته ، كما فصل ذلك في الباب الأول والثاني من (شرح الديباجة) المرفق.

ثامنا: ومن دواعي إنشاء الجمعية؛ كشف تواطؤ أغلب الدول الغربية المريب، تلك التي تتشدق بإثارة ملف حقوق الإنسان، عندما تختلف مع بعض الحكومات ، أسكتها نفط الخليج، على طريق الشاعر القديم:

في فمي نفط وهل ينطق من في فيه نفط

بل اعتبرت سلوك المملكة في مجال حقوق الإنسان يرشحها، لتكون ضمن مجلس حقوق الإنسان، مع أن القضاء السعودي يتجاهل المواثيق التي وقعت عليها المملكة، التي أوجزت في الباب الثاني من (شرح الديباجة) المرفق بل إن قضاة المحاكم وقضاة التحقيق معا، فضلا عن غيرهم ينتهكونها انتهاكا صريحا.

تاسعا: ومن أهم دواعي إنشاء الجمعية؛ أن من أسباب استشراء العنف غياب قاعدة الجهاد المدني السياسي السلمي، لأن كثيرا من المثقفين لا يثمنون العمل في مجال حقوق الإنسان، فضلا عن الفقهاء والوعاظ، ولا يثمنون أنه في أعلى درجات الأمر بالمعروف والنهي عن المنكر، بل هو جهاد عظيم، بل صرحت الشريعة بأنه أعظم أو خير الجهاد كما ورد في الحديث الصحيح أن رجلا سأل الرسول صلى الله عليه وسلم-وقد وضع رجله في الركاب/متجها إلى الجهاد العسكري- فقال يا رسول الله: ما أعظم الجهاد فقال الرسول صلى الله عليه وسلم أعظم الجهاد كلمة عدل عند سلطان جائر.

على أن مساعدة المظلوم، في ظل المجتمعات المدنية المتكاثرة السكان ، لا تتاح للأفراد المشغولين في خضم الحياة بأمورهم ، لأن الأفراد مهما كان حولهم ، لا يستطيعون القيام بالشفاعة والنصرة ، لأن جهودهم محدودة. ولذلك صار تعاون الأفراد في ما بينهم أمراً ضرورياً مشروعاً ، كما قال الله تعالى: (وَتَعَاوَنُوا عَلَى الْبِرِّ وَالتَّقْوَىٰ)،ولا بد من أن يتصدى مجموعات من الناس ، للتعاون في الحسبة ، كما قال تعالى: (وَلْتَكُن مِّنكُمْ أُمَّةٌ يَدْعُونَ إِلَى الْخَيْرِ وَيَأْمُرُونَ بِالْمَعْرُوفِ وَيَنْهَوْنَ عَنِ الْمُنكَرِ وَأُولَٰئِكَ هُمُ الْمُفْلِحُونَ) فجعل الآمرين بالمعروف الناهين عن المنكر جماعة، لأنه لا يتم مثل ذلك الواجب إلا بالجماعة، وما لا يتم الواجب إلا به فهو واجب ، ولذلك قال الرسول صلى الله عليه وسلم : " مثل المؤمنين في توادهم وتراحمهم وتعاطفهم مثل الجسد الواحد ، إذا اشتكى منه عضو تداعى له سائر الجسد بالسهر والحمى " (متفق عليه) ، وقال أيضاً : " المؤمن للمؤمن كالبنيان يشد بعضه بعضا"، كما فصل الباب الرابع من (شرح الديباجة) المرفق.

وقاعدة نصرة المظلوم قاعدة لها تطبيقات وآليات كثيرة غابت عن أكثر البلدان العربية الإسلامية ، على أن الشريعة الإسلامية قد قررت قاعدة التعاون على البر والتقوى عامة ، وقاعدة الحسبة خاصة، بل لقد أثنى الرسول صلى الله عليه وسلم على تعاون أهل الجاهلية في حلف الفضول ، من أجل رفع الظلم بل شارك في الحلف، وقال عنه : " ولو دعيت به في الإسلام لأجبت" (رواه الحميدي بسند صحيح)، وعند ابن إسحاق (ما أحب إن لي به حمر النعم)، وفي الحديث دلالة واضحة على أهمية التعاون مع كل الجهات والهيئات والشخصيات، في سبيل دفع المظالم، مهما كانت توجهاتها ومذاهبها وأديانها –كما في الباب الرابع من (شرح الديباجة) المرفق.

عاشرا: ومن أهم دواعي إنشاء الجمعية؛ أن الدولة بدلا من التحقيق في هذه الانتهاكات وتقديم المتهمين إلى محاكمات علنية، ساقت عشرات من دعاة حقوق الإنسان الى السجون، بدعاوى الارهاب ودعم الارهاب، أو تعرضوا لمضايقات أو تلفيقات تشل نشاطهم والناس لا يعلمون.

وطفح الكيل فصارت المنظمات الدولية؛ تصدر تقارير تترى عن تردي حالة حقوق الإنسان في البلاد من انتهاكات صارخة من تعذيب واكراه واعتقالات تعسفية ومعاملة مشينة تحط من كرامة الانسان وتهضم حقوقه وترهيب للناشطين في مجال حقوق الانسان والمجتمع المدني.

وصارت تهم العنف والارهاب تمتد حتى وصلت إلى دعاة العدل والشورى وحقوق الانسان، من كافة الأطياف، من أجل شل حركة المجتمع المدني، وضرب القيادات الفعالة، التي تتمتع بالمصداقية والثقة عند العموم، وشل الشخصيات القادرة على قيادة العمل السلمي، القادرة على طرح البديل الحقيقي للعنف والعنف المضاد.

من أجل ذلك صار لا بد من ما ليس منه بد، لا بد من تعليق الجرس ونفخ صفارة الإنذار، فلا دخان من غير نار، قبل أن تتكاثف انتهاكات حقوق الإنسان، حتى تحرق الجميع وتغرق السفينة بما فيها الربان والركاب.

من أجل ذلك قرر الموقعون أدناه من دعاة العدل والشورى وحقوق الانسان إنشاء هذه الجمعية

ب =أهداف الجمعية:

تسعى الجمعية إلى ما يلي:

١ - تأصيل ثقافة حقوق الإنسان السياسية إسلاميا ،باعتبار وسائل الحكم الشوري من أركان العقيدة السياسية الإسلامية، التي لا يجوز-شرعا-التنازل عنها، أو التفريط بها: كالعدالة والحرية والتعددية فكرية وسياسية والتسامح، وحصر حل كل خلاف بالأسلوب السلمي، وكون الأمة هي المخولة بتطبيق الشريعة، وقوامة الأمة على الحكومة، وتداول السلطة، وحفظ حقوق الأقلية، والتوافقية وحكم الأكثرية، وقيام مجلس نواب منتخب من عموم الشعب رجالا ونساء، يتولى الإشراف على الحكومة، ويراقب ويحاسب، والتزام الحاكم قرارات نواب الأمة المنتخبين، ومعاير استقلال القضاء ونزاهته كما في الباب الأول من (شرح الديباجة).)

٢ - تأصيل ثقافة حقوق الإنسان المدنية والاقتصادية إسلاميا، كالمساواة، وتكافؤ الفرص السياسية، والعدالة والمساواة الاقتصادية والاجتماعية، في السكن والعلاج والتعليم كما في الباب الأول من (شرح الديباجة).)

٣ - تأصيل ثقافة حقوق الإنسان والمتهم والسجين إسلاميا، وجلاء الغبار عن موقف الإسلام المشرف، في حفظ حقوق الإنسان، والمتهم والسجين، وشرع معايير وضمانات شرعية المحاكمات، كما في الباب الأول من (شرح الديباجة).)

٤ - نشر وتعميم وتعليم وتعميق مفاهيم ومبادئ حقوق الإنسان وحرياته الأساسية الواردة في البيان العالمي لحقوق الإنسان الصادر عن الأمم المتحدة في العاشر من كانون الأول عام 1948 ونشر الوثائق والاتفاقيات الدولية التي تتلاءم أهدافها مع البيان المذكور.

٥ - ومن أهداف الجمعية نشر ثقافة الجهاد المدني السلمي، باعتبارها ثقافة إسلامية أصيلة، ولأنها الأسلوب المضمون، مهما طال الطريق، وتكاثفت رمال الصحراء، وتعرجت وديانها، للوصول إلى دولة العدل والشورى وحقوق الإنسان، و تجريم العنف أسلوبا للاحتفاظ بالسلطة، وتركه أسلوبا للوصول إليها، وبيان أن التجمعات المدنية الأهلية، هي صمام الأمان من العنف والتطرف. لعل ذلك يسهم في تنبيه الغافلين والمتغافلين، الذين يظنون أن سبب العنف والتطرف هو الدين، وليس سببه الاستبداد والظلم وفساد الإدارة والاستئثار بالسلطة والثروة.

٦ - الإسهام في تأصيل ثقافة الدستور والمجتمع المدني الإسلامي ومفاهيمها، وإجراءاتها وآلياتها ونشرها، وتأكيد تأسيس تلك الثقافة على الإسلام بصفته عقيدة هذه الأمة وشريعتها.

٧ - المطالبة بالحقوق السياسية، كإنشاء مجلس نواب، وإصدار نظام فعال للجمعيات الأهلية وإنشاء أحزاب سياسية، وتعزيز استقلال القضاء، والفصل بين السلطات، وتحديدها، وإنشاء دواوين قضائية للمراقبة والمحاسبة المالية والإدارية

٨ - والمطالبة بالحقوق المدنية، كإصدار قوانين تكفل العناية بالطبقات والأقاليم المهمشة والفقيرة، سكنيا ومعيشيا وزراعيا وصحيا وتعليميا.

٩ - توثيق انتهاكات حقوق الإنسان والقيام بالأعمال المناسبة والتعاون مع الجهات المعنية من أجل دفعها والتقليل منها

١٠ - ترسيخ الإيمان بحقوق الإنسان وحرياته الأساسية وحمل كل فرد في المجتمع على أن يبذل جهده في تنمية احترام هذه الحقوق والحريات والاعتراف بها والدفاع عنها بكل الوسائل القانونية والأدبية.

ج=وسائل الجمعية:

١ - تأليف الكتب والأبحاث والدراسات

٢ - إصدار النشرات والبيانات والتقارير

٣ - التواصل مع القيادة السياسية، والفعاليات الاجتماعية

٤ - عقد الندوات والمحاضرات

٥ - إصدار تقارير وبيانات دورية عن الانتهاكات العامة للحقوق

٦ - فتح سجل لانتهاكات حقوق الإنسان على العموم، والمتهم والمعتقل على الخصوص ولاسيما الخطيرة منها، سواء أكانت انتهاكات سابقة أم حالية، لأن انتهاكات حقوق الإنسان لا تسقط بالتقادم.

وسيتكون السجل من ملفين:

الملف الأول رصد الانتهاكات العامة لحقوق الأمة

الملف الثاني يرصد الانتهاكات الخاصة بحقوق الأفراد ، ولاسيما:

١ - التعذيب الجسدي والنفسي

٢ - بقاء السجين فوق المدة المحكوم بها،

٣ - الاعتقال التعسفي وبقاء السجين في السجن أكثر من المدة التي قننتها الدولة ستة أشهر دون أن يطلق سراحه أو يحال الى محاكمة تتضمن الحد الأدنى من ضمانات العدالة ولاسيما العلانية كما نص النظام. (علما بأن القاعدة المقررة عند الفقهاء والدول الدستورية لا تتجاوز ثلاثة أشهر في أقصى الأحوال). ولا سيما

٤ - الأحكام القضائية التي تعارض القوانين المحلية التي أصدرتها الدولة أو التي تناقض المعاهدات الدولية التي صادقت عليها المملكة، ولاسيما الأحكام التي تعتبر الحقوق السياسية جرائم، وتعاقب عليها وتلفيق التهم أو إقامة محاكمات صورية تفتقد معايير المحاكمات العادلة ولاسيما العلانية وحرمان السجين من حقوقه التي نصت عليها المواثيق الدولية وإصدار أحكام قاسية لا يتناسب فيها العقاب مع الجريمة.

٥ - التهديد بالتصفية والاغتيال والإيذاء الجسدي

٦ - منع المعتقل أو السجين من الزيارة

٧ - انتهاك العرض أو التهديد بالانتهاك، أو التصرفات الجنسية أو الاقوال والاعمال البذيئة

٨ - الضغوط على السجين التي تفضي إلى الانهيار العصبي أو الجنون الناتج عن ممارسات المحققين أو السجانين

٩ - حالات الوفاة داخل السجون، نتيجة التعذيب أو إهمال الرعاية الصحية أو سوء التغذية

١٠ - حالات الاخفاء القسري لاسيما التي تستهدف الحقوقيين والسياسيين

١١ - الاغتيال بحوادث السيارات و نحوها

١٢ - التهديدات و المضايقات لاقارب الناشط السياسي والحقوقي، والسجين و لا سيما النساء والاطفال وحرمانهم من حقوقهم وارهابهم.

١٣ - منع الناشطين الحقوقيين والسياسيين من السفر لضمان سكوتهم وإشغالهم بأنفسهم عن المطالبة بحقوق الأمة

١٤ - منع الناشطين الحقوقيين والسياسيين من الكتابة والخطابة والاجتماع والطبع والنشر

١٥ - الفصل التعسفي من العمل أو المضايقة في طلب الرزق والتجارة

١٦ - تهديد الناشطين الحقوقيين والسياسيين بكف اليد عن العمل وتجميد الراتب لضمان سكوتهم

د -نداء إلى من لديه معلومات عن انتهاكات حقوق الإنسان:
ويرجو الموقعون على هذا البيان كل من تعرض لانتهاكات موثقة أو علم بها أن يبلغ أحد الموقعين على هذا البيان من أجل رصدها ورفعها لخادم الحرمين الشريفين، والجهات المعنية.
وعسى أن تسرع الدولة بتقديم المتهمين بانتهاك حقوق الناس المدنية والسياسية، أيا كانت مواقعهم ومراتبهم الى محاكمات علنية ومحاسبتهم ومعاقبتهم وحماية الضحايا والشهود حتى لا تتراكم وتتكاثر الانتهاكات في المستقبل، فيعمنا الله بالهلاك، وصدق الله العظيم" وما كان ربك مهلك القرى بظلم وأهلها مصلحون"
وفي الختام ليس لدينا أحلام يقظة ولا منام، وندرك أن الطريق مخيف، ولكن لا بد من شق الطريق، فإن سلمنا وسلمت الجمعية، سرنا-بعون الله- في طريق أهداف الجمعية، وإن قمعنا وقمعت الجمعية -كما قمعت (لجنة الدفاع عن الحقوق الشرعية) -عام 1413ه(1992م) ، فحسبنا أننا أضأنا من خلال ذلك شمعتين: إحداهما: الكلمة(شرح الديباجة) التي تحدد الهدف (اعرف حقوقك السياسية في الإسلام، من دون أوهام فقهاء الاستبداد ومثقفي الظلام) والثانية بالموقف الذي يحدد الوسيلة المضمونة للوصول: الجهاد المدني السلمي، ومن سار على الدرب وصل.
والسلام عليكم ورحمة الله وبركاته.

المؤسسون:
١ - سعود بن أحمد الدغيثر/ من نشطاء المجتمع المدني/الرياض
٢ - د/ عبدالرحمن بن حامد الحامد/ تخصص اقتصاد إسلامي، مدرس في الكلية التقنية/القصيم
٣ - د/ عبدالكريم بن يوسف الخضر/أستاذ الفقه المقارن في كلية الشريعة في القصيم/ ناشط في الدفاع عن حقوق الإنسان
٤ - د/عبدالله الحامد (أبو بلال)/أستاذ الأدب السابق في جامعة الإمام/ وعضو مؤسس لأول لجنة للدفاع عن الحقوق الشرعية (التي حظرتها الدولة وفصلت أعضاءها من وظائفهم وسجنتهم عام 1413هـ/1992)/الرياض
٥ - عيسى الحامد/ ناشط في الدفاع عن حقوق الإنسان/القصيم
٦ - فهد بن عبدالعزيز العريني السبيعي/ ناشط في الدفاع عن حقوق الإنسان والمجتمع المدني/الرياض
٧ - فوزان بن محسن الحربي/ ناشط في الدفاع عن حقوق الإنسان والمجتمع المدني/الرياض
٨ - محمد بن حمد بن عبد الله المحيسن/ من نشطاء المجتمع المدني/الرياض
٩ - د/محمد بن فهد القحطاني/أستاذ جامعي في الاقتصاد السياسي/ ناشط في الدفاع عن حقوق الإنسان/الرياض
١٠ - محمد بن صالح البجادي/ ناشط في الدفاع عن حقوق الإنسان/القصيم
١١ - مهنا بن محمد خليف الفالح/من نشطاء المجتمع المدني/الجوف
ملاحظة هامة: ننشر البيان التأسيسي وشرح الديباجة قبل استكمال التهذيب ، وقبل استكمال بقية توقيعات الأعضاء، تجنبا لمحاولات إجهاض إعلان الجمعية، بضربة استباقية، من الجهات التي تعوق الإصلاح، بالضغط على بعض الموقعين للانسحاب، وقد أجل ذكر أسماء الذين لم تصل توقيعاتهم، وسوف تنشر حين ورودها في المبيضة النهائية.
ملاحظة أخرى: تبلغنا برغبة من دعاة حقوق الإنسان الموقوفين التالية أسماؤهم في المشاركة:
١ - المحامي سليمان بن إبراهيم الرشودي/ قاض سابق وعضو مؤسس لأول لجنة للدفاع عن الحقوق الشرعية(حظرتها الدولة وفصلت أعضاءها من وظائفهم وسجنتهم عام 1413هـ/1992)، ومن قيادات الحركة الحقوقية والدستورية(معتقل-من دون محاكمة- منذ يوم الجمعة 14/1/1428هـ الموافق 2/2/2007م حتى يوم إعلان هذه الجمعية)
٢ - د/موسى بن محمد القرني/ أستاذ سابق لأصول الفقه في الجامعة الإسلامية في المدينة المنورة/ ومن قيادات الحركة الحقوقية والدستورية(معتقل -من دون محاكمة- منذ يوم الجمعة 14/1/1428هـ الموافق 2/2/2007م حتى يوم إعلان هذه الجمعية / المدينة المنورة.
٣ - منصور بن سالم العوذة (معتقل-من دون محاكمة- منذ يوم23/11/1428هـ الموافق 2/12/2007م حتى يوم إعلان هذه الجمعية).
وقد رؤي التريث في انضمامهم، لأنه قد يعرضهم إلى مزيد من المضايقات، فضلا عن أنه يحتاج إلى موافقات خطية قطعية.

Appendix B

English translation of HASM's founding declaration

The following is my translation of HASM's 2009 CE founding declaration, which can be found in Appendix A. The founding declaration concisely summarizes the main themes of the theory of the Islamic civil rights movement and gives an insight into the language and arguments that its members use.

Association for Civil and Political Rights
in the Kingdom of Saudi Arabia
(Founding Declaration)
ar-Riyadh, Monday, 23 10 1430 (12th Oct 2009 CE)

In the Name of God, the Most Gracious, the Most Merciful

Praised be God, the Lord of the inhabitants of the world, who rules justly; and prayers and peace be upon the noblest of the prophets and messengers, upon his family, his companions and his followers, who ruled according to the principles of justice and shura, until the Day of Resurrection.

Fourteen centuries before the appearance of the international laws which protect human rights and to which governments are committed the Islamic sharia came to protect human dignity, safeguard the rights of man and end injustice. The Almighty God said: 'We have conferred dignity on the children of Adam' [Quran 17:70, translation M. Asad] and 'Whenever you judge between people, judge with justice' [Quran 4:58, translation M. Asad], and in the sacred hadith [*ḥadīṯ qudsī*] He said: 'O My servants, I have forbidden oppression for myself and have made it forbidden amongst you, so do not oppress one another' (was transmitted by Muslim, at-Tirmiḏī and Ibn Māǧa and confirmed by al-Albānī, it comes via Abū Ḏurr – may God be pleased with him – from the Messenger of God – peace be upon him).

A. Preamble

Why an association for civil and political rights?

Firstly, the most important reason for the founding of the association is that human rights and basic freedoms, especially political ones, are subject to grave violations in the Kingdom of Saudi Arabia. These violations increased after the Gulf War because the peoples' awareness of their rights increased. As their awareness of their rights increased, the government increased its violence and after the second Gulf War it threw thousands of young people into prison. As it suppressed peaceful action as manifested in the Memorandum of Advice, the Letter of Demands or the founding of the Committee for the Defence of Legitimate Rights the explosions of Riyadh and Khobar happened. As the government alone took big political decisions on the domestic and external level without being mandated by society and without involving it, the events of 11 September and its aftermath happened.

Some influential members of the political system continue to marginalize society and continue to patronize it. They turn official television channels into theatre troupes, deceiving the people about the real reasons and basic elements of violence. Questions of violence and terrorism become something to be addressed by police measures and political remedies are ignored. The remedy is clear and simple and does not need many strategies and planning. It consists of allowing groups that want to end political paralysis and other parts of society to form political parties and organizations and to operate publicly in the open.

Oppression, torture, the violation of human rights and restrictions of freedoms are not only a great injustice, but they do not guarantee security and stability. Only justice and political reform which affirms the power of the community and its sovereignty over the government guarantee security, stability and prosperity. Suppressing the advocates of peaceful change raises the value of the shares of the advocates of violent change.

It is obvious that depriving the people of peaceful means of public expression leads to their seeking refuge in the forming of violent, secret organizations. It is well-known that violent movements are born in prisons which are known for heavy torture. The torture chambers supply the violent movements with members and together with restrictions on civil and political rights they increase the paralysis and subsequently produce rebellion, strife and the eternal circle of violence and counter-violence.

During the last three years, complaints about human rights violations have increased.

The regency of King Abdullah started with a welcome movement towards reform by freeing a number of political prisoners. People were pleased with his calls for fighting the vermin of injustice with the sword of justice and they were optimistic about some steps like the founding of the Human Rights Commission. However, these reforms came to a halt, and the human rights situation returned to its former state of violations because of the increased dominance of the Interior Ministry over the affairs of the people and the country.

Despite the weakness of the standards that the state enacted in the areas of human rights and the rights of the accused and the prisoners, it did not abide by them. A number of advocates of justice, shura and human rights wrote secret and public letters and declarations, but the Interior Ministry used the fight against terrorism as a pretext for cracking down on all ideas which prove that the real reasons for terrorism are political and that its real solution is political. Recently, talk about severe and blatant violations of human rights in general and the rights of the accused and prisoners in particular became more frequent and people exchanged numerous reports about them.

One of these reports is a declaration by the female protesters in al-Qasim on 2nd Rajab 1428 a.h. [16 July 2007 CE], in which they say that, before the protest, they had sent a report to the deputy Interior Minister, in which they described the physical and psychological torture that their family members had been subjected to, like heavy beatings, starvation, sleep deprivation, the use of electronic sticks, pressing of their heads into waste containers, humiliation by repeating insulting words and other forms of torture. These reports, if they are true, show the cruel treatment and uncover the ugly torture in the prisons of the General Investigation Directorate [*al-mabāḥiṯ al-ʿāmma*].

Some reports say that some interrogators transgressed all limits by insulting God himself and abusing the name of the Messenger, peace be upon him. Some reports suggest that many of those who were subjected to the cruel forms of torture like threats or morally degrading acts suffer from intense fear, hindering them from speaking out or exposing the injustice and torture that was done to them. This suggests that what can be found in the reports is only a small part of what is happening.

There is no smoke without fire, but secrecy prevents the pulling away of the veil and fear prevents the throats from complaining. Sometimes those whose rights are violated are too embarrassed to clearly speak about it because they fear a loss of face. Despite all this we have not heard of a judicial committee being formed to investigate these violations.

The government has continued its restrictions on civil assembly and has buried the project of civil associations, which are a safety valve for the future of the country and protect it from the dangers of violence and counter-violence. The fact that society remains without effective civil associations allows the Interior Ministry to give all other rights of the citizens the final blow and spread fear, depression and all other psychological illnesses that result from oppression. International reports have proven that 60 per cent of the Saudi people suffer from 'anxiety' (see the newspaper *ar-Riyāḍ*, 24 July 2009). There is a dialectic relationship between anxiety and terrorism.

Secondly, one of the most important reasons for the founding of the association is that the state presents the violations of political human rights in a deviant religious discourse, which outwardly applies the sharia. It makes oppression, coercion and the violation of human rights look good in front of the people. Many people do not know that Islam is innocent of all actions that bury the sovereignty of the community [*umma*] over the government and suppress freedom, pluralism, justice, consultation [*šūrā*] of the representatives of the community and tolerance. The first chapter of the 'Explanation of the Preamble' (*Šarḥ ad-dībāǧa*) probably demonstrates the large difference between the principles of human rights and especially political rights in Islam on the one hand and the claims of the government that it applies the sharia (our constitution is Islam) on the other hand.

Thirdly, one of the reasons for the founding of the association is that a number of international organizations is influenced by the Western view on human rights and does not display the Islamic view on human rights in an effective manner.

Fourthly, one of the most important reasons for the founding of the association is that the weakness of the citizens' awareness of their rights has exposed them to more violations and frustration. Socrates has marked the beginning of human self-consciousness through the saying 'Know thyself'. The slogan of collective self-consciousness is 'Know your rights'.

Fifthly, one of the reasons for the founding of the association is that many international organizations that speak about human rights violations in Arab countries focus on individual cases. They focus on arbitrary arrests, judicial monitoring, disappearances and torture. These things are important, but they reduce the problem, and they deal with topics that were defined in the West, namely the neglect of the necessary balance between civil and political rights on the one hand and economic, social and cultural rights on the other hand. They do not publish reports on the violation of general political and civil rights, like the absence of a parliament, the absence of a separation of powers, the lack of independence of the judiciary and the absence of civil associations, in addition to the absence of political parties, the disruption of a fair distribution of wealth and the absence of a change of power.

Sixthly, one of the reasons for the founding of the association is that the state presents the violations of human rights as well as the rights of the accused and the prisoner under the slogan of the implementation of the sharia. One of the reasons is the jurisprudence of secret, cruel pseudo-trials, which happens under the label of that which God has sent down [*mā anzala llāh*], as well as the fact that torture is being justified under the heading of safeguarding security and bringing truth to light. There is no alternative to revealing the wrong innovations [*bidaʿ*] of legitimizing torture and secret trials, as is shown in the third chapter of the attached 'Explanation of the Preamble'.

Seventhly, one of the reasons for the founding of the association is that the Saudi judiciary in its official structure – as well as its implementation – represents a clear disruption of the standards that the Islamic sharia has set up fourteen centuries before the international organizations enacted the international standards of the independence and integrity of the judiciary. This is laid out in detail in the first and second chapter of the attached 'Explanation of the Preamble'.

Eighthly, one of the reasons for the founding of the association is the discovery of a suspicious complicity of most Western states, who brag about campaigning for human rights, when there are conflicts with some governments, and then the oil of the Gulf silences them, like the old poet said: 'In my mouth, there is oil. Does someone who has oil in his mouth speak?'

The kingdom's conduct is considered sufficient to nominate it for the Human Rights Council, while the Saudi judiciary ignores the documents that the kingdom has signed. This is briefly explained in the second chapter of the attached 'Explanation of the Preamble'. In fact, the trial judges and the examining magistrates clearly violate them.

Ninthly, one of the most important reasons for the founding of the association is that one of the reasons for the spread of violence is the absence of a foundation for peaceful, political, civil jihad. Many intellectuals as well as Islamic legal scholars [*fuqahā'*] and preachers do not value working in the area of human rights. They do not understand that it is the highest degree of enjoining virtue and forbidding vice [*al-amr bi-l-ma'rūf wa-n-nahy 'an al-munkar*]. Indeed, it is a great jihad. The sharia clearly says that it is the greatest or the best jihad, as can be seen in the authentic hadith: 'A man who put his foot into the stirrup and was on his way to military jihad asked the Messenger – peace be upon him – and said: "Oh, Messenger of God, what is the greatest jihad?" The Messenger – peace be upon him – said: "The greatest jihad is a word of justice before an unjust ruler."'

Helping the oppressed in civilized societies with many inhabitants is nothing that single individuals, who are occupied with their affairs in life, can accomplish. No matter what his power, an individual cannot accomplish supplications and support, because his efforts are limited.

Therefore, cooperation between individuals in matters that concern them has become a necessity of the sharia, just like God Almighty said: 'Help one another in furthering virtue and God-consciousness' [Quran 5:2, translation M. Asad]. There is no alternative to groups of people cooperating for accountability [*ḥisba*], like God Almighty said: 'That there might grow out of you a community [of people] who invite unto all that is good, and enjoin the doing of what is right and forbid the doing of what is wrong: and it is they, who shall attain a happy state' [Quran 3:104, translation M. Asad]. Those who enjoin virtue and forbid vice are made into a group, because this duty can only be accomplished in a group. That without which an obligation is not accomplished is itself an obligation. Therefore, the Messenger – peace be upon him – said: 'In their mutual friendship and compassion and sympathy, the believers are like one body. If one organ complains, the rest of the body comes to protect and safeguard it' (Agreed upon). He also said: 'A believer is for the believer like a building, in which they strengthen each other.' This is laid out in detail in the fourth chapter of the attached 'Explanation of the Preamble'.

Supporting the oppressed and showing them compassion is based on implementations and mechanisms which are absent in most Islamic and Arab countries. The Islamic sharia emphasized the principle of cooperation in furthering virtue and God-consciousness in general and the principle of accountability [*ḥisba*] in particular. Indeed, the Messenger – peace be upon him – praised the cooperation with the people of ignorance [*ǧāhilīya*] in the 'League of the Virtuous' [*ḥilf al-fuḍūl*] in order to lift injustice. This is a clear indication for the importance of cooperation with all sides, organizations and individuals in order to lift injustice, no matter what their orientation, religious denomination or religion, like it can be seen in the fourth chapter of the attached 'Explanation of the Preamble'.

Tenthly, one of the most important reasons for the founding of the association is that, instead of investigating these violations and presenting the accused to public trials, the state has thrown tens of human rights advocates into prisons and accused them of terrorism or supporting terrorism. Others have been harassed or subjected to false accusations that paralyse their activism, and the people do not know it.

Enough is enough. International organizations publish reports that show the deterioration of the human rights situation in the country, in light of striking violations like torture, coercion, arbitrary arrests and degrading treatments that violate human dignity, curtail their rights and discourage those who are active in the field of human rights and civil rights.

The accusations of terrorism have even reached the advocates of justice, shura and human rights coming from all parties, in order to paralyse the civil society movement and crack down on effective leadership figures who enjoy credibility and the trust of the people. They want to crack down on people who are able to lead peaceful activism and who are able to present a true alternative to violence and counter-violence.

Therefore, there is no alternative to that to which there is no alternative. There is no alternative to ringing the alarm bell and sounding the alarm. There is no smoke without fire. [One has to act,] before the human rights violations increase even more, until all are burnt and the ship sinks with the captain and the passengers on board.

Therefore, the signing advocates of justice, shura and human rights have decided to establish this association.

B. Aims of the association

1. Laying an Islamic foundation for a culture of political human rights, while considering the means of shura rule one of the pillars of the Islamic political doctrine [*al-ʿaqīda s-siyāsīya l-islāmīya*], which – according to the sharia – cannot be abandoned or neglected. They include justice, freedom, ideological and political pluralism, tolerance, confining all conflicts to peaceful means, the community [*umma*] being mandated to implement the sharia, sovereignty of the community over the government, change of power, protecting the rights of minorities, rule of the majority by consensus and the establishment of a council of representatives elected by all the people, men and women, which oversees the government and holds it accountable, in addition to the commitment of the ruler to the decisions of the elected representatives of the community and the standards of independence and integrity of the judiciary, as described in the first chapter of the 'Explanation of the Preamble'.
2. Laying an Islamic foundation for a culture of civil and economic rights, like equality, equal political opportunities, economic and social justice and fairness in the areas of housing, healthcare and education, as described in the first chapter of the 'Explanation of the Preamble'.
3. Laying an Islamic foundation for a culture of human rights and rights of the accused and the prisoner, as well as removing the dust from the Islamic position on the protection of human rights and the rights of the accused and the prisoners; introducing legal measures and guarantees for trials, as described in the first chapter of the 'Explanation of the Preamble'.
4. Spreading, teaching and informing about the concepts and principles of human rights and basic freedoms as laid out in the International Declaration of Human Rights, which was adopted by the United Nations on 10 December 1948 CE;

publishing the international documents and agreements whose aims coincide with the mentioned declaration.

5. One of the aims of the association is spreading the culture of peaceful, civil jihad, which is considered an authentic Islamic culture, because it is the guaranteed way to reach the state of justice, shura and human rights, no matter how long the path, how dense the sand of the desert and how winding its wadis; declaring violence as a means to cling to power a crime and discarding it as a means to reach power. Civil society associations are a safety valve for preventing violence and extremism. Maybe this contributes to convincing the uninformed who believe that the reason for violence and extremism is religion and not oppression, injustice, administrative corruption and wanting to have power and wealth for themselves alone.
6. Contributing to laying the foundation for a constitutional culture and a culture of Islamic civil society, its concepts, measures and means; confirming that this culture is based on Islam, which is the doctrine [*ʿaqīda*] of this community and its sharia.
7. Demanding political rights, like the establishment of a council of representatives, the passing of an effective law for civil associations and the founding of political parties, strengthening the independence of the judiciary, separating and defining the state powers and establishing judicial offices for financial and administrative oversight and accountability.
8. Demanding civil rights, like the passing of laws which care for marginalized and poor minorities and supports them in the areas of housing, their livelihood, agriculture, healthcare and education.
9. Documenting violations of human rights and taking the appropriate actions as well as cooperating with the responsible bodies in order to prevent them and reduce them.
10. Ingraining the belief in human rights and basic freedoms and holding each individual of society responsible for doing what he can in order to increase the respect for these rights and freedoms and for recognizing and defending them with all legal means and means of behaviour.

C. Means of the association

1. Writing books, studies and papers
2. Publishing pamphlets, declarations and reports
3. Contact with political figures and leaders of society
4. Organizing panels and lectures
5. Publishing periodic reports and declarations about violations of rights in general
6. Opening a register for documenting violations of human rights in general and of the rights of the accused and the prisoner in particular, especially the grave ones, be it past or present violations, because human rights violations do not lapse after a certain period of time.

The register will consist of two records:

The first record documents general human rights violations.

The second record documents specific violations of the rights of individuals, especially:

1. Physical and psychological torture
2. Staying in prison longer than the sentence requires
3. Arbitrary arrests and the staying of the prisoners in prison longer than six months without being released or handed over to a court, which ensures a minimum of judicial guarantees, especially a public trial, like the judicial system requires. (It is pointed out that the basis that was approved by the Islamic legal scholars and the constitutional states does not exceed three months under the most extreme circumstances)
4. Sentences contradicting local laws that were passed by the state or contradicting international treaties which the kingdom has ratified; this especially applies to sentences which consider human rights a crime or interfere with them, to inventing accusations or holding pseudo-trials, which fall short of the standards of fair trials, like the publicness of the trial, as well as depriving the prisoner of his rights, which are written down in the international documents, and passing cruel judgements, in which the punishment and the crime do not match
5. Threatening with eliminations, murder and bodily harm
6. Barring the prisoner from receiving visitors
7. Violating someone's honour or threatening to violate it, as well as sexual acts or offensive words and acts
8. Pressuring the prisoner, which leads to a nervous breakdown or insanity resulting from the acts of the interrogators or the prison wards
9. Cases of death inside the prisons as a result of torture, neglect of healthcare or malnutrition
10. Cases of forced disappearance, especially targeting rights advocates and politicians
11. Murder by car accidents and similar means
12. Threats against and harassment of the family members of a political activist, rights advocate or prisoner, especially of women and children, like depriving them of their rights and terrorising them
13. Imposing a travel ban on rights activists and political activists to guarantee their silence and keeping them from demanding the rights of the community
14. Barring the rights activists and political activists from writing, speaking, gathering, printing and publishing
15. Arbitrary job dismissals or harassment in their daily livelihood or trade
16. Threatening the rights activists and political activists with freezing their salary in order to guarantee their silence

D. Call on everyone who has information on human rights violations

The signatories of this declaration ask everyone who is subject to proven violations or who knows of such violations to inform one of the signatories of this declaration, so that they can be recorded and brought to the attention of the Custodian of the Two Holy Mosques and the relevant authorities.

Maybe the state will be quick to present those who are accused of violating the civil and political rights of the people to public courts, no matter what their position or rank, so that they can be held accountable and punished and that the victims and the witnesses are protected so that the violations do not increase even further in the future and God does not leave us to the demise, as God the Almighty has said: ‘For, never would thy Sustainer destroy a community for wrong [beliefs alone] so long as its people behave righteously [towards one another]’ [Quran 11:117, translation M. Asad].

Finally, we do not have waking or sleeping dreams and we know that the road is terrifying. But there is no alternative to taking the road. If we are spared and if the association is spared, we will continue on the way towards the aims of the association, with the support of God. If we are suppressed and if the association is suppressed, like the Committee for the Defence of Legitimate Rights was suppressed in 1413 (1992 CE), we feel that we have thereby lighted two candles: The first is the word of the ‘Explanation of the Preamble’, which defines the aim as ‘Know thy political rights in Islam, without the fantasies of the Islamic legal scholars [*fuqahā'*] of oppression and the intellectuals of injustice’; the second is the position which defines the means that, by guarantee, lead to the desired result, namely peaceful, civil jihad. He who takes the path will arrive.

May the peace and mercy of God be with you!

The founders

1. Sa'ūd ibn 'Aḥmad ad-Duġaiṯir, civil society activist, Riyadh
2. Dr 'Abd ar-Raḥmān ibn Ḥāmid al-Ḥāmid, expert for Islamic economics and lecturer at the Technical Faculty, al-Qasim
3. Dr 'Abd al-Karīm ibn Yūsuf al-Ḫaḍr, professor for comparative Islamic jurisprudence at the Sharia Faculty in al-Qasim, activist for the defence of human rights
4. Dr 'Abdallāh al-Ḥāmid (Abu Bilāl), former professor for literature at al-Imām University, founding member of the first Committee for the Defence of Legitimate Rights (which the state banned and whose members were fired and imprisoned in 1413/1992 CE), Riyadh
5. 'Īsā al-Ḥāmid, activist for the defence of human rights
6. Fahd ibn 'Abd al-'Azīz al-'Arīnī as-Sabī'ī, activist for the defence of human rights and civil society, Riyadh
7. Fawzān ibn Muḥsin al-Ḥarbī, activist for the defence of human rights and civil society, Riyadh
8. Muḥammad ibn Ḥamad ibn 'Abdallāh al-Muḥaisin, civil society activist, ar-Riyadh
9. Dr Muḥammad ibn Fahd al-Qaḥṭāni, university professor for political economics, activist for the defence of human rights, Riyadh
10. Muḥammad ibn Ṣāliḥ al-Baǧādī, activist for the defence of human rights, al-Qasim
11. Muhannā ibn Muḥammad Ḫalīf al-Fāliḥ, civil society activist, al-Jauf

Important note

We publish the founding declaration and the 'Explanation of the Preamble' before the final touches have been completed and before the rest of the signatures of the members have been obtained, in order to thwart any attempt at derailing the publication of the declaration by a preventive strike on the part of the parties who impede reform and try to exert pressure on some signatories so that they withdraw. The mentioning of the names of those who's signature has not been obtained was postponed and we will publish them when they reach us in the final version.

Additional note:

We were informed about the wish of the following imprisoned human rights advocates to participate:

1. Lawyer Sulaymān ibn Ibrāhīm ar-Rašūdī, former judge and founding member of the first Committee for the Defence of Legitimate Rights (which the state forbid and whose members were fired and imprisoned in 1413/1992 CE), one of the leaders of the human rights movement and the constitutional movement (imprisoned, without trial, since Friday, 14th Muḥarram 1428, 2 February 2007 CE, until the day of the publication of this association)
2. Dr Mūsā ibn Muḥammad al-Qarnī, former professor for principles of Islamic jurisprudence [*uṣūl al-fiqh*] at the Islamic University in Medina, one of the leaders of the human rights movement and the constitutional movement (imprisoned, without trial, since Friday, 14th Muḥarram 1428, 2 February 2007 CE, until the day of the publication of this association), Medina
3. Manṣūr ibn Sālim al-ʿAuḏa (imprisoned, without trial, since 23rd Ḏū l-qāʿda 1428, 2 December 2007 CE, until the day of the publication of the association)

It was decided to wait with their admission, because it would subject them to more harassment, besides the need for clear, written consent.

Notes

Introduction

1

”فحي على فلك الجهاد المدني
للنقلة من الحكم العضوض إلى الشوري
فلا حقوق مدنية دون حقوق سياسية
ولا حقوق سياسية دون جهاد الاستبداد حتى الاستشهاد
أما نرى النمل كيف تشكل من أجسادها جسرا متيناً؟
أليست بعد عشرات الضحايا تعبر جدولا مترعا؟
أما ترى النحل كيف تقاوم زنبورا عملاقا؟
أليست بعد عشرات الضحايا تلقيه خارج الخلية؟
إن الانتقال من فقه حقوق السلطان إلى فقه حقوق الإنسان
هو بداية الخروج من قواقع الأدعية إلى مواقع التضحية.“

ʿAbdallāh al-Ḥāmid, *Ḥuqūq al-insān baina nūr al-islām wa-ġabaš al-mulk al-ʿaḍūḍ* (Bairūt: Bīsān li-n-našr wa-t-tawzīʿ wa-l-iʿlām, 2010), 3.

2 See, e.g., Asef Bayat, *Making Islam Democratic: Social Movements and the Post-Islamist Turn* (Stanford: Stanford University Press, 2007).

3 See, e.g., Abū l-Aʿlā Māḍī, *Ruʾyat ʻAl-Wasaṭʼ fī s-siyāsa wa-l-muǧtamaʿ* (al-Qāhira: Maktaba š-šurūq ad-duwalīya, 2005); and Gudrun Krämer, *Gottes Staat als Republik: Reflexionen zeitgenössischer Muslime zu Islam, Menschenrechten und Demokratie* (Baden-Baden: Nomos Verlagsgesellschaft, 1999), 151–7.

4 See, e.g., Ihsan Dagi, ‘Post-Islamism à la Turca’, in *Post-Islamism: The Changing Faces of Political Islam*, ed. Asef Bayat (Oxford: Oxford University Press, 2013), 71–108; and Cihan Tugal, ‘Islam and the Retrenchment of Turkish Conservatism’, in *Post-Islamism*, ed. Asef Bayat, 109–33.

5 See, e.g., Humeira Iqtidar, ‘Post-Islamist Strands in Pakistan: Islamist Spin-Offs and Their Contradictory Trajectories’, in *Post-Islamism*, ed. Asef Bayat, 257–76; and S. M. Zafar, ‘Accountability, Parliament, and Ijtihad’, in *Liberal Islam: A Sourcebook*, ed. Charles Kurzman (New York: Oxford University Press, 1998), 67–72.

6 See, e.g., Noorhaidi Hasan, ‘Post-Islamist Politics in Indonesia’, in *Post-Islamism*, ed. Asef Bayat, 157–82.

7 See, e.g., Maria Stephan (as editor), *Civilian Jihad: Nonviolent Struggle, Democratization, and Governance in the Middle East* (New York: Palgrave Macmillan, 2009).

8 For details concerning their view on human rights, see Chapter 7, ‘Islamic Human Rights’.

9 Stéphane Lacroix, ‘Saudi Arabia and the Limits of Post-Islamism’, in *Post-Islamism: The Changing Faces of Political Islam*, ed. Asef Bayat (Oxford: Oxford University Press, 2013), 277–97.

10 For more details on the problematic features of the term ‘Islamist’, see, e.g., Emin Poljarevic, ‘Islamism’, in *The Oxford Encyclopedia of Islam and Politics*, ed. Emad

El-Din Shahin (New York: Oxford University Press, 2014); Larbi Sadiki, *The Search for Arab Democracy. Discourses and Counter-Discourses* (London: Hurst, 2004), 98–100; and Martin Kramer, 'Coming to Terms. Fundamentalists or Islamists?', *Middle East Quarterly* 10, no. 2 (Spring 2003): 65–77.

11 See, e.g., Sulaymān al-Ḫarāšī, *Sȧalnī sā'il 'an ad-duktūr 'Abdallāh al-Ḥāmid* (published on said.net, without date, available online: http://www.saaid.net/Warathah/Alkharashy/m/43.htm, accessed 11 June 2020); and as-Sakīna, *Ǧam'īyat al-ḥuqūq al-madanīya wa-s-siyāsīya (ḥasm)* (published on assakina.com, 10 March 2013, available online: http://www.assakina.com/center/parties/22693.html, accessed 6 September 2019).

12 See Right Livelihood Foundation, *Laureates Abdullah al-Hamid, Waleed Abu al-Khair & Mohammad Fahad al-Qahtani* (published on rightlivelihoodaward.org, 2018, available online: https://www.rightlivelihoodaward.org/laureates/abdullah-al-hamid-waleed-abu-al-khair-mohammad-fahad-al-qahtani/, accessed 11 June 2020).

13 See, e.g., Amnesty International, *Saudi Arabia's ACPRA: How the Kingdom Silences Its Human Rights Activists* (published on amnesty.org, 10 October 2014, available online: https://www.amnesty.org/en/documents/MDE23/025/2014/en/, accessed 11 June 2020).

14 See Stéphane Lacroix, 'Between Islamists and Liberals: Saudi Arabia's New "Islamo-Liberal" Reformists', *Middle East Journal* 58, no. 3 (Summer 2004): 345–65; Stéphane Lacroix, *Les Islamistes Saoudiens. Une insurrection manquée* (Paris: Presses Universitaires de France, 2010); and Madawi al-Rasheed, *Muted Modernists: The Struggle Over Divine Politics in Saudi Arabia* (London: Hurst, 2015).

15 See The Economist, *The Saudi Revolution Begins: How to Ensure Muhammad ibn Salman's Reforms Succeed* (published on economist.com, 23 June 2018, available online: https://www.economist.com/leaders/2018/06/23/how-to-ensure-muhammad-bin-salmans-reforms-succeed, accessed 11 June 2020).

Chapter 1

1 For details about the life and doctrine of Muhammad ibn 'Abd al-Wahhāb, see, e.g., 'Abd Allāh Ṣāliḥ Al-'Uthaymīn, *Muhammad ibn 'Abd al-Wahhāb: The Man and His Works* (London: I.B. Tauris, 2009); David Dean Commins, *The Wahhabi Mission and Saudi Arabia* (London: I.B. Tauris, 2006); Madawi al-Rasheed, *Contesting the Saudi State: Islamic Voices from a New Generation* (New York: Cambridge University Press, 2007), 22–58; and Hamadi Redissi, *Le Pacte de Nadjd: Ou comment l'islam sectaire est devenu l'islam* (Paris: Éditions du Seuil, 2007), 122–37.

2 For more details about the issue of naming 'Wahhabism', see, e.g., Hamadi Redissi, 'The Refutation of Wahhabism in Arabic Sources: 1745–1932', in *Kingdom without Borders: Saudi Arabia's Political, Religious and Media Frontiers*, ed. Madawi al-Rasheed (London: Hurst, 2008), 157–81; David Commins, 'From Wahhabi to Salafi', in *Saudi Arabia in Transition: Insights on Social, Political, Economic and Religious Change*, ed. Bernard Haykel, Thomas Hegghammer and Stéphane Lacroix (Cambridge: Cambridge University Press, 2015), 151–66; and Rüdiger Lohlker, *Die Salafisten: Der Aufstand der Frommen, Saudi-Arabien und der Islam* (München:

C.H. Beck, 2017), 33–4; as well as Nabil Mouline, *The Clerics of Islam: Religion, Authority, and Political Power in Saudi Arabia* (New Haven/London: Yale University Press, 2014), 9.

3 For details about the origins of the Saud family and the alliance between Muhammad ibn Abd al-Wahhab and Muhammad ibn Saud, see, e.g., Madawi al-Rasheed, *A History of Saudi Arabia*, 2nd edn. (New York: Cambridge University Press, 2010), 13–20; Redissi, *Le Pacte de Nadjd*, 37–48; and Lohlker, *Die Salafisten*, 33–42.

4 For sources concerning the history of the second Saudi State, the emirate of Nadjd (1824–91 CE), see, e.g., al-Rasheed, *A History of Saudi Arabia*, 22–4; and Redissi, *Le Pacte de Nadjd*, 67–9. For sources concerning the genesis of the third Saudi state, the Kingdom of Saudi Arabia, see, e.g., al-Rasheed, *A History of Saudi Arabia*, 37–68; John S. Habib, 'Wahhabi Origins of the Contemporary Saudi State', in *Religion and Politics in Saudi Arabia: Wahhabism and the State*, ed. Mohammed Ayoob and Hasan Kosebalaban (Boulder: Lynne Rienner, 2009), 57–73; and Redissi, *Le Pacte de Nadjd*, 70–81.

5 See, e.g., al-Rasheed, *A History of Saudi Arabia*, 46–56.

6 For sources concerning the history of the Ikhwan and their role in the building of the Kingdom of Saudi Arabia, see, e.g., al-Rasheed, *A History of Saudi Arabia*, 56–68; Habib, 'Wahhabi Origins of the Contemporary Saudi State', 64–7; and Redissi, *Le Pacte de Nadjd*, 70–81.

7 For details about the institutionalization of 'Wahhabism' in the Saudi state, see, e.g., al-Rasheed, *Contesting the Saudi State*, 22–58; Nabil Mouline, 'Enforcing and Reinforcing the State's Islam', in *Saudi Arabia in Transition*, ed. Haykel, Hegghammer and Lacroix, 48–67; and Abdullah Hamidaddin, *Tweeted Heresies: Saudi Islam in Transformation* (New York: Oxford University Press, 2020), 42–9.

8 For details about the approval of the Wahhabi scholars for the suppression of the Ikhwan revolt, see, e.g., al-Rasheed, *A History of Saudi Arabia*, 66–8.

9 For details about their approval for the Saudi alliance with the United States during the Gulf War of 1990–1 CE, see., e.g., al-Rasheed, *A History of Saudi Arabia*, 163–6.

10 For details about the position of the 'Wahhabi' scholars concerning the demonstrations of the so-called Arab Spring, see, e.g., ar-Riyāḍ, *Hay'at kibār al-'ulamā': al-Iṣlāḥ lā yakūn bi-l-muẓāharāt wa-l-asālīb allatī tuṯīr al-fitan wa-tafarruq al-ǧamā'a* (published on alriyadh.com, 7 March 2011 CE, available online: http://www.alriyadh.com/611507, accessed 11 June 2020).

11 See, e.g., al-Rasheed, *A History of Saudi Arabia*, 197–210; Madawi al-Rasheed, *Xenophobia, Tribalism and Imagined Enemies: Mohammed Bin Salman's Brand of Saudi Nationalism* (published on middleeasteye.net, 5 September 2018, available online: https://www.middleeasteye.net/opinion/xenophobia- tribalism-and-imagined-enemies-mohammed-bin-salmans-brand-saudi-nationalism, accessed 11 June 2020).

12 For details on the 'institutionalization of sin' in Saudi politics, see, especially, Abdullah Hamidaddin's excellent observations in Hamidaddin, *Tweeted Heresies*, 39–64.

13 For details about the Ikhwan rebellion, see, e.g., Habib, *Wahhabi Origins of the Contemporary Saudi State*, 57–73; al-Rasheed, *A History of Saudi Arabia*, 63–8; Joseph Kostiner, 'On Instruments and Their Designers: The Ikhwan of Najd and the Emergence of the Saudi State', *Middle Eastern Studies* 21, no. 3 (1985): 298–323.

14 For details about the resistance movement in the Hijaz, see, e.g., J. E. Peterson, *Historical Dictionary of Saudi Arabia*, 2nd edn. (Lanham: The Scarecrow Press, 2003), 108.

15 For details concerning the Free Princes, see, e.g., al-Rasheed, *A History of Saudi Arabia*, 102–10; Habib, *Wahhabi Origins of the Contemporary Saudi State*, 60–1; Richard Dekmejian, 'The Liberal Impulse in Saudi Arabia', *The Middle East Journal* 57, no. 3 (Summer 2003): 400–13; Mamoun Fandy, *Saudi Arabia and the Politics of Dissent* (New York: Palgrave, 1999), 44–5; and Peterson, *Historical Dictionary of Saudi Arabia*, 108.

16 For details about socialist and Arab nationalist movements in Saudi Arabia from the 1950s until the 1970s CE, see, e.g., Toby Matthiesen, *The Other Saudis: Shiism, Dissent and Sectarianism* (New York: Cambridge University Press, 2015); Ghassane Salameh, 'Political Power and the Saudi State', *Middle East Research and Information Project (MERIP) Reports* no. 91 (October 1980): 20–1; Peterson, *Historical Dictionary of Saudi Arabia*, 109–10; and MERIP, 'The Arabian Peninsula Opposition Movements', *Middle East Research and Information Project (MERIP) Reports* no. 130 (February 1985): 13–15.

17 For details about Rejectionism and the siege of the Great Mosque in Mecca, see, e.g., Thomas Hegghammer and Stéphane Lacroix, 'Rejectionist Islamism in Saudi Arabia: The Story of Juhayman Al-ʿUtaybi Revisited', *International Journal of Middle Eastern Studies* 39 (2007): 107–8; al-Rasheed, *A History of Saudi Arabia*, 139–41; and Stéphane Lacroix, *Les Islamistes Saoudiens: Une insurrection manquée* (Paris: Presses Universitaires de France, 2010), 109–21.

18 For details about the Shia opposition activism since the 1970s CE, see, especially, Matthiesen, *The Other Saudis*; as well as Toby Craig, 'Rebellion on the Saudi Periphery: Modernity, Marginalization, and the Shiʿa Uprising of 1979', *International Journal of Middle East Studies* 38, no. 2 (May 2006): 213–33.

19 For details about the doctrine of Jihadism and its link to Saudi Arabia, see, e.g., Thomas Hegghammer, *Jihad in Saudi Arabia: Violence and Pan-Islamism since 1979* (Cambridge: Cambridge University Press, 2010); Thomas Hegghammer, '"Classical" and "Global" Jihadism in Saudi Arabia', in *Saudi Arabia in Transition*, ed. Haykel, Hegghammer and Lacroix, 207–28; and Thomas Hegghammer, *The Caravan: Abdallah Azzam and the Rise of Global Jihad* (Cambridge: Cambridge University Press, 2020).

20 For details about the rise of the Sahwa, see, e.g., Fandy, *Saudi Arabia and the Politics of Dissent*; Toby Craig Jones, 'Religious Revivalism and Its Challenge to the Saudi Regime', in *Religion and Politics in Saudi Arabia*, ed. Ayoob and Kosebalaban, 109–19; Lacroix, *Les Islamistes Saoudiens*, 64–89; and Stéphane Lacroix, 'Understanding Stability and Dissent in the Kingdom. The Double- Edged Role of the jama'at in Saudi Politics', in *Saudi Arabia in Transition*, ed. Haykel, Hegghammer and Lacroix, 167–80.

21 For details, see, e.g., al-Rasheed, *A History of Saudi Arabia*, 158–63; and Lacroix, *Les Islamistes Saoudiens*, 189–96.

22 For details on the 'Letter of Demands' of 1991 CE, see, e.g., Anonymous, *Ḫiṭāb al-maṭālib* (May 1991, available online: http://www.al-waie.org/archives/article/11370, accessed 11 June 2020); Lacroix, *Les Islamistes Saoudiens*, 214–19; Gilles Kepel, *Jihad. Expansion et déclin de l'islamisme* (Paris: Éditions Gallimard, 2000), 333–4; and Redissi, *Le Pacte de Nadjd*, 287–8. For details on the 'Memorandum of Advice', see, e.g., Anonymous, *Mudakkirat an-naṣīḥa* (September 1992, available online: https://libral.org/vb/archive/index.php/t-25264.html, accessed 11 June 2020); Fandy, *Saudi Arabia and the Politics of Dissent*, 50–60; as well as al-Rasheed, *A History of Saudi Arabia*, 163–6; Kepel, *Jihad*, 334–5; and Redissi, *Le Pacte de Nadjd*, 288.

23 See, e.g., Fandy, *Saudi Arabia and the Politics of Dissent*, 116; and Kepel, *Jihad*, 335.

24 For details about the reforms of 1992 CE, see, e.g., al-Rasheed, *A History of Saudi Arabia*, 166–9.

25 For details concerning the security and media campaign against the reformist wave of the early 1990s CE, see, e.g., al-Rasheed, *A History of Saudi Arabia*, 170–1.

26 For details on the collapse of the Islamically inspired political opposition wave of the 1990s CE, see, e.g., al-Rasheed, *A History of Saudi Arabia*, 222–33; al-Rasheed, *Contesting the Saudi State*, 81–101; Jones, 'Religious Revivalism and Its Challenge to the Saudi Regime', 109–20; and Lacroix, *Les Islamistes Saoudiens*, 313–14.

27 See, e.g., Stéphane Lacroix, 'Between Islamists and Liberals: Saudi Arabia's New "Islamo-Liberal" Reformists', *Middle East Journal* 58, no. 3 (Summer 2004): 345–65; and Lacroix, *Les Islamistes Saoudiens*, 293–7.

28 For details about the names and labels used to speak about the Islamic civil rights movement and the broader Islamo-reformist current, see Chapter 6, 'Names and labels'.

29 For details about the 'Riyadh Spring' of the 2000s CE, see, e.g., al-Rasheed, *A History of Saudi Arabia*, 242–74; and Franke Drewes, 'Das Nationale Dialogforum in Saudi-Arabien. Ausdruck politischer Reformen oder Stagnation?', in *Saudi Arabien: Ein Königreich im Wandel*, ed. Ulrike Freitag (Paderborn: Verlag Ferdinand Schöningh, 2010), 29–60.

30 For details about the petition 'Vision for the Present of the Homeland and Its Future' of January 2003 CE, see, e.g., Anonymus, *Ruʾyat li-ḥāḍir al-waṭan wa-mustaqbalihi* (January 2003, available online: http://www.mstayeb.com/index.php?option=com_content&view=article&id=145:ro2yalehaderalwatan&catid=2 0:isla7&Itemid=5, accessed 11 June 2020); Dekmejian, 'The Liberal Impulse in Saudi Arabia', 400–13; Lacroix, 'Between Islamists and Liberals', 345–65; al-Rasheed, *Contesting the Saudi State*, 232–4; and Lacroix, *Les Islamistes Saoudiens*, 293–97.

31 For details about the petition 'Calling on the Leadership and the People at the Same Time: Constitutional Reform First' of December 2003 CE, see, e.g., Anonymus, *Nidāʾan ilā l-qiyāda wa-š-šaʿb maʿan: al-Iṣlāḥ ad-dustūrī awwalan* (December 2003, available online: http://www.saudiaffairs.net/webpage/sa/issue12/article12l/issue12lt2.htm, accessed 11 June 2020); Stéphane Lacroix, 'Islamo-Liberal Politics in Saudi Arabia', in *Saudi Arabia in the Balance: Political Economy, Society, Foreign Affairs*, ed. Paul Aarts and Gerd Nonneman (New York: New York University Press, 2005), 35–56; al-Rasheed, *Contesting the Saudi State*, 234–5; and Lacroix, *Les Islamistes Saoudiens*, 296–7.

32 For details about the petition 'Milestones on the Way of a Constitutional Monarchy' of February 2007, see, e.g., Anonymus, *Maʿālim fī ṭarīq al-malakīya d-dustūrīya* (February 2007, available online: https://www.alquds.co.uk/نص-العريضة-الحديثة-التي-وجهها-الاصلاح/, accessed 11 June 2020); and Stefan Maneval, 'Die Liberal Reformbewegung in Saudi-Arabian. Analyse und Übersetzung der Reformpetition vom 2. Februar 2007', in *Saudi-Arabien*, ed. Freitag, 61–88; and Guido Steinberg, *Saudi-Arabien: Politik Geschichte Religion* (München: C.H. Beck, 2013), 61–88.

33 For details about the judicial reforms of 2007 CE, see, e.g., Maneval, 'Die Liberal Reformbewegung in Saudi-Arabian', 167–75.

34 For concrete examples concerning the persecution of opposition activists in the 2000s CE, see, e.g., Arabic Network for Human Rights Information (ANHRI), *Iʿtiqālāt ǧadīda fī l-mamlaka l-ʿarabīya s-suʿūdīya: Iʿtiqāl aḥada ʿašara munāḍil min afāḍil*

al-ǧazīra l-ʿarabīya (published on anhri.net, 17 March 2004, available online: http://www.anhri.net/mena/achr/pr040317.shtml, accessed 11 June 2020); Arabic Network for Human Rights Information (ANHRI), *Wa-yastamirr musalsal al-mumaṭala fī muḥakamat al-iṣlāḥiyīn aṯ-ṯalāṯa bi-s- suʿūdīya* (published on anhri.net, 17 February 2005, available online: http://www.anhri.net/saudi/spdhr/2005/pr0217.shtml, accessed 11 June 2020); and ar-Riyāḍ, *Tisaʿ sanawāt siğnan li-d-Dumaynī wa-sabaʿ li-l-Ḥāmid wa-sitta li-l-Fāliḥ* (published on alriyadh.com, 16 May 2005, available online: http://www.alriyadh.com/64858, accessed 11 June 2020).

35 For details about the reaction of the Saudi government to the Arab Spring, see, e.g., Guido Steinberg, *Leading the Counter-Revolution: Saudi Arabia and the Arab Spring* (research paper by the Stiftung Wissenschaft und Politik, 2014).

36 See, ar-Riyāḍ, *Hayʾat kibār al-ʿulamāʾ*.

37 For a detailed account of the most important planned protest and its failure, see, e.g., Madawi al-Rasheed, *Muted Modernists: The Struggle Over Divine Politics in Saudi Arabia* (London: Hurst, 2015), 42–7; Bernard Haykel, Thomas Hegghammer, and Stéphane Lacroix, 'Introduction', in *Saudi Arabia in Transition*, ed. Haykel, Hegghammer and Lacroix, 1–6; and Stéphane Lacroix, 'No Spring in Riyadh: Saudi Arabia's Seemingly Impossible Revolution', in *Taking to the Streets: The Transformation of Arab Activism*, ed. Lina Khatib and Ellen Lust (Baltimore: Johns Hopkins University Press, 2014), 311–17.

38 For details about the protests for the support of political prisoners of the 2010s CE, see, e.g., al-Rasheed, *Muted Modernists*, 47–8; and Stéphane Lacroix, *Saudi Islamists and the Arab Spring* (paper published by the London School of Economics Kuwait Programme on Development, Governance and Globalisation in the Gulf States, May 2014), 15–18. For details about women's rights protets in the 2010s CE, see, e.g., al-Rasheed, *Muted Modernists*, 48–9; and Nora Doaiji, 'From HASM to HAZM: Saudi Feminism Beyond Patriarchal Bargaining', in *Salman's Legacy: The Dilemmas of a New Era in Saudi Arabia*, ed. Madawi al-Rasheed (New York: Oxford University Press, 2018), 117–44.

39 For details about the petition 'Towards a State of Rights and Institutions' of February 2011 CE, see, e.g., Anonymous, *Bayān naḥwa daulat al-ḥuqūq wa-l-muʾassasāt* (February 2011, available online: https://libral.org/vb/archive/index.php/t-51378.html, accessed 11 June 2020); and Lacroix, *No Spring in Riyadh*, 309–11.

40 For details about the petition 'National Declaration of Reform' of March 2011, see, e.g., Anonymous, *Iʿlān waṭanī li-l-iṣlāḥ* (March 2011, available online: https://www.alawan.org/2013/12/08/إعلان-وطني-للاصلاح-نداء-من-مثقفين-سعو/, accessed 11 June 2020).

41 For details about the biography of Hakim al-Mutayri and the Salafist movement in Kuwait, see, e.g., Zoltan Pall, *Kuwaiti Salafism and Its Growing Influence in the Levant* (published by the Carnegie Endowment for International Peace, 7 May 2014, available online: https://carnegieendowment.org/files/kuwaiti_salafists.pdf, accessed 11 June 2020).

42 For details about al-Mutayri's theory, see, e.g., Ḥākim al-Muṭairī, *al-Ḥurrīya aw aṭ-ṭawfān* (Bairūt: al-Muʾassasa l-ʿarabīya li-d-dirāsāt wa-n-našr, 2004) and Ḥākim al-Muṭairī, *Taḥrīr al-insān wa-taǧrīd aṭ-ṭuġyān* (Bairūt: al-Muʾassasa l-ʿarabīya li-d-dirāsāt wa-n-našr, 2009).

43 For details about the biography of Salman al-Awda, see, e.g., al-Rasheed, *Muted Modernists*, 75–94; Mamoun Fandy, *Saudi Arabia and the Politics of Dissent* (New York: Palgrave, 2001), 89–113; John Calvert, *Islamism: A Documentary and Reference Guide* (Westport: Greenwood Press, 2008), 168–72; Amnesty

International, *Saudi Arabia: Prominent Reformist Cleric Faces Death Sentence for His Peaceful Activism* (published on amnesty.org, 26 July 2019, available online: https://www.amnesty.org/en/latest/news/2019/07/saudi-arabia-prominent-reformist-cleric-faces-death-sentence-for-his-peaceful-activism/, accessed 11 June 2020); and Nushin Atmaca, 'Die neue Mitte? Gegenwärtige Positionen Salman al-'Awdas zur Rolle der Frau, religiösem Extremismus und Gewalt', in *Saudi-Arabien,* ed. Freitag, 165–88.

44 See Salmān al-ʿAuda, *Asʾilat aṯ-ṯawra* (Bairūt: Markaz namāʾ li-l-buḥūṯ wa-d-dirāsāt, 2012).

45 For details about the biography of Muhammad al-Abd al-Karim see, e.g., al-Rasheed, *Muted Modernists*, 115–36; and Lacroix, *Saudi Islamists and the Arab Spring*, 8.

46 Muḥammad al-ʿAbd al-Karīm, *al-Iḥtisāb al-madanī: Dirāsa fī l-bināʾ al-maqāṣidī li-l-ʾiḥtisāb*, aṭ-ṭabʿa ṯ-ṯānīya (Bairūt: aš-Šabaka l-ʿarabīya li-l-ʾabḥāṯ wa-n-našr, 2013).

47 Muḥammad al-ʿAbd al-Karīm, *Tafkīk al-istibdād: Dirāsa fī fiqh at-taḥarrur min at-taġallub* (Bairūt: aš-Šabaka l-ʿarabīya li-l-abḥāṯ wa-n-našr, 2013).

48 For details about the biography of Abdallah al-Maliki, see, e.g., al-Rasheed, *Muted Modernists*, 95–113.

49 ʿAbdallāh al-Mālikī, *Siyādat al-umma qabla taṭbīq aš-šarīʿa: Naḥwa faḍāʾ amṯal li-taǧsīd mabādiʾ al-islām* (Bairūt: Aš-Šabaka l-ʿarabīya li-l-abḥāṯ wa-n-našr, 2012).

50 For details about the biography of Muhammad al-Ahmari, see, e.g., al-Rasheed, *Muted Modernists*, 137–55.

51 Muḥammad al-Aḥmarī, *ad-Dīmuqrāṭīya: al-Ǧuḏūr wa-iškālīyat at-taṭbīq* (Bairūt: aš-Šabaka l-ʿarabīya li-l-abḥāṯ wa-n-našr, 2012).

52 See ALQST's official website https://www.alqst.org/ar (accessed 11 June 2020).

53 See Diwan London's official website https://www.diwan.tv (accessed 11 June 2020).

54 See the National Assembly Party's official website https://the-naas.com/en (accessed 6 September 2021).

55

"فان الشريعة الإسلامية جاءت بحفظ كرامة الانسان وصيانة حقوقه ونهت عن الظلم، قبل أربعة عشر قرنا من ظهور القوانين الدولية التي كفلت حقوق الإنسان والتزمت بها الحكومات، كما قلا تعالى (ولقد كرّمنا بني آدم) وقال (وإذا حكمتم بين الناس أن تحكموا بالعدل)."

HASM, Al-Iʿlān at-taʾsīsī (published on acpra.org, 12 October 2009, available online: http://acpra.org/news.php?action=view&id=1, accessed 11 June 2020).

56 "الجهاد المدني السياسي السلمي"

Ibid.

57

"ويرجو الموقعون على هذا البيان كل من تعرض لانتهاكات موثقة أو علم بها أن يبلغ أحد الموقعين على هذا البيان من أجل رصدها ورفعها لخادم الحرمين الشريفين، والجهات المعنية."

Ibid.

58 See https://www.youtube.com/user/AcpraTube/videos (accessed 11 June 2020).

59 In 2012 CE, Muhammad al-Qahtani was mentioned as the forty-seventh most influential global thinker by *Foreign Policy* magazine. See al-Rasheed, *Muted Modernists*, 65; and Alicia P. Q. Wittmeyer, *The FP Top 100 Global Thinkers* (published on foreignpolicy.com, 26 November 2012, available online: https://foreignpolicy.com/2012/11/26/the-fp-top-100-global-thinkers-2/, accessed 11 June 2020).

60 See W3team, *Liqāʾ farīq waʿy maʿa ràìs ḥasm al-muhandis Fawzān al-Ḥarbī qabla iʿtiqālihi* (blog entry published on w3iteam.wordpress.com, 19 March 2014, available

online: https://w3iteam.wordpress.com/2014/03/19/لقاء-فريق-وعي-مع-رئيس-حسم-المهندس-
فوزان/, accessed 11 June 2020).

61 For more information on HASM's activities and its support for political prisoners during the first years of the existence of the association, see, e.g., al-Rasheed, *Muted Modernists*, 55–74; and Lacroix, 'Saudi Islamists and the Arab Spring', 16–18.

62 For details about the Human Rights Commission and the National Society for Human Rights, see, e.g., al-Rasheed, *A History of Saudi Arabia*, 250–3.

63 For details about the Human Rights Monitor in Saudi Arabia, see, e.g., Amnesty International, *Saudi Arabia: End Ill-treatment, Arbitrary Detention of Human Rights Defender, Waleed Abu al-Khair* (published on amnesty.org, 6 December 2019, available online: https://www.amnesty.org/en/latest/news/2019/12/saudi-arabia-end-ill-treatment- arbitrary-detention-of-human-rights-defender-waleed-abu-al-khair/, accessed 11 June 2020).

64 For details about the Adala Centre for Human Rights, see, e.g., Amnesty International, *Saudi Arabia Steps Up Ruthless Crackdown Against Human Rights Activists* (published on amnesty.org, 10 January 2017, available online: https://www.amnesty.org/en/latest/news/2017/01/saudi-arabia-steps-up-ruthless-crackdown-against-human- rights-activists/, accessed 11 June 2020).

65 For details about the Union for Human Rights, see, e.g., Human Rights Watch, *Saudi Arabia: New Rights Group Facing Harassment* (published on hrw.org, 7 May 2013, available online: https://www.hrw.org/news/2013/05/07/saudi-arabia-new-rights-group-facing-harassment, accessed 11 June 2020); and ALQST, *Terrorism Court Hands Down Seven- and 14-Year Jail Sentences for Starting a Human Rights Group* (published on alqst.org, 26 January 2018, available online: https://alqst.org/eng/terrorism-court-hands-seven-14-year-jail-sentences- starting-human-rights-group/, accessed 11 June 2020).

66 For details on the European Saudi Organisation for Human Rights and ALQST, see their websites https://www.esohr.org/en/ (accessed 11 June 2020) and https://alqst.org/eng/ (accessed 11 June 2020).

67 A video of the lecture by Sulayman ar-Rashudi can be found here: Acpra Tube, *Ḥukm al-muẓāharāt wa-l-iʿtiṣāmāt fī š-šarīʿa l-islāmīya* (published on youtube.com, 11 December 2012, available online: https://www.youtube.com/watch?v=JY8y6hIalig, accessed 11 June 2020).

68 For sources concerning the arrests and trials of HASM members after 2011 CE, see, e.g., Amnesty International, *Saudi Arabia's ACPRA: How the Kingdom Silences Its Human Rights Activists* (published on amnesty.org, 10 October 2014, available online: https://www.amnesty.de/downloads/saudi-arabias-acpra-how-kingdom-silences-its-human-rights-activists, accessed 11 June 2020); al-Karāma, *as-Suʿūdīya: Iʿtiqāl as-saiyid Muḥammad ibn Ġānim al-Qaḥṭānī wa-sitta šaḫṣiyāt uḫrā ʿalā ḫalafīyat ṭalab iʿtimād ḥizb siyāsī* (published on alkarama.org, 17 February 2011, available online: http://ararchive.alkarama.org/item/4061-2014-08-03-16-04-57, accessed 11 June 2020); al-Ǧazīra, *as-Suʿūdīya: Siǧn nāšiṭīn wa-iġlāq ḥasm* (published on aljazeera.net, 9 March 2013, available online: https://www.aljazeera.net/news/arabic/2013/3/9/السعودية-
سجن-ناشطين-وإغلاق-حسم, accessed 11 June 2020); and al-Yawm, *as-Siǧn 8 sanawāt li-ʿaḍw ḥasm li-daʿwātihi t-taḥrīḍīya* (published on alyaum.com, 25 June 2013, available online: https://www.alyaum.com/articles/878069/المملكة-اليوم/الدكتور-عبد-
الكريم-الخضر, accessed 11 June 2020).

69 See, e.g., Amnesty International, *Saudi Arabia's ACPRA*; The Right Livelihood Award, *Saudi Human Rights Trio Named 2018 Right Livelihood Award Laureates* (published on rightlivelihoodaward.org, 24 September 2018, available online: https://www.rightlivelihoodaward.org/wp-content/uploads/2018/09/Nr-2-Final-PR-EN-23-Sep-2018.pdf, accessed 11 June 2020); and ALQST's website 'Prisoners of Conscience', which is available online: https://moqsetoon.com/prisonersofconscience/en/prisoners-of-conscience/ (accessed 26 January 2020)

70 See, e.g., ar-Riyāḍ, *Aḥkām bi-siğn iṯnain min mu'assisī mā yaṭlaqu 'alayhi ğam'īyat ḥasm 11 wa-10 sanawāt wa-ḥall al-ğam'īya wa-iġlāq manāšiṭihā wa-muṣādarat mumtalakātihā* (published on al-riyadh.com, 10 March 2013, available online: http://www.alriyadh.com/816175, accessed 11 June 2020).

71 See HASM, *Bayān 'an waqā'i' al-ğalsa l-ḥādiya 'ašara (ğalsat an-naṭq bi-l-ḥukm) li-l-muḥākama s-siyāsīya li-l-muṭālibīn bi-šurūṭ al-bay'a š-šar'īya (sulṭat al-umma) wa-ḥuqūq al-insān* (published on acpra.org, 11 March 2013, available online: http://www.acpra.org/news.php?action=view&id=224&spell=0&highlight=%C8%ED%C7%E4+%DA%E4+%E6%DE%C7%C6%DA+%C7%E1%CC%E1%D3%C9+%C7%E1%CD%C7%CF%ED%C9+%DA%D4%D1, accessed 11 June 2020). For more details about the ideological battle between HASM and the establishment during the trials, see, e.g., al -Rasheed, *Muted Modernists*, 56–8.

72 For details on the court's sentence against HASM, see, e.g., Amnesty International, *Saudi Arabia's ACPRA*; al-Ğazīra, *as-Su'ūdīya: Siğn nāšiṭīn wa-iġlāq ḥasm* (published on aljazeera.net, 9 March 2013, available online: https://www.aljazeera.net/news/arabic/2013/3/9/السعودية-سجن-ناشطين-وإغلاق-حسم, accessed 11 June 2020); and ar-Riyāḍ, *Aḥkām bi-siğn iṯnain min mu'assisī mā yaṭlaqu 'alayhi ğam'īyat ḥasm*.

73 See, e.g., Sulaymān al-Ḫarāšī, *Sảalnī sā'il 'an ad-duktūr 'Abdallāh al-Ḥāmid* (published on saaid.net, without date, available online: http://www.saaid.net/Warathah/Alkharashy/m/43.htm, accessed 11 June 2020); and as-Sakīna: *Ğam'īyat al-ḥuqūq al-madanīya wa-s-siyāsīya (ḥasm)*.

74 See, e.g., the untitled calls for protests for 21 February 2013 CE published by Twitter accounts @Sit_ins and @bayfsad in January and February 2013 CE. The calls are available online: https://twitpic.com/c4a7u1 and https://twitpic.com/c50nhj (both accessed 11 June 2020).

75 See, e.g., al-Ğazīra, *Su'ūdīyūn yu'linūn wafāt "šayḫ al-ḥuqūqīyīn" 'Abdallāh al-Ḥāmid fī s-siğn ğirā'a l-ihmāl aṭ-ṭibbī* (published on aljazeera.net, 24 April 2020, available online: https://www.aljazeera.net/news/humanrights/2020/4/24/السعودية-أنباء-وفاة-عبد-الله-الحامد, accessed 11 June 2020); Amnesty International, *Saudi Arabia: Prisoner of Conscience Dr Abdullah al-Hamid Dies While in Detention* (published on anmesty.org, 24 April 2020, available online: https://www.amnesty.org/en/latest/news/2020/04/saudi-arabia-prisoner-of-conscience-dr-abdullah-alhamid-dies-while-in-detention/, accessed 11 June 2020); and BBC, *Saudi Arabia: Prominent Human Rights Activist 'Dies in Jail'* (published on bbc.com, 24 April 2020, available online: https://www.bbc.com/news/world-middle-east-52411453, accessed 11 June 2020). In June 2020 CE, a report by the UN's Office of the High Commissioner for Human Rights also stated that Abdallah al-Hamid's death was a direct result of his ill-treatment in prison and the fact that he was being denied the necessary medical treatment (see https://spcommreports.ohchr.org/TMResultsBase/DownLoadPublicCommunicationFile?gId=25310, accessed 4 August 2020).

Chapter 2

1 For details about the biography of Abdallah al-Hamid, see, e.g., Madawi al-Rasheed, *Muted Modernists: The Struggle Over Divine Politics in Saudi Arabia* (London: Hurst, 2015), 62–4; Amnesty International (AI), *Saudi Arabia's ACPRA: How the Kingdom Silences Its Human Rights Activists* (published on amnesty.org, 10 October 2014, available online: https://www.amnesty.org/en/documents/MDE23/025/2014/en/, accessed 11 June 2020); and W3iteam, *Nazra'u l-wa'y li-yaqṭafa l-muǧtama' al-'adl wa-n-namā'. 'Abdallāh al-Ḥāmid* (blog entry published on w3iteam.wordpress.com, 28 September 2014, available online: https://w3iteam.wordpress.com/2014/09/28/عبد-الله-الحامد/, accessed 11 June 2020).

2 See, e.g., al-Ǧazīra, *Su'ūdiyūn yu'linūna wafāt "šayḫ al-ḥuqūqiyīn" 'Abdallāh al-Ḥāmid fī s-siǧn ǧirā'a l-ihmāl aṭ-ṭibbī* (published on aljazeera.net, 24 April 2020, available online: https://www.aljazeera.net/news/humanrights/2020/4/24/السعودية-أنباء-وفاة-عبد-الله-الحامد-السجن-الإهمال-الطبي, accessed 11 June 2020); BBC, *Saudi Arabia: Prominent Human Rights Activist 'Dies in Jail'* (published on bbc.com, 24 April 2020, available online: https://www.bbc.com/news/world-middle-east-52411453?intlink_from_url=&link_location=live-reporting-story, accessed 11 June 2020); and Amnesty International (AI), *Saudi Arabia: Prisoner of Conscience Dr Abdullah al-Hamid Dies While in Detention* (published on amnesty.org, 24 April 2020, available online: https://www.amnesty.org/en/latest/news/2020/04/saudi-arabia-prisoner-of-conscience-dr-abdullah-alhamid-dies-while-in-detention/, accessed 11 June 2020). In June 2020 CE, a report by the UN's Office of the High Commissioner for Human Rights also stated that Abdallah al-Hamid's death was a direct result of his ill-treatment in prison and the fact that he was being denied the necessary medical treatment (see https://spcommreports.ohchr.org/TMResultsBase/DownLoadPublicCommunicationFile?gId=25310, accessed 4 August 2020).

3 For details about the biography of Muhammad al-Qahtani, see, e.g., al-Rasheed, *Muted Modernists*, 65; and Amnesty International (AI), *Saudi Arabia's ACPRA*.

4 For details about the biography of Sulayman ar-Rashudi, see, e.g., al-Rasheed, *Muted Modernists*, 64–5; Amnesty International (AI), *Saudi Arabia's ACPRA*; and W3iteam, *Sulaymān ar-Rašūdī, šayḫ al-iṣlāḥiyīn* (blog entry published on w3iteam.wordpress.com, 5 September 2014, available online: https://w3iteam.wordpress.com/2014/09/05/سليمان-الرشودي-شيخ-الإصلاحيين/, accessed 11 June 2020).

5 For details about the biography of Abd al-Karim al-Khadr, see, e.g., Amnesty International (AI), *Saudi Arabia's ACPRA*; and W3iteam, *'Abd al-Karīm al-Ḫaḍr* (blog entry published on w3iteam.wordpress.com, 16 December 2014, available online: https://w3iteam.wordpress.com/2014/12/16/عبد-الكريم-الخضر/, accessed 11 June 2020).

6 For details about the biography of Muhammad al-Bajadi, see, e.g., al-Rasheed, *Muted Modernists*, 65–6; Amnesty International (AI), *Saudi Arabia's ACPRA*; and W3iteam, *Man huwa Muḥammad al-Baǧādī* (blog entry published on w3iteam.wordpress.com, 31 March 2014, available online: https://w3iteam.wordpress.com/2014/03/31/من-هو-محمد-البجادي؟-الرجل-الذي-قال-كل-ا/, accessed 11 June 2020).

7 For details about the biography of Fawzan al-Harbi, Abd ar-Rahman al-Hamid and Abd al-Aziz ash-Shubayli, see, e.g., Amnesty International (AI), *Saudi Arabia's ACPRA*.

8 For details about the links between some women's activists and HASM members, see, e.g., Nora Doaiji, 'From HASM to HAZM. Saudi Feminism Beyond Patriarchal Bargaining', in *Salman's Legacy. The Dilemmas of a New Era in Saudi Arabia*, ed. Madawi al-Rasheed (New York: Oxford University Press 2018), 124–9.

9 Gilles Kepel, *Fitna. Guerre au coeur de l'islam* (Paris: Gallimard, 2004), 204 (my translation).

10 See, e.g., Madawi al-Rasheed, *Contesting the Saudi State. Islamic Voices from a New Generation* (New York: Cambridge University Press, 2007), 62–8; and Stéphane Lacroix, *Les Islamistes Saoudiens. Une insurrection manquée* (Paris: Presses Universitaires de France, 2010), 18–28.

11 This point has been made before, for example, in Abdullah Hamidaddin's study on the informal debate about Islam in Saudi Arabia. See, e.g., Abdullah Hamidaddin, *Tweeted Heresies: Saudi Islam in Transformation* (New York: Oxford University Press, 2020), 63.

12 See, e.g., Lacroix, 'Saudi Arabia and the Limits of Post-Islamism', in *Post-Islamism. The Changing Faces of Political Islam*, ed. Asef Bayat (Oxford: Oxford University Press, 2013), 292.

13 See, e.g., Asef Bayat, 'Post-Islamism at Large', in *Post-Islamism*, 3–32.

14 See, e.g., David Commins, 'Contestation and Authority in Wahhabi Polemics', in *Religion and Politics in Saudi Arabia. Wahhabism and the State*, ed. Mohammed Ayoob and Hasan Kosebalaban (Boulder: Lynne Rienner Publishers, 2009), 50; John Calvert, *Islamism. A Documentary and Reference Guide* (Westport: Greenwood Press, 2008), 4; and Dale Eickelman and James Piscatori, *Muslim Politics* (Princeton: Princeton University Press, 1996), 43–5.

15 See Hamadi Redissi, *Le Pacte de Nadjd: Ou comment l'islam sectaire est devenu l'islam* (Paris: Éditions du Seuil, 2007), 145–6.

16 This point has been made by German scholar of Islamic history Gudrun Krämer. See, e.g., Gudrun Krämer, *Gottes Staat als Republik: Reflexionen zeitgenössischer Muslime zu Islam, Menschenrechten und Demokratie* (Baden-Baden: Nomos Verlagsgesellschaft, 1999), 261.

17 See, e.g., Asef Bayat, *Making Islam Democratic: Social Movements and the Post-Islamist Turn* (Stanford: Stanford University Press, 2007); and Asef Bayat, 'The Making of Post-Islamist Iran', in *Post-Islamism. The Changing Faces of Political Islam*, ed. Asef Bayat (Oxford: Oxford University Press, 2013), 35–70.

18 See, e.g., Usaama al-Azami, *Islam and the Arab Revolutions: The Ulama Between Democracy and Autocracy* (London: Hurst, 2021).

Chapter 3

1 See HASM, *Al-I'lān at-tàsīsī* (published on acpra.org, 23 October 2009, available online: http://www.acpra.org/news.php?action=view&id=1, accessed 11 June 2020).

2 The aforementioned videos were published via the YouTube channel 'Acpra Tube', which is available online: https://www.youtube.com/channel/UC43mVXNncsuzVJsWFeMCalA (accessed 11 June 2020).

3

”أهم دواعي إنشاء الجمعية أن حقوق الإنسان والحريات الأساسية ولا سيما السياسية في المملكة العربية السعودية تتعرض لانتهاكات خطيرة، وقد ازدادت هذه الانتهاكات منذ حرب الخليج، لازدياد وعي الناس بحقوقهم، وعندما ازداد وعيهم بحقوقهم زادت الحكومة بطشا على بطش، فساقت آلاف الشباب إلى السجون، بعد حرب الخليج الثانية.“

HASM, *Al-Iʿlān at-taʾsīsī.*

A very similar point is made by HASM member Muhammad al-Qahtani in a lecture titled 'Human rights violations in Saudi Arabia', which was published in October 2012 CE on HASM's YouTube channel 'Acpra Tube'. See Acpra Tube, *Intihākāt ḥuqūq al-insān fī s-Suʿūdīya / D. Muḥammad al-Qaḥṭānī* (published on youtube.com, 2 October 2012, available online: https://www.youtube.com/watch?v=hj2f6vO8iCc, accessed 11 June 2020).

4

”عم فقه الاضطرار، ورسخ في النظام التعليمي والأكاديمي. [...] واعتبر الاستبداد شرا لا بد منه، وقد ظهر هذا الاتجاه في جيل الإمام أحمد بن حنبل، ثم ازداد يأس الفقهاء من بعدهم، واعتبروا الجور من طبيعة الدولة والرياسة، وقدموا الأمن البوليسي على العدالة.“

ʿAbdallāh al-Ḥāmid, *aṭ-Ṭarīq aṯ-ṯāliṯ: ad-Dustūr al-islāmī* (Dimašq: Markaz an-nāqid aṯ-ṯaqāfī, 2009), 18.

5 ”أن أخطر ما عانته أمتنا الإسلامية عبر العصور، هو تكاتف تحالف فقهاء الظلام وأمراء الاستبداد.“

ʿAbdallāh al-Ḥāmid, *Ḥuqūq al-insān baina nūr al-islām wa-ġabaš al-mulk al-ʿaḍūḍ* (Bairūt: Bīsān li-n-našr wa-t-tawzīʿ wa-l-iʿlām, 1996), 8.

6 For details about al-Hamid's analysis of the development of Islamic discourse from the time of the prophet Muhammad until the twentieth century CE, see especially the following two of his books: ʿAbdallāh al-Ḥāmid, *as-Salafīya l-wusṭā: al-ʿAdl ʿadīl aṣ-ṣalāt* (Dimašq: Markaz an-nāqid aṯ-ṯaqāfī, 2009); and ʿAbdallāh al-Ḥāmid, *Likay lā yakūnu l-qurʾān ḥammāl auğuh: al-Miṣbāḥ fī zuğāğa wa-miškāt* (self-published 2008, available online: http://www.acpra.org/download.php?action=view&id=11, accessed 11 June 2020).

7

”ومن ما زاد البلبلة فتكا، أن التناقض لم ينحصر في شق العقيدة الروحي، ولا في مسائل فرعية صغيرة أو ثانوية قليلة من شقها المدني، بل في قضايا كبرى وكثيرة. [...] وصار المستفتي يجد الرأي ونقيضه عند العالم والفقيه الواحد، بل يجد مثنى وثلاث من الآراء المتعارضة المتناقضة، أو غير المتجانسة، ليس في المذهب الواحد بل للعالم والفقيه الواحد.“

al-Ḥāmid, *Likay lā yakūnu l-qurʾān ḥammāl auğuh*, 55–6.

8

”من أجل ذلك نقول: إن الفقهاء المحافظون اليوم في عهد الإمبريالية الغربية على الصياغة العباسية للعقيدة والتربية والسياسة والثقافة، [...] إنما يحمون التخلف السياسي بخطاب ديني. [...] وإنهم يفتحون الباب الموارب لرياح العلمنة والفرنجة والتغريب والعولمة والهيمنة الأطلسية، كما فتحه فقهاء الدولة العثمانية الغافلون من قبل.“

al-Ḥāmid, *as-Salafīya l-wusṭā*, 235.

9 In the very poetic translation of Muhammad Asad, the Verse of Light reads: 'God is the Light of the heavens and the earth. The parable of His light is, as it were, that of a niche containing a lamp; the lamp is [enclosed] in glass, the glass [shining] like a radiant star: [a lamp] lit from a blessed tree – an olive-tree that is neither of the east nor of the west – the oil whereof [is so bright that it] would well-nigh give light [of itself] even though fire had not touched it: light upon light! God guides unto His light him that wills [to be guided]; and [to this end] God propounds parables unto men, since God [alone] has full knowledge of all things' (Quran 34:35, translation by Muhammad Asad).

10

"صياغة العقيدة ومقاصد الشريعة وروحها، صياغة تجدد للعودة إلى مصباح (صريح الشريعة نصوصا واستقراء) في زجاجة العهد النبوي والراشدي ومشكاة حقائق العلوم ولاسيما علوم الاجتماع، من أجل التركيز على العناصر التي تجابه التحديات الحديثة."

al-Ḥāmid, *Likay lā yakūnu l-qur'ān ḥammāl auǧuh*, 48.

11 See al-Ḥāmid, *as-Salafīya l-wusṭā*.

12

"مرونة المنهج السلفي، وكونه إطار يسمح بتجديد أصيل يجمع بين الحفاظ على الثوابت القطعية، والتجديد في الوسائل والصياغة والفروع والحركة والتطبيق. [...] أن السلفية منهج وأسلوب وليس مذهبا محددا. [...] أن كل سلفية فإنما هي تجديد آني، يشكل خلطة دواء، تركز على وباء ما، في زمنها ومكانها."

al-Ḥāmid, *as-Salafīya l-wusṭā*, 28.

13

"الحق يعرف بالدليل والبرهان، لا بقول فلان ولا فلان. [...] ولذلك أوجب الفقهاء الوعاة على كل مسلم قادر أن يجتهد في أمور دينه، ولا سيما الأمور الأساسية، فلا يجوز له أن يقلد."

al-Ḥāmid, *Ḥuqūq al-insān baina nūr al-islām wa-ġabaš al-mulk al-'aḍūḍ*, 78.

14

"وسنن الله المقروءة في كتاب الشريعة لا تخالف سننه المشاهدة في مسرح الاجتماع والطبيعة. فالفكر الإنساني الصحيح في علوم الاجتماع والطبيعة لا يخالف المنقول الصريح من علوم الشريعة، كما بين هذه القاعدة العظيمة ابن تيمية في كتاب (العقل والنقل)."

al-Ḥāmid, *Likay lā yakūnu l-qur'ān ḥammāl auǧuh*, 135.

15

"١. تأصيل ثقافة حقوق الإنسان السياسية إسلاميا، باعتبار وسائل الحكم الشوري من أركان العقيدة السياسية الإسلامية التي لا يجوز – شرعا – التنازل عنها، أو التفريط بها: كالعدالة والحرية والتعددية الفكرية والسياسية والتسامح. [...]
٢. تأصيل ثقافة حقوق الإنسان المدنية والاقتصادية إسلاميا، كالمساواة، وتكافؤ الفرص السياسية، والعدالة والمساواة الاقتصادية والاجتماعية. [...]
٣. تأصيل ثقافة حقوق الإنسان والمتهم والسجين إسلاميا."

HASM, *Al-I'lān at-ta'sīsī*.

16 Al-Hamid's view on Ali and the way he treated the Kharijites is explained in several of his books and lectures, e.g., al-Ḥāmid, *Ḥuqūq al-insān baina nūr al-islām wa-ġabaš al-mulk al-'aḍūḍ*, 81–3; and Acpra Tube, *al-Ta'addudīya baina hady ar-rāšidīn wa-hawā l-mustabiddin* (published on youtube.com, 21 February 2013, available online: https://www.youtube.com/watch?v=06ic4IBNeb4, accessed 11 June 2020).

17 'Min aǧl ḏālika yanbaġī an nataḏakkara an al-islām huwa dīn al-ḥuqūq wa-l-ḥurrīya wa-l-karāma wa-l-musāwā'a.'
Acpra Tube, *Naḥwa ḫiṭāb dīnī yaḥtaḍinu l-ḥukm aš-šūrī* (published on youtube .com, 19 November 2012, available online: https://www.youtube.com/watch?v =flpZmSsLIxI, accessed 11 June 2020), 26:36–26:47.

18 'Al-Ḥukm aš-šūrī huwa al-'alāma l-fāriqa baina ḥukm yantamī ilā hadi Muḥammad wa-ḥukm yantamī ilā hawā Ḫisraw wa-Qayṣar.'
Acpra Tube, *Naḥwa ḫiṭāb dīnī yaḥtaḍinu l-ḥukm aš-šūrī*, 34:18–34:28.

19

"أولها أن الإسلام أكد أن مركز الأمة فوق الحاكم، لا العكس. [. . .]
وثانيها أن الإمام إنما هو وكيل أدنى عن الأمة، وليس وكيلا عليها. [...]
وثالثها: ما دام الحاكم وكيلا، فأنه يجب عليه ما يجب على كل وكيل، أن يراعي أحكام الوكالة، فيرجع إلى موكلته (الأمة)، في كل شيء مهم. [...]
ورابعها: الحكم في الإسلام شوري انتخابي، ولا تجوز ولاية المتغلب، ولا مشروعية له. [...]

وخامسها: لا يجوز للحاكم استخدام العنف لا من أجل الوصول إلى السلطة ولا للاحتفاظ بها، ولا يجوز له مضايقة معارضيه. [...]
سادسها: الحاكم موظف وأجير، تنطبق عليه أحكام الإجارة. [...]
سابعها: ومن الحقوق السياسية في الإسلام تداول السلطة وتولية الأكفياء. [...]
ثامنها: القاضي كالوالي وكيل عن الأمة، لا عليها، ولا عن السلطان.
تاسعها: المواطنة – في دولة الإسلام – هي أساس الحقوق والواجبات.
عاشرها: الجهاد إنما هو ضد العدوان، لا ضد الكفر المجرد من العدوان، فأساس العلاقة بين الدولة الإسلامية ودول العالم الأخرى هي المسالمة."

al-Ḥāmid, *Ḥuqūq al-insān baina nūr al-islām wa-ġabaš al-mulk al-ʿaḍūḍ*, 123–6.

20 ".الأمة المهدية أنما هي أمة الأحرار"
ʿAbdallāh al-Ḥāmid, *al-Burhān bi-qawāmat al-umma wa-siyādatihā ʿalā s-sulṭān* (self-published, 2012, available online: http://www.acpra.org/download.php?action=view&id=26, accessed 11 June 2020), 30.

21
"فالإسلام يجعل طاعة الأمة من طاعة الله، لأن الأمة هي التي تجسد الإجماع السياسي، وهي التي خولا الله حفظ الملة والدولة، وهي بذلك أمة مرحومة، وهي بإجماعها معصومة، لأنها كما جاء في الحديث الصحيح (لا تجتمع على ضلالة)."
al-Ḥāmid, *Ḥuqūq al-insān baina nūr al-islām wa-ġabaš al-mulk al-ʿaḍūḍ*, 145.

22
"الحكم في الإسلام يقوم على عقد بين الدولة والمجتمع، يسمى (البيعة)، على كتاب الله وسنة نبيه صلى الله عليه وسلم، ومضمون ذلك أن الحاكم وكيل للأمة وأن مقتضى الوكالة أن يلتزم الحاكم بالآليات والوسائل المؤسسية (أي الدستورية) التي تضمن العدل في المال والإدارة، والشورى الجماعية الملزمة (السلطة النيابية)."
ʿAbdallāh al-Ḥāmid, *Ṯulāṯīyat al-muǧtamaʿ al-madanī: ʿAn sirr najāḥ al-ġarb wa-iḫfāq al-ʿarab* (Bairūt: ad-Dār al-ʿarabīya li-l-ʿulūm, 2004), 58.

23 See Acpra Tube, *Ḫurūǧ al-ḥākim ʿalā l-umma* (published on youtube.com, 30 October 2012, available online: https://www.youtube.com/watch?v=EVZW_GyOGbA, accessed 11 June 2020).

24 Quran 4:59, translation by Muhammad Asad.

25
"مجلس نواب الأمة هو الإجراء المناسب اليوم، لمفهوم أولي الأمر في القرآن ولمفهوم أهل الحل والعقد في التراث، فهم وحدهم إذن الذين يجسدون إجماع الأمة."
al-Ḥāmid, *Ṯulāṯīyat al-muǧtamaʿ al-madanī*, 60.

A similar point is made by Abd al-Karim al-Khadr in one of his lectures. See Acpra Tube, *Ūlī l-amr lā walī l-amr / D. ʿAbd al-Karīm al-Ḫaḍr* (published on youtube.com, 25 December 2012, available online: https://www.youtube.com/watch?v=qRcIY_w6e6A, accessed 11 June 2020).

26
"وأن النظام الشوري له تنظيمات وإجراءات وتفريعات، يجسدها (النظام الدستوري)، فـ(النظام الدستوري) هو التجلي لسيادة الأمة، الدستور هو التجلي لـ(النظام الشوري)، والدستور هو (الوهاب) الصالحيات (المناع) التجاوزات."
al-Ḥāmid, *Ṯulāṯīyat al-muǧtamaʿ al-madanī*, 73.

27
"الدستور كلمة عامة فالدستور يمكن أن يكون (علمانيا)، ويمكن أن يكون (بوذيا)، ويمكن أن يكون (اشتراكيا)، [...] ويمكن أن يكون (إسلاميا)، وملتزما يأمر بالمعروف وينهي عن المنكر."
al-Ḥāmid, *Ṯulāṯīyat al-muǧtamaʿ al-madanī*, 80.

28
"فتأسيس الجمعية عمل مشروع في الإسلام. لأنها من أدوات التعاون على البر والتقوى، والتعاون على الأمر بالمعروف والنهي عن المنكر، وهي داخلة في قوله تعالى (ولتكن منكم امة يدعون إلى الخير)."

ʿAbdallāh al-Ḥāmid, *Inšāʾ ǧamʿīyat ḥasm amr mašrūʿ bal farīḍa šarʿīya* (self-published 2012, at the time of writing no longer accessible via the internet, a copy is in my possession), 1.

29 For an example of the position of the Wahhabi scholars concerning the demonstrations of the so-called Arab Spring, see, e.g., ar-Riyāḍ, *Hayʾat kibār al-ʿulamāʾ: al-Iṣlāḥ lā yakūnu bi-l-muẓāharāt wa-l-asālīb allatī tuṯīru l-fitan wa-tafarruq al-ǧamāʿa* (published on alriyadh.com, 7 March 2011 CE, available online: http://www.alriyadh.com/611507, accessed 11 June 2020).

30 'Al-muẓāharāt wa-l-iʿtiṣāmāt min al-wasāʾil, wa-l-qāʿida l-fiqhīya taqūlu: Al-wasāʾil lahā ḥukm al-ġāyāt. Wa-mā dāmat al-wasīla hunā hiya al-muẓāharāt as-silmīya wa-l-maqṣūd minhā huwa rafʿ aẓ-ẓulm, wa-iḥqāq al-ḥaqq wa-l-ʿadl, allaḏī faraḍahu llāh ʿalā ʿibādihi ǧamīʿan. [. . .] Fa-d-daʿwa ilā l-muẓāharāt as-silmīya li-rafʿ aẓ-ẓulm wa-l-istibdād wa-izālat al-fasād wa-iʿṭāʾ aš-šaʿb ḥuqūqahu wa-ḥurrīyatahu l-maslūba wa-l-karāma l-muhāna, hāḏā min ad-daʿwa li-l-ḫayr wa-l-amr bi-l-maʿrūf wa-n-nahy ʿan al-munkar allaḏī šaraʿahu llāh. Wa-mā dāmat hāḏihi hiya l-ġāya l-mašrūʿa, fa-ayy wasīla mubāḥa tuwaṣṣilu ilayhā fa-hiya mašrūʿa, bal wāǧiba.'
Acpra Tube, *Ḥukm al-muẓāharāt wa-l-iʿtiṣāmāt fī š-šarīʿa l-islāmīya* (published on youtube.com, 11 December 2012, available online: https://www.youtube.com/watch?v=JY8y6hIalig, accessed 11 June 2020), 6:55–10:07.

31

"أما نحن العرب والمسلمين، فلا بد لنا لكي ننهض من تجديد مفهوم الجهاد، لا بد من خطاب يؤكد أن الجهاد صنوان: عسكري حربي يصد الغزاة ومدني سلمي يصد الطغاة."

ʿAbdallāh al-Ḥāmid, *al-Ǧihād ṣinwān. Silmī li-aṭr wulāt wa-ḥarbī li-dafʿ ġuzāt* (self-published 2011, at the time of writing no longer accessible via the internet, a copy is in my possession), 61.

32

"الجهاد العسكري فرض كفاية، إذا قام به من يكفي سقط الاثم عن الباقين، أما الجهاد السلمي، فهو فرض عين، لأن استمرار المواطنين في تقليم أظافر الطغيان كلما طالت، هو صمام الأمان، فاشتراك الناس في المظاهرات والاعتصامات والبينات وفي التصويت والترشح والتوشيح في الانتخابات، هو ضمان حقوقهم."

ʿAbdallāḥ al-Ḥāmid, *al-Kalima aqwā min ar-raṣāṣa: al-Ǧihād as-silmī l-akbar* (Bairūt: ad-Dār al-ʿarabīya li-l-ʿulūm, 2004), 8.

33

"فليستيقظ الشيوخ والشبان والكهول الذين يتوقون إلى الجهاد في سبيل الله، سائلين الله أن يمنحهم الشهادة [...] ظانين أن الجهاد لا يكون إلا في أفغانستان والفيليبين والبوسنة والشيشان، وأن لا يكون إلا ضد عدوان الكفار، وأن لا سبيل إليه إلا بالتدريب على حمل المدفع والرشاش، وركوب المدرعات والدبابات."

al-Ḥāmid, *al-Kalima aqwā min ar-raṣāṣa*, 54.

34 'Likay naqūlu li-hảūlāʾi š-šabāb allaḏīna yabḥaṯūna ʿan al-ǧihād wa-l-istišhād ḫāriǧ al-ǧazīra: Halummū ilā l-ǧihād as-silmī li-iqāmat al-ḥukm aš-šūrī dāḫil al-ǧazīra, wa-huwa awlā alf marra min al-ǧihād al-ʿaskarī ḫāriǧahā.'
Acpra Tube, *Halummū ilā l-ǧihād as-silmī badalan min al-ʿaskarī / ʿAbdallāh al-Ḥāmid* (published on youtube.com, 31 December 2012, available online: https://www.youtube.com/watch?v=hF4uX9O89Pw, accessed 11 June 2020), 4:00–4:18.

Chapter 4

1 For example, in his 2013 book *Civil ihtisab*, al-Abd al-Karim says: 'Civil jihad will break the power of the giants. In our fight we confront their tyranny with peaceful

action.' Muḥammad al-ʿAbd al-Karīm, *al-Iḥtisāb al-madanī: Dirāsa fī l-bināʾ al-maqāṣidī li-l-ʾiḥtisāb*, aṭ-ṭabʿa aṯ-ṯānīya (Bairūt: aš-Šabaka l-ʿarabīya li-l-ʾabḥāṯ wa-n-našr, 2013), 141. Abdallah al-Hamid started to draw up his theory of peaceful jihad in the mid-1990s CE and already mentions it in his 1996 CE book about human rights. See ʿAbdallāḥ al-Ḥāmid, *Ḥuqūq al-insān baina nūr al-islām wa-ġabaš al-mulk al-ʿaḍūḍ* (Bairūt: Bīsān li-n-našr wa-t-tawzīʿ wa-l-iʿlām, 1996).

2 See, e.g., Nora Doaiji, 'From HASM to HAZM. Saudi Feminism Beyond Patriarchal Bargaining', in *Salman's Legacy. The Dilemmas of a New Era in Saudi Arabia*, ed. Madawi al-Rasheed (New York: Oxford University Press 2018), 117–44.

3 See ʿUmar ibn ʿAbd al-ʿAzīz az-Zahrānī, *Barnāmağ fitna #102* (published on youtube.com, 18 October 2014, available online: https://www.youtube.com/watch?v=aSQcvAtKG6M, accessed 11 June 2020).

4 See Sahar al-Faifi, *Meet the Hero of Saudi Arabia's Silent Majority* (published on middleeastmonitor.com on 12 March 2019, available online: https://www.middleeastmonitor.com/20190312-meet-the-hero-of-saudi-arabias-silent-majority/, accessed 11 June 2020).

5 Amnesty International, *Joint Public Statement: Urgent Call for Release of Saudi Human Rights Defenders* (published on amnesty.org on 12 March 2018, available online: https://www.amnesty.org/download/documents/MDE2380392018ENGLISH.pdf, accessed 11 June 2020).

6 See, e.g., ALQST, *ALQST Renews Its Call to Recognize the Achievements of Saudi Human Rights Activists* (published on alqst.org, 29 November 2018, available online: https://alqst.org/eng/call_out_their_names/, accessed 11 June 2020).

7 See, e.g., as-Sakīna, *Ğamʿīyat al-ḥuqūq al-madanīya wa-s-siyāsīya (ḥasm)* (published on assakina.com, 10 March 2013, available online: http://www.assakina.com/center/parties/22693.html, accessed 6 September 2019). The same wording can be found in HASM's own report about the trial. See HASM, *Bayān ʿan waqāʾiʿ al-ğalsa l-ḥādiya ʿašara (ğalsat an-naṭq bi-l-ḥukm) li-l-muḥākama s-siyāsīya li-l-muṭālibīn bi-šurūṭ al-bayʿa š-šarʿīya (sulṭat al-umma) wa-ḥuqūq al-insān* (published on acpra.org, 11 March 2013, available online: http://www.acpra.org/news.php?action=view&id=224&spell=0&highlight=%C8%ED%C7%E4+%DA%E4+%E6%DE%C7%C6%DA+%C7%E1%CC%E1%D3%C9+%C7%E1%CD%C7%CF%ED%C9+%DA%D4%D1, accessed 11 June 2020).

8

"من تأمل حال المدعى عليهما وجدهما في حال عدم ثبات اعتقادي فمرة يجنحون إلى (مذهب المعتزلة) في انكار المنكر والأمر بالمعروف وتارة يجنحون الى (مذهب الخوارج) في اجازة الخروج على ولي الامر وتارة يذهبون الى (مذهب المرجئة) بتقسيم التوحيد إلى قسمين قسم روحي عموده الصلاة وقسم مدني عموده العدل والحكم الشوري وتارة اخرى الى (مذهب الفلاسفة) اليونانين في العقد الاجتماعي."

ar-Riyāḍ, *Aḥkām bi-siğn iṯnain min muʾassisī mā yaṭlaqu ʿalayhi ğamʿīyat ḥasm 11 wa-10 sanawāt wa-ḥall al-ğamʿīya wa-iġlāq manāšiṭihā wa-muṣādarat mumtalakātihā* (published on al-riyadh.com, 10 March 2013, available online: http://www.alriyadh.com/816175, accessed 11 June 2020).

9 See, e.g., ar-Riyāḍ, *Aḥkām bi-siğn iṯnain min muʾassisī mā yaṭlaqu ʿalayhi ğamʿīyat ḥasm*.

10 See Sulaymān ibn Ṣāliḥ al-Ḫarrāšī, *Sàalnī sāʾil ʿan ad-duktūr ʿAbdallāh al-Ḥāmid* (published on saaid.net, without date, available online: http://www.saaid.net/Warathah/Alkharashy/m/43.htm, accessed 11 June 2020). Similar arguments can be found in other articles, like Ibrahīm ibn ʿUmar as-Sakrān, *Man hum at-tanwīrīyūn?!* (published on islamway.net, 5 November 2014, available online: https://ar.islamway

.net/article/39497/من-هم-التنويريون, accessed 11 June 2020); and Nāṣir ibn Sa'īd as-Sayf, *at-Tanwīrīyūn fī s-Su'ūdīya baina l-wahm wa-l-ḥaqīqa* (published on almohtasb.com, 30 April 2013, available online: http://www.almohtasb.com/alhesba/Articles/14125, accessed 11 June 2020).

11 See as-Sakīna, *Ğam'īyat al-ḥuqūq al-madanīya wa-s-siyāsīya (ḥasm)*.

12 See, e.g., Ḫālid al-Maršūd, *Tawbat An-Na'īmī wa-inšiqāq Al-'Iyāšī 'an ğam'īyat ḥasm* (published on alweeam.com, 5 March 2013, available online: https://www.alweeam.com.sa/y2013/186638/عضوان-من-جمعية-حسم-يعلنان-الانشقاق-عن/, accessed 11 June 2020).

13 See, e.g., International Crisis Group, *Saudi Arabia Backgrounder. Who Are the Islamists?* (ICG Middle East Report No. 31, September 2014, available online: https://www.crisisgroup.org/middle-east-north-africa/gulf-and-arabian-peninsula/saudi-arabia/saudi-arabia-backgrounder-who-are-islamists, accessed 11 June 2020), 9–10.

14 See, e.g., Stéphane Lacroix, 'Between Islamists and Liberals: Saudi Arabia's New "Islamo-Liberal" Reformists', *Middle East Journal* 58, no. 3 (Summer 2004): 345–65; and Stéphane Lacroix, *Les Islamistes Saoudiens* (Paris: Presses Universitaires de France, 2010), 293–7.

15 See, e.g., Saud al-Sarhan, *The Neo-Reformists: A New Democratic Islamic Discourse* (published on mei.edu, 1 October 2009, available online: https://www.mei.edu/publications/neo-reformists-new-democratic-islamic-discourse, accessed 11 June 2020). In his article, al-Sarhan specifically refers to Muhammad al-Ahmari, but he also mentions HASM member Abdallah al-Hamid as someone who 'attempt[ed] to re-consider Islamic political theory and to make democracy compatible with Shari'a.'

16 See Amnesty International, *Saudi Arabia's ACPRA: How the Kingdom Silences Its Human Rights Activists*, published on amnesty.org, 10 October 2014, available online: https://www.amnesty.org/en/documents/MDE23/025/2014/en/, accessed 11 June 2020). Similar points are being made in AI's 2019 Saudi Arabia country report, which is available online: https://www.amnesty.org/en/countries/middle-east-and-north-africa/saudi-arabia/report-saudi-arabia/ (accessed 11 June 2020).

17 See Americans for Democracy & Human Rights in Bahrain, *Roads to Reform: The Enduring Work of the Saudi Association for Civil and Political Rights* (published on adhrb.org, 2017, available online: https://www.adhrb.org/wp-content/uploads/2017/03/2017.3.1_ADHRB_Roads_Web.pdf, accessed 11 June 2020).

18 See, e.g., BBC, *Saudi Arabia: Prominent human rights activist 'dies in jail'* (published on bbc.com, 24 April 2020, available online: https://www.bbc.com/news/world-middle-east-52411453, accessed 11 June 2020).

19 See, e.g., Amnesty International, *Saudi Arabia: Prisoner of Conscience Dr Abdullah al-Hamid Dies While in Detention* (published on amnesty.org, 24 April 2020, available online: https://www.amnesty.org/en/latest/news/2020/04/saudi-arabia-prisoner-of-conscience-dr-abdullah-alhamid-dies-while-in-detention/, accessed 11 June 2020).

20 See, e.g., al-Ğazīra, *Su'ūdīyūn yu'linūna wafāt "šayḫ al-ḥuqūqīyīn" 'Abdallāh al-Ḥāmid fī s-siğn ğirā'a l-ihmāl aṭ-ṭibbī* (published on aljazeera.net, 24 April 2020, available online: https://www.aljazeera.net/news/humanrights/2020/4/24/السعودية-أنباء-وفاة-عبد-الله-الحامد, accessed 11 June 2020).

21 See, e.g., ALQST, *ALQST Renews Its Call to Recognize the Achievements*.

22 Right Livelihood Foundation, *Celebrate 70th Anniversary of Human Rights – Support Reformists Instead of the Regime in Saudi Arabia* (published on rightlivelihoodaward

.org, 12 October 2018, available online: https://www.rightlivelihoodaward.org/media/celebrate-70th-anniversary-of-human-rights-support-reformists-instead-of-the-regime-in-saudi-arabia/, accessed 11 June 2020).

23 See The Right Livelihood Foundation, *Laureates Abdullah al-Hamid, Waleed Abu al-Khair & Mohammad Fahad al-Qahtani* (published on rightlivelihoodaward.org, December 2018, available online: https://www.rightlivelihoodaward.org/laureates/abdullah-al-hamid-waleed-abu-al-khair-mohammad-fahad-al-qahtani/, accessed 11 June 2020).

24 See, e.g., NRC, *Geuzenpenning naar Saoedische mensenrechtenorganisatie ACPRA* (published on nrc.nl, 16 January 2020, available online: https://www.nrc.nl/nieuws/2020/01/16/geuzenpenning-naar-saoedische-mensenrechtenorganisatie-acpra-a3987102, accessed 11 June 2020); and Amnesty International, *Prestigious Dutch Human Rights Prize Awarded to Saudi Arabian Human Rights Organization* (published on amnesty.nl, 16 January 2020, available online: https://www.amnesty.nl/prestigious-dutch-human-rights-prize-awarded-to-saudi-arabian-human-rights-organization, accessed 11 June 2020).

25 See, e.g., Da Dagsavisen, *Nobel: Stortingspolitikere krysser partigrenser for å hedre saudiarabiske aktivister* (published on dagsavisen.no, 11 February 2019, available online: https://www.dagsavisen.no/innenriks/nobel-stortingspolitikere-krysser-partigrenser-for-a-hedre-saudiarabiske-aktivister-1.1276328, accessed 11 June 2020).

Chapter 5

1

”أما الصياغة المعرفية تنظيرا وتطبيقا للفكر الاجتماعي عامة والسياسي خاصة، فإنما هي تراكم هرمي، يقف فيه اللاحق، على كتفي السابقين، فيرى ما هو أبعد من رؤيتهم.“

ʿAbdallāh al-Ḥāmid, *as-Salafīya l-wusṭā: al-ʿAdl ʿadīl aṣ-ṣalāt* (Dimašq: Markaz an-nāqid aṯ-ṯaqāfī, 2009), 202.

2 Quran 3:104 (translation Muhammad Asad).

3

”وأساس مشروعية التكتل للدفاع من المصالح العامة، قوله تعالى (ولتكن منكم أمة يدعون إلى الخير، ويأمرون بالمعروف وينهون عن المنكر، وأولئك هم المفلحون.) ولا معروف أعرف من العدل، ولا منكر أنكر من الظلم.“

ʿAbdallāh al-Ḥāmid, *Ṯulāṯīyat al-muǧtamaʿ al-madanī* (Bairūt: ad-Dār al-ʿarabīya li-l-ʿulūm, 2004), 116.

4 This argument is also mentioned in other texts of the movement. See, e.g., ʿAbdallāh al-Ḥāmid, *al-Kalima aqwā min ar-raṣāṣa: al-Ǧihād as-silmī l-akbar* (Bairūt: ad-Dār al-ʿarabīya li-l-ʿulūm, 2004), 85 and 189; Matrūk al-Fāliḥ, *al-Iṣlāḥ ad-dustūrī fī s-Suʿūdīya: al-Qaḍāyā wa-l-asʾila l-asāsīya* (Bārīs: al-Muʾassasa l-ʿarabīya l-ūrubīya li-n-našr, 2004), 25; and Muḥammad al-ʿAbd al-Karīm, *al-Iḥtisāb al-madanī: Dirāsa fī l-bināʾ al-maqāṣidī li-l-ʾiḥtisāb*, aṭ-ṭabʿa ṯ-ṯānīya (Bairūt: aš-Šabaka l-ʿarabīya li-l-ʾabḥāṯ wa-n-našr, 2013), 21 and 37.

5 Quran 42:38 (translation Muhammad Asad).

6

”ومحمد رشيد [رضا] ومحمد عبده يتوافقان في استنباط سلطة الأمة، وكون مجلس النواب يجسدها من آيتي (أولى الأمر) وآية الشورى (الشورى ٨٢).“

al-Ḥāmid, *Ṯulāṯīyat al-muǧtamaʿ al-madanī*, 59.

7 The same argument can also be found in other books of the movement. See, e.g., ʿAbdallāh al-Ḥāmid, *al-Burhān bi-qawāmat al-umma wa-siyādatihā ʿalā s-sulṭān* (self-published 2012, available online: http://www.acpra.org/download.php?action=view&id=26, accessed 11 June 2020), 16; and Ḥākim al-Muṭairī, *al-Ḥurrīya aw aṭ-ṭawfān* (Bairūt: al-Muʾassasa l-ʿarabīya li-d-dirāsāt wa-n-našr, 2004), 29.

8

"أفضل الجهاد كلمة عدل عند سلطان جائر أو أمير جائر."

Abū Dāwud Sulaymān ibn al-Ašʿaṯ As-Siǧistānī, *Sunan Abī Dāwud*, ed. Šuʿayb al-Arnaʾūṭ, Vol. 6 (Bairūt: Dār ar-risāla al-ʿālamīya, 2009), 400 (Hadith No. 4344).

9

"سيد الشهداء حمزة بن عبد المطلب، ورجل قام إلى إمام جائر فأمره ونهاه، فقتله."

Nāṣir ad-Dīn al-Albānī, *Ṣaḥīḥ at-tarġīb wa-t-tarhīb*, 2nd part (ar-Riyāḍ: Maktabat al-maʿārif li-n-našr wa-t-tawzīʿ, 2000), 574 (Hadith No. 2308).

10 For Abdallah al-Hamid's discussion of the two hadiths, see, especially, al-Ḥāmid, *al-Kalima aqwā min ar-raṣāṣa*, 5–6.

11 The same argument can be found in other texts. See, e.g., ʿAbdallāh al-Ḥāmid, *al-Ǧihād ṣinwān: Silmī li-aṭr wulāt wa-ḥarbī li-dafʿ ġuzāt* (self-published, 2011, at the time of writing not accessible via the internet anymore, a copy is in my possession), 83–4; al-ʿAbd al-Karīm, *al-Iḥtisāb al-madanī*, 38; Muḥammad al-ʿAbd al-Karīm, *Tafkīk al-istibdād: Dirāsa fī fiqh at-taḥarrur min at-taġallub* (Bairūt: aš-Šabaka l-ʿarabīya li-l-abḥāṯ wa-n-našr, 2013), 52; Salmān al-ʿAuda, *Asʾilat aṯ-ṯawra* (Bairūt: Markaz namāʾ li-l-buḥūṯ wa-d-dirāsāt, 2012), 153; al-Muṭairī, *al-Ḥurrīya aw aṭ-ṭawfān*, 46; and Ḥākim al-Muṭairī, *Taḥrīr al-insān wa-taǧrīd aṭ-ṭuġyān* (Bairūt: al-Muʾassasa l-ʿarabīya li-d-dirāsāt wa-n-našr, 2009), 23.

12

"رجعنا من الجهاد الأصغر إلى الجهاد الأكبر."

Mullā ʿAlī al-Qārī, *al-Asrār al-marfūʿa li-l-ʿallāma Nūr ad-Dīn ʿAlī ibn Muḥammad ibn Sulṭān al-mašhūr bi-l-Mullā ʿAlī Al-Qārī*, aṭ-ṭabʿa ṯ-ṯānīya, ed. Muḥammad ibn Luṭfī aṣ-Ṣabbāġ (Bairūt: al-Maktab al-islāmī, 1979), 211 (Hadith No. 211).

13

"هذا الأثر لم يثبت أنه حديث نبوي قاله النبي صلى الله عليه وسلم عند منصرفه من غزوة تبوك، ولكنه حديث سياسي صحيح، فإذا قصدنا به الجهاد السياسي السلمي، ولكنه غير صحيح اللفظ عند علماء الحديث."

al-Ḥāmid, *al-Kalima aqwā min ar-raṣāṣa*, 56.

14

"لا تجمع أمتي على ضلالة، ويد الله مع الجماعة."

Nāṣir ad-Dīn al-Albānī, *Ḍaʿīf sunan at-Tirmiḏī* (ar-Riyāḍ: Maktabat al-maʿārif li-l-našr wa-tawzīʿ, 2000), 211 (Hadith No. 2167).

15 See, e.g., ʿAbdallāh al-Ḥāmid, *Ḥuqūq al-insān baina nūr al-islām wa-ġabaš al-mulk al-ʿaḍūḍ* (Bairūt: Bīsān li-n-našr wa-t-tawzīʿ wa-l-iʿlām, 2010), 145.

16 The same argument can be found in other texts of the Islamo-reformist movement. See, e.g., al-Ḥāmid, *al-Burhān bi-qawāmat al-umma*, 29 and 102; and Muḥammad al-Aḥmarī, *ad-Dīmuqrāṭīya: al-Ǧuḏūr wa-iškālīyat at-taṭbīq* (Bairūt: aš-Šabaka l-ʿarabīya li-l-abḥāṯ wa-n-našr, 2012), 158.

17

"ينبغي أن نقسم رموز السلف العباسي والمملوكي والعثماني الصالح إلى مجددين ومقلدين. وأن المجددين منهم كانوا مجاهدين أحرار، كالأئمة أبو حنيفة، ومالك والشافعي وأحمد."

al-Ḥāmid, *as-Salafīya l-wusṭā*, 83.

18 See, e.g., al-Ḥāmid, *as-Salafīya l-wusṭā*, 43–4.
19 See, e.g., al-Ḥāmid, *as-Salafīya l-wusṭā*, 15–16.
20 See, e.g., al-Ḥāmid, *Ḥuqūq al-insān baina nūr al-islām wa-ġabaš al-mulk al-ʿaḍūḍ*, 88.
21 See, e.g., al-Fāliḥ, *al-Iṣlāḥ ad-dustūrī fī s-Suʿūdīya*, 29.
22 See, e.g., al-ʿAbd al-Karīm, *al-Iḥtisāb al-madanī*, 7.
23 See, e.g., al-Ḥāmid, *al-Kalima aqwā min ar-raṣāṣa*, 124; al-Ḥāmid, *al-Burhān bi-qawāmat al-umma*, 22 and 109–10; and al-Ḥāmid, *Ṯulāṯīyat al-muǧtamaʿ al-madanī*, 64 and 94.
24 See, e.g., al-Ḥāmid, *al-Kalima aqwā min ar-raṣāṣa*, 18–19 and 78; al-Ḥāmid, *as-Salafīya l-wusṭā*, 15–16 and 77; ʿAbdallāh al-Ḥāmid, *Likay lā yakūnu l-qurʾān ḥammāl auğuh: al-Mişbāḥ fī zuğāğa wa-miškāt* (self-published 2008, available online: http://www.acpra.org/download.php?action=view&id=11, accessed 11 June 2020), 314–15; and ʿAbdallāh al-Ḥāmid, *aṭ-Ṭarīq aṯ-ṯāliṯ: ad-Dustūr al-islāmī* (Dimašq: Markaz an-nāqid aṯ-ṯaqāfī, 2009), 50.
25 See, e.g., al-Ḥāmid, *al-Kalima aqwā min ar-raṣāṣa*, 30.
26 See, e.g., al-Ḥāmid, *al-Kalima aqwā min ar-raṣāṣa*, 128–9 and 198–9; and al-Ḥāmid, *al-Burhān bi-qawāmat al-umma*, 22.
27 See, e.g., al-Ḥāmid, *al-Burhān bi-qawāmat al-umma*, 36 and 90–1; al-Ḥāmid, *as-Salafīya l-wusṭā*, 52–3; and al-Ḥāmid, *Likay lā yakūnu l-qurʾān ḥammāl auğuh*, 304.
28

”وصرح به ابن تيمية في كتاب (السياسة الشرعية) فقال: (إن الله يقيم الدولة العادلة ولو كانت كافرة، ولا يقيم الدولة الظالمة ولو كانت مسلمة. [...] أذن لا يصح وصف أي دولة بأنها مسلمة، ما لم تقم شرطي البيعة الشرعية: الشورى والعدل.“

al-Ḥāmid, *al-Burhān bi-qawāmat al-umma*, 33–4.
29 See, e.g., al-Ḥāmid, *as-Salafīya l-wusṭā*, 52–3 and 153.
30 For more details about the different aspects of Ibn Khaldun's theory, see, e.g., Muḥammad ʿĀbid al-Ğābirī, *Fikr Ibn Ḫaldūn: al-ʿAṣabīya wa-d-daula*, aṭ-ṭabʿa ṯ-ṯāmina (Bairūt: Markaz dirāsāt al-waḥda l-ʿarabīya, 2008); Muhsin Mahdi, *Ibn Khaldūn's Philosophy of History: A Study in the Philosophic Foundations of the Science of Culture* (Chicago: University of Chicago Press, 1964); Abdesselam Cheddadi, *Ibn Khaldūn: L'homme et le théoricien de la civilisation* (Paris: Gallimard, 2006); Yves Lacoste, *Ibn Khaldoun: Naissance de l'Histoire, passé du tiers monde* (Paris: La Découverte, 1998); and Peter Enz, *Der Keim der Revolte: Militante Solidarität und religiöse Mission bei Ibn Khaldun* (Freiburg: Verlag Karl Alber, 2012).
31

”أجل يمكن التأسيس على الأفكار المضيئة، لنوابغ الإسلام كالشاطبي، وابن تيمية وابن القيم والغزالي، ولا سيما الن خلدون الذي ينبغي إبرازه شيخا للإسلام، في علم الاجتماع السياسي.“

al-Ḥāmid, *Likay lā yakūnu l-qurʾān ḥammāl auğuh*, 81.

See, also, al-Ḥāmid, *as-Salafīya l-wusṭā*, 15–16; and al-Ḥāmid, *Likay lā yakūnu l-qurʾān ḥammāl auğuh*, 115.
32

”فأعطوا الحكام سلطة مطلقة، واعتبروا الشورى غير ملزمة، وأشاعوا أقوالا تمجد الحكام، كأقوال الفضيل من عياض، والبربهاري وسهل بن عبدالله التستري، وابن أبي العز شارح الطحاوية ونحوها، ثم دسوها في نسيج العقيدة، كي لا يجرؤ أحد على مناقشتها.“

al-Ḥāmid, *aṭ-Ṭarīq aṯ-ṯāliṯ*, 53.

33 For details about al-Mawardi's 'Ordinances of Government' and other discourses about politics in Arabic-Islamic thought between the seventh and the eighteenth centuries CE, see, especially, Thomas Bauer's excellent chapter on the subject in Thomas Bauer, *Die Kultur der Ambiguität: Eine andere Geschichte des Islams* (Berlin: Verlag der Weltreligionen, 2011), 315–43.

34 See, e.g., al-Ḥāmid, *Likay lā yakūnu l-qur'ān ḥammāl auğuh*, 181; al-ʿAbd al-Karīm, *Tafkīk al-istibdād*, 156 and 218; and al-Muṭairī, *al-Ḥurrīya aw aṭ-ṭawfān*, 7.

35

"أسلافنا العباسيون كانوا يعيشون زمن تماس حضاري عنيف، اختلط فيه الجنس العربي، بالأجناس الفارسية والرومية والسريانية والقبطية والهندية، وأسلم من أسلم بخلفيته الثقافية وهويته القومية. [...] وكما فرضت الثقافة العلمانية نفسها علينا اليوم، فرضت بالأمس الثقافة الأجنبية نفسها على المثقفين. [...] وأنهم بأخطائهم كانوا ضحايا، ولكنهم بصوابهم كانوا روادا، وأخطاؤهم كانت جسرا عبر عليه الآخرين. [...] وهذا هو دور الكندي والفارابي وابن سينا أيضا ونحوهم."

al-Ḥāmid, *as-Salafīya l-wusṭā*, 205–6.

36 "كتلميذ في محراب أرسطو"

al-Ḥāmid, *Likay lā yakūnu l-qur'ān ḥammāl auğuh*, 72.

37

"أما دور ابن رشد في الثقافة الإسلامية، فلم يكن منتجا لأنه لم يجد يتجاوز دور شارح منبت لثقافة اليونان. [...] وكتابات أمثال ابن رشد [...] كانت بعيدة عن فهم الشريعة، كما كانت بعيدة عن الفلسفة العملية، أي أنها بعيدة هم العقلانية العملية، التي نهض بها الغرب بعد أن تخلص بيكن وأمثاله من وصاية أرسطو وأفلاطون."

al-Ḥāmid, *Likay lā yakūnu l-qur'ān ḥammāl auğuh*, 151.

38 See, e.g, al-Ḥāmid, *as-Salafīya l-wusṭā*, 56.

39

"ومن صورها السلفية الصحراوية عند محمد بن عبد الوهاب."

al-Ḥāmid, *Likay lā yakūnu l-qur'ān ḥammāl auğuh*, 184.

40

"والحكم النهائي هو درجة التغيير نحو الصلاح والنجاح، وهذا أمر قد تحقق للوهابية بقدر كبير جدا. ومحمد هم عبد الوهاب كان معياريا، عندما طبق أفكار ابن تيمية، فحارب خرافات العقيدة الروحية. وكان معياريا واقعيا في شق العقيدة المدني، عندما أدرك أن إقامة الحكم العادل من فروض الدين. [...] أراد ابن عبد الوهاب إقامة العدل من خلال نموذج المستبد العادل، لأنه كغير من المصلحين عبد الخلافة الراشدة، لم يثمنوا العلاقة بين العدل والشورى والتعددية والحرية والروح المعرفي، فكان تجديده مرحليا آنيا، يناسب مرحلة من مراحل مجتمع الجزيرة العربية الصحراوي."

al-Ḥāmid, *as-Salafīya l-wusṭā*, 57–8.

41

"وهذا يتطلب تعميقا وترويجا لمواصلة نحت خطاب النهضة الذي بدأه روادها، كالأفغاني وخير الدين التونسي والكواكبي ومحمد عبده [...] ومحمد رشيد رضا وحسن البنا."

al-Ḥāmid, *as-Salafīya l-wusṭā*, 140.

42 For example, al-Hamid refers to this idea in these passages: al-Ḥāmid, *al-Kalima aqwā min ar-raṣāṣa*, 124; al-Ḥāmid, *al-Burhān bi-qawāmat al-umma*, 29 and 36; and al-Ḥāmid, *Ṯulāṯīyat al-muğtamaʿ al-madanī*, 59–60.

43 See, e.g., al-Ḥāmid, *Ṯulāṯīyat al-muğtamaʿ al-madanī*, 94 and 142; and al-Ḥāmid, *al-Burhān bi-qawāmat al-umma*, 97.

44

"وقد تبني المفهوم الشيخان محمد عبده ورشيد رضا في تفسير المنار. واعتبر الشيخان محمد عبده ومحمد رشيد رضا التجمعات المدنية ومجلس النواب بمثابة الهياكل والوسائل في بلورة إرادة الأمة، لأنها تجسد المرجعية الاجتماعية للأمة، أي بعبارة سياسية: تجسد سلطة الأمة."

al-Ḥāmid, *Ṯulāṯīyat al-muğtamaʿ al-madanī*, 109.

45 ʿAbd ar-Raḥmān al-Kawākibī, *Ṭabāʾiʿ al-istibdād wa-maṣāriʿ al-istiʿbād, aṭ-ṭabʿa ṯ-ṯānīya* (al-Qāhira: Dār aš-šuruq, 2009).
46 See, e.g., al-Ḥāmid, *as-Salafīya l-wusṭā*, 15–16; al-Ḥāmid, *Likay lā yakūnu l-qurʾān ḥammāl auǧuh*, 182–5; al-ʿAbd al-Karīm, *Tafkīk al-istibdād*, 37; al-Aḥmarī, *ad-Dīmuqrāṭīya*, 190; and al-Muṭairī, *al-Ḥurrīya aw aṭ-ṭawfān*, 264.
47 See, e.g., al-Ḥāmid, *al-Burhān bi-qawāmat al-umma*, 29.
48 For more details on the hybrid discourse of Islamic Modernism, see, e.g., Larbi Sadiki, *The Search for Arab Democracy: Discourses and Counter-Discourses* (London: Hurst, 2004), 218–29; Muhammad Muslih and Michelle Browers, 'Democracy', in *The Oxford Encyclopaedia of the Islamic World*, ed. John L. Esposito (Oxford: Oxford University Press, 2009, also available online: http://oxfordislamicstudies.com/article/opr/t236/e0185, accessed 11 June 2020); and Nasr Hamid Abu Zeid, 'The Modernisation of Islam or the Islamisation of Modernity', in *Cosmopolitanism, Identity and Authenticity in the Middle East*, ed. Roel Meijer (Richmond: Curzon, 1999), 71–86.
49 For details on Sayyid Qutb's theory of the state and the role of democratic forms of government in it, see, e.g., Sayed Khatab, 'The Voice of Democratism in Sayyid Quṭb's Response to Violence and Terrorism', *Islam and Christian-Muslim Relations* 20, no. 3 (July 2009): 315–32; and Muslih and Browers, 'Democracy'.
50 See, e.g., al-Ḥāmid, *al-Kalima aqwā min ar-raṣāṣa*, 30; Ḥāmid, *as-Salafīya l-wusṭā*, 199 and 231; and al-Ḥāmid, *Likay lā yakūnu l-qurʾān ḥammāl auǧuh*, 182–5.
51 See, e.g., al-Ḥāmid, *al-Kalima aqwā min ar-raṣāṣa*, 113.
52 For details about the ideas of the 'centrist stream' with regard to the state, see, e.g., Sagi Polka, 'The Centrist Stream in Egypt and its Role in the Public Discourse Surrounding the Shaping of the Country's Cultural Identity', *Middle Eastern Studies* 39, no. 3 (July 2003): 39–64; Rachel Scott, *The Challenge of Political Islam: Non-Muslims and the Egyptian State* (Stanford: Stanford University Press, 2010), 34–63; and Muslih and Browers, 'Democracy'.
53 See, e.g., al-Ḥāmid, *Ḥuqūq al-insān baina nūr al-islām wa-ġabaš al-mulk al-ʿaḍūḍ*, 125 and 157; and al-Ḥāmid, *Ṯulāṯīyat al-muǧtamaʿ al-madanī*, 60.
54 See, e.g., the following passage from one of Abdallah al-Hamid's book: 'Al-Qaradawi said: "Demonstrations, if they aim at waking the umma, are the best jihad."'

"كما قال القرضاوي: المظاهرات إذا استهدفت إيقاظ الأمة، فهي خير الجهاد."

al-Ḥāmid, *al-Kalima aqwā min ar-raṣāṣa*, 8.
55 See, e.g., al-Aḥmarī, *ad-Dīmuqrāṭīya*, 190 and 217.
56 See, e.g., al-Ḥāmid, *al-Burhān bi-qawāmat al-umma*, 124; and al-Aḥmarī, *ad-Dīmuqrāṭīya*, 121.
57 See, e.g., al-Ḥāmid, *Likay lā yakūnu l-qurʾān ḥammāl auǧuh*, 288; ʿAbdallāh al-Mālikī, *Siyādat al-umma qabla taṭbīq aš-šarīʿa: Naḥwa faḍāʾ amṯal li-taǧsīd mabādiʾ al-islām* (Bairūt: aš-Šabaka l-ʿarabīya li-l-abḥāṯ wa-n-našr, 2012), 20; and al-Aḥmarī, *ad-Dīmuqrāṭīya*, 119.
58

"قال الإمام عبد العزيز بن باز رحمه الله تعالى: (وليس من منهج السلف التشهير بعيوب الولاة، وذكر ذلك على المنابر لأن ذلك يفضي إلى الفوضى.) [...] وصدور هذه القواعد من فقهاء صالحين كابن باز وابن عثيمين، رحمنا الله وإياهما، يدل على أن العالم المشهور المتفوق في العلوم الروحية أن لا يلزم أن تكون له بصيرة في شئون السياسة والإدارة والحضارة."

al-Ḥāmid, *al-Kalima aqwā min ar-raṣāṣa*, 93.

59 'Kaifa našа̄a amṯāl aš-šaiẖ Usāma ibn Lādin? Lā šakkan an aš-šayẖ Usāma ibn Lādin rağul ṣādiq šuğği'a 'alā l-ğihād fī Afġānistān, ẖayr al-ğihad, ṯumma 'āda ilā l-bilād wa-kāna yanbaġī an yakūna li-miṯlihi makān wa-dawr. [. . .] Kāna min ḥaqqihi an yušārika fī binā' baladihi wa-yanšа̄a ğam'īya silmīya, lākin al-qam' kāna lahu bi-l-mirṣād. Law iḥtaḍanahu wa-akramahu wa-i'tarafa bi-dawrihi wa-dawr amṯālihi. . ., lākinnahu lā yurīdu an yanfatiḥa li-l-ḥarāk as-silmī. Wa-suddat amāma Ibn Lādin as-subul wa-ḍuyyiqa fī kull makān fa-infağara ka-l-burqān.'
Acpra Tube, *Halummū ilā l-ğihād as-silmī badalan min al-'askarī / 'Abdallāh al-Ḥāmid* (published on youtube.com, 31 December 2012, available online: https://www.youtube.com/watch?v=hF4uX9O89Pw, accessed 11 June 2020), 16:37–17:42.

60
"الدولة الدستورية هي تعاقدية، أي التي تجسد (التزاما متبادلا بين الشعب والحكومة) أي (ميثاقا ما بين شعب وزعيم ورئيس ومرؤوسين) كما نظر روسو في كتاب العقد الاجتماعي، وكما أكد الإسلام من قبله في مفهوم (البيعة)."
al-Ḥāmid, *Ṯulāṯīyat al-muğtama' al-madanī*, 108.

61 See, e.g., al-Ḥāmid, *Ḥuqūq al-insān baina nūr al-islām wa-ġabaš al-mulk al-'aḍūḍ*, 64; and al-Ḥāmid, *Ṯulāṯīyat al-muğtama' al-madanī*, 38 and 97.

62 See, e.g., al-Ḥāmid, *Ṯulāṯīyat al-muğtama' al-madanī*, 27 and 38.

63
"في الدولة القامعة يسود نظام العلاقات الرأسي، القائم على الطبقية بين السادة والعبيد. وتقوم العلاقة على القسر والإكراه، فلا تستقر السلطة فيه إلا بمفهوم الأمن العسكري والبوليسي. [...] من أجل هذه المفاسد رفضه مفكرو الغرب ك(لوك) و(روسو) و(ديدرو) و(هيجل)، ونادوا بالمجتمع المدني الشوري."
al-Ḥāmid, *Ṯulāṯīyat al-muğtama' al-madanī*, 38.

64 See, e.g., 'Abdallāh al-Ḥāmid, *Ma'āyīr istiqlāl al-qaḍā' ad-duwalīya fī būtaqa š-šarī'a l-islāmīya* (Bairūt: ad-Dār al-'arabīya li-l-'ulūm nāširūn, 2004), 5.

65 See, e.g., aš-Šarq al-Ausaṭ, *Bad' a'māl mu'tamar al-'adāla l-'arabī fī l-Qāhira l-yaum* (published on aawsat.com, 21 February 2003, available online: https://archive.aawsat.com/details.asp?issueno=8800&article=154079#.XoiX_y2B3Vp, accessed 11 June 2020).

66
"وقد تتدخل الرأي العام الدولي، ففي عصر الإعلام المفتوح، لا يستطيع السفاح أن يتمادى. هذا أسلوب مدرسة غاندي، في التغيير السلمي."
al-Ḥāmid, *al-Kalima aqwā min ar-raṣāṣa*, 34.

67 See 'Abdallāh al-Ḥāmid, *Inšā' ğam'īyat ḥasm amr mašrū' bal farīḍa šar'īya* (self-published, 2012, at the time of writing no longer accessible via the internet, a copy is in my possession), 4–5; and al-Fāliḥ, *al-Iṣlāḥ ad-dustūrī fī s-Su'ūdīya*, 92.

Chapter 6

1 See, e.g., Madawi al-Rasheed, *Muted Modernists: The Struggle Over Divine Politics in Saudi Arabia* (London: Hurst, 2015), 58. A similar point is being made by Stéphane Lacroix in 'Saudi Arabia and the Limits of Post-Islamism', in *Post-Islamism. The Changing Faces of Political Islam*, ed. Asef Bayat (Oxford: Oxford University Press, 2013), 277–97.

2 See, e.g., Madawi al-Rasheed, *Contesting the Saudi State: Islamic Voices from a New Generation* (New York: Cambridge University Press, 2007), 257.

3 ”وهذا بتطلب الجمع بين النخبية والشعبية، في لغة الخطاب ومضمونه. [...] سيجيئ التعبير عن المفاهيم والأفكار بلغة مبسطة واضحة، سهلة يفهمها الناس، ولكنها أيضا علمية دقيقة رصينة هادئة مبرهنة، تتحرى الموضوعية والإقناع.“

ʿAbdallāh al-Ḥāmid, *al-Kalima aqwā min ar-raṣāṣa: al-Ǧihād as-silmī l-akbar* (Bairūt: ad-Dār al-ʿarabīya li-l-ʿulūm, 2004), 147.

4 See www.acpra.org (accessed 11 June 2020).

5 See, e.g., HASM, *Al-Iʿlān at-tàsīsī* (published on acpra.org, 23 October 2009, available online: http://www.acpra.org/news.php?action=view&id=1, accessed 11 June 2020).

6 See, e.g., HASM's English call for the release of prisoners in September 2013, HASM, *APCRA Demands the Release of All Prisoners of Conscience* (published on acpra.org, 28 September 2013, available online: http://www.acpra.org/news/view_251.html, accessed 11 June 2020).

7 See, e.g., HASM's report on the arrest of Abd ar-Rahman al-Hamid in April 2014, HASM, *Bayān ʿan iʿtiqāl ʿaḍw ğamʿīyat ḥasm: D. ʿAbd Ar-Raḥmān al-Ḥāmid* (published on acpra.org, 19 April 2014, available online: http://acpra.org/news_view_269.html, accessed 11 June 2020).

8 See, e.g., HASM's report on the ninth session of the trial against Fawzan al-Harbi, HASM, *Bayān al-ğalsa t-tāsiʿa min muḥākamat ʿaḍw ğamʿīyat ḥasm: Fawzān al-Ḥarbī* (published on acpra.org, 3 April 2014, available online: http://www.acpra.org/news_view_268.html, accessed 11 June 2020); HASM's report on the second session in the trial of Abd al-Karim al-Khadr, HASM, *Bayān al-ğalsa ṯ-ṯānīya min al-muḥākama s-siyāsīya ṯ-ṯānīya li-D. ʿAbd al-Karīm al-Ḫaḍr* (published on acpra.org, 22 May 2014, available online: http://www.acpra.org/news_view_273.html, accessed 11 June 2020); and HASM's report on the first session of the trial against Isa al-Hamid, HASM, *Bayān al-ğalsa l-ūlā min al-muḥākama s-siyāsīya li-ʿĪsā al-Ḥāmid* (published on acpra.org, 13 June 2014, available online: http://www.acpra.org/news_view_274.html, accessed 11 June 2020).

9 See, e.g., HASM, *al-Bayān 11 ʿan ğalsat an-naṭq bi-l-ḥukm fī l-muḥākama s-siyāsīya li-ʿaḍwai ḥasm, al-Ḥāmid wa-l-Qaḥṭānī wa-ṣudūr al-ḥukm* (published on acpra.org, 11 March 2013, available online: http://www.acpra.org/news_view_224.html, accessed 11 June 2020); and HASM, *Bayān ğalsat an-naṭq bi-l-ḥukm min al-muḥākama s-siyāsīya li-D. ʿAbd al-Karīm al-Ḫaḍr ʿadw ḥasm* (published on acpra.org, 28 June 2013, available online: http://www.acpra.org/news_view_242.html, accessed 11 June 2020).

10 See https://www.youtube.com/user/AcpraTube/videos (accessed 12 March 2020).

11 An important example is Sulayman ar-Rashudi's lecture on the legitimacy of demonstrations according to the Islamic sharia. See Acpra Tube, *Ḥukm al-muẓāharāt wa-l-iʿtiṣāmāt fī š-šarīʿa l-islāmīya* (published on youtube.com, 11 December 2012, available online: https://www.youtube.com/watch?v=JY8y6hIalig, accessed 11 June 2020).

12 See, e.g., Acpra Tube, *Taṣrīḥ al-Ḫaḍr wa-l-Ḥāmid fī ğalsat 1 li-muḥākamat ḥasm Al-Qaṣīm* (published on youtube.com, 4 February 2013, available online: https//www.youtube.com/watch?v=boD3Y_HieMI, accessed 11 June 2020); and Acpra Tube, *Taṣrīḥ ʿAbd Al-ʿAzīz Aš-Šubaylī baʿda l-ğalsa r-rābiʿa min muḥakamat ḥasm Al-Qaṣīm* (published on youtube.com, 24 April 2013, available online: https://www.youtube.com/watch?v=AbjTyR1twKI, accessed 11 June 2020).

13 For example ʿAbdallāh al-Ḥāmid, *Ṣarḫat ḫādim* (Bairūt: ad-Dār al-ʿarabīya li-l-ʿulūm, 2003); ʿAbdallāh al-Ḥāmid, *Ḫawāṭir tilmīḏ maqmūʿ* (Bairūt: ad-Dār al-ʿarabīya li-l-ʿulūm, 2003); and the play, ʿAbdallāh al-Ḥāmid, *al-Ḥasan al-Baṣrī wa-l-Ḥaǧǧāǧ fī āḫar az-zamān* (Bairūt: ad-Dār al-ʿarabīya li-l-ʿulūm, 2003).

14

”يا خادم الحرمين كل بلية / أسبابها رأي أتى محصورا
لا بد للحكام من شورى ولو / ملكوا عقولا فذة وحجورا
لو كان رأي مغنيا في فضلها / ما كان فيها المصطفى مجبورا
ما بيعة الإسلام تمت دونها / بل إنها مقرونة بالشورى [...]
هذا هو الإسلام شورى حرة / لم يغذ قهارا ولا مقهورا
والرأي في الأحرار هل مستعبد / أو خانع يستنبط المستورا؟
لا بد قبل الرأي من حرية / أوصى بها الإسلام قبل الشورى“

ʿAbdallāh al-Ḥāmid, *Ammā baʿda kawāriṯ al-ḫalīǧ* (self-published, May 2012, available online: https://www.scribd.com/document/324758098/أما-بعد-كوارث-الخليج, accessed 11 June 2020), 11.

15

”وأكد علماء الحشرات نزعة النمل والنحل، في التضحية بالنفس من أجل المجموعة، لا تكاد تظهر عند أي حيوان آخر، فهي على عكس الحشرات والحيوانات الأخرى، التي تتسم فالأنانية فيفضل أفرادها الهرب إذا تعرضت لأي خطر، فيأكلها العدو المهاجم واحدة بعد الأخرى، كالغنم والشياه.
وما معنى قوله تعالى (وأوحى ربك إلى النحل)؟
أليس معناه قول الشاعر:
يقضي المروءة أن نمد جسومنا، جسرا فقل لرفاقنا أن يعبروا.“

al-Ḥāmid, *al-Kalima aqwā min ar-raṣāṣa*, 47.

16

”فكيف يكون الإنسان اليوم سلفيا وهو لم يكتب ببنان ولم يتكلم بلسان، فضلا عن أن يشارك دعاة الإصلاح السياسي في إصدار بيان فضلا عن يعتصم ويتظاهر في ميدان.“

ʿAbdallāh al-Ḥāmid, *as-Salafīya l-wusṭā: al-ʿAdl ʿadīl aṣ-ṣalāt* (Dimašq: Markaz an-nāqid aṯ-ṯaqāfī, 2009), 215.

17 See, e.g., International Crisis Group, *Saudi Arabia Backgrounder. Who Are the Islamists?* (ICG Middle East Report No. 31, September 2014, available online: https://www.crisisgroup.org/middle-east-north-africa/gulf-and-arabian-peninsula/saudi-arabia/saudi-arabia-backgrounder-who-are-islamists, accessed 11 June 2020), 9–10.

18 See, e.g., Saud al-Sarhan, *The Neo-Reformists. A New Democratic Islamic Discourse* (published on mei.edu, 1 October 2009, available online: https://www.mei.edu/publications/neo-reformists-new-democratic-islamic-discourse, accessed 11 June 2020).

19 See, e.g., Rüdiger Lohlker, *Die Salafisten: Der Aufstand der Frommen, Saudi-Arabien und der Islam* (München: C.H. Beck, 2017), 155.

20 See, e.g., Stéphane Lacroix, 'Between Islamists and Liberals: Saudi Arabia's New "Islamo-Liberal" Reformists', *Middle East Journal* 58, no. 3 (Summer 2004): 345–65; and Stéphane Lacroix, *Les Islamistes Saoudiens: Une insurrection manquée* (Paris: Presses Universitaires de France, 2010), 293–7.

21 See, e.g., Abdullah Hamidaddin, *Tweeted Heresies. Saudi Islam in Transformation* (New York: Oxford University Press, 2020), 33.

22 See also, International Crisis Group, *Saudi Arabia Backgrounder*, 8–10.

23 See, e.g., al-Rasheed, *Muted Modernists*, 107.

24 See, e.g., ʿAbd al-Wahhāb Āl Ġaẓīf, *At-Tanwīr al-islāmī fī l-mašhad as-suʿūdī* (Ǧidda: Markaz taʾṣīl, 2013); Ibrāhīm ibn ʿUmar as-Sakrān, *Man hum at-tanwīrīyūn?!* (published on islamway.net, 5 November 2014, available online: https://ar.islamway.net/article/39497/من-هم-التنويريون, accessed 11 June 2020); and Nāṣir ibn Saʿīd as-Sayf, *At-Tanwīrīyūn fī s-Suʿūdīya baina l-wahm wa-l-ḥaqīqa* (published on almohtasb.com, 30 April 2013, available online: http://www.almohtasb.com/alhesba/Articles/14125, accessed 11 June 2020).

25 See, e.g., Lacroix, 'Between Islamists and Liberals', 345–65.

26 See, e.g., The Arabic Network for Human Rights Information, *Wa-yastamirru musalsal al-mumaṭala fī muḥakamat al-iṣlāḥiyīn aṯ-ṯalāṯa bi-s-suʿūdīya* (published on anhri.net, 17 February 2005, available online: http://www.anhri.net/saudi/spdhr/2005/pr0217.shtml, accessed 11 June 2020); and al-Ǧazīra, *Muḥākamāt muʿtaqalīn li-muṭālabatihim bi-iṣlāḥ fī s-Suʿūdīya* (published on Aljazeera.net, 3 October 2014, available online: https://www.aljazeera.net/news/arabic/2004/10/3/محاكمة-معتقلين-لمطالبتهم-بالإصلاح-في-السعودية, accessed 11 June 2020).

27 For details about the term reform in the writings of Muhammad Abduh and Muhammad Rashid Rida, see, e.g., A. Mera, Hamid Algar, N. Berkes and Aziz Ahmad, 'Iṣlāḥ', in *Encyclopaedia of Islam*, ed. P. Bearman et al., 2nd edn. (EI^2) (Leiden: Brill, 1954–2004, first published online 2009, available online: https://referenceworks.brillonline.com/entries/encyclopaedia-of-islam-2/islah-COM_0386, accessed 11 June 2020).

28 See, e.g., ʿAbdallāh al-Ḥāmid, *Likay lā yakūnu l-qurʾān ḥammāl awǧuh: al-Miṣbāḥ fī zuǧāǧa wa-miškāt* (self-published 2008, available online: http://www.acpra.org/download.php?action=view&id=11, accessed 11 June 2020), 91.

29 See, e.g., ʿAbdallāh al-Ḥāmid, *al-Burhān bi-qawāmat al-umma wa-siyādatihā ʿalā s-sulṭān* (self-published 2012, available online: http://www.acpra.org/download.php?action=view&id=26, accessed 11 June 2020), 8; ʿAbdallāh al-Ḥāmid, *Ṯulāṯīyat al-muǧtamaʿ al-madanī* (Bairūt: ad-Dār al-ʿarabīya li-l-ʿulūm, 2004), 22; and al-Ḥāmid, *al-Kalima aqwā min ar-raṣāṣa*, 19.

30 See, e.g., Matrūk al-Fāliḥ, *al-Iṣlāḥ ad-dustūrī fī s-Suʿūdīya: Al-qaḍāyā wa-l-asʾila l-asāsīya* (Bārīs: al-Muʾassasa l-ʿarabīya l-ūrubīya li-n-našr, 2004), 5.

31 See, e.g., al-Ḥāmid, *al-Kalima aqwā min ar-raṣāṣa*, 3.

32

"أثبت الفقهاء الأمويون وعيهم السياسي، وأثبتوا أن السلفية إصلاح سياسي، وأن منهج أهل السنة والجماعة، ليس الصبر على جور الحاكم وجبره، بل توصيته بالعدل والشورى، على ذلك قاومها الفقهاء الأوائل كالحسن البصري [...] وسفيان الثوري [...] وسعيد بن جبير، ومالك وأبي حنيفة الذي مات في السجن لأنه رفض القضاء."

ʿAbdallāh al-Ḥāmid, *aṭ-Ṭarīq aṯ-ṯāliṯ. ad-Dustūr al-islāmī* (Dimašq: Markaz an-nāqid aṯ-ṯaqāfī, 2009), 17.

33 See, e.g., this short passage from one of al-Hamids earlier books: 'Today, it is our great need as those, who belong to Salafism, to counter the darkness of our Islamic jurist colleagues of the Arab and Islamic state of oppression.'

"حاجتنا اليوم – نحن المنتسبون للسلفية – للتصدي اليوم لغبش زملائنا من فقهاء دولة الاستبداد العربية والإسلامية."

ʿAbdallāh al-Ḥāmid, *Ḥuqūq al-insān baina nūr al-islām wa-ġabaš al-mulk al-ʿaḍūḍ* (Bairūt: Bīsān li-n-našr wa-t-tawzīʿ wa-l-iʿlām, 1996), 130.

34

"ونحن اليوم في عهد الإمبريالية الغربية نواجه أعنف تحد وأعظمه وأخطره، بحاجة إلى مواصلة بناء صورة سلفية حضارية، بدأها رموز نهضة الأسلام الحديثة، التي أشعل منارها بالمناداة بالإصلاح

السياسي: جمال الدين الأفغاني والكواكبي وخير الدين التونسي، وتبلورت بعض مفرداتها في الاتجاه الإخواني."

al-Ḥāmid, *as-Salafīya l-wusṭā*, 213.

35 See, e.g., Ami Ayalon, *Language and Change in the Arab Middle East: The Evolution of Modern Political Discourse* (New York: Oxford University Press, 1987), 6.

A similar point is being made by Carsten Jürgensen in *Demokratie und Menschenrechte in der arabischen Welt: Positionen arabischer Menschenrechtsaktivisten* (Hamburg: Deutsches Orient-Instituts Hamburg, 1994), 60–1.

36 For details on this argument, see, especially, Ayalon, *Language and Change in the Arab Middle East*, 127–33. Muhammad Abid Al-Jabri makes a similar point with regard to the term "human rights" (ḥuqūq al-insān); see Muḥammad ʿĀbid Al-Jabri, 'The Concepts of Rights and Justice in Arab-Islamic Texts', in *Human Rights in Arab Thought. A Reader*, ed. Salma K. Jayyusi (London: I.B. Tauris, 2009), 17–61.

37 See Ayalon, *Language and Change in the Arab Middle East*, 21–3 and 26–8.

38

"عندما ترد كلمة (حقوق الإنسان)، يظن عدد غير قليل من الناس، أنها مفهوم دخيل على الإسلام، وأنها مرتبطة بالعلمانية. [...] حقوق الإنسان ليست مفهوما علمانيا، بل إن الأديان السماوية ولا سيما الإسلام قررتها وأكدتها وفرضتها."

ʿAbdallāh al-Ḥāmid, *Ḥuqūq al-insān baina nūr al-islām wa-ġabaš al-mulk al-ʿaḍūḍ* (Bairūt: Bīsān li-n-našr wa-t-tawzīʿ wa-l-iʿlām, 2010), 13.

39

"ومن دواعي إنشاء الجمعية، أن العديد من المنظمات الدولية متأثرة بالنظرة الغربية لحقوق الإنسان، ولم تبرز بشكل فعال النظرية الإسلامية لحقوق الإنسان."

HASM, *Al-Iʿlān at-taʾsīsī.*

40 See, e.g., Al-Jabri, 'The Concepts of Rights and Justice in Arab-Islamic Texts', 17–61.

41 The Verse of the Light can be translated as follows: 'God is the Light of the heavens and the earth. The parable of His light is, as it were, that of a niche containing a lamp; the lamp is [enclosed] in glass, the glass [shining] like a radiant star: [a lamp] lit from a blessed tree – an olive-tree that is neither of the east nor of the west – the oil whereof [is so bright that it] would well-nigh give light [of itself] even though fire had not touched it: light upon light! God guides unto His light him that wills [to be guided]; and [to this end] God propounds parables unto men, since God [alone] has full knowledge of all things' (Quran 34:35, translation by Muhammad Asad).

42

"صياغة العقيدة ومقاصد الشريعة وروحها، صياغة تجدد للعودة إلى مصباح (صريح الشريعة نصوصا واستقراءا) في زجاجة العهد النبوي والراشدي ومشكاة حقائق العلوم ولاسيما علوم الاجتماع، من أجل التركيز على العناصر التي تجابه التحديات الحديثة."

al-Ḥāmid, *Likay lā yakūnu l-qurʾān ḥammāl auǧuh*, 48.

43 See, e.g., online sources like Ḫālid ʿAbd al-Munʿim ar-Rifāʿī, *Maʿnā muqawwala: 'In al-qurʾān huwa ḥammāl auǧuh'* (published on islamway.net, 11 November 2012, available online: https://ar.islamway.net/fatwa/39877/معنى-مقولة-إن-القرآن-هو-حمال-أوجه, accessed 11 June 2020); and Muḥammad At-Tīǧānī, *Fa-isʾalū ahl aḏ-ḏikr. Aṣ-ṣafḥa 210* (published on shiaonlinelibrary.com, without date, available online: http://shiaonlinelibrary.com/الكتب/4606_فاسألوا-أهل-الذكر-الدكتور-محمد-التيجاني/الصفحة_205, accessed 11 June 2020).

44 For example, the term 'biting kingship' in the meaning of oppressive rule is mentioned in the following texts: ʿAbdallāh al-Ḥāmid, *al-Ǧihād ṣinwān: Silmī li-aṭr wulāt wa-ḥarbī li-dafʿ ġuzāt* (self-published 2011, at the time of writing not accessible via the

internet anymore, a copy is in my possession), 74; al-Ḥāmid, *Ṯulāṯīyat al-muǧtamaʿ al-madanī*, 30; al-Ḥāmid, *aṭ-Ṭarīq aṯ-ṯāliṯ*, 12; Ḥākim al-Muṭairī, *al-Ḥurrīya aw aṭ-ṭawfān* (Bairūt: al-Muʾassasa l-ʿarabīya li-d-dirāsāt wa-n-našr, 2004), 107; and Muḥammad al-ʿAbd al-Karīm, *Tafkīk al-istibdād: Dirāsa fī fiqh at-taḥarrur min at-taġallub* (Bairūt: aš-Šabaka l-ʿarabīya li-l-abḥāṯ wa-n-našr, 2013), 102.

45 This is the mentioned hadith: 'The prophethood will remain amongst you for as long as God wills it to be. Then God will raise it when he wills to raise it. Then there will be the caliphate upon the prophetic methodology. Then there will be biting kingship and it will remain for as long as God wills it to remain. Then God will raise it when he wills to raise it.'

"تكون النبوة فيكم ما شاء الله أن تكون، ثم يرفعها إذا شاء أن يرفعها، ثم تكون خلافة على منهاج النبوة، فتكون ملكا عاضا، فيكون ما شاء الله أن يكون، ثم يرفعها إذا شاء أن يرفعها."

Aḥmad ibn Ḥanbal, *Musnad al-Imām Aḥmad ibn Ḥanbal*, ed. ʿAbdallāh ibn ʿAbd al-Muḥsin at-Turkī, Vol. 30 (Bairūt: Al-Resalah Publishers 1999, also available online: https://archive.org/stream/waqmsnda/msnda30#page/n4/mode/2up, accessed 11 June 2020), 355–6.

46 An example is this passage from a book by Abdallah al-Hamid: 'The Muslims suffered defeats in the era of European imperialism [al-imbiryālīya al-ifranǧīya] since the last days of the Ottoman state.'

"وانهزم المسلمون في عصر الأمبريالية الإفرنجية، منذ أواخر أيام الدولة العثمانية."

al-Ḥāmid, *al-Ǧihād ṣinwān*, 15.

Another example is the following passage from another of al-Hamid's books: 'They are arguments which can be seen in the history of the modern European [ifranǧī], American and other civilisations.'

" وهي أدلة أيضا مشاهدة في تاريخ الحضارات الحديثة الإفرنجية والأمريكية وغيرها."

al-Ḥāmid, *al-Burhān bi-qawāmat al-umma*, 35.

47

"فقد صرحت نصوص أخرى بأن الإسلام قرر أن المسلم وغير المسلم سواء في كافة الحقوق القائمة على المواطنة، ولذلك اعتبر الاعتداء على الكفار كالاعتداء على المسلمين."

al-Ḥāmid, *Ḥuqūq al-insān baina nūr al-islām wa-ġabaš al-mulk al-ʿaḍūḍ*, 17.

48

"مشروعية الجهاد محصورة بالدفاع عل دولة العدل والشورى، لأنه لا فرق بين مستعبد محلي مسلم، ومستعبد أجنبي كافر."

al-Ḥāmid, *al-Ǧihād ṣinwān*, 77.

49

"بان الشريعة الإسلامية جاءت بحفظ كرامة الإنسان وصيانة حقوقه ونهت عن الظلم، قبل أربعة عشر قرنا من ظهور القوانين الدولية التي كفلت حقوق الإنسان والتزمت بها الحكومات، كما قال تعالى (ولقد كرمنا بني آدم) وقال (وإذا حكمتم بين الناس أن تحكموا بالعدل) وكما قال في الحديث القدسي 'يا عبادي إني حرمت الظلم على نفسي وجعلته بينكم محروما فلا ظالموا.'"

HASM, *Al-Iʿlān at-taʾsīsī*.

50

"فلعل الأجدى أن نفهمه من خلال (زجاجة) التطبيق النبوي والراشدي، لأنها التطبيق المعياري للدين، أي قبل عهود الاختلال الديني."

al-Ḥāmid, *al-Kalima aqwā min ar-raṣāṣa*, 6.

51

"وقال الفقهاء الثلاثة: إن علة الجهاد العسكري هو العدوان أو خوفه، ووافقهم فقهاء من بعدهم أشهرهم ابن تيمية. [...] وجرى على هذا الرأي جمهور الفقهاء وفقهاء السياسة الشرعية على الخصوص، كمحمد عبده ومحمد رشيد رضا وحسن البنا ومحمد الغزالي. [...]"

al-Ḥāmid, *al-Ǧihād ṣinwān*, 25.

52 See, e.g., al-Ḥāmid, *as-Salafīya l-wusṭā*, 67.

53

”فلن يكون لدعاة (الحكم الشوري) مصداقية شعبية، ما لم تكن لهم مصداقية دينية، ولن تكون لهم مصداقية دينية، ما لم تكن أفكارهم مؤصلا فقهيا، عبر العلوم الأربعة: أصول الفقه ومقاصد الشريعة والعقيدة والسياسة الشرعية.“

al-Ḥāmid, *al-Kalima aqwā min ar-raṣāṣa*, 168.

54 'Fa-l-ḥukm bi-t-taḥrīm wa-t-taḥlīl lā yağūzu illā bi-dalīl šarʿī wa-burhān ʿilmī wāḍiḥ. [. . .] Al-Aḥkām aš-šarʿīya tanqasimu ilā qismain. Al-qism al-awwal mā yataʿallaqu bi-l-ʿibādāt wa-l-ḥudūd wa-l-qurubāt allatī šaraʿahā llāh dīnan yataʿabbadu ʿibāduhu bi-hā wifqan mā šaraʿahu llāh bi kitābihi. [. . .] Al-qism aṯ-ṯānī mā yataʿallaqu bi-l-ʿādāt wa-šuʾūn al-ḥayāt al-madanīya. Fa-hāḏā l-aṣl fihi al-ibāḥa wifqan li-l-qāʿida l-uṣūlīya l-fiqhīya allatī taqūlu: Al-aṣl fī l-ašyāʾ al-ibāḥa. Wa-mawḍūʿunā fī hāḏihi l-layla, ḥukm al-iʿtiṣāmāt wa-l-taẓāhurāt fī š-šarīʿya l-islāmīya, huwa min hāḏā l-qism aṯ-ṯānī qaṭʿan.'

Acpra Tube, *Ḥukm al-muẓāharāt wa-l-iʿtiṣāmāt fī š-šarīʿa l-islāmīya*, 1:50–3:31.

55 'Al-muẓāharāt wa-l-iʿtiṣāmāt min al-wasāʾil, wa-l-qāʿida l-fiqhīya taqūlu: Al-wasāʾil lahā ḥukm al-ġāyāt. Wa-mā dāmat al-wasīla hunā hiya l-muẓāharāt as-silmīya wa-l-maqṣūd minhā huwa rafʿ aẓ-ẓulm, wa-iḥqāq al-ḥaqq wa-l-ʿadl, allaḏī faraḍahu llāḥ ʿalā ʿibādihi ğamīʿan. [. . .] Fa-d-daʿwa ilā l-muẓāharāt as-silmīya li-rafʿ aẓ-ẓulm wa-l-istibdād wa-izālat al-fasād wa-iʿṭāʾ aš-šaʿb ḥuqūqahu wa-ḥurrīyatahu l-maslūba wa-l-karāma l-muhāna, hāḏā min ad-daʿwa li-l-ḫāyr wa-l-amr bi-l-maʿrūf wa-n-nahy ʿan al-munkar allaḏī šaraʿahu llāh. Wa-mā dāmat hāḏihi hiya l-ġāya l-mašrūʿa, fa-ayy wasīla mubāḥa tuwaṣṣilu ilayhā fa-hiya mašrūʿa, bal wāğiba.'

Acpra Tube, *Ḥukm al-muẓāharāt wa-l-iʿtiṣāmāt fī š-šarīʿa l-islāmīya*, 6:55–10:07.

56 See, e.g., al-Ḥāmid, *Likay lā yakūnu l-qurʾān ḥammāl auğuh*, 91.

57 See, e.g., R. M. Gleave, 'Maḳāṣid al-Sharīʿa', in *Encyclopaedia of Islam*, ed. P. Bearman et al., 2nd edn. (Leiden: Brill, 1954–2004, first published online 2012, available online: https://referenceworks.brillonline.com/entries/encyclopaedia-of-islam-2/makasid-al-sharia-SIM_8809, accessed 11 June 2020); Wael B. Hallaq, *Law and Legal Theory in Classical and Medieval Islam* (Aldershot: Ashgate, 1994), 69–90; Jamaleddine Ben Abdeljelil and Serdar Kurnaz, *Maqāṣid aš-Šarīʿa: Die Maximen des islamischen Rechts*, Studienreihe Islam im Diskurs Band 1 (Berlin: EB-Verlag, 2014); and Mahmoud Bassiouni, *Menschenrechte zwischen Universalität und islamischer Legitimität* (Berlin: Suhrkamp Taschenbuch Wissenschaft, 2014), 141–82.

58

”وكل ما أجمعت الإنسانية الراقية على أنه ضوروة لحياة الناس، من أمور المعائش، وبناء المدن والدول، فإنما هو من الشريعة، وكل ما لا تقوم حياة الناس إلا به فهو معدود في أصول الدين، كما شرح الشاطبي هذا القاعدة في الموافقات.“

al-Ḥāmid, *al-Ğihād ṣinwān*, 79.

59

”فالنظر المقاصدي ينظر إلى المقصد الكلي الأسمى في حفظ الحقوق والحريات ومراعاة العدالة ومكافحة الفساد وتبني هموم الأصلاح، وإذا تم ذلك بأقل الطرق كلفة وأقربها وأقلها خسارة فهو أقرب إلى نفس الشريعة وروحها ومبادئها العامة.“

Salmān al-ʿAuda, *Asʾilat aṯ-ṯawra* (Bairūt: Markaz namāʾ li-l-buḥūṯ wa-d-dirāsāt, 2012), 27–8.

60 See, e.g., Ridwan Al-Sayyid, 'The Question of Human Rights in Contemporary Islamic Thought', in *Human Rights in Arab Thought*, ed. Jayyusi, 253–73. For an English language example of another contemporary Islamically inspired reformer

who refers to the aims of the sharia in his reasoning, see, e.g., Rachid Ghannouchi, 'Participation in Non-Islamic Government', in *Liberal Islam: A Sourcebook*, ed. Charles Kurzman (New York: Oxford University Press, 1998), 89–95.

61

"فأمور السمو المدني كإقامة الحياة والعمران والحضارة، يتأتى للعقول البشرية المستقلة بفهم أكثر مصالحها ومفاسدها، ويأتي الشرع كاشفا أو مقررا، ما أثبتته العقول."

al-Ḥāmid, *Likay lā yakūnu l-qur'ān ḥammāl auğuh*, 268.

62

"إن البشر يدركون أغلب المصالح في الشق المدني، بما وهبهم الله من الفطرة، وبما منحهم من نور البصيرة، وبما كشفت لهم التجربة والخبرة."

al-Ḥāmid, *Likay lā yakūnu l-qur'ān ḥammāl auğuh*, 310.

63

"فالمعقول القطعي إنسانيا أو حضاريا أو سياسيا، إذا كان محسوسا أو تجريبيا أو برهانيا، فإنما هو شرعي – بصورة تلقائية – فلك ما صح من علوم الإنسان والطبيعة، فإنه ينسجم مع الشريعة، وهو علم مشروع – إذا – كما ذكر ابن تيمية في كتاب العقل والنقل."

al-Ḥāmid, *Likay lā yakūnu l-qur'ān ḥammāl auğuh*, 304.

64

"فينهزم الجائر أمام ضميره في الجولة الأولى، لأن العدل والحق مزرعان في فطرة وعقل كل إنسان."

al-Ḥāmid, *al-Kalima aqwā min ar-raṣāṣa*, 33.

65 See, e.g., al-Ḥāmid, *as-Salafīya l-wusṭā*, 131.

66 See, e.g., al-Ḥāmid, *al-Kalima aqwā min ar-raṣāṣa*, 113.

67

"وهذا يدل على أن أساس مفاسد الأمة هو حصر مرجعية الأمة بثنائية (السلطان والفقهاء) ثم اعتبار الحكام والأمراء الأدرى بمصالح الأمة. [...] هذه هو الأدلة الشرعية من سنن الله المشاهدة في تاريخ الإسلام منذ العصر الأموي، وهي الأدلة المشاهدة في تاريخ الأمم القديمة، في الحضارات الفرعونية والبابلية والأشورية والفينيقية، وفي الصينية والهندية والفارسية، وفي اليونانية والرومانية والسكسونية، وهي أدلة أيضا مشاهدة في تاريخ الحضارات الحديثة الإفرنجية والأمريكية وغيرها."

al-Ḥāmid, *al-Burhān bi-qawāmat al-umma*, 35.

See, also, al-Ḥāmid, *al-Kalima aqwā min ar-raṣāṣa*, 58.

68 See, e.g., al-Ḥāmid, *al-Kalima aqwā min ar-raṣāṣa*, 104.

69

"أن الصريح من النصوص الشرعية لا يخالف الصحيح من علوم الإنسان والطبيعة، لإن الذي أنزل الشريعة، هو الذي خلق الطبيعة. [...] وغير الصريح في الكتاب والسنة يرد إلى الصحيح من علوم الإنسان والطبيعة، وغير الصريح من علوم الإنسان والطبيعة يرد إلى الصريح من الكتاب والسنة. فهذا قاعدة عظيمة ألم بها ابن تيمية في العقل والنقل."

al-Ḥāmid, *al-Burhān bi-qawāmat al-umma*, 90–1.

70

"في العصر العباسي جرى انزياح كبير في دلالات الألفاظ بحيث يبقى المصطلح، ولكن يغير الناس مفهومه، وهذا واضح في مصطلحات كثيرة، كالصبر والحكمة والأمر بالمعروف والنهي عن المنكر، وحفظ القرآن وتعليمه. [...] وكذلك مصطلح أولى الأمر، الذي ضيق معناه اللغوي الشامل، أهل الرأي والنظر وعرفاء الأمة وقصر على الفقهاء والأمراء."

al-Ḥāmid, *al-Burhān bi-qawāmat al-umma*, 52–3.

71 See, e.g., al-Ḥāmid, *al-Burhān bi-qawāmat al-umma*, 123.

72

"فالإسلام هو هوية الأمة الحضارية، وهذه مسألة مهمة، ينبغي مواصلة التذكير. فاستنساخ التنوير الأطلسي، ينطوي على موقف حضاري شاذج، لأن النتيجة هي سعي متعثر لإدماج هوية الأمة، لتكون طرفا في المركزية الأطليسة. [...] المشروع العلماني لم ينبثق من هوية الأمة."

al-Ḥāmid, *Likay lā yakūnu l-qur'ān ḥammāl auğuh*, 14–15.

73

"وترك الجهاد المدني أدى إلى ذهاب الأعراض والتعرض للفتن والانحراف، والأمراض النفسية والعقلية، وشيوع المخدرات، وتعرض المسلمين للفقر والجهل والقهر والمرض، مما جعلهم بيئة صالحة للقيم الامبريالية الإفرنجية الغلابة. ينبغي البدء بحماية المسلمين من الامبريالية والفرنجة والعلمنة والهيمنة الأجنبية."

al-Ḥāmid, *al-Kalima aqwā min ar-raṣāṣa*, 55.

74

"ومن الواضح أن للإمبريالية الأطلسية هدفا استراتيجيا بعيد المدى من امتلاك هذا السلاح، وهو إنشاء ذهنية الاستسلام والانهزام في عقولنا وقيمنا الاجتماعية، نحن العرب والمسلمين، حتى نعتقد أنه الحضارة الغربية وما في قيمها من فجور، هي قدرنا المكتوب."

al-Ḥāmid, *al-Ǧihād ṣinwān*, 53.

See, also, al-Ḥāmid, *Ḥuqūq al-insān baina nūr al-islām wa-ġabaš al-mulk al-ʿaḍūḍ*, 106.

75 See, e.g., al-Ḥāmid, *Ḥuqūq al-insān baina nūr al-islām wa-ġabaš al-mulk al-ʿaḍūḍ*, 9.

76 See, e.g., al-Ḥāmid, *Ḥuqūq al-insān baina nūr al-islām wa-ġabaš al-mulk al-ʿaḍūḍ*, 105.

77 See, e.g., al-Ḥāmid *al-Kalima aqwā min ar-raṣāṣa*, 73.

78

"السلام الصهيوني الذي تسوق له الإمبريالية الأطلسية اليوم، يشبه ما سمي بالسلام الروماني في الزمن القديم، انه سلام الدولة السيدة والدولة المستعبدة. [...] ومن الواضح للعيان ان دويلة الاحتلال الصهيوني ليست دولة عنصرية ولا عسكرية فحسب، بل هي دولة إجرامية يهدد السلم العالمي كافة، ويستمد اجرامه من عقيدة عنصرية. [...] الفكر الصهيوني في جذوره فكر عدواني."

al-Ḥāmid, *al-Ǧihād ṣinwān*, 79.

79

"لم تتصور بعض النخب العربية الحداثة السياسية والاجتماعية إلا محاكاة للنموذج الأوروبي، أي بتبني القيم الغربية الثلاث: العلمانية والليبرالية والرأسمالية، هذه القيم الثلاث لا تطابق الشريعة الإسلامية بل تناقضها في أمور جوهرية. [...] وأنه ينبغي لنا تأصيل قيم المفهوم في بوتقة الشريعة الإسلامية، بتحرير مفاهيمه الإنسانية من أوهام الخصوصية الأوروبية."

al-Ḥāmid, *Ṯulāṯīyat al-muǧtamaʿ al-madanī*, 130–1.

80 For more details about Islamic identity and authenticity in Islamic thought after the nineteenth century CE, see, e.g., al-Ridwan Sayyid, 'The Question of Human Rights in Contemporary Islamic Thought', 253–7; Nasr Hamid Abu Zeid, 'The Modernisation of Islam or the Islamisation of Modernity', in *Cosmopolitanism, Identity and Authenticity in the Middle East*, ed. Roel Meijer (Richmond: Curzon, 1999), 71–86; and Gudrun Krämer, *Demokratie im Islam: Der Kampf für Toleranz und Freiheit in der arabischen Welt* (München: C.H. Beck, 2011), 176–82.

81 See Larbi Sadiki, *The Search for Arab Democracy: Discourses and Counter-Discourses* (London: Hurst, 2004), 110–39.

82 See, e.g., Ridwan Al-Sayyid, 'Islamic Movements and Authenticity: Barriers to Development', in *Cosmopolitanism, Identity and Authenticity in the Middle East*, ed. Meijer, 109–11.

83 See, e.g., Fandy, *Saudi Arabia and the Politics of Dissent*, 116–17; Gilles Kepel, *Jihad: Expansion et déclin de l'islamisme* (Paris: Editions Gallimard, 2000), 335–7; and Lacroix, *Les Islamistes Saoudiens*, 222–3.

84 See http://www.acpra.org/news.php?action=list&cat_id=12 (accessed 11 June 2020).

85 See, e.g., HASM, *ACPRA Demands the Immediate Unconditional Release of Its Co-Founder, Mohammed Al-Bjady* (published on acpra.org, 24 March 2011 CE, available online: http://www.acpra.org/news_view_117.html, accessed 11 June 2020).

86 See, e.g., HASM, *ACPRA Demands the Release of All Prisoners of Conscience* (published on acpra.org, 28 September 2013, available online: http://www.acpra.org/news_view_251.html, accessed 11 June 2020).
87 See, e.g., HASM, *ACPRA Invites People to Attend the 6th Trial Hearing of Its Co-founders: al-Hamid and al-Qahtani*, published on acpra.org, 19 November 2012, available online: http://www.acpra.org/news_view_198.html, accessed 11 June 2020).
88 See HASM, *ACPRA Sends Letters to Top Saudi Officials, and UNHCR about HR Violations* (published on acpra.org, 14 August 2011, available online: http://www.acpra.org/news_view_140.html, accessed 11 June 2020).
89 See HASM, *Saudi Civil & Political Rights Association (An Establishing Declaration)* (published on acpra.org, 1 February 2010, available online: http://www.acpra.org/news_view_5.html, accessed 11 June 2020).
90 This is the mentioned passage: 'One of the most important reasons for the founding of the association is that the state presents the violations of political human rights in a deviant religious discourse, which outwardly applies the sharia. [. . .] Many people do not know that Islam is innocent of all actions that bury the sovereignty of the Muslim community over the government and suppress freedom, pluralism, justice and shura.'

”ومن اهم دواعي إنشاء الجمعية، أن الدولة تقدم انتهاكات حقوق الإنسان السياسية بخطاب ديني محرف ظاهره تطبيق الشريعة ، [...] وكثير من الناس لا يدركون أن الإسلام بريء من كل ممارسة لوأد قوامة الأمة على الحكومة، وقمع الحرية والتعددية والعدالة والشورى.“

HASM, *Al-I'lān at-ta'sīsī.*

91 This is exemplified by the following passage: 'One of the most important reasons for the founding of the association is that one of the reasons for the spreading of violence is the absence of a basis for peaceful, political, civil jihad. [. . .] Therefore, cooperation between individuals in matters that concern them has become a necessity of the sharia.'

”ومن أهم دواعي إنشاء الجمعية، أن من أسباب استشراء العنف غياب قاعدة الجهاد المدني السياسي السلمي. [...] ولذلك صار تعاون الأفراد في ما بينهم أمرا ضروريا شرعيا.“

See HASM, *Al-I'lān at-ta'sīsī.*

92

”ومن دواعي إنشاء الجمعية، كشف تواطؤ أغلب الدول الغربية المريب، تلك التي تتشدق بإثارة ملف حقوق الإنسان عندما تختلف مع بعض الحكومات، أسكتها نفط الخليج.“

HASM, *Al-I'lān at-ta'sīsī.*

93

”ومن دواعي إنشاء الجمعية، أن العديد من المنظمات الدولية متأثر بالنظرة الغربية لحقوق الإنسان، ولم تبرز بشكل فعال النظرية الإسلامية لحقوق الإنسان.“

HASM, *Al-I'lān at-ta'sīsī.*

94 HASM, *Saudi Civil & Political Rights Association.*

95

”تأصيل ثقافة حقوق الإنسان السياسية إسلاميا، باعتبار وسائل الحكم الشوري من أركان العقيدة السياسية الإسلامية، التي لا يجوز – شرعا – التنازل عنها، أو التفريط بها: كالعدالة والحرية والتعددية الفكرية والسياسية والتسامح، وحصر حل كل خلاف بالأسلوب السلمي“

HASM, *Al-I'lān at-ta'sīsī.*

Chapter 7

1

” أهم دواعي إنشاء الجمعية أن حقوق الإنسان والحريات الأساسية ولا سيما السياسية في المملكة العربية السعودية تتعرض لانتهاكات خطيرة. [...] فالقمع والتعذيب وانتهاكات حقوق الانسان ومصادرة الحريات

فضلا عن كونها ظلما كبيرا لا تضمن الامن والاستقرار وانما الذي يضمن الامن والاستقرار والازدهار
هو العدل والإصلاح السياسي."

HASM, *Al-I'lān at-tàsīsī* (published on acpra.org, 23 October 2009, available online: http://www.acpra.org/news.php?action=view&id=1, accessed 11 June 2020).

2 'Naḥnu nurakkizu, ʿalā fikra, ʿalā l-intihākāt al-ğismānīya li-š-šaḫs, yaʿnī bi-maʿnā l-iʿtiqāl at-taʿassufī, at-taʿḏīb, al-iḫtifāʾ al-qasrī, al-ḥirmān min al-ḥuqūq. Lākin fī l-ḥaqīqa lamā tanẓuru ilā manẓumat al-ḥuqūq hiya awsaʿ min al-intihākāt al-ğismānīya wa-n-nafsīya. Wa-allaḏī tawallada min ğamīʿ haḏihi al-ašyāʾ huwa l-ḥirmān min al-ḥuqūq as-siyāsīya. Limāḏā fī baladinā tantaširu miṯl haḏihi l-iʿtiqālāt at-taʿassufīya bi-niṭāq wāsiʿ? Hiya murṭabita bi-š-šakl as-siyāsī. Li-māḏā fī l-buldān ad-dīmuqrāṭīya lā yūğadu miṯl haḏihi l-intihākāt?'

Acpra Tube, *Intihākāt ḥuqūq al-insān fī s-Suʿūdīya / D. Muḥammad al-Qaḥṭānī* (published on youtube.com, 2 October 2012, available online: https://www.youtube.com/watch?v=hj2f6vO8iCc, accessed 11 June 2020), 6:57–7:40.

3

"يعيش المسلمون اليوم والعرب خاصة [...] أسوأ صور العبودية لغير اللهو هذه العبودية التي تتجلى اليوم
في خضوع أكثر شعوبهم وخنوعهم شبه المطلق للطغاة. [...] يخضع نحو ثلاثمائة مليون عربي من الخليج
إلى المحيط كعبيد بلا أغلال تحت سيطرة أنظمة حكم هو من أسوء الأنظمة السياسية في العالم، وأكثر ظلما
وفسادا."

Ḥākim al-Muṭairī, *Taḥrīr al-insān wa-tağrīd aṭ-ṭuġyān* (Bairūt: al-Muʾassasa l-ʿarabīya li-d-dirāsāt wa-n-našr, 2009), 7.

4

"وانهزم المسلمون في عصر الإمبريالية الإفرنجية، منذ أواخر أيام الدولة العثمانية، عندما جهلوا طبيعة
التحدي والعدوان الإفرنجي الإمبريالي. [...] لماذا انهزم العرب والمسلمون أمام الإمبريالية الإفرنجية؟ لأن
الطغيان الداخلي دمر عوامل قوة الأمة المعرفية والحضارية، بسبب غيبة ثقافة الجهاد المدني، التي تصون
المجتمع عن الاستسلام، والدولة عن التغول."

ʿAbdallāh al-Ḥāmid, *al-Ğihād ṣinwān: Silmī li-aṭr wulāt wa-ḥarbī li-dafʿ ġuzāt* (self-published, 2011, at the time of writing not accessible via the internet anymore, a copy is in my possession), 15.

5 See, e.g., ʿAbdallāh al-Ḥāmid, *al-Kalima aqwā min ar-raṣāṣa: al-Ğihād as-silmī l-akbar* (Bairūt: ad-Dār al-ʿarabīya li-l-ʿulūm, 2004, also available online: https://archive.org/details/wordstrongerthanbullet/mode/2up, accessed 11 June 2020), 169.

6

"شاركت الروح الصحراوية التي حملها العرب من الجزيرة في إضاعتها أولا، وثانيا الروح الفرعوني
التي اقتبسوها من مدائن كسرى وقيصر وفرعون، هذا الزواج بين فرعون والصحراء أنتج الأزمة
السياسية، التي أفسدت التربية السياسية، وأفرزت تيارين لم يستطيعا إحراز إي قدر من النجاح"
الفئة الأولى: فقهاء الاحتساب السياسي الصحراوي الذين راموا إصلاح الدولة بالسلاح، من دون إعداد
فكري. [...]
الفئة الثانية: فقهاء المسكنة الذين استسلموا للاستبداد والفرعنة."

ʿAbdallāh al-Ḥāmid, *Ḥuqūq al-insān baina nūr al-islām wa-ġabaš al-mulk al-ʿaḍūḍ* (Bairūt: Bīsān li-n-našr wa-t-tawzīʿ wa-l-iʿlām, 2010), 127.

7 See, e.g., al-Ḥāmid, *al-Kalima aqwā min ar-raṣāṣa*, 55 and 61; and ʿAbdallāh al-Ḥāmid, *as-Salafīya l-wusṭā: al-ʿAdl ʿadīl aṣ-ṣalāt* (Dimašq: Markaz an-nāqid aṯ-ṯaqāfī, 2009), 196.

8 See, e.g., al-Ḥāmid, *al-Kalima aqwā min ar-raṣāṣa*, 114.

9

"إنها المذهبية الشورية وفروعه كالعدل والحرية والتعددية من لباب العقيدة، وأنها أولى من تلك الصراعات
المذهبية. ومن أجل ذلك خاض الناس صراعا اجتماعيا دمويا، [...] لا يترتب على تقرير الصواب فيها
عدل ولا شورى."

al-Ḥāmid, *al-Kalima aqwā min ar-raṣāṣa*, 108.

10

”جهود متميزة، تنفض عن الفقه السياسي ما شابه من التأويل والتحريف، وتعيد بناءه نظرياته وآلياته على صريح ما أوحاه الله عز وجل عبر الشريعة، وصحيح ما أوحاه الله عز وجل إلى الطبائع عبر حقائق علوم الإنسان والشريعة.“

al-Ḥāmid, *al-Kalima aqwā min ar-raṣāṣa*, 169.

11 See, e.g., Ridwan Al-Sayyid, ‘Islamic Movements and Authenticity: Barriers to Development’, in *Cosmopolitanism, Identity and Authenticity in the Middle East*, ed. Roel Meijer (Richmond: Curzon, 1999), 106–11; Sagi Polka, ‘The Centrist Stream in Egypt and Its Role in the Public Discourse Surrounding the Shaping of the Country’s Cultural Identity’, *Middle Eastern Studies* 39, no. 3 (July 2003): 52–8; and Rüdiger Lohlker, *Die Salafisten: Der Aufstand der Frommen, Saudi-Arabien und der Islam* (München: C.H. Beck, 2017), 135.

12 See, e.g., Thomas Bauer, *Die Kultur der Ambiguität: Eine andere Geschichte des Islams* (Berlin: Verlag der Weltreligionen, 2011), 192–223.

13

”لا يمكن إذن فقه نصوص الشريعة من دون إدراك النظام الكلي لها، لا يمكن ذلك لأن إدراك النظام الكلي لأي شيء يسبق معرفة وظائف أجزائه ويلهم إلى إدراك العلاقات بين الوحدات. [...] لكل قطعة وظيفة، سواء أكانت صغيرة أم كبيرة والله – في سننه الإنسانية – قد جعل أهميتها بحسب دورها في تحقيق الخير للبشر في الدنيا والآخرة.“

al-Ḥāmid, *al-Ğihād ṣinwān*, 21.

14

”لا بد – إذا – من مواصلة تأسيس خطاب إسلامي يوازن بين شقي الإسلام: الشق الروحي والمدني.“

al-Ḥāmid, *al-Ğihād ṣinwān*, 62.

15 See, e.g., Muḥammad al-ʿAbd al-Karīm, *al-Iḥtisāb al-madanī: Dirāsa fī l-bināʾ al-maqāṣidī li-l-ʾiḥtisāb*, aṭ-ṭabʿa aṯ-ṯānīya (Bairūt: aš-Šabaka l-ʿarabīya li-l-ʾabḥāṯ wa-n-našr, 2013), 78–9.

16

”منذ أمد آثر التفكير الديني عالم الغيب على عالم الشهادة، وترك العلم العملي الذي يحل مشكلات الإنسان على الأرض، إلى العلم التجريدي الذي لا يفضي التعمق فيه إلى عمل.“

ʿAbdallāh al-Ḥāmid, *Likay lā yakūnu l-qurʾān ḥammāl awğuh: al-Miṣbāḥ fī zuğağa wa-miškāt* (self-published 2008, available online: http://www.acpra.org/download.php?action=view&id=11, accessed 11 June 2020), 75.

See, also, al-Ḥāmid, *al-Ğihād ṣinwān*, 84.

17

”بل العقيدة السديدة أن نعمل عملا صالحا.“

al-Ḥāmid, *as-Salafīya l-wusṭā*, 80.

18 Karl Marx, *Thesen über Feuerbach*, in Karl Marx and Friedrich Engels, *Karl Marx – Friedrich Engels Studienausgabe*, Band 1 (Frankfurt: Fischer Bücherei, 1966), 141 (my translation).

19

”كل مصلح عندما يجدد تختلط في تجديده عنصران: معياري مطلق هو أساس الإصلاح في كل زمان ومكان، وهو صريح الإسلام وصحيح الحكمة، ونسبي آني عالج به مشكلة قائمة، ومن العنصرين تتكون خلطة التجديد.“

al-Ḥāmid, *as-Salafīya l-wusṭā*, 92.

20

”المتغير لا بد أن يتغير، لأنه مرتبط بالحركة الاجتماعية للبشر، إذ يحتاج الناس إلى صياغة دينية متغيرة، تواكب حركة التغير الثقافي والاجتماعي والحضاري. [...] إذا تغيرت الأسئلة والمشكلات والمعطيات، فلا بد من أن تتغير الأوجبة والحلول، ولا تكون الحلول مشروعة، إلا بالعودة إلى صيدلية القرآن والسنة.“

al-Ḥāmid, *as-Salafīya l-wusṭā*, 104.

21 For details about the concept of the sharia in the Sunni mainstream, see, e.g., N. Calder and M. B. Hooker, ‘Sharīʿa’, in *Encyclopaedia of Islam*, ed. P. Bearman et al., 2nd edn. (Available online: https://referenceworks.brillonline.com/entries/encyclopaedia-of-islam-2/sharia-COM_1040, accessed 11 June 2020), and Mahmoud Bassiouni, *Menschenrechte zwischen Universalität und islamischer Legitimität* (Berlin: Suhrkamp Taschenbuch Wissenschaft, 2014), 40–9.

22 See, e.g., W. Madelung, ‘Murd̲jiʾa’, in *Encyclopaedia of Islam*, ed. P. Bearman et al., 2nd edn. (Available online: https://referenceworks.brillonline.com/entries/encyclopaedia-of-islam-2/murdjia-COM_0801, accessed 11 June 2020).

23 See, e.g., Jochen Lobah, ‘Der Salafismus zwischen Reformdiskurs und Extremismus’, in *Demokratie und Islam: Theoretische und empirische Studien*, ed. Ahmet Cavuldak, Oliver Hidalgo, Philipp W. Hildmann and Holger Zapf (Wiesbaden: Springer, 2014), 86–7.

24 See, e.g., Polka, ‘The Centrist Stream in Egypt’, 39–64.

25 See, e.g., Polka, ‘The Centrist Stream in Egypt’, 42; and Bauer, *Die Kultur der Ambiguität*, 341–3.

26

”ولكم سنن الله الطبيعية – كما قال سيد قطب – هي (النواميس التي تحكم حياة البشر، وفق مشيئة الله، التي أصبحت سننا جارية مطردة لا تتخلف، بحيث إن ما وقع منها في الماضي يقع مثيله في الحاضر، إذا أصبحت حال الحاضرين مثل حال السابقين.) والسير على مقتضى سنن الله السياسية، هو طريق عودة الأمة إلى قوتها ووحدتها.“

al-Ḥāmid, *al-Kalima aqwā min ar-raṣāṣa*, 113.

27

”وسنن الله المقروءة في كتاب الشريعة، لا تخالف سننه المشاهدة في مسرح الاجتماع والطبيعة. فالفكر الإنساني الصحيح في علوم الاجتماع والطبيعة لا يخالف المنقول الصريح من علوم الشريعة.“

ʿAbdallāh al-Ḥāmid, *al-Burhān bi-qawāmat al-umma wa-siyādatihā ʿalā s-sulṭān* (self-published, 2012, available online: http://www.acpra.org/download.php?action=view&id=26, accessed 11 June 2020), 36.

28 See, e.g., al-Ḥāmid, *al-Burhān bi-qawāmat al-umma*, 91.

29

”فقد جرت العقول السليمة بمقتضى الفطرة والخبرة، في الأمم المدنية [...] على إدراك أن (الحكم الشوري) شرط في أي حكومة، وأن التجمعات الأهلية المدنية هي ضمانة (الحكم الشوري)، وأن حيوية المجتمع تظاهرات واعتصامات وبيانات هو ضمان حقوق الشعب وحرياته، وأن جو الحرية السامية، هو المناخ التي تنمو فيه المجتمعات، هذه أمور عرفتها كم أمة وملة ودولة، مسلمة وغير مسلمة.“

al-Ḥāmid, *al-Kalima aqwā min ar-raṣāṣa*, 197.

30

”فينهزم الجائر أمام ضميره في الجولة الأولى، لأن العدل والحق مزرعان في فطرة وعقل كل إنسان.“

al-Ḥāmid, *al-Kalima aqwā min ar-raṣāṣa*, 33.

31 See, e.g., al-Ḥāmid, *al-Kalima aqwā min ar-raṣāṣa*, 102.

32

”وكل ما هو فطري في الجبلة إنما هو حق مقدس من حقوق الناس، لأن الإسلام – كأي دين سماوي – هو دين الفطرة.“

al-Ḥāmid, *Ḥuqūq al-insān baina nūr al-islām wa-ġabaš al-mulk al-ʿaḍūḍ*, 142. See, also, ʿAbdallāh al-Ḥāmid, *T̲ulāt̲īyat al-muğtamaʿ al-madanī* (Bairūt: ad-Dār al-ʿarabīya li-l-ʿulūm, 2004), 70.

33 See, e.g., al-Ḥāmid, *Likay lā yakūnu l-qurʾān ḥammāl auğuh*, 253.

34 See, especially, Shahab Ahmed’s insightful comments on the subject in Shahab Ahmed, *What Is Islam? The Importance of Being Islamic* (Princeton: Princeton University Press, 2016), 430–5.

35 For more details about the use of 'innate nature' (fiṭra) in the history of Islamic thought, see, e.g., D. B. Macdonald, 'Fiṭra', in *Encyclopaedia of Islam*, ed. P. Bearman et al., 2nd edn. (Available online: https://referenceworks.brillonline.com/entries/encyclopaedia-of-islam-2/fitra-SIM_2391, accessed 11 June 2020).

36 See, e.g., Ahmad S. Moussalli, 'Islamism: Modernisation of Islam or Islamisation of Knowledge', in *Cosmopolitanism, Identity and Authenticity in the Middle East*, ed. Roel Meijer (Richmond: Curzon, 1999), 87–101; and Polka, 'The Centrist Stream in Egypt', 42–4.

37 Quran 24:35.

38

"السلفية: هي المناداة بفهم مصباح القرآن والسنة، من خلال صفاء زجاجة التطبيق النبوي والراشدي، ومشكاة حقائق علوم الإنسان والطبيعة."

al-Ḥāmid, *as-Salafīya l-wusṭā*, 62.

39

"السلفية متفقة في منهج الاستدلال، ولكنها شتى الصياغات والمعالجات. [...] وجاءت اتجاهات السلفية حسب احتياجات المجتمعات وذهنيات الأشخاص والجغرافيا والمناخ الاجتماعي. فكانت حركة إصلاح للتفكير عند أبي حنيفة ومالك والشافعي وابن تيمية وحركة رفض للدخيل عند أحمد بن حنبل، وحركة نقض للفلسفة اليونانية عند الغزالي، [...] وحركة تأصيل للفكر الاجتماعي عند ابن خلدون، وحركة بناء لمقاصد الشريعة الكلية القطعية عند الشاطبي في الموافقات، وعند الدهلوي في كتابه حجة الله البالغة، وحركة تنوير وتحرير للهوية من الجمود والتغريب عند محمد عبده ومحمد رشيد رضا والمودودي والكواكبي وحسن البنا وسيد قطب، وحركة استقلال سياسي للهوية عند محمد عن عبد الوهاب، [...] وهي حركة دعوة إلى قيم المجتمع المدني وتجمعاته الأهلية، وضمانات الحكم العادل والمطالبة بالدستور في اتجاهات بدأت منذ الكواكبي وخير الدين التونسي والأفغاني وغيرهم."

al-Ḥāmid, *as-Salafīya l-wusṭā*, 15–16.
A similar, albeit not as comprehensive, list can be found in al-Ḥāmid, *Likay lā yakūnu l-qurʾān ḥammāl auğuh*, 182–5.

40

"بيان مرونة المنهج السلفي، وكونه إطارا يسمح بتجديد أصيل يجمع فين الحفاظ على الثوابت القطعية، والتجديد في الوسائل والصياغة والفروع والحركة والتطبيق. [...] السلفية منهج وأسلوب وليس مذهبا محددا في زمن أموي أو عباسي أو مملوكي أو عثماني. كل سلفية فإنما هي تجديد آني، يشكل خلطة دواء، تركز على وباء ما، في زمنها ومكانها."

al-Ḥāmid, *as-Salafīya l-wusṭā*, 28.

41

"فالسلفيات الأموية والعباسية والمملوكية والعثمانية، ليست هي المرجعية وإنما هي حركات وصياغات ومعالجات تنتسب إلى السلفية. [...] فليس ميزان السلفية ما قال أحمد بن حنبل أو الأشعري، ولا ما قال ابن تيمية أو الغزالي، ولا ما قال محمد بن عبد الوهاب أو سيد قطب، بل الميزان هو [ما] قاله الله و[ما] قاله الرسول [وما] قاله الصحابة السابقون."

al-Ḥāmid, *as-Salafīya l-wusṭā*, 124–5.

42

"فكيف يكون الإنسان اليوم سلفيا وهو لم يكتب ببنان ولم يتكلم بلسان، فضلا عن أن يشارك دعاة الإصلاح السياسي في إصدار بيان فضلا عن يعتصم ويتظاهر في ميدان، وهو يرى المنكرات الكبرى في الدولة العربية القامعة داخليا، المنقمعة خارجيا."

al-Ḥāmid, *as-Salafīya l-wusṭā*, 215.

43 See Henri Lauzière, *The Making of Salafism: Islamic Reform in the Twentieth Century* (New York: Columbia University Press, 2015), 27–59.

44 See, e.g., P. Shinar and W. Ende, 'Salafiyya', in *Encyclopaedia of Islam*, ed. P. Bearman et al., 2nd edn. (Available online: https://referenceworks.brillonline.com/entries/encyclopaedia-of-islam-2/salafiyya-COM_0982, accessed 11 June 2020); and Lohlker, *Die Salafisten*, 16–32.

45 See Lauzière, *The Making of Salafism*, 27–59.
46 See, e.g., Itzchak Weismann, 'A Perverted Balance: Modern Salafism between Reform and Jihād', *Die Welt des Islams* 57, no. 1 (2017): 41–2.
47 See, e.g., Weismann, 'A Perverted Balance'.
48 See, e.g., Roel Meijer, 'Yūsuf al-ʿUyairī and the Making of a Revolutionary Salafī Praxis', *Die Welt des Islams* 47, no. 3 (2007): 422–59; and Lohlker, *Die Salafisten*, 143–5.
49 For details about this categorization, see, e.g., Joas Wagemakers, 'Salafism', in *Oxford Research Encyclopedias* (August 2016, available online: https://oxfordre.com/religion/view/10.1093/acrefore/9780199340378.001.0001/acrefore-9780199340378-e-255#acrefore-9780199340378-e-255-div1-8, accessed 17 October 2020).
50 See, e.g., Yūsuf al-Qaraḍāwī, *Awlawiyāt al-ḥaraka l-islāmīya fī l-marḥala l-qādima* (al-Qāhira: Muʾassasat ar-risāla, 1991), 104–7.
51 Lohlker, *Die Salafisten*, 162 (my translation).
52

"بل الإسلام اعتبر تنازل الإنسان عن حريته شركا. [...] الناس الذين يعبدون الله صاروا بعبوديتهم لله أحرارا من سواه. [...] وأن الناس لا تنقسمون إلى أحرار وعبيد، بل الناس كلهم عبيد لله، وهم إذن أحرار أنداد لإخوانهم البشر الأحرار."

al-Ḥāmid, *Ḥuqūq al-insān baina nūr al-islām wa-ġabaš al-mulk al-ʿaḍūḍ*, 15.
53

"جوهر الرسالة المحمدية التحرير."

Muḥammad al-ʿAbd al-Karīm, *Tafkīk al-istibdād: Dirāsa fī fiqh at-taḥarrur min at-taġallub* (Bairūt: aš-Šabaka l-ʿarabīya li-l-abḥāṯ wa-n-našr, 2013), 211.
54

"نحتاج في زمننا إلى أن نفهم الإسلام خطاب تحرير للناس في حياتهم وعقولهم وأفكارهم."

Muḥammad al-Aḥmarī, *ad-Dīmuqrāṭīya: al-Ǧuḏūr wa-iškālīyat at-taṭbīq* (Bairūt: aš-Šabaka l-ʿarabīya li-l-abḥāṯ wa-n-našr, 2012), 144.
55

"لقد جاء الإسلام لتحرير الإنسانية كلها من كل أشكال العبودية لغير الله، وجعل التوحيد شعار التحرير (لا إله إلا الله)، فلا ملوك، ولا قياصرة، ولا أكاسرة، ولا فراعنة، ولا جبابرة."

al-Muṭairī, *Taḥrīr al-insān wa-taǧrīd aṭ-ṭuġyān*, 16.
56 See, e.g., al-Ḥāmid, *Ḥuqūq al-insān baina nūr al-islām wa-ġabaš al-mulk al-ʿaḍūḍ*, 78.
57

"عندما أوجب الإسلام الشورى نظاما سياسيا، بني ذلك على استقرارها نظاما تربويا، أي أنه عندما قرر (الشورى)، فإنما هي شورى الأحرار الأنداد، لكل حاكم شوري، لا شورى العبيد والأوغاد، لكل طاغية جلاد، شورى المفكرين المجتهدين لا المقلدين."

al-Ḥāmid, *Ḥuqūq al-insān baina nūr al-islām wa-ġabaš al-mulk al-ʿaḍūḍ*, 141.
58

"مفهوم الحرية في الإسلام يشبه المفهوم العلماني في مسألة، ويخالفه في أخرى، فهو يشبهه في أن حرية الإنسان تنتهي حيث تبتدئ حريات الآخرين. ويخالفه في أخرى، وهو أن الحرية في الإسلام مرتبطة بالفطرة، فالإسلام – والأديان السماوية غير المحرفة – هو دين الفطرة، فكل ما هو طيب في الفطرة، كالزواج والعفة والأمانة هو طيب في الإسلام، وكل ما هو خبيث في الفطرة الإنسانية، فهو في الإسلام خبيث."

al-Ḥāmid, *Ḥuqūq al-insān baina nūr al-islām wa-ġabaš al-mulk al-ʿaḍūḍ*, 114.
59

"والحرية في التصور الإسلامي تتمثل بالإنسان المتحرر من سلطة البشر لإجل سلطة رب البشر، فهو لا يريد من الحرية سوى الدفاع عن معبوده."

al-ʿAbd al-Karīm, *Tafkīk al-istibdād*, 181.

60 For details about the term ‘sharia caveat’, see, e.g., Anna Würth, *Dialog mit dem Islam als Konfliktprävention? Zur Menschenrechtspolitik gegenüber islamisch geprägten Staaten* (Studie des Deutschen Instituts für Menschenrechte, September 2003), 39.

61 In fact, this is the whole point of al-Maliki’s book *The Sovereignty of the Umma before the Implementation of the Sharia* (see ʿAbdallāh al-Mālikī, *Siyādat al-umma qabla taṭbīq aš-šarīʿa: Naḥwa faḍāʾ amṯal li-taǧsīd mabādiʾ al-islām* [Bairūt: Aš-Šabaka l-ʿarabīya li-l-abḥāṯ wa-n-našr, 2012]). In some passages of his book, al-Ahmari implies that he, too, might be sympathetic to this thought, although he does not explicitly state so (see, e.g., al-Aḥmarī, *ad-Dīmuqrāṭīya*, 140).

62 For details about al-Ghannouchi’s view on freedom, see, e.g., Lino Klevesatz, ‘Religious Freedom in Current Political Islam: The Writings of Rachid al-Ghannouchi and Abu al-’Ala Madi’, in *Demokratie und Islam*, ed. Cavuldak, Hidalgo, Hildmann and Zapf, 45–64. For details about at-Turabi’s view on the issue, see, e.g., Ḥasan at-Turābī, ‘The Islamic State’, in John Calvert, *Islamism. A Documentary and Reference Guide* (Westport: Greenwood Press, 2008), 51–5. For details about Yusuf al-Qaradawi’s opinions concerning freedom, see, e.g., Yūsuf al-Qaraḍāwī, *al-Islām wa-l-ḥurrīya* (published on al-qaradawi.net, 10 January 2019, available online: https://www.al-qaradawi.net/node/3637, accessed 11 June 2020).

63 For details about the political theory of Murtaza Mutahhari, see, e.g., Vanessa Martin, *Creating an Islamic State: Khomeini and the Making of a New Iran* (London: I.B. Tauris, 2000), 81–92.

64 For example, ʿAbdallāh al-Ḥāmid, *aṭ-Ṭarīq aṯ-ṯāliṯ: ad-Dustūr al-islāmī* (Dimašq: Markaz an-nāqid aṯ-ṯaqāfī, 2009); and Matrūk al-Fāliḥ, *al-Iṣlāḥ ad-dustūrī fī s-Suʿūdīya: al-Qaḍāyā wa-l-asʾila l-asāsīya* (Bārīs: al-Muʾassasa l-ʿarabīya l-ūrubīya li-n-našr, 2004).

65

”ولكي نضمن تحقيق العدل والقضاء على الاستبداد، فإننا بحاجة إلى آليات وهياكل. [...] وتلك الوسائل والآليات والهياكل والإجراءات والعناصر التي يكمن أن تحقق لنا العدل وتقضي على الاستبداد وتضمن حقوق الناس وحرياتهم يوفرها ويتضمنها الدستور. والدستور بهذا المعنى ليس كفرا ولا إيمانا، بل هو آليات وهياكل وإجراءات وعناصر محايدة لإقامة حياة مدنية إسلامية.“

al-Fāliḥ, *al-Iṣlāḥ ad-dustūrī fī s-Suʿūdīya*, 31.

66 See, e.g., al-Fāliḥ, *al-Iṣlāḥ ad-dustūrī fī s-Suʿūdīya*, 9.

67

”وإذا قلنا (النظام الدستوري الإسلامي)، جاء في حوالي عشر نقاط:
١ – مقتضى قوامة الأمة أن بيعة الأمة الحاكم على الكتاب والسنة، هي عقد اجتماعي يقون على تعادل الحقوق والواجبات، والتزامه بقوامتها عليه. [...]
[٢] – ومن وسائل قوامة الأمة على الحاكم قيام (مجلس نواب منتخب) يرسم الخطوط التربوية والسياسية والمالية ويشرع النظم والوسائل، التي تكفل تطبيق الشريعة، ويراقب أداء الحكومة. [...]
[٣] - ومن وسائل قوامة الأمة على الحكام تحديد صلاحياتهم بكونها (تنفيذية).
[٤] - ومن وسائل قوامة الأمة على الحكام استقلال القضاء. [...]
[٥] - ومن وسائل قوامة الأمة على الحكام الفصل بين السلطات الثلاث.
[٦] - ومن وسائل قوامة الأمة على الحكام قيام أحزاب سياسية، وتداول السلطة، لأن ذلك ضمان تجنب الناس اللجوء إلى التغيير الدموي.
[٧] - ومن وسائل قوامة الأمة على الحكام حرية الرأي والتعبير والتجمع. [...]
[٨] - ومن وسائل قوامة الأمة على الحكام قيام جمعيات أهلية، دون وصاية الحكومة.
[٩] - ومن وسائل قوامة الأمة على الحكام اعتماد الانتخابات والاستفتاء.“

al-Ḥāmid, *al-Kalima aqwā min ar-raṣāṣa*, 59–60.

Similar, if not as comprehensive, lists of the content of an 'Islamic constitution' can be found in other books by members of the Islamic civil rights movement. See, e.g., al-Ḥāmid, *al-Burhān bi-qawāmat al-umma*, 9–10; and al-Fāliḥ, *al-Iṣlāḥ ad-dustūrī fī s-Su'ūdīya*, 6–9.

68

"(النظام الشوري) في كل أمة يجسد (عقيدتها) وقيمها، وأعرافها الدينية والاجتماعية الراسخة، فإن أنشأت دولة متقدمة غير مسلمة علمانية أو بوذية أو شيوعية دستورا، سمي دستورها علمانية أو بوذيا أو شيوعيا، وحققت العدل والشورى، وهما أساس الاستقرار والازدهار في الحياة الدنيا، سياسيا واجتماعيا واقتصاديا.
[...] وإن أنشأت (النظام الشوري) أمة مسلمة على الشريعة، جمعت فين خيري الدنيا والآخرة. [...]
وسمي دستورها (إسلاميا)."

al-Ḥāmid, *aṭ-Ṭarīq aṯ-ṯāliṯ*, 110.

69

"ولكي تتجلى صورة إسلامية الدستور، ننص على شرطين [...]:
الأول: ولا يكون الدستور إسلاميا، إذا لم تنضبط طاعة أولي الأمر بطاعة الله ورسوله. [...] وإذا ينبغي أن تكون سلطة الأمة مؤطرة بقطعيات الشريعة، ليكون الدستور تجسيدا لسلطة الأمة الملتزمة بالشريعة. [...]
كل قانون تصدره الدولة وهو غير شرعي، فهو غير دستوري. [...]
الشرط الثاني: الالتزام بقطعيات الشريعة الإسلامية في التربية والقضاء والشؤون الأسرية خاصة والشؤون الاجتماعية عامة."

al-Ḥāmid, *Ṯulāṯīyat al-muğtama' al-madanī*, 83–4.
See, also, al-Ḥāmid, *aṭ-Ṭarīq aṯ-ṯāliṯ*, 111.

70 For details about the term 'sharia caveat', see, e.g., Würth, *Dialog mit dem Islam als Konfliktprävention?*, 39.

71 "Ad-Dustūr al-islāmī, ad-dustūr al-munbaṯiq min ta'ālīm al-islām, lā nurīdu dasātīr waḍ'īya ġarbīya, lā, nurīdu dustūran yanbaṯiqu min ta'ālīm al-islām."
Acpra Tube, *Asbāb azamāt al-umma, wa-hal ad-du'āt waḥduhu kāfin li-taḥqīq an-naṣr?* (published on youtube.com, 7 June 2013, available online: https://www.youtube.com/watch?v=QRWq1s0c8dw, accessed 11 June 2020), 10:05–10:17.

72 For details concerning the lexical development of the term 'dustūr', see, e.g., Ed. Lewis, M. Khadduri, A. K. S. Lambton, J. A. M. Caldwell, A. Gledhill and Ch. Pellat, 'Dustūr', in *Encyclopaedia of Islam*, ed. P. Bearman et al., 2nd edn. (Available online: https://referenceworks.brillonline.com/entries/encyclopaedia-of-islam-2/dustur-COM_0199, accessed 11 June 2020); and Ami Ayalon, *Language and Change in the Arab Middle East: The Evolution of Modern Political Discourse* (New York: Oxford University Press, 1987), 94–6.

73 See, e.g., Lorenz Müller, *Islam und Menschenrechte: Sunnitische Muslime zwischen Islamismus, Säkularismus und Modernismus* (Hamburg: Deutsches Orient-Institut Hamburg, 1996), 193–210.

74 For details about the Charter of Medina, see, e.g., Carsten Jürgensen, *Demokratie und Menschenrechte in der arabischen Welt: Positionen arabischer Menschenrechtsaktivisten* (Hamburg: Deutsches Orient-Institut Hamburg, 1994), 63–5; and Müller, *Islam und Menschenrechte*, 203–5.

75 See, e.g., Naser Ghorbannia, 'The Influence of Religion on Law in the Iranian Legal System', in *Mixed Legal Systems, East and West*, ed. Vernon Palmer, Mohamed Mattar and Anna Koppel (London: Routledge, 2014), 209–12; and Saīd Amir Arjomand, 'Shari'a and Constitution in Iran: A Historical Perspective', in *Shari'a: Islamic Law in the Contemporary Context*, ed. Abbas Amanat and Frank Griffel (Stanford: Stanford University Press, 2009), 156–64.

76 See, e.g., Mara Revkin, 'Egypt's Constitution in Question', *Middle East Law and Governance* 5, no. 3 (2013): 331–43; Cornelius Hulsman (ed.), *The Egyptian*

Constitution: Perspectives from Egypt (Baden-Baden: Tectum Wissenschaftsverlag, 2017); and Francois Sureau, ‘Égypte: une constitution entre deux mondes’, *Pouvoirs: Revue francaise d’etudes constitutionelles et politiques* 149, no. 2 (February 2014): 151–67.

77

"تسعي الجمعية إلى ما يلي:
١ – تأصيل ثقافة حقوق الإنسان السياسية إسلاميا، باعتبار وسائل الحكم الشوري من أركان العقيدة السياسية الإسلامية، التي لا يجوز – شرعا – التنازل عنها، أو التفريط بها."

HASM, *Al-I'lān at-tàsīsī.*

78

"أي أن كل دولة لا تطبق الشورى النيابية، لا تعتبر إسلامية، وإن كان شعبها مسلما، أو أنها تحكم بغير ما أنزل الله."

al-Ḥāmid, *al-Burhān bi-qawāmat al-umma*, 24.

79 See, e.g., al-Ḥāmid, *Ṯulāṯīyat al-muǧtama' al-madanī*, 51.

80 See, e.g., al-Ḥāmid, *al-Burhān bi-qawāmat al-umma*, 23–4.

81

"لا يمكن ضمان شورى الأمة في دولة، إلا من خلال نقبائها وممثليها، وعرفائها المتبوعين فيها. إذن فإن إقامة مجلس لنواب الأمة داخل في الواجبات الكبرى في أي دولة إسلامية."

al-Ḥāmid, *al-Burhān bi-qawāmat al-umma*, 113.

82

"الديمقراطية مشهد من أنجح محاولات الإنسان لإدارة مجتمعه وترتيب علاقاته. [...] ومن حصاد هذا النص أن ما يسمى اليوم بالديمقراطية ليس اختراعا أثينيا ولا يونانيا، وإن كان لتوثيق تجربتهم. [...] هذه التجربة الديمقراطية سنة بشرية، جربها العالم في مناطق عديدة، منذ أقدم سجلات التصويت والانتخاب البشري في الأمم."

al-Aḥmarī, *ad-Dīmuqrāṭīya*, 11.

83

"الديموقراطية – إذا – هي ثمرة التجربة الإنسانية وهي صيغ متعددة. [...] ولا شك أن النظام الديموقراطي خير بمراحل من الأنظمة الاستبدادية، ومن أجمل ما فيه تحقيق قدر من العدالة والتراضي والتداول الطوعي للسلطة، كما هو مشهود في معظم بلاد العالم."

al-'Auda, *As'ilat aṯ-ṯaura*, 135–6.

84

"فإنه لا يمكن إنقاذ الجماهير من التخلف والركود إلا بتجديد الخطاب الديني، وكشف التحريف الذي نسج في المناخ الأموي والعباسي، الذي لوى أعناق [...] تطبيق الأمم المتحضرة، منذ العصور اليونانية والرومانية، لوسائل الحكم الشوري (الديمقراطية)."

al-Ḥāmid, *al-Kalima aqwā min ar-raṣāṣa*, 104.

85

"الدمقراطية الغربية مبدأ من مبادئ (العلمانية)، وهي فرع ل (أيديولوجية)، ولا يمكن فك ارتباط الغصن بشجرته. هذه الدمقراطية الغربية لا يمكن أن تقبلها إلا الأمم التي لا أصل لها، [...] لأنها تؤدي بطبيعتها فرع من العلمانية. أما الدمقراطية وسيلة إنسانية لتطبيق مبادئ الإدارة الاجتماعية والسياسية، فهي لا تعارض أي عقيدة شيوعية أو بوذية أو إسلامية، بل تنسجم معها، لأنها كالثوب للجسد، فهذه من ضمانات العدل وسيادة الأمة على حكامها، ومن مكارم الأخلاق السياسية. ولا بأس علينا من الاقتباس، إذا لزمنا الاحتراس وقيدناها بلفظ مانع فقلنا (الدمقراطية الإسلامية)."

al-Ḥāmid, *Likay lā yakūnu l-qur'ān ḥammāl auǧuh*, 146.

86 Quran 42:38 (translation Muhammad Asad).

87 For details concerning the meaning of the concept of consultation (*šūrā*) in ‘classical’ Islamic thought before the nineteenth century CE, see, e.g., C. E. Bosworth, Manuela Marín and Ami Ayalon, ‘Shūrā’, in *Encyclopaedia of Islam*, ed. P. Bearman et al., 2nd edn. (Available online: https://referenceworks.brillonline.com/entries/encyclopaedia-of-islam-2/shura-COM_1063, accessed 11 June 2020).

88 For details about Muhammad Abduh's and Muhammad Rashid Rida's ambiguous interpretation of consultation (šūrā), see, e.g., Ayalon, *Language and Change in the Arab Middle East*, 119–23.

89 For details about the concept of shura in twentieth-century Islamic thought, see, e.g., John L. Esposito and John O. Voll, *Islam and Democracy* (New York: Oxford University Press, 1996), 11–32; Ahmad S. Mousalli, 'Islamic Democracy and Pluralism', in *Progressive Muslims: On Justice, Gender, and Pluralism*, ed. Omid Safi (Oxford: Oneworld Publications, 2003), 286–305; Gudrun Krämer, *Gottes Staat als Republik: Reflexionen zeitgenössischer Muslime zu Islam, Menschenrechten und Demokratie* (Baden-Baden: Nomos Verlagsgesellschaft, 1999), 121–9; and Jürgensen, *Demokratie und Menschenrechte in der arabischen Welt*, 60–5.

90 See, e.g., Sayed Khatab, 'The Voice of Democratism in Sayyid Quṭb's Response to Violence and Terrorism', *Islam and Christian-Muslim Relations* 20, no. 3 (July 2009): 330. For a more general overview of Sayyid Qutb's political theory, see, e.g., Sayed Khatab, *The Power of Sovereignty: The Political and Ideological Philosophy of Sayyid Qutb* (New York: Routledge, 2006).

91 See, e.g., Yūsuf al-Qaraḍāwī, *ad-Dīn wa-s-siyāsa: Tàṣīl wa-radd šubuhāt* (Dūblin: al-Mağlis al-ūrubī li-l-iftā᾽ wa-l-buḥūṯ, 2007), 145.

92 See, e.g., Hasan Al-Turabi, 'The Islamic State', in *Voices of Resurgent Islam*, ed. John L. Esposito (New York: Oxford University Press, 1983), 247–51.

93 See, e.g., Rachid Ghannouchi, 'Participation in Non-Islamic Government', in *Liberal Islam: A Sourcebook*, ed. Charles Kurzman (New York: Oxford University Press, 1998), 91–5.

94 See, e.g., Muḥammad Ḫalaf Allāh, *al-Qur᾽ān wa-d-daula* (al-Qāhira: Maktabat al-Anğlū l-Maṣrīya, 1973).

95 See, e.g., S. M. Zafar, 'Accountability, Parliament, and Ijtihad', in *Liberal Islam*, ed. Kurzman, 67–72.

96 See, e.g., Sadek J. Sulaiman, 'Democracy and Shura', in *Liberal Islam*, ed. Kurzman, 96–8.

97 See, e.g., Vanessa Martin's excellent study on the thought of the Islamic Revolution in Iran: Martin, *Creating an Islamic State*, 75–99. A somewhat biased, but nevertheless very interesting, discussion of the relationship between democracy and Islam according to the state doctrine of the Islamic Republic of Iran can be found in, Hamid Reza Yousefi (ed.), *Demokratie im Islam: Analysen – Theorien – Perspektiven* (Münster: Waxmann, 2014).

98 See, e.g., Asef Bayat, *Making Islam Democratic: Social Movements and the Post-Islamist Turn* (Stanford: Stanford University Press, 2007); and Asef Bayat, 'The Making of Post-Islamist Iran', in *Post-Islamism. The Changing Faces of Political Islam*, ed. Asef Bayat (Oxford: Oxford University Press, 2013), 35–70.

99 See, e.g., Imad Mustafa, *Der Politische Islam: Zwischen Muslimbrüdern, Hamas und Hizbollah* (Wien: ProMedia, 2013), 133–55.

100

”يرى الحزب أن الشورى (الديمقراطية) مبدأ أساسي تقوم عليه الدولة بكل مؤسساتها فهي ليست مجرد مبدأ سياسي يحكم أشكال العلاقات السياسية فحسب.. بل هي نمط سلوك ومنهج عام لإدارة مختلف جوانب الحياة في الدولة. [...] والشورى التي نؤمن بها ونسعى إلى تحقيقها وتأسيس نظام الحكم عليها ليست قالبا حامدا ولكنها تعني إرساء مبدأ تداول السلطة وحق الشعب في تقرير شؤونه واختيار نوابه وحكامه ومراقبتهم ومحاسبتهم.“

Hizb al-ḥurrīya wa-l-ʿadāla, *Barnāmağ ḥizb al-ḥurrīya wa-l-ʿadāla* (published by the Freedom and Justice Party, 2011, available online: https://kurzman.unc.edu/files/2011/06/FJP_20111.pdf, accessed 11 June 2020), 14.

101 ''أن الأمة هي ولية أمرها، وأن لها السيادة والقوامة على الدولة عامة والحكومة خاصة، وأن الأمة هي الحافظة للشريعة لا الحكام. [...] أن الحاكم ليس مرجع فصل النزاع، وأن الأمة هي (مرجعية) الدولة.''
al-Ḥāmid, *al-Burhān bi-qawāmat al-umma*, 7.

102 See, e.g., al-Ḥāmid, *al-Burhān bi-qawāmat al-umma*, 15.

103 ''الحكم يقوم على (عقد اجتماعي)، على عقد بيعة الاختيار الشوري بين الأمة والحاكم، يقر به الحاكم بسلطة الأمة، وأنه وكيل عنها، ولا صحة ولا مشروعية لنظام الحكم الأحادي المطلق القائم على التغلب وبيعة الاضطرار الجبرية.''
al-Ḥāmid, *al-Kalima aqwā min ar-raṣāṣa*, 136.

104 ''عقد البيعة، كسائر العقود، وهو عن الفقهاء أشبه بعقد الوكالة أو الإجارة، حيث إن الأمة هي الأصل، ومن تختاره حاكما لها هو الوكيل عنها.''
al-Mālikī, *Siyādat al-umma qabla taṭbīq aš-šarīʿa*, 134.

105 ''فالعلاقة لين الأمة والإمام تقوم على أساس عقد بين طرفين، تكون الأمة فيه هي الأصيل، والإمام هو الوكيل عنها في إدارة شؤونها.''
Ḥākim al-Muṭairī, *al-Ḥurrīya aw aṭ-ṭawfān* (Bairūt: al-Muʾassasa l-ʿarabīya li-d-dirāsāt wa-n-našr, 2004), 21.

106 'Fī n-naẓar ilā hāḏā al-ittihām allaḏī wuǧǧiha ʿādatan ilā l-afrād, naǧidu huwa ittihām qāṣir fī aḥyān kaṯīra. Ḏālikā, annā hunāka ǧuzʾ āḫar li-hāḏā l-ittihām, wa-huwa ḫurūǧ al-ḥākim ʿalā l-umma. al-ʿAlāqa baina l-ḥākim wa-baina l-umma hiya ʿalāqa taʿāqudīya tusammā fī š-šārīʿa l-islāmīya bi-l-bayʿa š-šārʿīya. Wa-l-bayʿa š-šarʿīya man ḫalafa fīhā, siwā an ḫālafa al-ḥākim mā bāyaʿa ʿalaihi l-umma aw ḫālafat al-umma mā bāyaʿa ʿalaihā al-ḥākim, yakūnu man ḫālafa fīhā qad ḫaraǧa ʿalā l-āḫar.'
Acpra Tube, *Ḫurūǧ al-ḥākim ʿalā l-umma* (published on youtube.com, 30 October 2012, available online: https://www.youtube.com/watch?v=EVZW_GyOGbA, accessed 11 June 2020), 1:10–2:00.

107 For details about Abdallah al-Hamid's refutation of the opinion that 'those who have been entrusted with authority' (ūlī al-amr) are the despotic rulers, see, e.g., al-Ḥāmid, *al-Burhān bi-qawāmat al-umma*, 37–44 and 62–4; and al-Ḥāmid, *al-Kalima aqwā min ar-raṣāṣa*, 90–1.

108 See, e.g., al-Ḥāmid, *al-Burhān bi-qawāmat al-umma*, 99–100.

109 ''سمات أولي الأمر الخمسة:
[. . .]
١. أصحاب رأي وحنكة وبصيرة، وعلم وحسن التدبير، وهذا هو المعنى الأصلي.
٢. أصحاب إيثار ونصح وإخلاص للأمة، وهو معنى تابع.
٣. أصحاب شجاعة متميزة، وهذا معنى تابع.
٤. أصحاب نزاهة واستقامة في السلوك، وهذا معنى تابع.''
al-Ḥāmid, *al-Burhān bi-qawāmat al-umma*, 46.

110 This argument is also mentioned in texts by other members of the Islamic civil rights movement, like Abd al-Karim al-Khadr, and in texts by members of the broader Islamo-reformist current, like Hakim al-Mutayri. See, e.g., Acpra Tube, *Ūlī l-amr lā walī al-amr / D. ʿAbd al-Karīm al-Ḫaḍr* (published on youtube.com, 25 December 2012, available online: https://www.youtube.com/watch?v=qRcIY_w6e6A, accessed 11 June 2020); and al-Muṭairī, *al-Ḥurrīya aw aṭ-ṭawfān*, 63–4.

111

"فأهل الحل والعقد هم حسب العقدة التي تحتاج إلى حل. [...] فإن كانت في أمر منصوص عليه في الشريعة، فلا إشكال في أنهم الفقهاء، وإن كانت في اجتهاد لا يدركه إلا الفقهاء، فهم – أيضا – أهل حله وعقده. وإن كانت في اجتهاد لا يدركه إلا الاقتصاديون، فأهل الحل والعقد إنما هم أهل الاقتصاد. وإن كانت في مشكل تربوي، فإنما هم أهل التربية. وهم أيضا المهندسين المعماريون في تخصصهم، والتقنيون في التقانة أو الأطباء في الطب والغذاء، أو أهل السياسة والإدارة والاجتماع في شؤون السياسة والإدارة والاجتماع، فكل أهل اختصاص بفرع من فروع المعرفة، هم أهل الحل والعقد في هذا التخصص."

al-Ḥāmid, *al-Burhān bi-qawāmat al-umma*, 109.

112

"إن أقرب إلى تطبيق مفهوم (أولي الأمر) في الدولة الإسلامية الحديثة، قالبان أساسيان:
القالب الأول: مجلس النواب، وهو أهمها وأولها بالمفهوم، فهو الجهاز الذي يقوم بوضع الخطط العريضة لسياسة الدولة الداخلية والخارجية. [...] ويتضمن إصدار القوانين السارية في الدولة، ويجسد بذلك كبراء القوم في المجتمع المدني الأهلي، من المتبوعين من الذين يتسمون وأصحاب العلم والحنكة والإيثار والنصح للأمة، والشجاعة، والنزاهة. [...]
القالب الثاني: التجمعات المدنية الأهلية، وهي جماع رأي الأمة وخلاصة تفكيرها في أمر من الأمور، وأولو الأمر في هذه الحالة هم التجمعات والجماعات والروابط والمنتديات، وسائر التجمعات."

al-Ḥāmid, *al-Burhān bi-qawāmat al-umma*, 120–1.

113 Muhammad ʿAbid Al-Jabiri, 'The Concepts of Rights and Justice in Arab-Islamic Texts', in *Human Rights in Arab Thought: A Reader*, ed. Salma K. Jayyusi (London: I.B. Tauris 2009), 31.

114 See, e.g., Madawi al-Rasheed, *Contesting the Saudi State: Islamic Voices from a New Generation* (New York: Cambridge University Press, 2007), 45–54.

115 See, e.g., Esposito and Voll, *Islam and Democracy*, 48.

116 See, e.g., Krämer, *Gottes Staat als Republik*, 104–17 and 182–92.

117 See, e.g., al-Rasheed, *Contesting the Saudi State*, 45–54.

118 See, e.g., Ayalon, *Language and Change in the Arab Middle East*, 57–8.

119 See, e.g., Fauzī Ḫalīl, *Daur ahl al-ḥall wa-l-ʿaqd fī n-namūḏaǧ al-islāmī li-niẓām al-ḥukm* (al-Qāhira: al-Maʿhad al-ʿālamī li-l-fikr al-islāmī, 1981); and Jürgensen, *Demokratie und Menschenrechte in der arabischen Welt*, 60–5.

120 This thought can be found in several texts by the members of the Islamic civil rights movement and the broader Islamo-reformist current. See, e.g., al-Ḥāmid, *al-Kalima aqwā min ar-raṣāṣa*, 97; al-Aḥmarī, *ad-Dīmuqrāṭīya*, 188; and Salmān al-ʿAuda, *Asʾilat aṯ-ṯawra* (Bairūt: Markaz namāʾ li-l-buḥūṯ wa-d-dirāsāt, 2012), 118–19.

121

"حكى الأصوليون في حجية الإجماع مسألتين: الإجماع العام والإجماع الخاص، فالإجماع العام، الذي هو إجماع الأمة في الأمور العامة، سياسية واقتصادية، وإدارية، تجارية. [...] وفي العادة يكون هذا الإجماع عن طريق (العرفاء)، وهو الذين تثق بهم جماعات الشعب، وتصدرهم ليمثلوها. [...] وهم الذين يجسدون مفهوم أهل الحل والعقد، كما ذهب إلى ذلك محمد عبده ومحمد رشيد رضا وحسن البنا ومحمد ضياء الريس. أما الإجماع الخاص، فهو إجماع المجتهدين في علم من العلوم، أو تخصص من التخصصات، كإجماع الفقهاء وإجماع المحدثين وإجماع الأصوليين، وإجماع النحاة وإجماع علماء السياسة، وإجماع الأطباء، وإجماع الاقتصاديين. [...] وأما إجماع الأمة فهو بيت القصيد، فهو من مبادئ السياسة الشرعية، فقد صرح الحديث الشريف بمرجعية أغلبية الأمة في قوله صلى الله عليه وسلم: 'اتبعوا السواد الأعظم.'"

al-Ḥāmid, *al-Burhān bi-qawāmat al-umma*, 29.

122

"الإسلام حدد طاعة الحاكم لأنها في إطار طاعة الأمة، لأن الأمة هي المخولة بحفظ الشريعة، فالإسلام يجعل طاعة الأمة من طاعة الله، لأن الأمة هي التي تجسد الإجماع السياسي، وهي التي خولها الله حفظ الملة والدولة، وهي بذلك أمة مرحومة، وهي بإجماعها معصومة، لأنها كما جاء في الحديث الصحيح 'لا تجتمع على ضلالة'."

al-Ḥāmid, *Ḥuqūq al-insān baina nūr al-islām wa-ġabaš al-mulk al-ʿaḍūḍ*, 145.

123 ".أن الأمة مهدية، فلو ضل بعضها، لما ضل أكثرها"
al-Ḥāmid, *al-Burhān bi-qawāmat al-umma*, 30.
A similar, if not as enthusiastic, endorsement of the rightly guiding power of the consensus of the people can be found in other texts of members of the broader Islamo-reformist current. See, e.g., al-Mālikī, *Siyādat al-umma qabla taṭbīq aš-šarīʿa*, 126–7; al-Aḥmarī, *ad-Dīmuqrāṭīya*, 201 and 268; and al-ʿAuda, *Asʾilat aṯ-ṯawra*, 134.

124 See, e.g., Muhammad Iqbal, *The Reconstruction of Religious Thought in Islam* (Stanford: Stanford University Press, 2013); Esposito and Voll, *Islam and Democracy*, 29–30; and Mairaj U. Syed, 'Ijmaʿ', in *The Oxford Handbook of Islamic Law*, ed. Anver E. Emon and Rumee Ahmed (Oxford: Oxford University Press, 2018), 278–98.

125 See, e.g., al-Qaraḍāwī, *ad-Dīn wa-s-siyāsa*; and David H. Warren and Christine Gilmore, 'Citizenship and Compatriotism in the Islamic Civil State: The Emerging Discourse of Yusuf al-Qaradawi and the "School of the Middle Way"', in *Islam and Democracy: Perspectives on the Arab Spring*, ed. Aylin Unver Noi (Newcastle upon Tyne: Cambridge Scholars Publishing, 2013).

126 See, e.g., at-Turābī, *The Islamic State*, in Calvert, *Islamism*, 51–5.

127 See, e.g., Rāšid al-Ġannūšī, *Al-Ḥurrīyāt al-ʿāmma fī d-daula l-islāmīya* (Bairūt: Markaz dirāsāt al-waḥda l-ʿarabīya, 1993).

128 See, e.g., Abū l-Aʿlā Māḍī, *Ruʾyat "Al-Wasaṭ" fī s-siyāsa wa-l-muǧtamaʿ* (al-Qāhira: Maktaba š-šurūq ad-duwalīya, 2005).

129 See, e.g., Sami Zemni, 'Moroccan Post-Islamism: Emerging Trend of Chimera?', in *Post-Islamism: The Changing Faces of Political Islam*, ed. Asef Bayat (Oxford: Oxford University Press, 2013), 134–56.

130
"النضال في سبيل الدفاع عن حرية الاجتهاد في الرأي والتعبير جزء من العقيدة."
al-Ḥāmid, *as-Salafīya l-wusṭā*, 42.

131
"أن مبدأ الحرية والتعددية والتسامح من أركان العقيدة الإسلامية."
al-Ḥāmid, *as-Salafīya l-wusṭā*, 186.

132
"فمن حق أي فرد أو مجموعة أن تفهم التنزيل بقدر ما تستطيع، ومن حقها أن تضلل وتبدع، من دون غلو ولا تطرف، ولا تكفير."
al-Ḥāmid, *as-Salafīya l-wusṭā*, 198.

133
"الحق يعرف بالدليل والبرهان، لا بقول فلان ولا علان. [...] ولذلك أوجب الفقهاء الوعاة على كل مسلم قادر أن يجتهد في أمور دينه، ولا سيما الأمور الأساسية، فلا يجوز له أن يقلد."
al-Ḥāmid, *Ḥuqūq al-insān baina nūr al-islām wa-ġabaš al-mulk al-ʿaḍūḍ*, 78.

134 See, e.g., al-Ḥāmid, *as-Salafīya l-wusṭā*, 169; and al-Aḥmarī, *ad-Dīmuqrāṭīya*, 276.

135 ".وما دام الإسلام قد أباح الاجتهاد فقد أباح الاختلاف"
al-Ḥāmid, *Ḥuqūq al-insān baina nūr al-islām wa-ġabaš al-mulk al-ʿaḍūḍ*, 88.

136 'Min maẓāhir ġulūwihim annahum yaʿtabirūna man ḫalafa l-qurʾān bi-ʿamal aw rầy fa-aḫṭảa innamā huwa murtakib kabīra. Wa-man irtakaba kabīra ʿindahum fa-huwa kāfir, kamā ḏakara Ibn Taymīya fī fatāwāhi. Bināʾan ʿalā haḏihi l-muqaddima kaffarū ʿUṯmān wa-ʿAlī wa-aṣḥāb al-ǧamal wa-l-ḥakamayn wa-kull man raḍiya bi-t-taḥkīm. [. . .] Kaifa taʿāmala ʿAlī maʿahum? Qāla lahum: 'Innā lakum ʿindanā ṯalāṯan mā ṣaḥabtumūnā. Lā namnaʿukum masāǧid allāh an taḏkurū fīhā ismuhu, wa-lā l-fayʾ mā damat aidīkum maʿā aidīnā, wa-la nuqātilukum ḥattā tabdảunā', kamā ḏakara

ḏalika ṭ-Ṭabarī fī tàrīḫihi. [. . .] Wa-kull man awwala lam yaḫruğu min al-islām wa lā yaqmaʿūhum wa lam yamnaʿūhum ḥuqūqahum al-madanīya.'
Acpra Tube, *al-Taʿaddudīya baina hady ar-rāšidīn wa-hawā l-mustabiddīn* (published on youtube.com, 21 February 2013, available online: https://www.youtube.com/watch?v=06ic4IBNeb4, accessed 11 June 2020), 6:37–8:56.
A similar interpretation of Ali's treatment of the Kharijites can be found in other writings of Islamo-reformist authors. See, e.g., al-Muṭairī, *al-Ḥurrīya aw aṭ-ṭawfān*, 58–61.

137 See, e.g., al-Ġannūšī, *al-Ḥurrīyāt al-ʿāmma fī d-daula al-islāmīya*; Mousalli, 'Islamic Democracy and Pluralism', 286–305; and Krämer, *Gottes Staat als Republik*, 138–9.

138 See, e.g., Krämer's study on the subject in Krämer, *Gottes Staat als Republik*, 98–9.

139 See, e.g., Müller's thorough study on human rights in Islam in Müller, *Islam und Menschenrechte*, 199–203.

140 See, e.g., Krämer, *Gottes Staat als Republik*, 137–8.

141 See, again, Krämer's study in Krämer, *Gottes Staat als Republik*, 151–7.

142

"المواطنة هي أساس الحقوق، وفي إطارها تنشأ قيم التعددية والحوارية والتسامح والأغلبية والشورى والتعايش."

al-Ḥāmid, *al-Kalima aqwā min ar-raṣāṣa*, 135.

143

"في البداية ينبغي التنبيه إلى أن الإسلام يركز (الإنسانية) مصدرا للحقوق والواجبات، وعلى مفهوم الكرامة الإنسانية، وجعل ذلك جوهر المواطنة. [...] جعل في العهد النبوي اليهود والنصارى داخلين في مفهوم الأمة. [...] فأساس استحقاق الحقوق في الإسلام إنسانية لكل من يقيم في الوطن، وغير المسلمين يستحقون نفس الحقوق، ما داموا غير محاربين."

al-Ḥāmid, *Ḥuqūq al-insān baina nūr al-islām wa-ġabaš al-mulk al-ʿaḍūḍ*, 66–7.

144

"أعطى اليهود الحق في اتباع أحكام دينهم، فهم أمة دينية لها خصوصيتها العقدية والثقافية، متميزة عن أمة المسلمين، ولكنها في الوقت نفسه، أمة من ضمن الأمة السياسية ذات الدائرة الواسعة: (أمة الدولة)، بمعنى أنه كان هناك تمايز في الأمة الدينية، وتمازج وتعاون في الأمة السياسية."

al-Mālikī, *Siyādat al-umma qabla taṭbīq aš-šarīʿa*, 25.

145 See, e.g., Ayalon, *Language and Change in the Arab Middle East*, 51–3.

146 See, e.g., Ayalon, *Language and Change in the Arab Middle East*, 27–8.

147 See, e.g., Krämer, *Gottes Staat als Republik*, 167–8.

148 See, e.g., Krämer, *Gottes Staat als Republik*, 172–3.

149 See, Yūsuf al-Qaraḍāwī, *Ġayr al-muslimīn fī l-muğtamaʿ al-islāmī*, at-tabʿa ṯ-ṯāliṯa (al-Qāhira: Maktabat wahba, 1992); and Krämer, *Gottes Staat als Republik*, 168–70.

150 See, Yūsuf al-Qaraḍāwī, *al-Waṭan wa-l-muwāṭana fī ḍaw' al-uṣūl al-ʿaqadīya wa-l-maqāṣid aš-šārīʿīya* (al-Qāhira: Dār aš-šurūq, 2010).

151 See Muḥammad Salīm al-ʿAwwā, *Fī n-niẓām as-siyāsī li-d-daula l-islāmīya* (al-Qāhira: Dār aš-šurūq, 2007); Ṭāriq al-Bišrī, *Baina l-ğāmiʿa ad-dīnīya wa-l-ğāmiʿa l-waṭanīya fī l-fikr as-siyāsī* (al-Qāhira: Dār aš-šurūq, 1998); and Fahmī Huwaydi, *Muwāṭinūn lā ḏimmīyūn* (al-Qāhira: Dār aš-šurūq, 2004).

152 See, Rāšid al-Ġannūšī, *ad-Dīmuqrāṭīya wa-ḥuqūq al-insān fī l-islām* (Bairūt: ad-Dār al-ʿarabīya li-l-ʿulūm nāširūn, 2012).

153 See, e.g., Warren and Gilmore, 'Citizenship and Compatriotism in the Islamic Civil State'; and Müller, *Islam und Menschenrechte*, 203–5.

154

”وقاعدة نصرة المظلوم قاعدة لها تطبيقات وآليات كثيرة غابت عن أكثر البلدان العربية، على أن الشريعة الإسلامية قد قررت قاعدة التعاون على البر والتقوى عامة، وقاعدة الحسبة خاصة.“

al-Ḥāmid, *Inšā᾿ ǧam῾īyat ḥasm amr mašrū῾ bal farīḍa šar῾īya* (self-published, 2012, at the time of writing not accessible via the internet anymore, a copy is in my possession), 2.

155

”وكلمة الحق والعدل والخير في هذه الحالة، إنما هي أمر بالمعروف ونهي عن المنكر، فلا معروف أعلى من العدل، ولا منكر أشفع من الظلم.“

al-Ḥāmid, *al-Kalima aqwā min ar-raṣāṣa*, 16.

156

”أن الاحتساب على السلطة من باب الأمر بالمعروف والنهي عن المنكر، ويركز على الأمر بالمعروف السياسي والنهي عن المنكر السياسي، وأهم أمر بالمعروف السياسي، هو إقامة العدل والأمر به، والدعوة إليه كتابة وخطابة أو تقديم رؤى.“

al-Fāliḥ, *al-Iṣlāḥ ad-dustūrī fī s-Su῾ūdīya*, 28.

157

”إن الاحتساب على السلطة في المجال السياسي لا يحتاج إلى إذن وموافقة منها، كما قال في ذلك عديد من الفقهاء كابن تيمية وأبو حامد الغزالي وغيرهم، لأن القيام بالاحتساب حق للفرد والجماعة، بل إنه يتجاوز الحق إلى كونه واجبا لمن لديه قدرة.“

al-Fāliḥ, *al-Iṣlāḥ ad-dustūrī fī s-Su῾ūdīya*, 29.
See, also, al-Ḥāmid, *Ṯulāṯīyat al-muǧtama῾ al-madanī*, 142.

158

”مساعدة المظلوم، في ظل المجتمعات المدنية المتكاثرة السكان، لا تتاح للأفراد المشغولين في خضم الحياة بأمورهم، لأن الأفراد مهما كان حولها، لا يستطيعون القيام بالشفاعة والنصرة، لأن جهودهم محدودة.
ولذلك صار تعاون الأفراد في ما بينهم أمرا ضروريا مشروعا، [...] كما قال الله تعالى: (ولتكن منكم أمة يدعون إلى الخير ويأمرون بالمعروف وينهون عن المنكر وأولئك هم المفلحون) فجعل الآمرين بالمعروف الناهين عن المنكر جماعة، لأنه لا يتم مثل ذلك الواجب ألا بالجماعة، وما لا يتم الواجب إلا به فهو واجب.“

HASM, *Al-I῾lān at-tȧsīsī.*
Similar arguments can be found in the books by Abdallah al-Hamid. See, e.g., al-Ḥāmid, *Ḥuqūq al-insān baina nūr al-islām wa-ġabaš al-mulk al-῾aḍūḍ*, 155–6.

159 See, e.g., al-Ḥāmid, *al-Kalima aqwā min ar-raṣāṣa*, 189 and al-῾Abd al-Karīm, *al-Iḥtisāb al-madanī*, 35–7.

160

”ومفهوم المجتمع المدني الذي نهض به الغرب، هو طريق التقدم في كل زمان ومكان، ومصطلح (المجتمع المدني) مصطلح غربي، [...] أما المفهوم فهو مفهوم حضاري عالمي إنساني، عرفه الناس قبل الإسلام، وأقره الإسلام.“

al-Ḥāmid, *Ṯulāṯīyat al-muǧtama῾ al-madanī*, 4.

161 See, e.g., Krämer, *Gottes Staat als Republik*, 97–8.

162 See, e.g., Mousalli, 'Islamic Democracy and Pluralism', 286–305.

163 See, e.g., Martin, *Creating an Islamic State*, 88.

164 See, e.g., Yūsuf al-Qaraḍāwī, *Šar῾īyat al-muẓāharāt as-silmīya* (published on al -qaradawi.net, 24 April 2016, available online: https://al-qaradawi.net/node/3885, accessed 11 June 2020).

165

”أن حقوق الأنسان والحريات الأساسية [...] – في المملكة العربية السعودية – تتعرض لانتهاكات خطيرة“

HASM, *Al-I῾lān at-tȧsīsī.*

166 ”تأصيل ثقافة حقوق الإنسان السياسية إسلاميا“
HASM, *Al-I῾lān at-tȧsīsī.*

"يمكن تحديد الحقوق الأساسية للمواطنين بأنها بضع عشرة: العدالة والمساواة والشورى (المشاركة
الشعبية في القرار السياسي) والحرية والتعددية والكرامة والالتزام بالروح السلمية وحل الخلافات بالحوار،
والتعلم، والأمن، وقيام الحكم على رأي الأكثرية، مع ضمان حقوق الأقلية، والأمر بالمعروف والنهي عن
المنكر، والتعاون على البر والتقوى، والتراحم، وسائر حقوق الأنسان التي عرفها البشر بالطبيعة، وأقرتها
الشريعة، قبل تنادي الأمم الحديثة إليها."

al-Ḥāmid, *Ṯulāṯīyat al-muğtamaʿ al-madanī*, 28.

168

"وكل ما هو فطري في الجبلة إنما هو حق مقدس من حقوق الناس، لأن الإسلام – كأي دين سماوي – هو
دين الفطرة."

al-Ḥāmid, *Ḥuqūq al-insān baina nūr al-islām wa-ġabaš al-mulk al-ʿaḍūḍ*, 142.
Similar arguments can be found in other texts by Abdallah al-Hamid or authors
of the Islamo-reformist current. See, e.g., al-Ḥāmid, *aṭ-Ṭarīq aṯ-ṯāliṯ*, 60;
al-ʿAbd al-Karīm, *al-Iḥtisāb al-madanī*, 80; and al-Muṭairī, *al-Ḥurrīya aw
aṭ-ṭawfān*, 87–8.

169

"عندما ترد كلمة (حقوق الإنسان)، يظن عدد غير قليل من الناس، أنها مفهوم دخيل على الإسلام، وأنها
مرتبطة فالعلمانية. [...] والحق أن حقوق الأنسان ليست مفهوما علمانيا، بل إن الأديان السماوية ولا سيما
الإسلام قررتها وأكدتها وفرضتها."

al-Ḥāmid, *Ḥuqūq al-insān baina nūr al-islām wa-ġabaš al-mulk al-ʿaḍūḍ*, 13.

170

"ومن دواعي إنشاء الجمعية، أن العديد من المنظمات الدولية متأثرة بالنظرة الغربية لحقوق الإنسان، ولم
تبرز بشكل فعال النظرية الإسلامية لحقوق الإنسان."

HASM, *Al-Iʿlān at-tāsīsī*.

171

"كما أن مفهوم الإسلام لحقوق الإنسان يختلف عن مفهومه العلماني، فالفرنجة يحل لهم برلمانهم أهواءهم،
وما تراه عقولهم حلالا، فقد يحل لهم الزنا واللواط وشرب الخمور والربا، فتعتبر هذه الأمور داخلة في
مفهوم الحرية، [...] لأن الحقيقة في العقيدة العلمانية نسبية، فما يراه قوم سيئا، قد يراه آخرون حسنا، أما
الحقيقة في الإسلام فهي مطلقة، فكل ما استقبحته الفطرة قبيح حرام، وكل ما استحسنته الفطرة فهو حسن
مباح."

al-Ḥāmid, *Ḥuqūq al-insān baina nūr al-islām wa-ġabaš al-mulk al-ʿaḍūḍ*, 115.
Similar arguments can be found in other writings by members of the Islamic civil
rights movement in particular and of the broader Islamo-reformist current in general.
See, e.g., al-Ḥāmid, *Ṯulāṯīyat al-muğtamaʿ al-madanī*, 130–1; al-Ḥāmid, *aṭ-Ṭarīq
aṯ-ṯāliṯ*, 133; al-Ḥāmid, *Likay lā yakūnu l-qurʾān ḥammāl auğuh*, 327–8; and
al-Muṭairī, *al-Ḥurrīya aw aṭ-ṭawfān*, 292–3.

172

"أن يكون صاحب الرأي [...] متسقا في رأيه مع الضوابط الشرعية، وهذا معنى تقديم طاعة الله وطاعة
الرسول، فلا عبرة برأي يقول مثلا إن الاختلاط (المشبوه) بين الرجال والنساء ليس له مضار في هذا
العصر، أو إن المرأة ينبغي أن تتحرر من الحجاب، أو أنه يجوز لها أن تسافر من دون محرم، أو لا باس
لو وجدت في خلوة مع رجل أجنبي عنها."

al-Ḥāmid, *al-Burhān bi-qawāmat al-umma*, 115.

173

"والمساواة في الأصل بين البشر لا تلغي أيضا التمايز بين الرجال والنساء نتيجة الاختلاف في تكوينهم
الفسيولوجي والنفسي ولذلك ترتب عليه اختلاف في بعض الحقوق والواجبات، كما أشار إلى ذلك القرآن
في قضايا الإرث والشهادة والطلاق."

al-Fāliḥ, *al-Iṣlāḥ ad-dustūrī fī s-Suʿūdīya*, 19.

174 For more details on the phases of the human rights debate in the Islamic world,
see, e.g., Sami A. Aldeeb Abu-Salieh, *Les Musulmans face aux droits de l'homme:
Religion & Droit & Politique* (Bochum: Verlag Dr. Dieter Winkler, 1994), 15–17.

175 See, e.g., Jürgensen, *Demokratie und Menschenrechte in der arabischen Welt*, 23–5.

176 For details about the global human rights debate, see, e.g., Jack Donnelly, 'Cultural Relativism and Universal Human Rights', *Human Rights Quarterly* 6, no. 4 (November 1984): 400–19.

177 For examples, see, e.g., Abdullahi An-Naʿim, *Toward an Islamic Reformation: Civil Liberties, Human Rights, and International Law* (Syracuse: Syracuse University Press, 1990), 34–44; Bassam Tibi, *Im Schatten Allahs: Der Islam und die Menschenrechte* (München: Piper, 1994), 41–5; Burhan Ghalyoun, 'Human Rights in Contemporary Arabic Thought', in *Human Rights in Arab Thought: A Reader*, ed. Salma K. Jayyusi (London: I.B. Tauris, 2009), 360–8; and Heiner Bielefeldt, 'Islam und Menschenrechte: Eine Problemskizze', in *Menschenrechte und Entwicklung: Globale Politik zwischen universalen Normen und kultureller Identität*, ed. Heiner Bielefeldt et al. (Bonn: Stiftung Entwicklung und Frieden Werkstattpapier, 1992), 33–6.

178 For details, see Bassiouni, *Menschenrechte zwischen Universalität und islamischer Legitimität*, 78–9.

179

"أن الجهاد السياسي جهاد سلمي، أداته القلم واللسان، والتكتل الاجتماعي عبر المظاهرات والإضراب والاعتصام، لا ينفجر فيه مسدس ولا رشاش، ولا يرفع أصحابه سوطا ولا عصا. [...] أنه في الغالب جهاد داخلي. [...] فالجهاد الداخلي يهدف إلى مقاومة انهيار الأمة الداخلي وانحرافها، لأن غيبة روح الشورى تؤدي إلى الاستبداد، والاستبداد يؤدي إلى الاستعباد والاضطهاد."

al-Ḥāmid, *al-Kalima aqwā min ar-raṣāṣa*, 7–8.

180

"ومن أهداف الجمعية نشر ثقافة الجهاد المدني السلمي، باعتبارها ثقافة إسلامية أصيلة، ولأنها الأسلوب المضمون، مهما طال الطريق، وتكاثفت رمال الصحراء، وتعرجت وديانها، للوصول إلى دولة العدل والشورى وحقوق الإنسان."

HASM, *Al-Iʿlān at-tàsīsī.*

181

"كلمة الخير والحق والعدل وسائر الوسائل السلمية، لها حالتان:
الحالة الدنيا، درجة الاحتساب: [...] وكلمة الحق والعدل والخير في هذه الحالة، إنما هي أمر بالمعروف ونهي عن المنكر، فلا معروف أعلى من العدل، وال منكر أشفع من الظلم، كما قال الشيخ محمد عبده.
ولكنها ليست جهادا، لأن عنصر المشقة والمخاطرة والمغامرة مفقود، وإنما هي في المرتبة الثانية.
الحالة العليا، درجة الجهاد: [...] والكلمة – في هذه الصورة – مغامرة ومخاطرة [...] وفي هذه الحالة تصبح الكلمة وسائر الوسائل السلمية جهادا، أي في المرتبة العليا."

al-Ḥāmid, *al-Kalima aqwā min ar-raṣāṣa*, 16.

182

"أما نحن العرب والمسلمين، فلا بد لنا لكي ننهض من تجديد مفهوم الجهاد، لا بد من خطاب يؤكد أن الجهاد صنوان: عسكري حربي يصد الغزاة ومدني سلمي يصد الطغاة."

al-Ḥāmid, *al-Ǧihād ṣinwān*, 61.

183 This argument can be found in several of Abdallah al-Hamid's texts. See, e.g., al-Ḥāmid, *al-Kalima aqwā min ar-raṣāṣa*, 7–9; al-Ḥāmid, *al-Ǧihād ṣinwān*, 16–17 and 24; and Acpra Tube, *Halummū ilā l-ǧihād as-silmī badalan min al-ʿaskarī / ʿAbdallāh al-Ḥāmid* (published on youtube.com, 31 December 2012, available online: https://www.youtube.com/watch?v=hF4uX9O89Pw, accessed 11 June 2020).

184 See, e.g., al-Ḥāmid, *al-Kalima aqwā min ar-raṣāṣa*, 61.

185 See, e.g., al-Ḥāmid, *al-Kalima aqwā min ar-raṣāṣa*, 62–3.

186 See, e.g., al-Ḥāmid, *al-Kalima aqwā min ar-raṣāṣa*, 63.

187 See, e.g., al-Ḥāmid, *al-Kalima aqwā min ar-raṣāṣa*, 65.

188 See, e.g., al-Ḥāmid, *al-Ğihād ṣinwān*, 70.

189

"الجهاد العسكري فرض كفاية، إذا قام به من يكفي سقط الاثم عن الباقين، أما الجهاد السلمي، فهو فرض عين، لأن استمرار المواطنين في تقليم أظافر الطغيان كلما طالت، هو صمام الأمان، فاشتراك الناس في المظاهرات والاعتصامات والبينات وفي التصويت والترشح والتوشيح في الانتخابات، هو ضمان حقوقهم."

al-Ḥāmid, *al-Kalima aqwā min ar-raṣāṣa*, 8.

190

"الجهاد المدني ولا سيما السياسي للمطالبة ب(الحكم الشوري) جهاد مفتوح لكل قادر عليه، فلم يرد في الشريعة الإلهية (فضلا عن الطبيعة البشرية) ما يقصر الأمر بالخير والنهي عن الشر على فريق دون فريق."

al-Ḥāmid, *al-Kalima aqwā min ar-raṣāṣa*, 201–2.

191

"فالمجاهد السلمي إذن يأمر الحاكم وينهاه دون تذلل وخضوع، لأن الله خوله مباشرة، بأن يأمر بالمعروف وينهى عن المنكر، وهو قوي بهذا التخويل الرباني. وذلك أمر من ما أوحت به الفطرة السوية، والطبيعة المستقيمة."

al-Ḥāmid, *al-Kalima aqwā min ar-raṣāṣa*, 119.

192

"لماذا نصف الجهاد السياسي بأنه الجهاد المدني الأكبر؟
أولا: لأن الإسلام وضع لذلك مبدأ عظيما، مبدأ يقرر أن الكلمة أقوى من الرصاصة، فجاء في الحديث الصحيح: 'سيد الشهداء حمزة بن عبد المطلب، ورجل قام إلى إمام جائر، فأمره ونهاه فقتله الإمام الجائر.' فهذا الحديث الذي يضع قائل كلمة عديلا لحمزة، إنما يدل دلالة ظاهرة على أن قائل كلمة في مجلس عندما يقتل، في مرتبة سيد الشهداء، لا في مرتبة شهيد عادي. [...]
الثاني: وفي الأدلة النصية، جاء أيضا 'خير الجهاد كلمة عدل أمام سلطان جائر.' وهذا النص ظاهر الدلالة على أن الجهاد السياسي أفضل أنواع الجهاد."

al-Ḥāmid, *al-Kalima aqwā min ar-raṣāṣa*, 57–8.

193 For a summary and analysis of Abdallah al-Hamid's concept of jihad, see also, Peter Enz-Harlass, '"Peaceful Civil Jihad" – Saudi Arabia's Islamic Civil Rights Movement and Its Concept of Jihad', *Middle Eastern Studies* (DOI: 10.1080/00263206.2021.1926995, published online on 3 June 2021, available online: https://www.tandfonline.com/doi/full/10.1080/00263206.2021.1926995, accessed 3 June 2021).

194 See, e.g., Gavin Picken, 'The "Greater" Jihad in Classical Islam', in *Twenty-First Century Jihad: Law, Society and Military Action*, ed. Elisabetz Kendall and Ewan Stein (London: I.B. Tauris 2015), 126–40.

195 For details about the concept of jihad in 'classical' Islamic thought until the nineteenth century CE, see, e.g., E. Tyan, 'D̲jihād', in *Encyclopaedia of Islam*, ed. P. Bearman et al., 2nd edn. (Available online: https://referenceworks.brillonline.com/entries/encyclopaedia-of-islam-2/djihad-COM_0189, accessed 11 June 2020); and Rudolf Peters, 'Jihād', in *The Oxford Encyclopedia of the Islamic World*, ed. John L. Esposito (Oxford: Oxford University Press, also available online: http://oxfordislamicstudies.com/article/opr/t236/e0418, accessed 11 June 2020).

196 See, e.g., Sayyid Quṭb, *as-Salām al-ʿālamī wa-l-islām* (al-Qāhira: Dār aš-šurūq, 1974), 174; Yvonne Haddad, 'Sayyid Qutb. Ideologue of Islamic Revival', in *Voices of Resurgent Islam*, ed. John L. Esposito (New York: Oxford University Press, 1983), 67–98; Gilles Kepel, *Jihad: Expansion et déclin de l'islamisme* (Paris: Gallimard, 2000), 69; and Krämer, *Gottes Staat als Republik*, 217.

197 See, e.g., Hossam Tammam, 'The Muslim Brotherhood and Jihad', in *Twenty-First Century Jihad*, ed. Kendall and Stein, 164–75; and Ewan Stein, 'Jihad Discourse in

Egypt under Muhammad Mursi', in *Twenty-First Century Jihad*, ed. Kendall and Stein, 176–200.

198 For details about Abdallah Azzam's theory of Jihadism, see, e.g., Hegghammer, Thomas, *Jihad in Saudi Arabia: Violence and Pan-Islamism since 1979* (Cambridge: Cambridge University Press, 2010), 38–58; and Stéphane Lacroix, *Les Islamistes Saoudiens: Une insurrection manquée* (Paris: Presses Universitaires de France, 2010), 133–7.

199 For details about the doctrine of 'Global Jihadism', see, e.g., Thomas Hegghammer, '"Classical" and "Global" Jihadism in Saudi Arabia', in *Saudi Arabia in Transition: Insights on Social, Political, Economic and Religious Change*, ed. Bernard Haykel, Thomas Hegghammer and Stéphane Lacroix (Cambridge: Cambridge University Press, 2015), 207–28; Hegghammer, *Jihad in Saudi Arabia*, 99–129; al-Rasheed, *Contesting the Saudi State*, 106–20; and Kepel, *Jihad*, 321–64.

200 See, e.g., Peters, 'Jihād'.

201 See, e.g., Brynjar Lia, *The Society of the Muslim Brothers in Egypt: The Rise of an Islamic Mass Movement 1928–1942* (Reading: Ithaca Press, 1997), 83; Calvert (ed.), *Islamism*, 15–25; and Martin, *Creating an Islamic State*, 143.

202 See, e.g., Youssef M. Choueiri, *Islamic Fundamentalism* (Boston: Twayne Publishers, 1990), 137–8; Calvert (ed.), *Islamism*, 26–30; and Martin, *Creating an Islamic State*, 143.

203 See, e.g., Kepel, *Jihad*, 95; and Hamadi Redissi, *Le Pacte de Nadjd: Ou comment l'islam sectaire est devenu l'islam* (Paris: Éditions du Seuil, 2007), 227.

204 See, e.g., Na'eem Jeenah, 'Jihad as a Form of Struggle in the Resistance to Apartheid', in *Twenty-First Century Jihad*, ed. Kendall and Stein, 201–15.

205 See, e.g., Abū l-Ḥasan An-Nadwī, *at-Tafsīr as-siyāsī li-l-islām fī mirāt kitābāt al-ustāḏ Abī l-Aʿlā al-Mawdūdī wa-š-šahīd Sayyid Quṭb* (al-Qāhira: Dār āfāq al-ġad, 1980); and Krämer, *Gottes Staat als Republik*, 226.

206 See, e.g., ʿAlī Ǧarīša, *al-Mašrūʿīya l-islāmīya l-ʿulyā*, aṭ-ṭabʿa ṯ-ṯānīya (al-Manṣūra: Dār al-wafāʾ, 2007); and Krämer, *Gottes Staat als Republik*, 247.

207 See, e.g., AOAbu Malek, *Fiqh al-ḥayāt al-ǧuzʾ al-awwal aš-šayḫ al-Qaraḍāwī – al-Ḥalqa 16/29* (published on youtube.com, 21 February 2013, available online: https://www.youtube.com/watch?v=8OeZTsi3oDg, accessed 11 June 2020), 1:48–4:28. A slightly adapted transcript of the interview can be found here, an-Nīlīn, *al-Qaraḍāwī: al-Muẓāharāt iḏā istahdafat īqāẓ al-umma fa-hiya ǧihād* (published on alnilin.com, without date, available online: https://www.alnilin.com/153591.htm, accessed 11 June 2020).

208

”نعني به: الجهاد الذي يلبي حاجات المجتمع المختلفة، ويعالج مشكلاته المتنوعة، ويغطي مطالبه المادية والمعنوية، وينهض له في سائر المجالات، حتى يتبوأ مكانته اللائقة به، وهو يشمل مجالات عدة: المجال العلمي أو الثقافي، والمجال الاجتماعي، والمجال الاقتصادي، والمجال التعليمي والتربوي، والمجال الصحي والطبي، والمجال البيئي، والمجال الحضاري بصفة عامة. [...] إن من واجب هذا الجهاد: أن نسعى جاهدا – ببذل الجهد، وبتحمل الجهد – حتى يعلم الجاهل، ويشغل العاطل، ويدرب العامل، ويشبع الجائع، ويكسو العاري، ويؤوي المشرد، ويداوي المريض، ويوفر تمام الكفاية لكل محتاج.“

Yūsuf al-Qaraḍāwī, *Fiqh al-ǧihād: Dirāsa muqārana li-aḥkāmihi wa-falsafatihi fī ḍawʾ al-qurʾān wa-s-sunna*, al-Ǧuzʾ al-awwal (al-Qāhira: Maktaba wahba, 2009), 232–3.

209 See, e.g., al-Qaraḍāwī, *Šarʿīyat al-muẓāharāt as-silmīya*.

210 See, e.g., Rachid al-Ghannouchi, 'What Is New about Yusuf al-Qaradawi's Jihad?', in *Twenty-First Century Jihad*, ed. Kendall and Stein, 334–50.

211 See al-Ḥāmid, *al-Kalima aqwā min ar-raṣāṣa*, 8.

Chapter 8

1 See Anna Würth, *Dialog mit dem Islam als Konfliktprävention? Zur Menschenrechtspolitik gegenüber islamisch geprägten Staaten* (Studie des Deutschen Instituts für Menschenrechte, September 2003), 39.

2 See Shahab Ahmed, *What Is Islam? The Importance of Being Islamic* (Princeton: Princeton University Press, 2016) and Thomas Bauer, *Die Kultur der Ambiguität: Eine andere Geschichte des Islams* (Berlin: Verlag der Weltreligionen, 2011).

3 See, especially, Bauer, *Die Kultur der Ambiguität*, 52 and Ahmed, *What Is Islam?*, 537.

4

"فلعل الأجدى أن نفهمه من خلال (زجاجة) التطبيق النبوي والراشدي، لأنها التطبيق المعياري للدين، أي قبل عهود الاختلال الديني."

ʿAbdallāh al-Ḥāmid, *al-Kalima aqwā min ar-raṣāṣa: al-Ǧihād as-silmī l-akbar* (Bairūt: ad-Dār al-ʿarabīya li-l-ʿulūm, 2004), 6.

5

"لعل ما يساعد على الفرز، أن نتذكر أن الثقافة العربية الإسلامية، التي نمتح منها في أمهات كتب التراث وبناتها، ليست هي الثقافة الإسلامية الصافية المحكمة، بل هي صياغة عباسية ومملوكية وعثمانية للثقافة الإسلامية جنحت إلى التأويل البعيد المرجوح والفاسد. [...] وصار الفكر الإسلامي – في الجملة – إسفنجيا زئبقيا، يفتقد الصلابة والمعيارية، مجزأ متناقضا، يفتقد الوحدة والانسجام، لأن النص – في ظل هشاشة الخلفية المعرفية – صار نصا مفتوحا، قابلا شتى التأويلات الفاسدة والبعيدة الاتجاهات."

ʿAbdallāh al-Ḥāmid, *as-Salafīya l-wusṭā: al-ʿAdl ʿadīl aṣ-ṣalāt* (Dimašq: Markaz an-nāqid aṯ-ṯaqāfī, 2009), 193–5.

6 See, e.g., ʿAbdallāh al-Ḥāmid, *Ḥuqūq al-insān baina nūr al-islām wa-ġabaš al-mulk al-ʿaḍūḍ* (Bairūt: Bīsān li-n-našr wa-t-tawzīʿ wa-l-iʿlām, 2010), 115.

7 See Chapter 6, 'Identity, culture war and antisemitism', of this book.

8 For details about Thomas Bauer's analysis of the different political discourses of 'classical' Islam, see Bauer, *Die Kultur der Ambiguität*, 315–43.

9 See, e.g., Bauer, *Die Kultur der Ambiguität*, 315–43; and Ridwan Al-Sayyid, 'Islamic Movements and Authenticity: Barriers to Development', in *Cosmopolitanism, Identity and Authenticity in the Middle East*, ed. Roel Meijer (Richmond: Curzon, 1999), 109–11.

10 See, e.g., Yūsuf al-Qaraḍāwī, *Min fiqh ad-daula fī l-islām* (al-Qāhira: Dār aš-šurūq, 1997); Rachel Scott, *The Challenge of Political Islam: Non-Muslims and the Egyptian State* (Stanford: Stanford University Press, 2010), 97; and Gudrun Krämer, *Gottes Staat als Republik: Reflexionen zeitgenössischer Muslime zu Islam, Menschenrechten und Demokratie* (Baden-Baden: Nomos Verlagsgesellschaft, 1999), 257–62.

11 For a thorough discussion of this view, see, e.g., Larbi Sadiki, *The Search for Arab Democracy: Discourses and Counter-Discourses* (London: Hurst, 2004), 61–3.

12

"وينبغي نبذ الصياغة العباسية، ذات النزعات الصحراوية والفرعونية والسفسطائية، التي جمدت مفهوم الإسلام والعقيدة في الشق الروحي، وهمشت شق العقيدة السياسي والحضاري."

al-Ḥāmid, *al-Kalima aqwā min ar-raṣāṣa*, 61.

13 The same thought can be found in the writings of other authors of the Islamo-reformist current. See, e.g., Muḥammad al-ʿAbd al-Karīm, *Tafkīk al-istibdād: Dirāsa fī fiqh at-taḥarrur min at-taġallub* (Bairūt: aš-Šabaka l-ʿarabīya li-l-abḥāṯ wa-n-našr, 2013), 165–6.

14

"الدمقراطية الغربية مبدأ من مبادئ (العلمانية)، وهي فرع ل (أيديولوجية)، ولا يمكن فك ارتباط الغصن بشجرته. هذه الدمقراطية الغربية لا يمكن أن تقبلها إلا الأمم التي لا أصل لها، [...] لأنها تؤدي بطبيعتها فرع من العلمانية. أما الدمقراطية وسيلة إنسانية لتطبيق مبادئ الإدارة الاجتماعية والسياسية، فهي لا

تعارض أي عقيدة شيوعية أو بوذية أو إسلامية، بل تنسجم معها، لأنها كالثوب للجسد، فهذه من ضمانات العدل وسيادة الأمة على حكامها، ومن مكارم الأخلاق السياسية. ولا بأس علينا من الاقتباس، إذا لزمنا الاحتراس وقيدناها بلفظ مانع فقلنا (الدمقراطية الإسلامية).“

ʿAbdallāḥ al-Ḥāmid, *Likay lā yakūnu l-qurʾān ḥammāl auğuh: al-Miṣbāḥ fī zuğāğa wa-miškāt* (self-published 2008, available online: http://www.acpra.org/download.php?action=view&id=11, accessed 11 June 2020), 146.

15

”ولكي تتجلى صورة إسلامية الدستور، ننص على شرطين [...]:
الأول: ولا يكون الدستور إسلاميا، إذا لم تنضبط طاعة أولي الأمر بطاعة الله ورسوله. [...] وإذا ينبغي أن تكون سلطة الأمة مؤطرة بقطعيات الشريعة، ليكون الدستور تجسيدا لسلطة الأمة الملتزمة بالشريعة. [...]
كل قانون تصدره الدولة وهو غير شرعي، فهو غير دستوري. [...]
الشرط الثاني: الالتزام بقطعيات الشريعة الإسلامية في التربية والقضاء والشؤون الأسرية خاصة والشؤون الاجتماعية عامة.“

ʿAbdallāh al-Ḥāmid, *Ṯulāṯīyat al-muğtamaʿ al-madanī* (Bairūt: ad-Dār al-ʿarabīya li-l-ʿulūm, 2004), 83–4.

16 See, e.g., al-Ḥāmid, *Ḥuqūq al-insān baina nūr al-islām wa-ġabaš al-mulk al-ʿaḍūḍ*, 115.

17 See, e.g., Matrūk al-Fāliḥ, *al-Iṣlāḥ ad-dustūrī fī s-Suʿūdīya: al-Qaḍāyā wa-l-asʾila l-asāsīya* (Bārīs: al-Muʾassasa l-ʿarabīya l-ūrubīya li-n-našr, 2004), 19.

Conclusion

1 See Madawi al-Rasheed, *Muted Modernists: The Struggle Over Divine Politics in Saudi Arabia* (London: Hurst, 2015), 58.

2 See Stéphane Lacroix, ‘Saudi Arabia and the Limits of Post-Islamism’, in *Post-Islamism: The Changing Faces of Political Islam*, ed. Asef Bayat (Oxford: Oxford University Press, 2013), 277–97.

Bibliography

The following pages list all sources mentioned in this book, first primary sources, then secondary sources and finally news articles and reports. Within each category, they are arranged in alphabetical order (by language, author and title). Arabic sources are written in transcription and ordered according to the Latin, rather than the Arabic, alphabet. In this alphabetical arrangement, I ignored the diacritical signs that are used to translate Arabic letters into the transcription alphabet. For example, 'H' (ه), 'Ḥ' (ح) and 'Ḫ' (خ) are treated the same with regard to the alphabetical arrangement. Arabic letters that are not represented by Latin letters in the transcription, like ʾ (ء) and ʿ (ع), are also ignored in the arrangement.

Primary sources

Arabic

Acpra Tube. *Asbāb azamāt al-umma, wa-hal ad-duʿāʾ waḥduhu kāfin li-taḥqīq an-naṣr?*. Published on youtube.com, 7 June 2013. Available online: https://www.youtube.com/watch?v=QRWq1s0c8dw (accessed 11 June 2020).

Acpra Tube. *at-Taʿaddudīya baina hady ar-rāšidīn wa-hawā al-mustabiddin*. Published on youtube.com, 21 February 2013. Available online: https://www.youtube.com/watch?v=06ic4IBNeb4 (accessed 11 June 2020).

Acpra Tube. *Halummū ilā l-ǧihād as-silmī badalan min al-ʿaskarī / ʿAbdallāh al-Ḥāmid*. Published on youtube.com, 31 December 2012. Available online: https://www.youtube.com/watch?v=hF4uX9O89Pw (accessed 11 June 2020).

Acpra Tube. *Ḥukm al-muẓāharāt wa-l-iʿtiṣāmāt fī š-šarīʿa l-islāmīya*. Published on youtube.com, 11 December 2012. Available online: https://www.youtube.com/watch?v=JY8y6hIalig (accessed 11 June 2020).

Acpra Tube. *Ḫurūǧ al-ḥākim ʿalā l-umma*. Published on youtube.com, 30 October 2012. Available online: https://www.youtube.com/watch?v=EVZW_GyOGbA (accessed 11 June 2020).

Acpra Tube. *Intihākāt ḥuqūq al-ʾinsān fī s-Suʿūdīya/D. Muḥammad al-Qaḥṭānī*. Published on youtube.com, 2 October 2012. Available online: https://www.youtube.com/watch?v=hj2f6vO8iCc&t=2s (accessed 11 June 2020).

Acpra Tube. *Naḥwa ḫiṭāb dīnī yaḥtaḍinu l-ḥukm aš-šūrī*. Published on youtube.com, 19 November 2012. Available online: https://www.youtube.com/watch?v=flpZmSsLIxI (accessed 11 June 2020).

Acpra Tube. *Taṣrīḥ ʿAbd al-ʿAzīz aš-Šubailī baʿda l-ǧalsa r-rābiʿa min muḥakamat ḥasm al-Qaṣīm*. Published on youtube.com, 24 April 2013. Available online: https://www.youtube.com/watch?v=AbjTyR1twKI (accessed 11 June 2020).

Acpra Tube. *Taṣrīḥ al-Ḫaḍr wa-l-Ḥāmid fī ǧalsat 1 li-muḥākamat ḥasm al-Qaṣīm*. Published on youtube.com, 4 February 2013. Available online: https//www.youtube.com/watch?v=boD3Y_HieMI (accessed 11 June 2020).
Acpra Tube. *Ūlī l-amr lā walī l-amr / D. ʿAbd al-Karīm al-Ḫaḍr*. Published in youtube.com, 25 December 2012. Available online: https://www.youtube.com/watch?v=qRcIY_w6e6A (accessed 11 June 2020).
al-ʿAbd al-Karīm, Muḥammad. *al-Iḥtisāb al-madanī: Dirāsa fī l-bināʾ al-maqāṣidī li-l-ʾiḥtisāb*. aṭ-Ṭabʿa ṯ-ṯānīya. Bairūt: aš-Šabaka l-ʿarabīya li-l-ʾabḥāṯ wa-n-našr, 2013.
al-ʿAbd al-Karīm, Muḥammad. *Azmat aṣ-ṣirāʿ as-siyāsī baina aǧniḥa l-usra l-ḥākima fī s-Suʿūdīya*. Published on paldf.net, 24 November 2010. Available online: https://www.paldf.net/forum/showthread.php?t=703821 and http://www.inbaa.com/أزمة-الصراع-السياسي-بين-الأجنحة-الحاك/ (accessed 11 June 2020).
al-ʿAbd al-Karīm, Muḥammad. *Ṣaḥwat at-tawḥīd: Dirāsa fī azmat al-ḫiṭāb as-siyāsī l-islāmī*. Bairūt: aš-Šabaka l-ʿarabīya li-l-ʾabḥāṯ wa-n-našr, 2012.
al-ʿAbd al-Karīm, Muḥammad. *Tafkīk al-ʾistibdād: Dirāsa fī fiqh at-taḥarrur min at-taġallub*. Bairūt: aš-Šabaka l-ʿarabīya li-l-ʾabḥāṯ wa-n-našr, 2013.
al-Aḥmarī, Muḥammad. *ad-Dīmuqrāṭīya: al-Ǧuḏūr wa-iškālīyat at-taṭbīq*. Bairūt: aš-Šabaka l-ʿarabīya li-l-ʾabḥāṯ wa-n-našr, 2012.
al-Albānī, Nāṣir ad-Dīn. *Ḍaʿīf sunan at-Tirmiḏī*. ar-Riyāḍ: Maktabat al-maʿārif li-l-našrww wa-tawzīʿ, 2000.
al-Albānī, Nāṣir ad-Dīn. *Ṣaḥīḥ at-tarġīb wa-t-tarhīb*. ar-Riyāḍ: Maktabat al-maʿārif li-n-našr wa-t-tawzīʿ, 2000.
al-Arnāʾūṭ, Šuʿayb, ed. *Sunan Abī Dāwud*. Bairūt: Dār ar-risāla l-ʿālamīya, 2009.
al-ʿAuda, Salmān. *ʾAsʾilat aṯ-ṯawra*. Bairūt: Markaz namāʾ li-l-buḥūṯ wa-d-dirāsāt, 2012.
al-ʿAuda, Salmān. *Law kuntu ṭayran*. ar-Riyāḍ: Muʾassasat al-islām al-yaum, 2012.
al-ʿAwwā,Muḥammad Salīm. *Fī n-niẓām as-siyāsī li-d-daula l-islāmīya*. al-Qāhira: Dār aš-šurūq, 2007.
al-Bišrī, Ṭāriq. *Baina l-ǧāmiʿa ad-dīnīya wa-l-ǧāmiʿa l-waṭanīya fī l-fikr as-siyāsī*. al-Qāhira: Dār aš-šurūq, 1998.
al-Būṭī, Muḥammad Saʿīd Ramaḍān. *al-Ǧihād fī l-islām: Kaifa nafhamuhu wa-kaifa numārisuhu*. Dimašq: Dār al-fikr, 1993.
al-Būṭī, Muḥammad Saʿīd Ramaḍān. *as-Salafīya marḥala zamanīya mubāraka lā maḏhab islāmī*. Dimašq: Dār al-fikr, 1988.
al-Fāliḥ, Matrūk. *al-Iṣlāḥ ad-dustūrī fī s-Suʿūdīya: al-Qaḍāyā wa-l-asʾila l-asāsīya*. Bārīs: al-Muʾassasa l-ʿarabīya l-ūrubīya li-n-našr, 2004.
al-Ǧābirī, Muḥammad ʿĀbid. *Fikr Ibn Ḫaldūn: al-ʿAṣabīya wa-d-daula*. aṭ-Ṭabʿa ṯ-ṯāmina. Bairūt: Markaz dirāsāt al-waḥda l-ʿarabīya, 2008.
al-Ġannūšī, Rāšid. *ad-Dīmuqrāṭīya wa-ḥuqūq al-insān fī l-islām*. Bairūt: ad-Dār al-ʿarabīya li-l-ʿulūm nāširūn, 2012.
al-Ġannūšī, Rāšid. *al-Ḥurrīyāt al-ʿāmma fī d-daula l-islāmīya*. Bairūt: Markaz dirāsāt al-waḥda l-ʿarabīya, 1993.
al-Ġaẓīf, ʿAbd al-Wahhāb. *at-Tanwīr al-islāmī fī l-mašhad as-suʿūdī: Uṣūluhu l-fikrīya wa-mawqifuhu min al-qaḍāyā š-šarʿīya*. Ǧidda: Markaz at-tȧṣīl li-d-dirāsāt wa-l-buḥūṯ, 2013.
al-Ḥāmid, Abdallah. *al-Burhān bi-qawāmat al-umma wa-siyādatihā ʿalā s-sulṭān*. Self-published, 2012. Available online: http://www.acpra.org/download.php?action=view&id=26 (accessed 11 June 2020).

al-Ḥāmid, Abdallah. *al-Ǧihād ṣinwān: Silmī li-aṭr wulāt wa-ḥarbī li-dafʿ ġuzāt*. Self-published 2011. At the time of writing not accessible via the internet anymore, a copy is in my possession.

al-Ḥāmid, Abdallah. *al-Ḥasan al-Baṣrī wa-l-Ḥaǧǧāǧ fī āḫar az-zamān*. Bairūt: ad-Dār al-ʿarabīya li-l-ʿulūm, 2003.

al-Ḥāmid, Abdallah. *al-Kalima aqwā min ar-raṣāṣa: al-Ǧihād as-silmī l-akbar*. Bairūt: ad-Dār al-ʿarabīya li-l-ʿulūm, 2004. Available online: https://archive.org/details/wordstrongerthanbullet/mode/2up (accessed 11 June 2020).

al-Ḥāmid, Abdallah. *Ammā baʿda kawāriṯ al-ḫalīǧ*. Self-published, 2012. Available online: https://www.scribd.com/document/324758098/أما-بعد-كوارث-الخليج (accessed 11 June 2020).

al-Ḥāmid, Abdallah. *as-Salafīya l-wusṭā: al-ʿAdl ʿadīl aṣ-ṣalāt*. Dimašq: Markaz an-nāqid aṯ-ṯaqāfī, 2009.

al-Ḥāmid, Abdallah. *aṭ-Ṭarīq aṯ-ṯāliṯ: ad-Dustūr al-islāmī*. Dimašq: Markaz an-nāqid aṯ-ṯaqāfī, 2009.

al-Ḥāmid, Abdallah. *Ḫawāṭir tilmīḏ maqmūʿ*. Bairūt: ad-Dār al-ʿarabīya li-l-ʿulūm, 2003.

al-Ḥāmid, Abdallah. *Ḥuqūq al-insān baina nūr al-islām wa-ġabaš al-mulk al-ʿaḍūḍ*. Bairūt: Bīsān li-n-našr wa-t-tawzīʿ wa-l-iʿlām, 2010.

al-Ḥāmid, Abdallah. *Inšāʾ ǧamʿīyat ḥasm amr mašrūʿ bal farīḍa šarʿīya*. Self-published, 2012. At the time of writing not accessible via the internet anymore, a copy is in my possession.

al-Ḥāmid, Abdallah. *Likay lā yakūnu l-qurʾān ḥammāl ʾawǧuh: al-Miṣbāḥ fī zuǧāǧa wa-miškāt*. Self-published 2008. Available online: http://www.acpra.org/download.php?action=view&id=11 (accessed 11 June 2020).

al-Ḥāmid, Abdallah. *Maʿāyīr istiqlāl al-qaḍāʾ ad-duwalīya fī būtaqa š-šarīʿa l-islāmīya*. Bairūt: ad-Dār al-ʿarabīya li-l-ʿulūm nāširūn, 2004.

al-Ḥāmid, Abdallah. *Ṣarḫat ḫādim*. Bairūt: ad-Dār al-ʿarabīya li-l-ʿulūm, 2003.

al-Ḥāmid, Abdallah. *Ṯulāṯīyat al-muǧtamaʿ al-madanī: ʿAn sirr najāḥ al-ġarb wa-iḫfāq al-ʿarab*. Bairūt: ad-Dār al-ʿarabīya li-l-ʿulūm, 2004.

al-Ḫarāšī, Sulaymān b. Ṣaliḥ. *Sàalnī sāʾil ʿan ad-duktūr ʿAbdallāh al-Ḥāmid*. Published on saaid.net, without date. Available online: http://www.saaid.net/Warathah/Alkharashy/m/43.htm (accessed 11 June 2020).

al-Kawākibī, ʿAbd ar-Raḥmān. *Ṭabāʾiʿ al-istibdād wa-maṣāriʿ al-istiʿbād*. aṭ-Ṭabʿa ṯ-ṯānīya. al-Qāhira: Dār aš-šuruq, 2009.

al-Māliki, ʿAbdallah. *Siyādat al-umma qabla taṭbīq aš-šarīʿa*. Bairūt: aš-Šabaka l-ʿarabīya li-l-ʾabḥāṯ wa-n-našr, 2011.

al-Maršūd, Ḫālid. *Taubat an-Naʿīmī wa-inšiqāq al-ʿIyāšī ʿan ǧamʿīyat ḥasm*. Published on alweeam.com, 5 March 2013. Available online: https://www.alweeam.com.sa/y2013/186638/عضوان-من-جمعية-حسم-يعلنان-الانشقاق-عن/ (accessed 11 June 2020).

al-Muṭayrī, Ḥākim. *al-Ḥurrīya aw aṭ-ṭawfān*. Bairūt: al-Muʾassasa l-ʿarabīya li-d-dirāsāt wa-n-našr, 2004.

al-Muṭayrī, Ḥākim. *Taḥrīr al-insān wa-taǧrīd aṭ-ṭuġyān*. Bairūt: al-Muʾassasa l-ʿarabīya li-d-dirāsāt wa-n-našr, 2009.

al-Qaraḍāwī, Yūsuf. *ad-Dīn wa-s-siyāsa: Tàṣīl wa-radd šubuhāt*. Dūblin: al-Maǧlis al-ūrubī li-l-iftāʾ wa-l-buḥūṯ, 2007.

al-Qaraḍāwī, Yūsuf. *al-Islām wa-l-ḥurrīya*. Published on al-qaradawi.net, 10 January 2019. Available online: https://www.al-qaradawi.net/node/3637 (accessed 11 June 2020).

al-Qaraḍāwī, Yūsuf. *al-Waṭan wa-l-muwāṭana fī ḍaw' al-uṣūl al-'aqadīya wa-l-maqāṣid aš-šārī'īya*. al-Qāhira: Dār aš-šurūq, 2010.

al-Qaraḍāwī, Yūsuf. *Fiqh al-ǧihād: Dirāsa muqārana li-aḥkāmihi wa-falsafatihi fī ḍaw' al-qur'ān wa-s-sunna*. Al-ǧuz' al-awwal. al-Qāhira: Maktabat wahba, 2009.

al-Qaraḍāwī, Yūsuf. *Ġayr al-muslimīn fī l-muǧtama' al-islāmī*. aṭ-Ṭab'a ṯ-ṯāliṯa. al-Qāhira: Maktabat wahba, 1992.

al-Qaraḍāwī, Yūsuf. *Min fiqh ad-daula fī l-islām*. al-Qāhira: Dār aš-šurūq, 1997.

al-Qaraḍāwī, Yūsuf. *Šar'īyat al-muẓāharāt as-silmīya*. Published on al-qaradawi.net, 24 April 2016. Available online: https://al-qaradawi.net/node/3885 (accessed 11 June 2020).

an-Nadwī, Abū l-Ḥasan. *at-Tafsīr as-siyāsī li-l-islām fī mirāt kitābāt al-ustāḏ Abī l-A'lā al-Mawdūdī wa-š-šahīd Sayyid Quṭb*. al-Qāhira: Dār āfāq al-ġad, 1980.

Anonymous. *Bayān naḥwa daulat al-ḥuqūq wa-l-mu'assasāt*. February 2011. Available online: https://libral.org/vb/archive/index.php/t-51378.html (accessed 11 June 2020).

Anonymous. *Ḫiṭāb al-maṭālib*. May 1991. Available online: http://www.al-waie.org/archives/article/11370 (accessed 11 June 2020).

Anonymous. *I'lān waṭanī li-l-iṣlāḥ*. March 2011. Available online: https://www.alawan.org/2013/12/08/إعلان-وطني-للاصلاح-نداء-من-مثقفين-سعو/ (accessed 11 June 2020).

Anonymous. *Ma'ālim fī ṭarīq al-malakīya d-dustūrīya*. February 2007. Available online: https://www.alquds.co.uk/نص-العريضة-الحديثة-التي-وجهها-الاصلاح/ (accessed 11 June 2020).

Anonymous. *Muḏakkirat an-naṣīḥa*. September 1992. Available online: https://libral.org/vb/archive/index.php/t-25264.html (accessed 11 June 2020).

Anonymous. *Nidā'an ilā l-qiyāda wa-š-ša'b ma'an: al-Iṣlāḥ ad-dustūrī awwalan*. December 2003. Available online: http://www.saudiaffairs.net/webpage/sa/issue12/article12l/issue12lt2.htm (accessed 11 June 2020).

Anonymous. *Ru'yat li-ḥāḍir al-waṭan wa-mustaqbalihi*. January 2003. Available online: http://www.mstayeb.com/index.php?option=com_content&view=article&id=145:ro2yalehaderalwatan&catid=20:isla7&Itemid=5 (accessed 11 June 2020).

AOAbu Malek. *Fiqh al-ḥayāt al-ǧuz' al-awwal aš-šayḫ al-Qaraḍāwī – al-Ḥalqa 16/29*. Published on youtube.com, 21 February 2013. Available online: https://www.youtube.com/watch?v=8OeZTsi3oDg (accessed 11 June 2020).

ar-Rifā'ī, Ḫālid 'Abd Al-Mun'im. *Ma'nā muqawwala: 'Inna l-qur'ān huwa ḥammāl auǧuh'*. Published on islamway.net, 11 November 2012. Available online: https://ar.islamway.net/fatwa/39877/معنى-مقولة-إن-القرآن-هو-حمال-أوجه (accessed 11 June 2020).

ar-Rīkī, Ḥasan ibn Ǧamāl. *Lam' aš-šihāb fī ṣirāt aš-šayḫ Muḥammad ibn 'Abd al-Wahhāb*. Ed. Aḥmad Musṭafā Abū Ḥakīma. Bairūt: Dār aṯ-ṯaqāfāt, 1967.

aṣ-Ṣabbāġ, Muḥammad ibn Luṭfī, ed. *al-Asrār al-marfū'a li-l-'allāma Nūr ad-Dīn 'Alī ibn Muḥammad ibn Sultān al-mašhūr bi-l-Mullā 'Alī Al-Qārī*. aṭ-Ṭab'a ṯ-ṯānīya. Bairūt: al-Maktab al-islāmī, 1979.

as-Sakīna. *Ǧam'īyat al-ḥuqūq al-madanīya wa-s-siyāyīya (ḥasm)*. Published on assakina.com, 10 March 2013. Available online: http://www.assakina.com/center/parties/22693.html (accessed 6 September 2019).

as-Sakrān, Ibrāhīm b. 'Umar. *Man hum at-tanwīriyūn?!* Published on islamway.net, 5 November 2014. Available online: https://ar.islamway.net/article/39497/من-هم-التنويريون (accessed 11 June 2020).

as-Saif Naṣir b. Sa'īd. *at-Tanwīrīyūn fī s-Su'ūdīya baina al-wahm wa-l-ḥaqīqa*. Published on almohtasb.com, 30 April 2013. Available online: http://www.almohtasb.com/alhesba/Articles/14125 (accessed 11 June 2020).

at-Tīğānī, Muḥāmmad. *Fa-is ʾalū ahl aḏ-ḏikr aṣ-ṣafḥa 210*. Published on shiaonlinelibrary.com, without date. Available online: http://shiaonlinelibrary.com/الكتب/4606_فاسألوا-أهل-الذكر-الدكتور-محمد-التيجاني/الصفحة_205 (accessed 11 June 2020).

at-Turkī, ʿAbdallāh ibn ʿAbd al-Muḥsin, ed. *Musnad al-Imām Aḥmad ibn Ḥanbal*. Vol. 30. Bairūt: Al-Resalah Publishers, 1999.

aẓ-Ẓahrānī, ʿUmar ibn ʿAbd Al-ʿAzīz. *Barnāmağ fitna No.102*. Published on youtube .com, 18 October 2014. Available online: https://www.youtube.com/watch?v =aSQcvAtKG6M (accessed 11 June 2020).

Ğamʿīyat al-ḥuqūq al-madanīya wa-s-siyāsīya fī s-Suʿūdīya. *al-Bayān 11 ʿan ğalsat an-naṭq bi-l-ḥukm fī l-muḥakama s-siyāsīya li-ʿaḍwai ḥasm, al-Ḥāmid wa-l-Qaḥṭānī wa-ṣudūr al-ḥukm*. Published on acpra.org, 11 March 2013. Available online: http:// www.acpra.org/news_view_224.html (accessed 11 June 2020).

Ğamʿīyat al-ḥuqūq al-madanīya wa-s-siyāsīya fī s-Suʿūdīya. *al-Iʿlān at-tàsīsī*. Published on acpra.org, 12 October 2009. Available online: http://www.acpra.org/news.php ?action=view&id=1 (accessed 11 June 2020).

Ğamʿīyat al-ḥuqūq al-madanīya wa-s-siyāsīya fī s-Suʿūdīya. *Bayān al-ğalsa l-ūlā min al-muḥakama s-siyāsīya li-ʿĪsā al-Ḥāmid*. Published on acpra.org, 13 June 2014. Available online: http://www.acpra.org/news_view_274.html (accessed 11 June 2020).

Ğamʿīyat al-ḥuqūq al-madanīya wa-s-siyāsīya fī s-Suʿūdīya. *Bayān al-ğalsa ṯ-ṯānīya min al-muḥakama s-siyāsīya ṯ-ṯānīya li-D. ʿAbd al-Karīm al-Ḫaḍr*. Published on acpra.org, 22 May 2014. Available online: http://www.acpra.org/news_view_273.html (accessed 11 June 2020).

Ğamʿīyat al-ḥuqūq al-madanīya wa-s-siyāsīya fī s-Suʿūdīya. *Bayān al-ğalsa t-tāsiʿa min muḥākamat ʿaḍw ğamʿīyat ḥasm: Fawzān al-Ḥarbī*. Published on acpra.org, 3 April 2014. Available online: http://www.acpra.org/news_view_268.html (accessed 11 June 2020).

Ğamʿīyat al-ḥuqūq al-madanīya wa-s-siyāsīya fī s-Suʿūdīya. *Bayān ʿan iʿtiqāl ʿaḍw ğamʿīyat ḥasm: D. ʿAbd Ar-Raḥmān al-Ḥāmid*. Published on acpra.org, 19 April 2014. Available online: http://acpra.org/news_view_269.html (accessed 11 June 2020).

Ğamʿīyat al-ḥuqūq al-madanīya wa-s-siyāsīya fī s-Suʿūdīya. *Bayān ʿan waqāʾiʿ al-ğalsa l-ḥādiya ʿašara (ğalsat an-naṭq bi-l-ḥukm) li-l-muḥakama s-siyāsīya li-l-muṭālibīn bi-šurūṭ al-bayʿa š-šarʿīya (sulṭat al-umma) wa-ḥuqūq al-insān*. Published on acpra.or g, 11 March 2013. Available online: http://www.acpra.org/news.php?action=view&id =224 (accessed 11 June 2020).

Ğamʿīyat al-ḥuqūq al-madanīya wa-s-siyāsīya fī s-Suʿūdīya. *Bayān ğalsat an-naṭq bi-l-ḥukm min al-muḥakama s-siyāsīya li-D. ʿAbd al-Karīm al-Ḫaḍr ʿadw ḥasm*. Published on acpra.org, 28 June 2013. Available online: http://www.acpra.org/news_view_242 .html (accessed 11 June 2020).

Ğamʿīyat al-ḥuqūq al-madanīya wa-s-siyāsīya fī s-Suʿūdīya. *Bayān ğalsat an-naṭq bi-l-ḥukm min muḥākamat ʿaḍw ğamʿīyat ḥasm: Fawzān al-Ḥarbī*. Published on acpra.org, 30 June 2014. Available online: http://www.acpra.org/news_view_275.html (accessed 11 June 2020).

Ğarīša, ʿAlī. *al-Mašrūʿīya l-islāmīya l-ʿulyā*. aṭ-Ṭabʿa ṯ-ṯānīya. al-Manṣūra: Dār al-wafāʾ, 2007.

Ḫalaf Allāh, Muḥammad. *al-Qurʾān wa-d-daula*. al-Qāhira: Maktabat al-Anğlū l-Maṣrīya, 1973.

Ḫalīl, Fawzī. *Daur ahl al-ḥall wa-l-ʿaqd fī n-namūḏağ al-islāmī li-niẓām al-ḥukm*. al-Qāhira: al-Maʿhad al-ʿālamī li-l-fikr al-islāmī, 1981.

Haykal, Muḥammad Ḫayr. *al-Ǧihād wa-l-qitāl fī s-siyāsa š-šar'īya*. Bairūt: Dār al-Bayāriq, 1992.
Hizb al-ḥurrīya wa-l-'adāla. *Barnāmaǧ ḥizb al-ḥurrīya wa-l-'adāla*. Published by the Freedom and Justice Party, 2011. Available online: https://kurzman.unc.edu/files/2011/06/FJP_20111.pdf (accessed 11 June 2020).
Hizb al-umma l-islāmīya. *an-Niẓām al-asāsī li-l-ḥizb*. Published on islamicommaparty.org, without date. Available online: https://islamicommaparty.org/partys-basic-system/ (accessed 11 June 2020).
Hizb an-nūr. *Barnāmaǧ*. Published by the Nur Party, 2011. Available online: https://kurzman.unc.edu/files/2011/06/AlNour_2011_brnameg_alnoor.pdf (accessed 11 June 2020).
Ḥizb at-taǧammu' al-waṭanī. *I'lān tàsīs ḥizb at-taǧammu' al-waṭanī*. Published on the-naas.com, 23 September 2020. Available online: https://the-naas.com/ar (accessed 24 March 2020).
Huwaidī, Fahmī. *Muwāṭinūn lā ḏimmīyūn*. al-Qāhira: Dār aš-šurūq, 2004.
Ittihād quwā l-mu'āraḍa fī ǧazīrat al-'arab. *I'lān tàsīs*. Published on justpaste.it, 24 June 2017. Available online: https://justpaste.it/Unionofoppositionforces (accessed 11 June 2020).
Māḍī, Abū l-'Alā. *Ru'yat "Al-Wasaṭ" fī s-siyāsa wa-l-muǧtama'*. al-Qāhira: Maktabat aš-šurūq ad-duwalīya, 2005.
Quṭb, Sayyid. *as-Salām al-'ālamī wa-l-islām*. al-Qāhira: Dār aš-šurūq, 1974.
W3iteam, *'Abd al-Karīm al-Ḫaḍr*. Blog entry published on w3iteam.wordpress.com, 16 December 2014. Available online: https://w3iteam.wordpress.com/2014/12/16/عبد-الكريم-الخضر/ (accessed 11 June 2020).
W3iteam. *Liqā' farīq wa'y ma'a ràīs ḥasm al-muhandis Fawzān al-Ḥarbī qabla i'tiqālihi*. Blog entry published on w3iteam.wordpress.com, 19 March 2014. Available online: https://w3iteam.wordpress.com/2014/03/19/لقاء-فريق-وعي-مع-رئيس-حسم-المهندس-فوزان/ (accessed 11 June 2020).
W3iteam. *Man huwa Muḥammad al-Baǧādī*. Blog entry published on w3iteam.wordpress.com, 31 March 2014. Available online: https://w3iteam.wordpress.com/2014/03/31/الرجل-الذي-قال-كل-امن-هو-محمد-البجادي-؟/ (accessed 11 June 2020).
W3iteam. *Nazra'u l-wa'y li-yaqṭafa l-muǧtama' al-'adl wa-n-namā': 'Abdallāḥ al-Ḥāmid*. Blog entry published on w3iteam.wordpress.com, 28 September 2014. Available online: https://w3iteam.wordpress.com/2014/09/28/عبد-الله-الحامد/ (accessed 11 June 2020).
W3iteam. *Sulaymān ar-Rašūdī, šayḫ al-iṣlāḥiyīn*. Blog entry published on w3iteam.wordpress.com, 5 September 2014. Available online: https://w3iteam.wordpress.com/2014/09/05/سليمان-الرشودي-شيخ-الإصلاحيين/ (accessed 11 June 2020).

English

al-Faifi, Sahar. *Meet the Hero of Saudi Arabia's Silent Majority*. Published on middleeastmonitor.com, 12 March 2019. Available online: https://www.middleeastmonitor.com/20190312-meet-the-hero-of-saudi-arabias-silent-majority/ (accessed 11 June 2020).
Iqbal, Muhammad. *The Reconstruction of Religious Thought in Islam*. Stanford: Stanford University Press, 2013.

German

Marx, Karl and Friedrich Engels. *Karl Marx – Friedrich Engels Studienausgabe*. Band 1. Frankfurt: Fischer Bücherei, 1966.

Secondary sources

English

Aarts, Paul and Gerd Nonneman (as editors). *Saudi Arabia in the Balance: Political Economy, Society, Foreign Affairs*. New York: New York University Press, 2005.

Ahmed, Shahab. *What is Islam? The Importance of Being Islamic*. Princeton: Princeton University Press, 2016.

al-Azami, Usaama. *Islam and the Arab Revolutions: The Ulama Between Democracy and Autocracy*. London: Hurst, 2021.

al-Rasheed, Madawi. *A History of Saudi Arabia*. 2nd edn. New York: Cambridge University Press, 2010.

al-Rasheed, Madawi. *Contesting the Saudi State: Islamic Voices from a New Generation*. New York: Cambridge University Press, 2007.

al-Rasheed, Madawi, ed. *Kingdom without Borders: Saudi Arabia's Political, Religious and Media Frontiers*. London: Hurst, 2008.

al-Rasheed, Madawi. *Muted Modernists: The Struggle Over Divine Politics in Saudi Arabia*. London: Hurst, 2015.

al-Rasheed, Madawi, ed. *Salman's Legacy: The Dilemmas of a New Era in Saudi Arabia*. New York: Oxford University Press, 2018.

al-Rasheed, Madawi. *Xenophobia, Tribalism and Imagined Enemies: Mohammed Bin Salman's Brand of Saudi Nationalism*. Published on middleeasteye.net, 5 September 2018. Available online: https://www.middleeasteye.net/opinion/xenophobia-tribalism-and-imagined-enemies-mohammed-bin-salmans-brand-saudi-nationalism (accessed 11 June 2020).

al-ʿUthaymīn, ʿAbd Allāh Sāliḥ. *Muhammad ibn ʿAbd al-Wahhāb: The Man and His Works*. London: I.B. Tauris, 2009.

Amanat, Abbas and Frank Griffel (as editors). *Islamic Law in the Contemporary Context*. Stanford: Stanford University Press, 2009.

an-Naʿim, Abdullahi. *Toward an Islamic Reformation: Civil Liberties, Human Rights, and International Law*. Syracuse: Syracuse University Press, 1990.

as-Sarhan, Saud. *The Neo-Reformists: A New Democratic Islamic Discourse*. Published on mei.edu, 1 October 2009. Available online: http://www.mei.edu/content/neo-reformists-new-democratic-islamic-discourse (accessed 11 June 2020).

Ayalon, Ami. *Language and Change in the Arab Middle East: The Evolution of Modern Political Discourse*. New York: Oxford University Press, 1987.

Ayoob, Mohammed and Hasan Kosebalaban (as editors). *Religion and Politics in Saudi Arabia: Wahhabism and the State*. Boulder: Lynne Rienner Publishers, 2008.

Bayat, Asef. *Making Islam Democratic: Social Movements and the Post-Islamist Turn*. Stanford: Stanford University Press, 2007.

Bayat, Asef, ed. *Post-Islamism: The Changing Faces of Political Islam*. Oxford: Oxford University Press, 2013.

Bearman, P. J., Th. Bianquis, C. E. Bosworth, E. van Donzel and W. P. Heinrichs, ed. *The Encyclopedia of Islam*. 2nd edn. Leiden: Brill, 1954–2004.

Beinin, Joel and Frédéric Vairel, ed. *Social Movements, Mobilization and Contestation in the Middle East and North Africa*. 2nd edn. Palo Alto: Stanford University Press, 2013.

Calvert, John. *Islamism: A Documentary and Reference Guide*. Westport: Greenwood Press, 2008.

Choueiri, Youssef M. *Islamic Fundamentalism: The Story of Islamist Movements*. Boston: Twayne Publishers, 1990.

Commins, David Dean. *The Wahhabi Mission and Saudi Arabia*. London: I.B. Tauris, 2006.

Crawford, M. J. 'The Daʿwa of Ibn ʿAbd al-Wahhāb before the Al Saʿūd'. *Journal of Arabian Studies* 1, no. 2 (2011): 147–61.

Dekmejian, Richard. 'The Liberal Impulse in Saudi Arabia'. *Middle East Journal* 57, no. 3 (Summer 2003): 400–13.

Donnelly, Jack. 'Cultural Relativism and Universal Human Rights'. *Human Rights Quarterly* 6, no. 4 (November 1984): 400–19.

Eickelman, Dale and James Piscatori. *Muslim Politics*. Princeton: Princeton University Press, 1996.

Emad El-Din, Shahin, ed. *The Oxford Encyclopedia of Islam and Politics*. New York: Oxford University Press, 2014.

Emon Anver, M. et al., ed. *The Oxford Handbook of Islamic Law*. Oxford: Oxford University Press, 2018.

Enz-Harlass, Peter. '"Peaceful Civil Jihad" – Saudi Arabia's Islamic Civil Rights Movement and Its Concept of Jihad'. *Middle Eastern Studies*. DOI: 10.1080/00263206.2021.1926995. Published online on 3 June 2021, Available online: https://www.tandfonline.com/doi/full/10.1080/00263206.2021.1926995 (accessed 3 June 2021).

Esposito, John L., ed. *The Oxford Encyclopedia of the Islamic World*. Oxford: Oxford University Press, 2009. Available online: https://www.oxfordreference.com/view/10.1093/acref/9780195305135.001.0001/acref-9780195305135 (accessed 11 June 2020).

Esposito, John L., ed. *Voices of Resurgent Islam*. New York: Oxford University Press, 1983.

Esposito, John L. and John O. Voll. *Islam and Democracy*. New York: Oxford University Press, 1996.

Fandy, Mamoun. *Saudi Arabia and the Politics of Dissent*. New York: Palgrave, 2001.

Fleet, Kate et al., ed. *Encyclopaedia of Islam*. 3rd edn. Brill, 2007. Available online: https://referenceworks.brillonline.com/browse/encyclopaedia-of-islam-3 (accessed 11 June 2020).

Gawhar, Altaf. *The Challenge of Islam*. London: Islamic Council of Europe, 1978.

Hallaq, Wael B. *Law and Legal Theory in Classical and Medieval Islam*. Aldershot: Ashgate, 1994.

Hamidaddin, Abdullah. *Tweeted Heresies: Saudi Islam in Transformation*. New York: Oxford University Press, 2020.

Haykel, Bernard, Thomas Hegghammer and Stéphane Lacroix (as editors). *Saudi Arabia in Transition: Insights on Social, Political, Economic and Religious Change*. Cambridge: Cambridge University Press, 2015.

Hegghammer, Thomas. *Jihad in Saudi Arabia: Violence and Pan-Islamism since 1979*. Cambridge: Cambridge University Press, 2010.

Hegghammer, Thomas. *The Caravan: Abdallah Azzam and the Rise of Global Jihad.* Cambridge: Cambridge University Press, 2020.
Hegghammer, Thomas and Stéphane Lacroix. 'Rejectionist Islam in Saudi Arabia: The Story of Juhayman Al-ʿUtaybi Revisited'. *International Journal of Middle East Studies* 39 (2007): 103–22.
Hulsman, Cornelius, ed. *The Egyptian Constitution: Perspectives from Egypt.* Baden-Baden: Tectum Wissenschaftsverlag, 2017.
Jayyusi, Salma Khadra, ed. *Human Rights in Arab Thought: A Reader.* London: I.B. Tauris, 2008.
Jones, Toby Craig. 'Rebellion on the Saudi Periphery: Modernity, Marginalization, and the Shiʿa Uprising of 1979'. *International Journal of Middle East Studies* 38, no. 2 (May 2006): 213–33.
Kendall, Elisabeth and Ewan Stein (as editors). *Twenty-first Century Jihad: Law, Society and Military Action.* London: I.B. Tauris, 2015.
Khatab, Sayed. *The Power of Sovereignty: The Political and Ideological Philosophy of Sayyid Qutb.* New York: Routledge, 2006.
Khatab, Sayed. 'The Voice of Democratism in Sayyid Qutb's Response to Violence and Terrorism'. *Islam and Christian-Muslim Relations* 20, no. 3 (2009): 315–32.
Khatib, Lina et al., ed. *Taking to the Streets: The Transformations of Arab Activism.* Baltimore: Johns Hopkins University Press, 2014.
Kostiner, Joseph. 'On Instruments and Their Designers: The Ikhwan of Najd and the Emergence of the Saudi State'. *Middle Eastern Studies* 21, no. 3 (1985): 298–323.
Kramer, Martin. 'Coming to Terms: Fundamentalists or Islamists?'. *Middle East Quarterly* 10, no. 2 (Spring 2003): 65–77.
Kurzman, Charles, ed. *Liberal Islam: A Sourcebook.* New York: Oxford University Press, 1998.
Lacroix, Stéphane, 'Between Islamists and Liberals: Saudi Arabia's New "Islamo-Liberal" Reformists'. *Middle East Journal* 58, no. 3 (Summer 2004): 345–65.
Lacroix, Stéphane. *Saudi Islamists and the Arab Spring.* Paper published by the London School of Economics (LSE) Kuwait Programme on Development, Governance and Globalisation in the Gulf States, May 2014.
Lauzière, Henri. *The Making of Salafism: Islamic Reform in the Twentieth Century.* New York: Columbia University Press, 2015.
Lia, Brynjar. *The Society of the Muslim Brothers in Egypt: The Rise of an Islamic Mass Movement 1928–1942.* Reading: Ithaca Press, 1997.
Mahdi, Muhsin. *Ibn Khaldūn's Philosophy of History.* Chicago: University of Chicago Press, 1964.
Martin, Vanessa. *Creating an Islamic State: Khomeini and the Making of a New Iran.* London: I.B. Tauris, 2000.
Mattar, Mohamed Y. and Anna Koppel (as editors). *Mixed Legal Systems, East and West.* London: Routledge, 2014.
Matthiesen, Toby. *The Other Saudis: Shiism, Dissent and Sectarianism.* New York: Cambridge University Press, 2015.
Meijer, Roel, ed. *Cosmopolitanism, Identity and Authenticity in the Middle East.* Richmond: Curzon, 2013.
Meijer, Roel. 'Yūsuf al-ʿUyairī and the Making of a Revolutionary Salafī Praxis'. *Die Welt des Islams* 47, no. 3 (2007): 422–59.
Mouline, Nabil. *The Clerics of Islam: Religion, Authority, and Political Power in Saudi Arabia.* New Haven/London: Yale University Press, 2014.

Niblock, Tim, ed. *State, Society and Economy in Saudi Arabia*. London: Croom Helm, 1982.

Noi, Aylin Ünver, ed. *Islam and Democracy: Perspectives on the Arab Spring*. Newcastle upon Tyne: Cambridge Scholars, 2013.

Pall, Zoltan. *Kuwaiti Salafism and Its Growing Influence in the Levant*. Published by the Carnegie Endowment for International Peace, 7 May 2014. Available online: https://carnegieendowment.org/files/kuwaiti_salafists.pdf (accessed 11 June 2020).

Peterson, J. E. *Historical Dictionary of Saudi Arabia*. 2nd edn. Lanham: The Scarecrow Press, 2003.

Polka, Sagi. 'The Centrist Stream in Egypt and Its Role in the Public Discourse Surrounding the Shaping of the Country's Cultural Identity'. *Middle Eastern Studies* 39, no. 3 (July 2003): 39–64.

Revkin, Mara. 'Egypt's Constitution in Question'. *Middle East Law and Governance* 5, no. 3 (2013): 331–43.

Sadiki, Larbi. *The Search for Arab Democracy: Discourses and Counter-Discourses*. London: Hurst, 2004.

Safi, Omid, ed. *Progressive Muslims: On Justice, Gender, and Pluralism*. Oxford: Oneworld Publications, 2003.

Salameh, Ghassane. 'Political Power and the Saudi State'. *Middle East Research and Information Project Reports* 91 (October 1980): 5–22.

Schmale, Wolfgang, ed. *Human Rights and Cultural Diversity*. Goldbach: Keip Publishing, 1993.

Scott, Rachel M. *The Challenge of Political Islam: Non-Muslims and the Egyptian State*. Stanford: Stanford University Press, 2010.

Steinberg, Guido. *Leading the Counter-Revolution: Saudi Arabia and the Arab Spring*. Research paper of the Stiftung Wissenschaft und Politik, 2014.

Stephan, Maria, ed. *Civilian Jihad: Nonviolent Struggle, Democratization, and Governance in the Middle East*. New York: Palgrave Macmillan, 2009.

Wagemakers, Joas. 'Salafism'. In *Oxford Research Encyclopedias*, August 2016. Available online: https://oxfordre.com/religion/view/10.1093/acrefore/9780199340378.001.0001/acrefore-9780199340378-e-255#acrefore-9780199340378-e-255-div1-8 (accessed 17 October 2020).

Weismann, Itzchak. 'A Perverted Balance: Modern Salafism between Reform and Jihād'. *Die Welt des Islams* 57, no. 1 (2017): 33–66.

French

Abu-Sahlieh, Sami A. Aldeeb. *Les musulmans face aux droits de l'homme*. Bochum: Verlag Dieter Winkler, 1994.

Cheddadi, Abdesselam. *Ibn Khaldūn: L'homme et le théoricien de la civilisation*. Paris: Gallimard, 2006.

Kepel, Gilles. *Fitna: Guerre au cœur de l'islam*. Paris: Gallimard, 2004.

Kepel, Gilles. *Jihad: Expansion et déclin de l'islamisme*. Paris: Gallimard, 2000.

Khayati, Mustapha. 'Un disciple libre penseur de Al-Afghani : Adib Ishaq'. *Revue des mondes musulmans et de la Méditerranée* 52, no. 1 (1989): 138–49.

Lacoste, Yves. *Ibn Khaldoun: Naissance de l'Histoire, passé du tiers monde*. Paris: La Découverte, 1998.

Lacroix, Stéphane. *Les Islamistes Saoudiens: Une insurrection manqué*. Paris: Presses Universitaires de France, 2010.

Redissi, Hamadi. *Le Pacte de Nadjd: Ou comment l'islam sectaire es devenu l'islam.* Paris: Éditions du Seuil, 2007.
Sureau, François. 'Égypte : une constitution entre deux mondes'. *Pouvoirs: Revue francaise d'etudes constitutionelles et politiques* 149, no. 2 (February 2014): 151–67.

German

Ben Abdeljelil, Jamaleddine and Serdar Kurnaz. *Maqāṣid aš-Šarīʿa: Die Maximen des islamischen Rechts.* Berlin: EB-Verlag, 2014.
Bassiouni, Mahmoud. *Menschenrechte zwischen Universalität und islamischer Legitimität.* Berlin: Suhrkamp Taschenbuch Wissenschaft, 2014.
Bauer, Thomas. *Die Kultur der Ambiguität: Eine andere Geschichte des Islams.* Berlin: Verlag der Weltreligionen, 2011.
Bielefeldt, Heiner et al., ed. *Menschenrechte und Entwicklung: Globale Politik zwischen universalen Normen und kultureller Identität.* Bonn: Stiftung Entwicklung und Frieden Werkstattpapier, 1992.
Cavuldak, Ahmet et al. (as editors). *Demokratie und Islam: Theoretische und empirische Studien.* Wiesbaden: Springer, 2014.
Elliesie, Hatem, ed. *Beiträge zum Islamischen Recht VII: Islam und Menschenrechte.* Frankfurt am Main: Peter Lang-Verlag, 2010.
Enz, Peter. *Der Keim der Revolte: Militante Solidarität und religiöse Mission bei Ibn Khaldun.* Freiburg: Verlag Karl Alber, 2012.
Enz, Peter. 'Religion und Rebellion: Ibn Khaldun und die revolutionäre Bewegung'. *Polylog. Zeitschrift für interkulturelles Philosophieren* 30 (2013): 105–15.
Jürgensen, Carsten. *Demokratie und Menschenrechte in der arabischen Welt.* Hamburg: Deutsches Orient-Institut Hamburg, 1994.
Krämer, Gudrun. *Demokratie im Islam: Der Kampf für Toleranz und Freiheit in der arabischen Welt.* München: C.H. Beck, 2011.
Krämer, Gudrun. *Gottes Staat als Republik: Reflexionen zeitgenössischer Muslime zu Islam, Menschenrechten und Demokratie.* Baden-Baden: Nomos Verlagsgesellschaft, 1999.
Lohlker, Rüdiger. *Die Salafisten: Der Aufstand der Frommen, Saudi-Arabien und der Islam.* München: C.H. Beck, 2017.
Müller, Lorenz. *Islam und Menschenrechte: Sunnitische Muslime zwischen Islamismus, Säkularismus und Modernismus.* Hamburg: Deutsches Orient-Institut Hamburg, 1996.
Mustafa, Imad. *Der politische Islam: Zwischen Muslimbrüdern, Hamas und Hizbollah.* Wien: Promedia, 2013.
Stahmann, Christian. *Islamische Menschenrechtskonzepte.* Würzburg: Ergon-Verlag, 2005.
Steinberg, Guido. *Saudi-Arabien: Politik Geschichte Religion.* 2. Auflage. München: C.H. Beck, 2013.
Tibi, Bassam. *Im Schatten Allahs: Der Islam und die Menschenrechte.* München: Piper, 1994.
Würth, Anna. *Dialog mit dem Islam als Konfliktprävention? Zur Menschenrechtspolitik gegenüber islamisch geprägten Staaten.* Studie des Deutschen Instituts für Menschenrechte, September 2003.
Yousefi, Hamid Reza, ed. *Demokratie im Islam: Analysen – Theorien – Perspektiven.* Münster: Waxmann, 2014.

News articles and reports

Arabic

al-Ǧazīra. *as-Suʿūdīya: Siǧn nāšiṭīn wa-iġlāq ḥasm*. Published on aljazeera.net, 9 March 2013. Available online: https://www.aljazeera.net/news/arabic/2013/3/9/السعودية-سجن-ناشطين-وإغلاق-حسم (accessed 11 June 2020).

al-Ǧazīra. *Muḥākamāt muʿtaqalīn li-muṭālabatihim bi-iṣlāḥ fī s-Suʿūdīya*. Published on aljazeera.net, 3 October 2014. Available online: https://www.aljazeera.net/news/arabic/2004/10/3/محاكمة-معتقلين-لمطالبتهم-بالإصلاح-في-السعودية (accessed 11 June 2020).

al-Ǧazīra. *Suʿūdīyūn yuʿlinūna wafāt "šayḫ al-ḥuqūqīyīn" ʿAbdallāh al-Ḥāmid fī s-siǧn ǧirāʾa l-ihmāl aṭ-ṭibbī*. Published on aljazeera.net, 24 April 2020. Available online: https://www.aljazeera.net/news/humanrights/2020/4/24/السعودية-أنباء-وفاة-عبد-الله-الحامد (accessed 11 June 2020).

al-Nilin. *al-Qaraḍāwī: al-Muẓāharāt iḏā istahdafat īqāẓ al-umma fa-hiya ǧihād*. Published on alnilin.com, without date. Available online: https://www.alnilin.com/153591.htm (accessed 11 June 2020).

al-Yaum. *as-Siǧn 8 sanawāt li-ʿaḍw ḥasm li-daʿwātihi at-taḥrīḍīya*. Published on alyaum.com, 25 June 2013. Available online: https://www.alyaum.com/articles/878069/المملكة-اليوم/الدكتور-عبد-الكريم-الخضر (accessed 11 June 2020).

ar-Riyāḍ. *Aḥkām bi-siǧn iṯnain min muʾassisī mā yaṭlaqu ʿalayhi ǧamʿīyat ḥasm 11 wa-10 sanawāt wa-ḥall al-ǧamʿīya wa-iġlāq manāšiṭihā wa-muṣādarat mumtalakātihā*. Published on alriyadh.com, 10 March 2013. Available online: http://www.alriyadh.com/816175 (accessed 11 June 2020).

ar-Riyāḍ. *Hayʾat kibār al-ʿulamāʾ: al-Iṣlāḥ lā yakūnu bi-l-muẓāharāt wa-l-asālīb allatī tuṯīru l-fitan wa-tafarruq al-ǧamāʿa*. Published on alriyadh.com, 7 March 2011 CE. Available online: http://www.alriyadh.com/611507 (accessed 11 June 2020).

aš-Šarq al-awsaṭ. *Badʾ aʿmāl muʾtamar al-ʿadāla l-ʿarabī fī l-Qāhira l-yaum*. Published on aawsat.com, 21 February 2003. Available online: https://archive.aawsat.com/details.asp?issueno=8800&article=154079#.XoiX_y2B3Vp (accessed 11 June 2020).

English

ALQST. *ALQST Renews Its Call to Recognize the Achievements of Saudi Human Rights Activists*. Published on alqst.org, 29 November 2018. Available online: https://alqst.org/eng/call_out_their_names/ (accessed 11 June 2020).

ALQST. *Terrorism Court Hands Down Seven- and 14-Year Jail Sentences for Starting a Human Rights Group*. Published on alqst.org, 26 January 2018. Available online: https://alqst.org/eng/terrorism-court-hands-seven-14-year-jail-sentences-starting-human-rights-group/ (accessed 11 June 2020).

Americans for Democracy & Human Rights in Bahrain. *Roads to Reform: The Enduring Work of the Saudi Association for Civil and Political Rights*. Published on adhrb.org, 2017. Available online: https://www.adhrb.org/wp-content/uploads/2017/03/2017.3.1_ADHRB_Roads_Web.pdf (accessed 11 June 2020).

Amnesty International. *Joint Public Statement: Urgent Call for Release of Saudi Human Rights Defenders*. Published on amnesty.org, 12 March 2018. Available online: https://www.amnesty.org/download/documents/MDE2380392018ENGLISH.pdf (accessed 11 June 2020).

Amnesty International. *Prestigious Dutch Human Rights Prize Awarded to Saudi Arabian Human Rights Organization*. Published on amnesty.nl, 16 January 2020. Available online: https://www.amnesty.nl/prestigious-dutch-human-rights-prize-awarded-to-saudi-arabian-human-rights-organization (accessed 11 June 2020).

Amnesty International. *Saudi Arabia: End Ill-Treatment, Arbitrary Detention of Human Rights Defender, Waleed Abu al-Khair*. Published on amnesty.org, 6 December 2019. Available online: https://www.amnesty.org/en/latest/news/2019/12/saudi-arabia-end-ill-treatment-arbitrary-detention-of-human-rights-defender-waleed-abu-al-khair/ (accessed 11 June 2020).

Amnesty International. *Saudi Arabia: Prisoner of Conscience Dr Abdullah al-Hamid Dies While in Detention*. Published on amnesty.org, 24 April 2020. Available online: https://www.amnesty.org/en/latest/news/2020/04/saudi-arabia-prisoner-of-conscience-dr-abdullah-alhamid-dies-while-in-detention/ (accessed 11 June 2020).

Amnesty International. *Saudi Arabia: Prominent Reformist Cleric Faces Death Sentence for His Peaceful Activism*. Published on amnesty.org, 26 July 2019. Available online: https://www.amnesty.org/en/latest/news/2019/07/saudi-arabia-prominent-reformist-cleric-faces-death-sentence-for-his-peaceful-activism/ (accessed 11 June 2020).

Amnesty International. *Saudi Arabia Steps Up Ruthless Crackdown Against Human Rights Activists*. Published on amnesty.org, 10 January 2017. Available online: https://www.amnesty.org/en/latest/news/2017/01/saudi-arabia-steps-up-ruthless-crackdown-against-human-rights-activists/ (accessed 11 June 2020).

Amnesty International. *Saudi Arabia's ACPRA. How the Kingdom Silences Its Human Rights Activists*. Published on amnesty.org, 10 October 2014. Available online: https://www.amnesty.org/en/documents/MDE23/025/2014/en/ (accessed 11 June 2020).

BBC. *Saudi Arabia: Prominent Human Rights Activist 'Dies in Jail'*. Published on bbc.com, 24 April 2020. Available online: https://www.bbc.com/news/world-middle-east-52411453 (accessed 11 June 2020).

HASM. *ACPRA Demands the Immediate Unconditional Release of Its Co-Founder, Mohammed Al-Bjady*. Published on acpra.org, 24 March 2011 CE. Available online: http://www.acpra.org/news_view_117.html (accessed 11 June 2020).

HASM. *APCRA Demands the Release of All Prisoners of Conscience*. Published on acpra.org, 28 September 2013. Available online: http://www.acpra.org/news/view_251.html (accessed 11 June 2020).

HASM. *ACPRA Invites People to Attend the 6th Trial Hearing of Its Co-Founders: al-Hamid and al-Qahtani*. Published on acpra.org, 19 November 2012. Available online: http://www.acpra.org/news_view_198.html (accessed 11 June 2020).

HASM. *ACPRA Sends Letters to Top Saudi Officials, and UNHCR about HR Violations*. Published on acpra.org, 14 August 2011. Available online: http://www.acpra.org/news_view_140.html (accessed 11 June 2020).

HASM. *Saudi Civil & Political Rights Association (An Establishing Declaration)*. Published on acpra.org, 1 February 2010. Available online: http://www.acpra.org/news_view_5.html (accessed 11 June 2020).

Human Rights Watch. *Saudi Arabia: New Rights Group Facing Harassment*. Published on hrw.org, 7 May 2013. Available online: https://www.hrw.org/news/2013/05/07/saudi-arabia-new-rights-group-facing-harassment (accessed 11 June 2020).

International Crisis Group. *Saudi Arabia Backgrounder. Who are the Islamists?*. ICG Middle Eastern Report No. 31, September 2014. Available online: https://www.crisisgroup.org/middle-east-north-africa/gulf-and-arabian-peninsula/saudi-arabia/saudi-arabia-backgrounder-who-are-islamists (accessed 11 June 2020).

Middle East Research and Information Project. 'The Arabian Peninsula Opposition Movements'. *Middle East Research and Information Project (MERIP) Reports* 130 (February 1985).

Right Livelihood Foundation. *Celebrate 70th Anniversary of Human Rights – Support Reformists Instead of the Regime in Saudi Arabia.* Published on rightlivelihoodaward.org, 12 October 2018. Available online: https://www.rightlivelihoodaward.org/media/celebrate-70th-anniversary-of-human-rights-support-reformists-instead-of-the-regime-in-saudi-arabia/ (accessed 11 June 2020).

Right Livelihood Foundation. *Laureates Abdullah al-Hamid, Waleed Abu al-Khair & Mohammad Fahad al-Qahtani.* Published on rightlivelihoodaward.org, December 2018. Available online: https://www.rightlivelihoodaward.org/laureates/abdullah-al-hamid-waleed-abu-al-khair-mohammad-fahad-al-qahtani/ (accessed 11 June 2020).

Right Livelihood Foundation. *Saudi Human Rights Trio Named 2018 Right Livelihood Award Laureates*. Published on rightlivelihoodaward.org, 24 September 2018. Available online: https://www.rightlivelihoodaward.org/wp-content/uploads/2018/09/Nr-2-Final-PR-EN-23-Sep-2018.pdf (accessed 11 June 2020).

The Economist. *The Saudi Revolution Begins: How to Ensure Muhammad bin Salman's Reforms Succeed.* Published on economist.com, 23 June 2018. Available online: https://www.economist.com/leaders/2018/06/23/how-to-ensure-muhammad-bin-salmans-reforms-succeed (accessed 11 June 2020).

Wittmeyer, Alicia P. Q. *The FP Top 100 Global Thinkers*. Published on foreignpolicy.com, 26 November 2012. Available online: https://foreignpolicy.com/2012/11/26/the-fp-top-100-global-thinkers-2/ (accessed 11 June 2020).

Other languages

Da Dagsavisen. *Nobel: Stortingspolitikere krysser partigrenser for å hedre saudiarabiske aktivister*. Published on dagsavisen.no, 11 February 2019. Available online: https://www.dagsavisen.no/innenriks/nobel-stortingspolitikere-krysser-partigrenser-for-a-hedre-saudiarabiske-aktivister-1.1276328 (accessed 11 June 2020).

NRC. *Geuzenpenning naar Saoedische mensenrechtenorganisatie ACPRA*. Published on nrc.nl, 16 January 2020. Available online: https://www.nrc.nl/nieuws/2020/01/16/geuzenpenning-naar-saoedische-mensenrechtenorganisatie-acpra-a3987102 (accessed 11 June 2020).

Index

www.ingramcontent.com/pod-product-compliance
Lightning Source LLC
Chambersburg PA
CBHW050413280326
41932CB00013BA/1849